JUVENILES IN JUSTICE
A BOOK OF READINGS

About the Editor

H. Ted Rubin is one of the nation's leading authorities on juvenile justice. As judge of the Denver Juvenile Court, 1965–71, he pioneered due process reforms and community-based rehabilitation programs during that period. He architected the major provisions of the model Colorado Children's Code enacted in early 1967. Previously, as a Colorado state legislator, Rubin developed forestry camp programs for delinquent youths and mental health/retardation legislation.

Director for Juvenile Justice for the Institute for Court Management, Denver, since 1971, he is currently Senior Associate for Juvenile and Criminal Justice for the Institute. He has taught at the University of Colorado, Boulder, and has served as Visiting Professor, School of Criminal Justice, State University of New York at Albany. Rubin has been a consultant to the President's Commission on Law Enforcement and Administration of Justice, the Joint Commission on Correctional Manpower and Training, the Institute of Judicial Administration-American Bar Association Juvenile Justice Standards Project, and the National Advisory Committee on Criminal Justice Standards and Goals.

He holds graduate degrees in both law and social work, earlier worked in children's agencies, and has published over thirty articles, mostly focused on juvenile justice, court, and rehabilitation issues. He is the author of *The Courts: Fulcrum of the Justice System* (Goodyear, 1976) and *Juvenile Justice: Policy, Practice, and Law* (Goodyear, 1979).

JUVENILES IN JUSTICE
A BOOK OF READINGS

Edited by

H. Ted Rubin

Institute for Court Management, Denver

Goodyear Publishing Company, Inc. • Santa Monica, California

Library of Congress Cataloging in Publication Data
Main entry under title:

Juveniles in justice.

1. Juvenile courts — United States.   2. Juvenile justice,
Administration of — United States.   I. Rubin, H. Ted,
1926-   II. Title.
KF9794.J88   345'.73'08   79-24922
ISBN 0-8302-4959-1

Current Printing (last digit):

10 9 8 7 6 5 4 3 2 1

Y-4959-6

Text designer: Linda M. Robertson
Compositor: Composition Type/Playa del Rey
Production Editor: Pam Tully
Copyeditor: LaDonna Wallace
Printed in the United States of America

Preface

This book centers on a changing American institution, the juvenile court. The book encompasses issues and practices that precede the court's function and extend beyond it. It also considers legislative policy, police procedures, and programmatic alternatives to juvenile detention, juvenile court, and juvenile institutionalization. It presents a reassessment of the court's workload and rationale for intervention. Its emphasis is the front end and what might be called the middle of the juvenile justice system, although certain policy aspects and legal dimensions of institutionalization are considered. This work also concerns children, the more than a million youngsters who experience one or more stages of the juvenile justice process each year.

The readings included here, all of them products of the 1970s, begin with the juvenile court and its past, present, and uncertain future. Considerations follow as to policy concerns and practices on the continuum of the court's workload from serious offenses and repetitive delinquency to status offenses or noncriminal misbehaviors, leading to an examination of the system from the arrest stage to the entry door of the fenced-in state institution.

The evolving policies which affect the court and influence the system's capability and motivation within the community are stressed. While the percentage of juvenile offenders who are dispatched to state institutions or enter the criminal justice system is comparatively small, these young people constitute an extremely important group who have been given up on for now by judges and policy makers. Policies that influence the number and type of such youths, some of whom have caused significant harm and others of whom hold an insufficiently tapped potential for community-based rehabilitation, are reviewed. The institutional experience does not receive substantial portrayal due to space limitations and the community-level emphasis.

The issues addressed are those at the cutting edge of the juvenile justice process. Some of the directions presented would disturb the status quo and disrupt the homeostatic balance of the juvenile justice world. Other articles represent evaluations of present juvenile justice practices: reporting critically on the juvenile court promise, assessing more neutrally what is happening out there, or researching the degree to which certain hopeful schemes are faring.

The impactful decision *In re Gault*, issued by the United States Supreme Court on May 15, 1967, incorporated social science data and evaluations to support a revisionist foundation to compel constitutional protections for juvenile offenders. This book draws on more recent data and reports to enrich our understanding of contemporary juvenile justice practice.

What is right about juvenile justice and also what is wrong receive ample attention. Traditional arguments in support of the court are excluded; the swiftly changing juvenile justice picture merits searching analysis rather than blind defense.

Introductory notes to each of the five sections and the several subsections construct a background for the articles or comment on the writings, most of which are by authors trained in law or social science. The editor's objective, for the student, professional, and general readership of this book, is to promote a deeper understanding of critical issues and developments in juvenile justice. The dominant value is constitutional fairness. A justice perspective compels accountability and enlightenment from those granted the authority to deal with youths who have been less than just in their actions toward others. Beyond delivering due process, juvenile justice agents must deliver themselves from the temptations of moralistic judgments and rhetorical promises.

Contents

section THREE
The Front End of the Juvenile Justice System

section FOUR
The Juvenile Court Treatment Rationale: Restriction and Expansion

section FIVE
Community Intervention with Juvenile Court Youths

Epilogue

CROSS-REFERENCE TABLE: Using *Juveniles in Justice: A Book of Readings* with Juvenile Justice Texts (Reading Number for *Juveniles in Justice*)

TEXT, CHAPTER	RUBIN *Juvenile Justice: Policy, Practice, and Law* (Goodyear, 1978)	COX & CONRAD *Juvenile Justice* (Brown, 1978)	JOHNSON *Introduction to the Juvenile Justice System* (West, 1975)	KATKIN, HYMAN & KRAMER *Juvenile Delinquency and the Juvenile Justice System* (Duxbury, 1976)
1	5-7, 26	1, 4	1	—
2	8-10	21	3, 8-10	—
3	11-13	3	25	1, 2
4	14-16	7	14-16, 18, 19, 20	19
5	17-19	8-10	3	8
6	3, 21, 23, 24, 26	14-16, 18-20	18, 23-26	11, 13
7	22	11-13	11-13	14-16
8	4	2	—	4, 20, 21
9	2	17	17	3, 18
10	—	—	5, 22	5-7, 9, 10, 22-26
11	1-4, 25	5, 6, 22-26	2	12, 17
12	20	4	4, 6, 7, 21	—
13	—	—	—	—
14	—	—	—	—
15	—	—	—	—
16	—	—	—	—
17	—	—	—	—
18	—	—	—	—
19	—	—	—	—

CROSS-REFERENCE TABLE: Using Juveniles in Justice: A Book of Readings with Juvenile Justice Texts (Reading Number for Juveniles in Justice)

TEXT CHAPTER	BARTOLLAS & MILLER The Juvenile Offender: Control, Correction, and Treatment Holbrook, 1978	EMPEY American Delinquency: Its Meaning and Construction Dorsey, 1978	PHELPS Juvenile Delinquency Goodyear, 1976	SENNA & SIEGEL Juvenile Law West, 1976
1	5	—	1, 2	1-4, 8-10
2	8-10	—	3, 8-10	11-13
3	11-13	—	—	14-19
4	1, 2, 18, 20	1	12, 17, 19	5-7
5	3	2	11-13	2, 20
6	23, 24, 25	3, 7	14-16	21, 23-26
7	17, 19	—	3, 4, 18, 20, 23-26	22
8	14-16	—	5-7, 21, 22	—
9	22	—	—	—
10	22	—	—	—
11	—	—	—	—
12	—	—	—	—
13	7, 21	17, 19	—	—
14	6	—	—	—
15	—	11-13	—	—
16	4, 26	14-16, 18, 20, 25	—	—
17	—	5, 6, 22	—	—
18	—	9, 10, 23, 24, 26	—	—
19	—	4, 8, 21	—	—

Perspectives of the Juvenile Court

INTRODUCTION

American society has never lacked divergent opinions as to how children should be disciplined, both within and outside the family unit. Even dominant child care philosophies shift and are reshaped with changing social conditions. The consensus which long supported the juvenile court construct has yielded to contemporary skepticism and proposals to substantially modify or even terminate specialized judicial processing for juvenile offenders.

More than eight decades ago, a reconsideration of how the judicial system should deal with youngsters who offended criminal laws and children who needed protection through the law led the Illinois legislature to create the nation's first statutory children's court, the Juvenile Division of the Circuit Court of Cook County, Illinois, in 1899. A separate judge was assigned to officiate over juvenile hearings; the housing of juvenile with adult offenders was to be eliminated; probation officers were authorized to represent children's best interests and to facilitate the achievement of court objectives; and a broad purpose to do better for children was promulgated. The juvenile court concept caught on, and in time juvenile court acts were approved in all states. The laws differed as to the particular court structure, jurisdictional age, delinquency definition, and other matters. But common to all were liberal entry criteria, a strong treatment rationale, wide latitude in decision making, and the casting of the judge in a very powerful role.

The 1960s began an intensified review of juvenile court procedures and attainments. A blanket of constitutional protections was mandated for youngsters brought into this forum. The rising incidence of serious and repetitive delinquent offenses, part of the disturbing crime problem of the 1960s and 1970s, precipitated significant changes in official response to offending juveniles and troubled youngsters and to the purposes and practices of juvenile courts and juvenile justice systems. The treatment rationale was wounded, though not mortally; a punishment rationale found increased acceptance; the differentiation of sanction, based on offense severity, achieved new support; the movement to curb court intervention with juvenile non-criminal misbehavior accelerated sharply.

The four articles which follow chart the inheritance of the juvenile court past, mark contemporary directions, and ponder an uncertain juvenile court future.

The Schultz article affirms the humanism of the original legislation as utilitarian to present day objectives. Director of the Institute of Judicial Administration-American Bar Association Juvenile Justice Standards Project for one cycle of its lengthy enterprise, Schultz challenges the revisionist critique that juvenile court origins were conceptually flawed and were motivated by a wish to straightjacket immigrant children. He suggests that the probation function, born in Massachusetts but ensconced by the Illinois Juvenile Act, was a notable invention which provided a vehicle for a community-based corrections, a high value in a humanistic juvenile rehabilitation enterprise. He finds commonality between early and more contemporary reforms in strengthening the family unit and in dealing with youngsters within their own homes or substitute community facilities. While the first cycle of reformers failed to appreciate current concerns about coercive intervention and procedural irregularity, Schultz applauds the initial conceptualization of a separate juvenile system, finds that the system's flexibility continues to provide benefits for its clientele, and observes that the statutory objectives for juvenile court acts have been translated into a standard from which "right to treatment" cases have brought more suitable conditions for institutionalized youths.

The Rubin article describes different organizational models for juvenile courts and reviews the juvenile caseflow process. The movement in a number of states to eliminate limited purpose trial courts and to unify all trial courts into either a single level or two-tier trial court system predicts that juvenile courts which are separately organized and administered will merge into lower or upper trial courts as specialized divisions. The Massachusetts model charted in the article has become outmoded by legislation which took effect in January, 1979. The historic, separate Boston Juvenile Court is now the Boston Division of the Juvenile Court Department of the Trial Court of the Commonwealth of Massachusetts. Further, the Connecticut separate statewide juvenile court system was transformed in 1978 into the juvenile division of the superior court.

Juvenile intake systems, designed over many years to restrict formal court processing to the more needful youngsters, is undergoing very rapid change. Legislative distrust of decision making by probation intake officers has triggered increased participation by the prosecutor at this vital stage. California amendments effective January, 1977 converted the California process described in the article to a model resembling Florida's second level prosecutor screening approach, although the California prosecutor does not review complaints rejected by the intake officer unless the complainant appeals.

This article sketches certain of the major trends of juvenile justice: a more legalistic and lawyer dominated court; the shift away from coercive intervention with status offense youths; the extension of community-based programming; and a more professional and accountable court.

These directions and others are reflected in the 1977 annual report of the Juvenile Division of the Superior Court for Pima County, Tucson, Arizona. The report describes how one juvenile court backed boldly away from locking up youngsters at local detention and state institutional levels, effectuated the goal to retain the child in his own family wherever possible, an objective which has been underemphasized by many juvenile courts, and found the funds and citizen and professional support to fulfill a community's responsibility to its youngsters. In a fast growing county, a changed philosophy and skilled leadership reduced state commitments from 280 in 1969 to 37 in 1977, slashed the detention of status offenders from 979 in 1974 to 16 in 1977, expanded the purchase of private residential placements, and innovated projects such as Mobile Diversion and the Street Program. This reformulation of what a juvenile court is all about did not occur without conflict or backlash. The local prosecutor expressed severe opposition to the community-based approach. At the end of 1978, the juvenile court judge was reassigned by his colleagues to the criminal division of the general court, following the rupture of the relationship between the judge and his court services director, who accepted a position elsewhere. Under different judicial leadership, the Tucson court soon began "locking them up" again.

The final article in this section, also by the editor, reviews the basic principles and describes certain of the major directions set forth by the Institute of Judicial

Administration-American Bar Association Juvenile Justice Standards Project. Several of these — proportionality in sanctions, determinate sentences, and repeal of status offense jurisdiction — would radically change the juvenile court we have known. The article reviews and analyzes five published papers which, because of the reach of these standards or because these standards have not gone far enough, argue that delinquent youths should be processed in criminal courts, and that juvenile courts, as such, should be abolished. These writers argue that due process safeguards can better be accorded by criminal courts, and that the substitution of a punishment for a treatment rationale removes the underpinnings of a specialized juvenile forum. The author rejects these arguments, preferring IJA-ABA reform directions and a juvenile court organized as a division of the general trial court; he cites the substantial deficiencies in adult misdemeanor courts that would inherit the bulk of the current juvenile court workload. Yet the abolitionist perspective is a haunting one which may influence policy makers of the future.

1 *The Cycle of Juvenile Court History*
J. Lawrence Schultz

Until recently there has been little challenge to the consensus that, at least for historical purposes, juvenile courts can be discussed as a group and that their collective birth date is April 21, 1899, when "an Act to regulate the treatment and control of dependent, neglected, and delinquent children"[1] was passed in Illinois. The rapid proliferation of legislated juvenile courts immediately after 1899 nourished that consensus.[2] Until recently, when sociologist Anthony M. Platt, in *The Child Savers: The Invention of Delinquency,*[3] and law professor Sanford J. Fox, in "Juvenile Justice Reform: An Historical Perspective,"[4] challenged many of the traditional assumptions about the "first juvenile court," the circumstances of the passage of the Illinois Act were not examined in detail.

THE 1899 JUVENILE COURT ACT

Although popularized and widely identified today as the "Juvenile Court Act," the germinal 1899 legislation in Illinois included other provisions, in addition to those establishing special court proceedings, for protecting children.[5] The provisions that

From *The Serious Juvenile Offender,* Proceedings of a National Symposium, September 19 and 20, 1977, Minneapolis, Minnesota. Office of Juvenile Justice and Delinquency Prevention, Law Enforcement Assistance Administration, U.S. Department of Justice (Washington, D.C.: Government Printing Office, 1978), pp. 32–50. Reprinted by permission.

Reprinted, with permission of the National Council on Crime and Delinquency, from J. Lawrence Schultz, "The Cycle of Juvenile Court History," *Crime and Delinquency,* October 1973, pp. 457-76.

stirred national interest, however, were those governing the hearing and disposition of cases involving children under the age of sixteen alleged to be either "dependent and neglected" or "delinquent," the latter category defined in 1899 as including any child "who violates any law of this state or any city or village ordinance."[6]

The innovative (for Illinois) provisions designated one circuit judge in Cook County to hear all cases under the Act, decreed that all these cases would be heard in a special separate courtroom, established a "summary" proceeding, mandated the separation of children from adults whenever both were confined in the same institution, and prohibited committing a child under twelve to a jail or a police station. Perhaps most significant, the Act vested authority in the new court to appoint probation officers (not paid by the state[7]), who would investigate cases when required by the court, "represent the interests of the child when the case [was] heard," provide any information the judge might request, and, following disposition, supervise children placed on probation.[8]

Finally, more important to this Act than purpose clauses usually are was its concluding section:

> This act shall be liberally construed, to the end that its purpose may be carried out, to wit: That the care, custody, and discipline of a child shall approximate as nearly as may be that which should be given by its parents, and in all cases where it can properly be done the child be placed in an improved family home and become a member of the family by legal adoption or otherwise.[9]

Significant amendments in 1901,[10] 1905,[11] and 1907[12] reveal a pattern of (1) expansion of the definition of juvenile deliquency,[13] (2) progressively greater concern with regulating the quality of treatment accorded juveniles confined in institutions by the juvenile court,[14] and (3) increasing public funding for the probation system.[15]

REVISIONISM: PLATT AND FOX

Earlier writers, while recognizing that the Illinois Act did not spring full-grown from the shores of Lake Michigan, have extolled the combination of elements incorporated in it or the central "philosophy" embodied in it as "revolutionary"[16] or "radically new."[17] Both Platt and Fox disagree. Although their interpretations are dissimilar in other ways, each concludes that the 1899 legislation served primarily conservative, middle-class interests and resulted in no important innovations, either in concept or in detail.

Although both writers share the view that the Act was essentially conservative and not innovative, the evidence each relies upon differs in some important respects. Fox's approach is to trace specific precedents for practices and concepts incorporated in the 1899 legislation, demonstrating that many of these were neither new nor liberal. Platt tends more toward bringing to the surface the conservative intellectual concepts and characteristics of the social structure of the late nineteenth century that influenced the shape of the Act.

Fox concentrates primarily on three themes. First, he contends that two important provisions of the Act — summary proceedings for children and a bias in favor of treatment as similar as possible to family life — were common in the nineteenth century. Second, he demonstrates, as Platt does, that in important respects the 1899

Act represented a failure in attempted reform, because the would-be reformers were defeated by vested interests in important causes: improving conditions of incarceration for children and severing public handling of children from the influence of sectarian organizations. The failure of the attempt to reform prison conditions is represented, according to Fox, by the defeat of a provision that would have removed children from the poorhouse and by the refusal of the legislature to appropriate any money to build a juvenile detention center, thus apparently pulling the teeth of the new prohibition against putting children younger than twelve in jails used by adults.

The third leg of Fox's argument is that the Act was not even progressive in concept. Far from being anything unusual, he argues, the *parens patriae* concept was at least as old as the House of Refuge, incorporated in 1824 by the New York legislature to care for both delinquent and wayward children. Most crucial, "the 1899 Illinois Act . . . restated the belief in the value of coercive predictions."[18] That is, the legislation approached the problems of delinquency, dependency, and neglect by assuming, as had all legislatures before, that government must devise methods to identify "predelinquent" children and force them to accept treatments designed by the state to correct their wayward tendencies.

Platt complements Fox's analysis by exploring currents of thought, reflected in the 1899 Act, which had come to dominate criminal and penological reform in the nineteenth century. He argues that these concepts were old hat by 1899 and that many of them served the interests of middle-class groups in maintaining their established institutions and their value systems. Paramount among these ideas (or biases) was *hostility* — hostility to the cities, to the new waves of East European immigrants, and even to their children, whom the reformers professedly wished to save from criminality and immorality.

According to Platt, the Social Darwinist conception that lower classes were inherently inferior and thus doomed to a life of poverty and license had been successfully resisted, but the identification of poverty with crime, and of both with immorality, remained. The corollary of attributing poor children's difficulties to an evil city environment was that they would best be treated if they were removed from their homes and placed in the more healthful countryside, preferably in a western state, where they would be exposed to the virtues of middle-class life: sobriety, thrift, industry, prudence, and piety. Training in agricultural and industrial pursuits would be imparted in small institutions approximating family structures, or in foster homes. Thus the unfortunate immigrant child would be assimilated to the American way of life. Prominent among the reformers were "middle-class women who extended their housewifely roles into public service and used their extensive political contacts and economic resources to advance the cause of child welfare."[19]

To summarize:

> Child saving may be understood as a crusade which served symbolic and ceremonial functions for native, middle-class Americans. The movement was not so much a break with the past as an affirmation of faith in traditional institutions. Parental authority, home education, rural life, and the independence of the family as a social unit were emphasized because they seemed threatened at this time by urbanism and industrialism. The child savers elevated the nuclear family, especially women as stalwarts of the family, and defended the family's right to supervise the socialization of youth.[20]

While Platt and Fox supplement each other in discussions of the middle-class orientation of the 1899 reform movement, Platt introduces a different and important theme not paralleled in Fox's article. The 1899 Act, he asserts, did not merely revise procedures and institutions but created "new categories of youthful misbehavior," bringing within the ambit of governmental control "a set of youthful activities that had been previously ignored or handled informally."[21]

To the extent that they reveal the tangle of motivations that drove the reform, Platt and Fox successfully demythologize the origins of the juvenile court movement. But the evidence they put forward does not seem to justify assuming an entirely debunking air. Furthermore, other evidence available about the first juvenile court acts — in Illinois and elsewhere — reveals other interpretations of the juvenile court movement.[22]

"Nothing Radically New"

Neither Fox nor Platt disputes the conventional understanding that important precursors of the juvenile courts included the equity jurisdiction of the English chancery court and common law doctrines limiting the legal responsibility of children for their criminal acts.[23] In addition, both authors point out that almost all the important aspects of the Illinois law of 1899 can be traced to legislative precedents in other states, including separate confinement of children who committed minor offenses (in the House of Refuge) and the use of probation (Massachusetts, 1860).[24]

Massachusetts was clearly the foremost source of inspiration for the reformers.[25] But then the reformers themselves never denied this: they were well aware that each major element of the Illinois Juvenile Court Act could be traced to nearly indistinguishable antecedents in other states, especially in Massachusetts. Indeed, the reliance on precedent was so clear that the reformers themselves made no effort to claim that the major elements of the legislation — separate trials and calendars, separation of juveniles from adults before trial, and probation — were unique or original.

It is true that some reformers stressed the claim that the new law brought these elements together for the first time and made explicit the conception that a child who broke the law was to be "treated as a child" rather than as a criminal.[26] Thus, these juvenile court reformers did claim orginality for the legislative embodiment of the idea that the criminal law was inappropriate for handling juvenile lawbreakers.

To assess the validity and significance of this claim requires, first, a discussion of specific elements of the juvenile court system created in 1899. But it is important to appreciate the limited nature of the claim itself. It is also important to realize that many of those judges and probation officers who participated in the first juvenile courts were in no sense overoptimistic, as so many later commentators have caricatured them. The tenor of many reformers' assessments of the juvenile courts' potential is represented by a comment from one of the most enthusiastic juvenile court judges, Ben Lindsey, of Denver: "Too much cannot be expected of the juvenile court. . . . It is a success . . . if it is only better than the old method."[27]

Religious Influence

It does seem true that in one specific respect the reformers were indeed defeated. The 1899 legislature continued the influence of private sectarian organizations, supported by state funds, which received referrals from the new juvenile courts: Section 17 of the Act required that the court place the child with custodians who had the same religious beliefs as the child's parents.

Penal Reform

Probably a more serious defeat for the reformers was their apparent failure to change conditions significantly in the institutions where children were placed after final court action. On the other hand, although these institutions were not abolished and new institutions were not authorized in 1899, the reformers did succeed in securing, in 1901, a certification procedure for all institutions receiving children under the Act and, in 1907, a mechanism for judicial review of the treatment given every committed juvenile.[28] It is impossible to evaluate the effectiveness of these measures without empirical evidence, which does not appear in the Platt and Fox studies.

Pretrial Detention

Of far more general importance is the claim that Illinois failed to effect reform in interim detention of juveniles pending final court action because the Act did not provide funds to build a juvenile detention home. To many reformers outside Illinois, reducing the number of children detained before final court action or a petition and providing a special "home" for the detention of children separate from adults accused of crimes were important — and sometimes overriding — goals.[29]

Both Platt and Fox are right in stating that under the 1899 Act not a penny from public funds would be spent to construct a new facility for detaining children pending final disposition of their cases, even though the statute said children under twelve could not be in jails. The legislators' refusal to pay for running the machinery it had set up seems in retrospect particularly ominous for the future of juvenile courts, whose supporters have often claimed that chronic fiscal neglect frustrated the original intent of the reformers.[30]

Portentous as the failure to finance the system may have been, however, it is possible to overestimate its significance from today's perspective, in a time when one does not think of private philanthropy salvaging a government-created program that the legislature leaves destitute. In Illinois at the turn of the century, public money was the relative newcomer, supplementing the investment of private charitable organizations. Where public money fell short, even in support of a public program, it seems that private funds could sometimes be expected to take up at least some of the slack. In this case, although no publicly supported detention facility was built under the 1899 law, children were placed in a building made available by a prisoner's aid society. Other children were lodged in a county hospital.[31]

Thus, it simply is not true that the prohibition against jail detention was defeated by legislative niggardliness, although this fact leaves open the more important question of whether it is desirable as a matter of policy to create a special system for detaining children apart from adults. In sum, the reformers did succeed in their purpose — children were in fact placed in separate detention facilities — but the nature and significance of the purpose itself remains at issue. Much the same can be said of two other specific aspects of the reform that were generally considered crucial, both in Illinois and elsewhere: the creation of a probation system as an investigative, fact-presenting, and correctional arm of the court; and the eschewing of "formal" court procedures in favor of "informal" ones.

Probation

Other than to note that Illinois borrowed its probation system from Massachusetts and that the legislature in 1899 refused to appropriate money for probation officers, neither Fox nor Platt discusses the significance of probation to the reform. Fox dismisses the creation of the probation system as a "token" aspect of the Illinois Act.[32]

Yet statements by reformers, early juvenile court judges, and early probation officers abound to the effect that throughout the nation — not just in Illinois — probation was considered more important than any other single element of the first juvenile court acts.[33] Specifically, both of the first juvenile court judges in Chicago isolated the probation system as the most important element of the Act.[34] With it, other reforms could wait, as they did in St. Louis; [35] without it, the other reforms were insufficient, as in Buffalo.[36]

These subjective evaluations are buttressed by the intimate historical relationship between the probation and the juvenile court movements. Although probation was never limited to juveniles before or after 1899, that date is almost as important to the growth of probation nationally as it is to the growth of juvenile courts. The use of probation had been sporadic and desultory until it became tied with the juvenile reform movement. It then spread to every state that enacted juvenile court legislation. By 1927, all but two states — Maine and Wyoming — had juvenile court laws, and every state except Wyoming had a juvenile probation system.[37]

That probation was the essential condition of juvenile justice reform is not difficult to understand. It was the tool that permitted juvenile court judges to extend their knowledge, and their dispositional authority, beyond the courthouse. The arm of the probation department that would supervise children who remained in their homes after disposition would give the judge an attractive middle course between incarceration and release. It was noted earlier that removing children from adult prisons was a central aim of many who pressed for juvenile court laws. By drawing on other community resources, probation would, at least in theory, provide the leverage to make possible a wide variety of different dispositions to match the variety of juveniles and their problems. Finally, probation would humanize and personalize the court's fact-finding process.

In partial response to the argument that the Juvenile Court Act continued the nineteenth-century faith in substitute families, the use of probation implies a commitment by the state to treat children in their homes and to try to correct their delinquent tendencies without removing them from their "evil" environments.[38] The compilation of social studies by probation workers may also be interpreted as an attempt to understand individual children personally, including their immigrant traits, instead of as a class.

Probation cannot be dismissed as irrelevant to the 1899 Act on the ground that the legislature refused to appropriate money to pay probation officers. Just as they provided the separate detention facility that the legislature would not fund, private philanthropists enlisted a corps of volunteer probation officers. Thus, despite the legislature's frugality, by the end of the Chicago court's first year, six probation officers were privately supported by the Juvenile Court Committee of the Chicago Woman's Club.[39]

In addition, one policeman in each police district was recruited to spend part of his on-duty time as a probation officer. As a result, the following scene occurred on the day that the Juvenile Court Act became effective:

> On July 1, 1899, Judge Tuthill met with the captains of the various police districts in Chicago and described the nature of the work which the new probation officers were expected to do:
> "What I desire from you gentlemen is your hearty cooperation in this work of preventing the growth of criminality among the young. You are so situated that you, even more than the justices, can get at the underlying facts in each particular case brought before you by the officers in your command. I shall want you to select some good reliable officers from each district to attend to the work of investigating the juvenile cases. The law contemplates that these officers shall discard their uniforms while investigating the cases."[40]

By 1904, fifteen policemen served as probation officers, ten to fifteen more officers were supported by the Woman's Club of Chicago, and several others were furnished by individual philanthropists.[41] Furthermore, as noted earlier, the absence of public financial support for probation persisted for only six years in Cook County, and for eight years elsewhere in Illinois.[42] By 1907 all probation officers in Illinois were publicly paid.

Procedures

Second in importance only to the role of probation in understanding juvenile court reform is the significance of the "informal" procedures mandated in the 1899 Act and its imitators. Fox reasons that this informality was not innovative because children had been dealt with informally before — especially in lower municipal courts. The argument is valid only if the "informality" of a police court is to be equated with the kind of "informality" contemplated for the juvenile court. Fox quite reasonably surmises that, in the nineteenth century, children tried for committing crimes were routinely processed primarily by lower municipal courts, which presumably did not adhere to the most libertarian conceptions of due process and adversary rights, especially in their dealings with children. With respect to commitments to training, industrial, and reform schools, it does not appear that children enjoyed any procedural rights whatever — even the rudimentary hearing that they would receive in the criminal courts.[43]

By contrast, thanks to private contributions, children in the Chicago juvenile court had the benefit of probation officers charged by law with the duty to represent their interests. (They also had a statutory right to a jury trial in every case.)[44] Children in juvenile court also enjoyed the benefit of apparently well-qualified judges, including Richard S. Tuthill and Julian Mack (later a Circuit Court judge). This is not to say that the absence of formal procedural provisions is irrelevant to the quality of the hearing children would receive in the long run, but the published facts do not warrant equating the atmosphere of the Illinois juvenile court in 1899 with what might reasonably be supposed to have been the nature of Chicago's petty criminal court proceedings.

Indeed, contrary to the assertion that "informality" was not an innovation in the juvenile courts, it is probably more accurate to say that juvenile courts represented in part an attempt to make procedure in one sense less informal — *less* summary and impersonal — by giving the court the time and manpower to conduct a full, personalized investigation in every case. There is good reason to believe that an important aim of the early reformers was to *improve* the quality of fact-finding in children's cases. Further, this purpose represented a reaction against the perceived sloppy, nonadversary assembly-line procedures in lower municipal courts.[45]

Thus, that juvenile court procedures would be "nonadversary" — without notice of specific charges and an opportunity to present a defense — was at most a minor, subsidiary aspect of juvenile court reform generally. For example, of all the authors who contributed to a 1904 collection of essays on the early juvenile courts, only Judge Ben Lindsey touched on the informality of procedures, and then only very briefly. Yet even he, like the other authors in the same collection, was far more impressed with the need for reforming correction and treatment programs than with making court procedures nonadversary.[46] As for the other authors, the following assertions can be made:[47]

1. None of them saw the creation of informal procedures as an important goal of juvenile court laws.
2. Formal, adversary procedures were not specifically regarded as inconsistent with the major purposes of the juvenile court laws (namely, to separate children from adults during detention, to individualize treatment, and to create a probation system).
3. Some of the authors expressly singled out a need for more thorough fact-finding as one important reason for creating juvenile courts.

Expansion of the Law's Writ

Platt's contention that the Act *expanded* the sphere of governmental intrusion in the lives of children complements Fox's argument that procedural "informality" was not "innovative" — and is just as vulnerable.

First, available evidence does not indicate that juvenile court laws expanded the categories of children *potentially* subject to state coercion. Similarly, it seems that a high proportion of children *in fact* incarcerated before the 1899 Act had not committed any crime — that same pattern the Platt says was created by the Act itself.

Specifically, Platt remarks that the juvenile courts were originally intended to handle "crime without victims" and that 50 percent of the delinquency cases in Cook County in the early years after passage of the Act arose from "disorderly behavior," "immorality," "truancy," and "incorrigibility," with the most common type of offense apparently being truancy. But it will be recalled that these broad status and juvenile offenses were added by amendments after 1899. More important, it is difficult to see how this pattern differs from that before the Act, in view of Platt's own findings. Thus, for instance, following the establishment of a State Reform School at Pontiac in 1867, children were committed, in part at the discretion of their parents and guardians, to indeterminate sentences for being "destitute of proper parental care, or growing up in mendicancy, ignorance, idleness or vice."[48] In 1898, the superintendent of a Chicago training school for boys, operated by the Board of Education "within the city prison," reported that his institution processed an average of 1,300 juveniles, "of which over a quarter were truants."[49]

Apart from incarceration in training, reform, and industrial schools on the basis of statutory criteria as vague and all-embracing as anything in the 1899 Act, children were systematically committed to adult jails for "disorderly conduct," a charge that could apparently encompass any act that might have served as a basis for juvenile court jurisdiction:

> From the first of January, 1899, when the legislature met which enacted the measure popularly known as the Juvenile Court Law, until the first of July, 1899, when the law went into effect, 332 boys between the ages of nine and sixteen years were sent to the city prison. Three hundred and twenty of them were sent up on the blanket charge of disorderly conduct, which covered offenses from burglary and assault with a deadly weapon to picking up coal on the railway tracks, building bonfires, playing ball in the streets, or "flipping trains," that is, jumping on and off moving cars . . . .[50]

Thus, a logical interpretation of the amendment expanding the jurisdiction of the Chicago juvenile court would be that it remedied a defect in the earlier legislation by bringing within the court children previously handled coercively by government agencies other than the juvenile court.

Nor does it follow, from the defeat of the reformers' attempt to effect a substantial improvement of children's conditions of confinement, that this effort failed totally or that children were treated more harshly by juvenile court judges than they had been by the criminal courts. Before the Act, according to Platt, the reform school at Pontiac was "in every sense a minor penitentiary."[51] An 1869 study of the state's jail system found ninety-eight juveniles jailed with more than four hundred adults, most of them awaiting trial, in institutions described as "moral plague spots" and breeding grounds for criminals. In the first six months of 1898, before the new Act barred the practice, 332 boys under sixteen were confined with adults in Chicago jails.[52]

If the use of probation and the presumption in the Act favorable to family treatment succeeded at all in reducing the confinement of children in adult penal institutions — and there is some evidence that the Act may in fact have had this effect — it would be difficult to argue that it served only to perpetuate the status quo.

Thus, most children referred to the new juvenile court were handled informally by probation officers. Only one-fourth were scheduled for a court appearance.[53]

Similarly, of 554 children placed on probation in the first two years under the original juvenile court act in Denver, 5.5 percent were subsequently committed to a training school. Of those brought to juvenile court on delinquency petitions, only 10 percent were initially sentenced to the schools, compared to 75 percent of those children who had appeared in criminal court before the 1903 law. Judge

Lindsey estimated that the less frequent resort to reform schools saved the state more than $100,000.[54]

Some of this evidence refutes the contention that in fact more children were brought under state control as a result of juvenile court acts. Probation may have kept some children out of training schools. However, it may also have permitted states to assume control over more children for longer periods of time than previously.[55] To make the case one way or the other requires objective evidence comparing what actually happened to children before and after the passage of juvenile court acts. Subjective evaluations and estimates by the reformers show only their own state of mind, and this is the primary evidence relied upon by Platt and Fox.

The Use of Coercion

Whether or not the Act affirmatively expanded state control, there remains to be considered the central idea of the Fox-Platt analysis that those responsible for the 1899 Act were able to propose only coercive measures as alternatives to the existing coercive system. A related argument is that the reliance on coercion reflected a partially suppressed hostility to immigrant cultures, a hostility that also interfered with the reformers' capacity to tailor programs for dealing with neglected and dependent children to values other than their own.

That the juvenile courts were and remain coercive institutions is self-evident. Juvenile courts deal with both crime and noncriminal problems by imposing conditions and restrictions of probation, assessing fines, removing children from their natural homes, and confining them in institutions. The broad coercive power of the juvenile court lurking constantly in the background also strengthens the hand of parents, teachers, police, welfare agencies, and adults generally in trying to make children behave differently from the way they want to behave. Thus, the juvenile court reformers created a system to force children to accept help against their wills and sometimes against the wills of their parents.

In stressing coercion and imposed "middle-class values," Platt and Fox's version of the juvenile court movement is similar to one view of the development of compulsory education in the latter half of the century.[56] The same kind of criticism is also commonly made of liberal good-government reforms dating from the same period.[57] These arguments hold that the main purpose of late nineteenth-century "reforms" was to instill habits of obedience and submission in order to protect the public peace, generate a docile labor force, and ensure the security of private property. Compulsory work for welfare recipients and civil commitment of people found both insane and dangerous illustrate other coercive techniques often attacked on roughly the same grounds.

In the future, it would be well if juvenile court historians attempted to relate juvenile courts and their problems to some of these other, similar forms of coercive government regulation of individual behavior. They might also consider bringing to the surface the intellectual currents of the day that made the air congenial to the growth of new legal instruments of social amelioration. Paramount among these were the reaction against Social Darwinism[58] and the rise of sociological jurisprudence.[59] In general, there is a need to reduce the conceptual isolation of juvenile courts, both vertically in time and horizontally across related institutions. Fox and Platt have made an important step toward meeting the former need; their accent on coercion suggests an approach to the latter need.

Imposed Middle-Class Values?

Nonetheless, despite the importance and validity of stressing coercion as the key aspect of juvenile court legislation, the leap to concluding that these laws — and other parallel progressivist measures — reflected class repression either is an act of faith or requires more objective evidence than Fox and Platt provide.

Assuming that greater social control over what was seen as undesirable lower-class disorder was indeed the promise, if not the immediate effect, of the juvenile court movement, one would like to know whether this phenomenon would have been entirely uncongenial to the lower-class groups themselves. Might not immigrants, racial minorities, and the poor have greeted an expansion of the state's police power as a vehicle for imposing middle-class ideals on ungovernable children, for relieving the burdens of underfinanced child-rearing, and for bringing a greater measure of order to turbulent neighborhoods? There is strong evidence that such a reaction would have been likely among many immigrants, although the answer may have varied according to different ethnic groups in different localities.[60] It is at least reasonable to assume that residents of crime-ridden neighborhoods in 1899 demanded, or at least desired, an intensity of even-handed police protection commensurate with the higher degree of lawlessness in their communities, as they do today. And it has not been shown that those largely excluded from benefits that accrue to the middle class scorn such attributes as discipline and self-denial.[61] In short, demonstrating that the middle class dominated the reforms does not also demonstrate that the lower class was harmed or offended.

Finally, the greatest obstacle to interpreting juvenile court acts as instruments of class oppression is the evidence that *parents* liberally availed themselves of the courts' broad jurisdiction and easy access by turning in their own children.

Thus, for example, both Judge Murphy and Judge Robert J. Wilkin, of the Children's Court of Brooklyn,[62] characterized, as the most difficult cases to come before them, those where the parents wanted only to rid themselves of a child, who was to be "branded as a disorderly or ungovernable child, when in reality such is not the case."[63] According to Judge Murphy, "in very many cases it is the parent who first despairs of controlling the boy at home, and it is the probation officer who stands by the child to save him from the reformatory."

WHAT DIFFERENCE DOES IT MAKE?

Of what significance is the preceding discussion of the history of juvenile court law? A glance back shows how little we have advanced in seventy-five years.

Procedures

This paper has dealt at some length upon the procedural aspect of the original juvenile court because the assumption that "informality" in the court hearing process is central to the "idea" of the juvenile court continues to exert an inordinate influence. There has been a tendency among writers on juvenile justice not to distinguish clearly between correction and treatment techniques on the one hand and procedures leading to dispositions on the other. One of the dangers exposed by a strong judge like Ben Lindsey is his confidence in the judge's power to act as investigator, adjudicator, and therapist. It is this conception, perhaps more than any other, that has fostered resistance to procedural change in the juvenile court. If the purpose of the initial court procedure was *itself* to treat, and not merely to establish the legality and desirability of one kind of treatment or another, then procedures that would interfere with the personal influence of the judge on the personality of the child would be entirely inconsistent with "the juvenile court idea."

Just such reasoning was recently relied upon by the Second Circuit Court of Appeals to justify denying a right of jury trial to juveniles charged with offenses for which they might subsequently be committed — and were in fact committed — to an adult prison.[64]

The crucial point is that this is the only conception of the juvenile court that is inherently inimical to adversary procedures: only if the person-to-person contact between judge and child during the hearing process is itself regarded as therapeutic, and only if that therapy is considered central to the function of the juvenile court, must adversary procedures be viewed as repugnant. Yet this view was apparently idiosyncratic among reformers and juvenile court judges at the time the first juvenile courts were established — indeed the circle of judges who embraced this idea with any fervor may not have extended beyond Ben Lindsey himself.

There is a second theoretical view of the juvenile court in which the presumed "informality" of "ideal" juvenile court procedures exercises a possibly baneful influence. The idea of the juvenile court has been characterized as a contract between government on one side and parents and children on the other, by which the full protection of procedural safeguards was relinquished in return for various promises amounting to a pledge that court intervention would help, not hurt (that is, children would not be stigmatized; the family would be strengthened; children removed from their homes would be treated as much as possible as they should be in good homes; and children would receive therapeutic treatment). If these promised benefits are not forthcoming, the theory continues, due process safeguards must be restored.[65] Evidence of substantive failures in juvenile court systems undoubtedly hastened the recent injection of procedural requirements, but this does not imply that procedural requirements preceding substantial coercion should vary with the "success" of the coercion, so long as the coerced individual himself objects. There is no opportunity here to explore the merits of the problem, but statements by reformers do not support the proposition that they had any *quid pro quo* in mind.

Substance: Jurisdiction and the
Use of Coercion

A historian of histories would find much evidence in the written accounts of the "first juvenile court law" to justify the conclusion that the accounts say more about the people who wrote them and their times than about anything that happened in Illinois in 1899. When juvenile courts were fresh, so were their histories; now, skepticism and cynicism are the accepted moods of the day, attitudes hastened by the criticisms leveled at juvenile courts by the President's Commission on Law Enforcement and Administration of Justice and the Supreme Court's *Gault* decision.[66]

The new reformist wisdom is that we are only beginning to learn that the juvenile courts were stillborn. It is no longer sufficient, by this view, to say that they have not been given the "resources" to do the job. The job cannot be done. A court cannot undertake both to protect the citizenry against lawlessness and to reform the lawbreaker. Coercive treatment premised on condemnation is punishment. We do not know enough — and even if we did we do not care enough — to do what is necessary to change children's behavior. To change children, we have to change society. In the meantime, we keep children out of the juvenile courts, where they are illegally coerced under hopelessly vague statutes and "stigmatized" (a popular word conjuring up a red letter on the breast but very difficult to define). The indictment should sound familiar: it is 1899 all over again. The "criminal" process (i.e., coercive, "stigmatizing" juvenile court) is no good. The jails and prisons (now, the training schools) "are training schools for crime."

Until recently, not only the indictment but also the agenda for reform was the same as it was in Jane Addams' Chicago: (1) keep kids out of big, coercive institutions and put them into small, community-based facilities (a variation of the idea behind probation); (2) replace the juvenile courts with "radical alternatives" like community councils on the "Scandinavian model," for kids who need help (that was the idea behind an "informal procedure" in Cook County); (3) "divert" kids from juvenile courts into programs run by expert child-serving institutions called "youth service bureaus" or "child advocacy centers" (i.e., develop individualized "treatment programs"). Even procedural reform, as argued above, is consistent with the main current of turn-of-the-century thinking.

The extent of the congruence between the present liberal agenda and that of the first reformers is captured with an ironic twist by the 1967 Crime Commission report, which echoed the usual mistaken characterization of the juvenile court movers as carried away by visions of beckoning scientific utopias. The Crime Commission vigorously condemned almost every aspect of present juvenile court practices — in the main those summarized above, to which the first reformers would also have objected — but concluded that on balance the juvenile court system should be preserved because it was better for kids than the criminal courts.[67] But this is all that the reformers themselves generally hoped the juvenile courts would be able to accomplish. It may be that it is the present reforming generation that is fooling itself, believing that any more than "better than the criminal courts" can be accomplished without a major reallocation of resources.

Moreover — perhaps in tacit recognition that the "liberal" agenda sketched above mimics the 1899 reform — one trend today seems to be to respond to many of the problems of children and adolescents by doing little or nothing unless severely provoked: (1) eliminate altogether the jurisdiction of juvenile courts over misbehavior of children that either defines a vague status ("incorrigible" and the like) or is peculiarly defined as misbehavior only for children (such as truancy); (2) bring only the most serious lawbreakers before the juvenile courts, referring others to entirely voluntary agencies and counseling, job placement, and "peer-group activities"; (3) commit juveniles to brief, determinate terms in coercive programs instead of indeterminate terms that may stretch on for many years, sometimes longer than an adult could receive for the same offense.

All of which may be an improvement but avoids the central dilemmas that gave rise to the 1899 law and which sustain juvenile courts today — how to respond to real needs appropriately and fairly, taking into account the dependency, vulnerability, and changeable nature of children and youth. The question is what (or whether any) program for reform will protect children's and parents' rights to fair proceedings, satisfy the universally felt need for enforcement of laws against serious offenders, protect children against harm from parents and guardians, use coercion where coercion is needed — but only where it is needed — and stop using coercion when it has done all it justifiably can do.

At least the latest alternative agenda does not rely on coercion and so is indeed different from the 1899 approach, which sought to replace one kind of coercion (jails, the criminal law) with another (probation, treatment). The trouble is that we do not know whether doing less will accomplish more. It does not purport to offer solutions to the real problems of children and youth; the danger is that the mere avoidance of making things worse will become the overriding measure of success. And we may find that the retreat from official coercion will leave a vacuum that only unofficial hidden coercion — by teachers, police, parents, runaway homes, and "youth service bureaus" — will fill as arbitrarily and destructively as any juvenile court.

In an atmosphere of skepticism that coercive social intervention can be trusted to help children, it may be that the most impressive justifications for the new approaches — emphasizing voluntariness, small scale, and above all reluctance to intervene coercively — are that they are cheaper and that they increase children's control of their own lives. Both of these may be taken as good in themselves. They were not the predominant attitudes of 1899. Seventy-five years from now we may know whether they are any wiser.

In Massachusetts the major institutions for delinquents have been closed. Institutional reform, at the top of the agenda in 1899, may now be at hand. Yet neither Massachusetts nor any other state, despite persistent rumblings, has implemented the new common wisdom in favor of greatly restricting juvenile courts' jurisdiction. Whether this represents continued middle-class hegemony, however, can be doubted; more likely it is a reflection of the enormous pressure generated by parents who no longer can or want to take care of their kids. It is the family problem we have yet to solve, and this was the sticking point in 1899.

Which brings us back to the issue raised earlier, the meaning and significance of the reformers' claim that at least in 1899 a state committed itself to handling law-violating children as children with problems rather than as criminals.

Three positive observations will close this discussion:

First, as the Crime Commission conceded despite its generally gloomy assessment of juvenile courts, kids do seem better off in those courts than they would be in adult criminal courts. This is true primarily because children's prisons as a whole are not as bad as adult prisons; because fewer children are sent to them, and for shorter periods of time; and because society seems to give juvenile courts a greater opportunity than criminal courts to handle even serious offenders by placing them in group or foster homes, in drug programs, or on probation instead of in prisons.

Second, the existence of a separate system committed on paper to treatment rather than punishment has permitted such innovations as former Commissioner Jerome Miller's reforms in Massachusetts, which seem now to have prepared the ground for reform of adult prisons in that state as well. The use of probation and the commitment to diversion at intake are similar flexible measures that were spawned in juvenile courts and later migrated to the adult system.

Finally, the purpose clause committing juvenile courts to ideal family treatment has proved a convenient handle in some cases for implementing the "right to treatment" idea, which otherwise must be pegged to more cumbersome and judicial restraint-inspiring constitutional doctrines.[68] Depending partly on the extent to which courts are willing to assess legislatures to pay for needed resources, these purpose clauses may yet provide a way to realize some of the promise of the original acts other than merely to treat children a little less badly than we treat criminals.

NOTES

1. Law of April 21, 1899 [1899] Ill. Laws 131.
2. By 1925 there were "juvenile courts" (although differing widely in essential attributes) in all but two states. — P. TAPPAN, JUVENILE DELINQUENCY xx (1949).
3. A. PLATT, THE CHILD SAVERS: THE INVENTION OF DELINQUENCY (1969).
4. FOX, *Juvenile Justice Reform: An Historical Perspective*, 22 STAN L. REV. 1187 (1970).
5. These additional measures provided for inspection of an annual reporting by foster homes, institutions, and private associations to whom children would be referred under the Act (*supra* note 1, §§ 12–14, 18, at 135), and regulated the deportation of dependent, neglected, and delinquent children to private agencies in Illinois by courts of other states (*id.*, § 16 at 136).
6. Delinquents more than ten years of age, unlike dependent and neglected children, could be committed to the state reformatory or Home for Juvenile Female Offenders. Dependent and neglected children, as well as delinquents, could be placed in a foster home, a state training school, or some accredited private institution. —*Id.*, §§ 7, 9.
7. See notes 24, 25, and 32 *infra* and related text.

8. Other procedural aspects of the Act are worth noting. "[A]ny reputable person" who in a petition alleged facts sufficient to invoke the court's jurisdiction could initiate a proceeding. — Law of April 21, 1899, *supra* note 1, § 4. This provision has contributed to the image of all juvenile proceedings — including those alleging commission of a crime — as "civil" in nature. Section 2 of the Act permitted any "interested person" to demand trial of any case brought under the Act by a "jury of six." This provision was probably included primarily to safeguard the constitutionality of the Act and was probably never used.

9. *Id.*, § 21, at 137.

10. Act of May 11, 1901 [1901] Ill. Laws 141.

11. Act of May 13, 1905, [1905] Ill. Laws 151.

12. Act of June 4, 1907, [1907] Ill. Laws 70.

13. Thus, the 1901 law broadened "delinquency" to embrace both a list of peculiarly juvenile offenses (e.g., frequenting places where "any gaming device" was operated) and the apparently all-encompassing "status" offenses of incorrigibility and "growing up in idleness or crime." — Act of May 11, 1901, *supra* note 10, § 2, at 142. The 1907 law extended the list of "juvenile" offenses to include, among other things, running away from home, loitering, and using profanity. — Act of June 4, 1907, *supra* note 12, § 2[1], at 76.

14. The 1901 law established a certification procedure, requiring that an outside public agency (the Board of State Commissioners of Public Charities) "pass" annually on the "fitness" of all institutions that received juveniles under the Act and forbidding commitment of children to institutions not approved by the agency as "competent" and having "adequate facilities to care for such children." — Act of May 11, 1901, *supra* note 10, § 13, at 143. In 1907, the new legislation permitted the court to inquire into the treatment accorded any adjudicated juvenile, to remove children from unsatisfactory institutions, and to return a committed juvenile to his home, if the home were later found suitable, "it being the intention of this Act that no child shall be taken away or kept out of his home . . . any longer than is reasonably necessary to preserve the welfare of such child and the interest of the state. . . ." — Act of June 4, 1907, *supra* note 12, §§ 9d – e, at 77.

15. The 1905 amendment provided public compensation (from county funds) for probation officers in Cook County. — Act of May 13, 1905, *supra* note 11, § 6, at 151. The 1907 legislature extended public remuneration to all probation officers in Illinois. — Act of April 19, 1907, § 6, [1907] Ill. Laws 69.

16. Handler, *The Juvenile Court and the Adversary System: Problems of Function and Form*, 1965, 1965 Wisc. L. Rev. 7.

17. Note, *Rights and Rehabilitation in the Juvenile Courts*, 14 Colum. L. Rev. 281 (1967). However, Julian Mack, the second juvenile court judge in Chicago, wrote in 1909 that he saw "nothing radically new" in probation or any other feature of the Act. — Mack, *The Juvenile Court*, 23 Harv. L. Rev. 104, 116 (1909). He viewed the work of juvenile courts generally as "at the best, palliative, curative." —*Id.*, at 122. This view was shared by many other judges and probation officers involved in the first juvenile courts. See notes 27 – 36 *infra* and related text.

18. Fox, *supra* note 4, at 1229.

19. Platt, *supra* note 3, at 83.

20. *Id.*, at 98.

21. *Id.*, at 3, 139.

22. In particular, a collection of essays by several of the first juvenile court judges and probation officers was published in 1904. — International Prison Commission, Children's Courts in the United States: Their Origin, Development, and Results, H.R. Doc. No. 701, 58th Cong., 2d, Sess. at x – xi (1904) (hereinafter cited as Children's Courts).

23. See President's Commission on Law Enforcement and Administration of Justice, Task Force Report: Juvenile Delinquency and Youth Crime 2-4 (1967). See also 4 W. Blackstone, Commentaries 21-22.

24. The chronology is summarized in Task Force Report, *Id.*, at 2–4. The House of Refuge is analyzed in R. Pickett, The House of Refuge (1969).

25. An 1869 statute there required the presence of a state agent or his deputy in cases of juveniles accused of crime whenever the child might be placed in a reformatory. His duties were to search for alternatives (e.g., placement in another family, indenture) and to visit the child periodically after disposition to see that the court's plan was being carried out. In addition, the state agent or his

assistant was to investigate juvenile criminal cases, "attend the trial and protect the interest of, or otherwise provide for, such child."

Juvenile hearings separate from criminal hearings were established in Suffolk County in 1870. In 1872 separate trials for juveniles were extended statewide, with various judges (justices of the peace, municipal and district judges, police courts) being called for the first time "trial justices of juvenile offenders." Separate sessions, court records, and dockets were established in 1872. In 1891, judges were required to appoint probation officers (the mayor of Boston had previously had discretionary authority to do this) to investigate cases of juveniles accused of crime and to visit them after disposition. In Boston, juvenile cases were heard separately, after criminal cases had been disposed of. Usually the judge examined the child privately in an anteroom in the presence of the state visiting agent.

Massachusetts' practices, and especially its probation system, as observed and reported upon by Lucy L. Flowers in 1895, was the specific and expressly recognized model for the Chicago Woman's Club's campaign for a juvenile court bill. The advocates of the bill did not themselves appear to consider their proposed juvenile court to be substantially different from the Massachusetts system, except for the section requiring that the state provide children removed from their homes with care as nearly as possible like that which should be given by parents. Mrs. Flowers herself thought that probation was clearly the most important concrete feature of the reform, an element directly borrowed from Massachusetts. — See J. HAWES, CHILDREN IN URBAN SOCIETY: *Juvenile Delinquency in Nineteenth-Century America* ch. x (1971).

26. HURLEY, CHILDREN'S COURTS, *op. cit. supra* note 22, at 8.

27. LINDSEY, *The Juvenile Courts of Denver,* in CHILDREN'S COURTS, *op. cit. supra* note 22, at 120. See also note 17 *supra*.

28. See notes 5 and 14 *supra*.

29. See Tuthill, *History of the Children's Court in Illinois,* in CHILDREN'S COURTS, *op. cit. supra* note 22, at 1; Lindsey, *supra* note 27, at 64 – 65; Skinner, *History of the Children's Court in Newark,* in CHILDREN'S COURTS, *id.,* at 148.

30. E.g., Alexander, *Constitutional Rights in the Juvenile Court,* in JUSTICE FOR THE CHILD, at 85 (M. Rosenheim ed. 1962).

31. See Kelsey, *The Juvenile Court of Chicago and Its Work,* 17 ANNALS, at 301 (1901).

32. Fox, *supra* note 4, at 1229.

33. According to Judge Tuthill, *supra* note 29, at 4, the character of the probation officer was absolutely central to the success of the court. Probation officers must be like "wise, patient, and loving parents." Thomas Murphy most sharply defined the central role of probation in *History of the Juvenile Court of Buffalo* in CHILDREN'S COURTS, *op. cit. supra* note 22, at 10. Despite earlier legislative provisions for separate and secret trials for juveniles, Judge Murphy reported, the key date for measuring the beginning of the juvenile court movement in New York was 1904, when probation was extended statewide —*Id.,* at 11.

Hannah Kent Schoof (president of the National Congress of Mothers and chairman of the Juvenile Court Committee of the New Century Club, Philadelphia), *A Campaign for Childhood,* in CHILDREN'S COURTS, *id.,* at 133, added still another opinion to all of those who conceived of probation as essential: "The success of the system would depend principally on the character of the probation work. . . ." As in Illinois, see notes 39 – 42 *infra,* the Pennsylvania legislature did not appropriate money for the probation officers it authorized the court to appoint. As in Chicago, private philanthropists, as well as charitable and women's organizations, bailed the court out.

Judge Stubbs, in *The Mission of the Juvenile Court of Indianapolis,* in CHILDREN'S COURTS, *op. cit. supra* note 22, at 149, swelled the chorus of those citing probation as central to the reform laws. Since he was apparently responsible for initiating the juvenile court law, some weight must be given to his assertion that the primary defect of police court treatment of children before the law was passed was the lack of any disposition midway between commitment to an institution and outright release. Because it filled that gap, the provision for probation officers was "the best feature of the statute." Although in Indiana the state paid for two probation officers in cities over 100,000, almost all of the important work was performed by a corps of nearly two hundred volunteers.

The importance of volunteers in probation was also underscored by Helen M. Rogers in *The Probation System of the Juvenile Court of Indianapolis,* in CHILDREN'S COURTS, *op. cit. supra* note 22, at 152. In her view, public money for enough supervising probation officers would never be sufficient to support enough manpower to do the kind of personal work with children that was essential to the system's success. Volunteers had been forthcoming most readily among business and professional men; volunteering for probation work had become so popular among the community's leaders that Mrs. Rogers could begin "to see afar off on the horizon the danger that it will become too fashionable."

In St. Louis, according to Eliot, _The Change Brought by the Juvenile Probation System in St. Louis,_ in CHILDREN'S COURTS, _op. cit. supra_ note 22, at 162, attempts to revamp the system of handling delinquent children was scrapped in 1903 in favor of one essential reform: a juvenile probation system.

34. See note 33 _supra;_ Mack, _supra_ note 17, at 116; Kelsey, _supra_ note 31, at 121.

35. See Eliot, supra note 33.

36. See Murphy, _supra_ note 33.

37. H. LOU, JUVENILE COURTS IN THE UNITED STATES 24 (1927).

38. At the same time that the Illinois legislature established the juvenile court, it undertook to regulate the massive importation of dependent, neglected, delinquent, and generally unwanted children placed in Illinois by the courts of other states. See Kelsey, _The Importation of Delinquent Children,_ 18 ANNALS 90 (1901). The purpose of this effort was to force resident states to care for their own children rather than dumping them in the West and was thus consistent with the intent of probation.

39. The first probation officer in Illinois was Alzina P. Stevens, a resident of Hull House. Like John Augustus, the first probation officer in the United States, Mrs. Stevens began as a volunteer. That probation systems were originally conceived as dependent on volunteers renders the Illinois legislature's failure to appropriate public money for Chicago's probation officers innocuous.

40. R. KOBETZ, THE POLICE AND JUVENILE DELINQUENCY 148 (1971), quoting the Chicago Tribune, July 2, 1899.

41. Tuthill, _supra_ note 29, at 2.

42. See note 15 _supra._

43. See D. ROTHMAN, THE DISCOVERY OF THE ASYLUM 209 (1971).

44. See note 17 _supra._

45. Contrary to traditional formulations of the "original juvenile court idea" that juvenile court judges were concerned with a youth's condition rather than with particular acts, in Judge Murphy's court (see note 33 _supra)_ the next step following the filing of the petition was the plea taking, and juveniles who pleaded not guilty were given an immediate hearing before any thought was given to disposition. The only children sentenced in Judge Murphy's court were those found guilty of a violation of the state penal code.

Mrs. Schoof, _supra_ note 33, was also moved to press for reform by the arbitrariness of criminal court procedures: "Any magistrate could commit a child to a reformatory on the parent's statement of incorrigibility, and no effort was ever made to prove the parent's statement. The child's side of the case was never heard." —_Id.,_ at 134–35. Children were processed through the overcrowded, impersonal criminal courts that disposed summarily of their cases without having the time or resources to dispose of any case other than arbitrarily.

B. Hall shared Mrs. Schoof's distaste for the summary and "flippant manner that usually characterizes proceedings in the police courts of our large cities" and cited this as a major concern of those whose efforts resulted in the juvenile court law enacted in 1902. — CHILDREN'S COURTS, _op. cit. supra_ note 22, at 144 – 45.

Judge Alfred F. Skinner, _History of the Children's Court in Newark, New Jersey,_ in CHILDREN'S COURTS, _op. cit. supra_ note 22, at 147, enumerated and stressed the importance of such procedural safeguards as a specific written complaint, a formal pleading, advising of the right to jury trial and to a grand jury presentment, assignment of counsel, and trial of the factual question of criminal law violation.

46. Lindsey, _supra_ note 27, expressed great faith in almost every part of the system, including his own moral force and the capacity of reform and industrial schools — institutions that he likened in importance to the best universities. —_Id.,_ at 29 – 30. But he also considered probation to be of paramount importance, and commitment to a training school as an admission of failure and a sign that the home environment of the child placed there was "hopeless." He also realistically assessed the industrial school as "as much of a horror" to the juvenile as "a penitentiary to an adult." —_Id.,_ at 38.

Lindsey's views of proper juvenile procedure are a paradigm of the _parens patriae_ position: Lawyers should never be appointed to represent a child because "the court is their defender and protector as well as corrector." —_Id.,_ at 64. Rules of evidence were out of place because they would allow the release of children whose guilt the judge knew of with certainty or could easily discover by shaming them into confessing. Letting guilty boys go free because of failure of formal proof, when the judge knew they were guilty, would only breed cynicism and reward concealment of the truth. —*Id.*, at 107.

47. See note 45 *supra*.

48. PLATT, *supra* note 3, at 103.

49. *Id.*, at 129.

50. Lathrop, Introduction, in S. BRECKENRIDGE & E. ABBOTT, THE DELINQUENT CHILD AND THE HOME 2 (1912).

51. PLATT, *supra* note 3, at 103.

52. *Id.*, at 127.

53. HAWES, *supra* note 25, ch. 10. In support of the claimed success of the system, Judge Tuthill, *supra* note 29, presented statistics showing that of 1,301 delinquency cases brought before him between Feb. 1 and Nov. 1, 1903, more than half (715) were placed on probation, 505 were sentenced to the John Worthy School, 58 cases were dismissed, 17 were sentenced to other courts, and 6 were placed in institutions for dependents. Of the 505 children placed in the school, 467 had previously been before the court at least once and 141 had been there at least twice. Thus, only about 38 children were placed in the school as a result of their first delinquency petition.

54. Lindsey, *supra* note 27, at 33. In Philadelphia, as in every other city surveyed in CHILDREN'S COURTS, *op. cit. supra* note 22, institutions were to be used only as a "last resort." Children were to remain at home unless the home was found "absolutely unsuitable," in which case some other home would be preferable to institutional placement. During 20.5 months, of 2,438 cases that came before the Philadelphia juvenile court, 1,726 alleged delinquency and 743 alleged dependency. About three-fifths (1,375) of these children were placed on probation.Of these, 54 subsequently returned to court. Only 166 children were placed in the House of Refuge. The others are unaccounted for. Presumably they were simply left in their homes, either after their cases had been dismissed or as one form of disposition, perhaps after a warning from the judge. — Schoof, *supra* note 33, at 140–41.

55. For instance, in five months, as a result of the juvenile court act according to an early probation officer in St. Louis, the St. Louis police and circuit courts placed on probation 255 children, of whom 8 percent were returned to court. The author speculates that many of these children would previously have been committed to the reform school, but she also praises probation because it would extend society's control over trouble-making juveniles: "formerly many children were released by the police at the stationhouse; while now it is their duty to report the arrest of every child to the probation officers for investigation. Children who are drifting into evil ways are checked and restrained." — Eliot, *supra* note 33.

56. For example, C. SILBERMAN, CRISIS IN THE CLASSROOM 55–58 (1970), taking to task the present system of public schools, includes a critical discussion of the roots of compulsory education in the United States that is similar to Fox's and Platt's analysis of juvenile court reform. It views most schools around the turn of the century as primarily engaged in proselytizing middle-class values and overtly antagonistic to minorities. "We were becoming Americans by learning how to be ashamed of our parents." —*Id.*, at 58.

Interestingly, although he records that Illinois instituted compulsory education in 1883, Platt blames the juvenile courts, rather than compulsory education itself, for inventing truancy as a form of juvenile misbehavior— even though truants were important subjects of state compulsion in Illinois before 1899.

A new compulsory education law enacted in Illinois in 1899 resulted partly from efforts of the Chicago Woman's Club (the group that initiated the juvenile court movement), which was concerned with enforcing school attendance as a method of reducing delinquency at that time. It succeeded only in strengthening the status quo: incorrigible truants, instead of being tolerated, were expelled. – HAWES, *supra* note 25, Ch. 10.

57. A major reform of the Chicago city government preceded the Juvenile Court Act by just three years. See King, *The Reform Movement in Chicago,* 25 ANNALS 235 (1905). This movement also had a nationwide impact. The same kind of incapacity of reform government, relative to the bossism it tried to oust, to give immigrants a sense that political power was responsive to their concrete everyday needs and wishes has plagued attempts to "clean up City Hall" from the beginning of the progressive era in the late nineteenth century. See R. HOFSTADTER, *The Age of Reform* 182–84 (1955).

58. It can be argued that the juvenile court that emerged at the turn of the century embodied two

germinal concepts of the late nineteenth-century reaction against Social Darwinism. Against no one was the Social Darwinist equation of physical weakness with moral inferiority more uncomfortable to sustain than against the impoverished child. Even if charity toward adults was scorned as a reward for weakness, charity toward children could be sustained as merely preserving a life until it was mature enough to prove its worth. In addition, the instrument of probation and the disenchantment with institutional care gave legal expression to the vision of the human personality as rooted in and maturing through creative interaction with other individuals. Probation maintained the child in his natural social environment but also introduced a new strong personality into the child's life, thus preserving his cultural world while exposing him to influences that might allow him to cope with a dominant culture different from his own.

59. See Pound, *The Scope and Purpose of Sociological Jurisprudence,* 25 HARV. L. REV. 140 (1911), 489 (1912).

60. See N. GLAZER & D. MOYNIHAN, BEYOND THE MELTING POT 82–83 (importance of religion to blacks), 124–125 (strict Puerto Rican morality in dealing with children), 195 (Italian indifference to U.S. moral code) (1963).

61. O. HANDLIN, THE UPROOTED 254 (paper ed. 1951): "In [the immigrants'] eyes, the young Americans were undisciplined and ungrateful, good only at throwing stones and snow at strangers."

62. *History of the Children's Court, Borough of Brooklyn, City of New York,* in CHILDREN'S COURTS, *op. cit. supra* note 22, at 25.

63. *Id.,* at 26.

64. United States ex rel. Murray v. Owens, Nos. 72-1474, 72-1514 at 4346-47 (2d Cir. Aug. 10, 1972).

65. The idea that less procedural "formality" leaves courts free to be more flexible in giving individual treatment to children in trouble was reflected recently in *McKeiver v. Pennsylvania,* 402 U.S. 528 (1971), holding there is no Fourteenth Amendment right to a jury in juvenile delinquency cases that may lead to lengthy incarceration.

66. *In re* Gault, 387 U.S. 1 (1967).

67. PRESIDENT'S COMMISSION ON LAW ENFORCEMENT AND ADMINISTRATION OF JUSTICE, THE CHALLENGE OF CRIME IN A FREE SOCIETY 81 (1967): "As trying as are the problems of the juvenile courts, the problems of the criminal courts, particularly those of the lower courts that would fall heir to much of the juvenile court jurisdiction, are even graver. . . ."

68. See United States v. Alsbrook, 336 F. Supp. 973 (D.C.D.C. 1971); Gough, *The Beyond-Control Child and the Right to Treatment: An Exercise in the Synthesis of Paradox,* 61 St. LOUIS U.L.J. 182 (1971).

2 *The Juvenile Courts*

H. Ted Rubin

The juvenile court is a special institution in American society. It receives considerable attention from the general public, and its efforts in behalf of children, families, and the community involve a wide web of collaborating agencies and citizens. It touches the lives of many of the poor. Teachers and school personnel are intensely aware of its presence. The middle and upper class citizens who work to improve social services for children and families learn to solicit the juvenile court judge's support for their efforts. Police officials and the juvenile court staff maintain an ambivalent working relationship — they approach their functions differently, although

From H. Ted Rubin, *The Courts: Fulcrum of the Justice System* (Santa Monica, Calif.: Goodyear Publishing Company, Inc., 1976) pp. 66–102.

they share certain common objectives. The judge of this court is far more active, generally, than other judges in exploiting his status to secure the expansion of needed health and welfare services. Serious crimes committed by youth disturb our image that this is the court of the lesser violation.

This court is a far more complex instrument than outsiders imagine. It is law, and it is social work; it is control, and it is help; it is the good parent and, also, the stern parent; it is both formal and informal. It is concerned not only with the delinquent, but also with the battered child, the runaway, and many others. It is undergoing substantial change, possibly more change than any other court. Criminal courts have projected a more predictable role to the public. The juvenile court has been all things to all people. It should probably narrow its scope and more carefully define its purpose.

One starting point for beginning to comprehend the juvenile court is to focus on the question of what the role of the juvenile court should be in this society. To project this role into the future requires an examination of the present and the past. And the examination of the present should focus initially on the structure and jurisdiction of this court. By structure is meant the place of the juvenile court in relation to other courts. By jurisdiction is meant the legislative provision as to those matters which can lawfully be considered by this court. The structure and jurisdiction of the juvenile court vary from state to state.

THE STRUCTURE OF JUVENILE COURTS

Factors useful in understanding the structure of the juvenile court, and in ascertaining its relative status among the various courts, include whether it is organized as a higher, lower, or separate court; the comparative pay of its judges; and whether appeals from its decisions are taken to the general trial court or to the state's appellate court system.

In California the juvenile court is really the juvenile division of the Superior Court. The Superior Court is the highest court of general trial jurisdiction. A presiding judge of the Superior Court typically assigns one or more judges to serve in the juvenile division. These judges were appointed as Superior Court judges. They frequently serve a year in the juvenile division and are then reassigned to a different division. Appeals taken from any division of the Superior Court go to an appellate court. The juvenile division, however, does not always have a status which is really equal to the other divisions, and better judges are not always willing to be assigned to the juvenile bench.

In Utah the juvenile court is a separate, statewide juvenile court system. Its judges are appointed by the governor, and throughout their term hear only juvenile cases. A term of office in this juvenile court is six years. The Utah equivalent of the California Superior Court is called the District Court. Utah juvenile court judges receive the same pay as the District Court judges. Appeals from both Utah juvenile courts and District Courts are taken to the Utah Supreme Court.

In Colorado, until 1965, there was one separate juvenile court in Denver; in the other sixty-two counties of that state, juvenile matters were heard in the county court. It was not required that the county court judge be a lawyer except in about ten of the largest counties. The great percentage of judges hearing juvenile cases were not lawyers, though probably the majority of juvenile cases were considered by lawyer judges. The Colorado equivalent to the California Superior Court is the District Court. While a Denver juvenile court judge received the same pay as a District Court judge before 1965, a county court judge was paid less. Further, appeals from the county court were taken to the next court up, the District Court, rather than directly to a state appellate court. The county court was ranked as an inferior court. A 1962 constitutional amendment, followed by implementing legislation in 1964, removed this structural inferiority and placed the juvenile function in the District Court throughout the state except in Denver, where a separate court has been retained.

The Juvenile Court for the District of Columbia, a separate court for many decades, was abolished in 1970 and its functions were transferred to a family division of the new Superior Court for the District of Columbia. In 1972 Delaware created a statewide family court, somewhat similar to Utah, but with a jurisdiction handling a wider array of family-related matters. The District of Columbia and the State of Delaware illustrate the two major structural directions in juvenile court reorganization. The first is the movement to place the juvenile jurisdiction, and to retain its specialness, either as a juvenile or a family division, but within the larger court organization. The latter is the movement to extend the separateness of a juvenile or family court as an independent structure. Massachusetts and Kansas are other states where new and separate juvenile courts have been approved in several communities in recent years. These two directions are in conflict. They may be termed the "Unified Trial Court Movement," and the "Specialized Trial Court Movement." Nationally, there seems to be more support for the former.

There are a variety of other structures for courts of juvenile jurisdiction. One is Maine, where a juvenile court is part of the lower district court in each of the districts of that state. Another includes states like Michigan, where a probate judge (the probate court is responsible for the administration of the estates of deceased and mentally incompetent persons and has jurisdiction over mental illness and retardation commitment procedures), also presides over the juvenile jurisdiction. In a number of states there are separate juvenile or family courts in larger counties, but in the remainder of the state the juvenile function is either in the court of highest general trial jurisdiction (Georgia) with the requirement of lawyer judges, or in a county-level court (Alabama, Mississippi) which does not require a lawyer judge, and where appeals go not to the state appellate court system but to the highest court of general trial jurisdiction.

Figures 2-1 through 2-7 illustrate different models of juvenile court and probation organization.

THE JURISDICTION OF JUVENILE COURTS

There is enormous variation in the types of matters which can be brought before juvenile courts. In California, four major types of cases are heard by juvenile courts: the delinquent child (Section 602 of the Welfare and Institutions Code), the

ORGANIZATION OF COURT OF JUVENILE JURISDICTION AND OF JUVENILE PROBATION AND RELATED SERVICES

Figure 2-1 Alaska Model

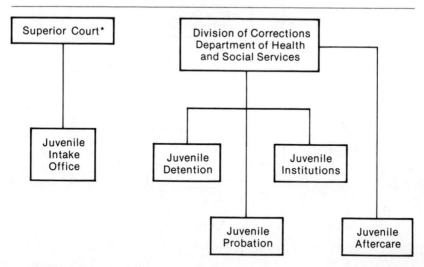

*Highest court of general trial jurisdiction.

Figure 2-2 California Model

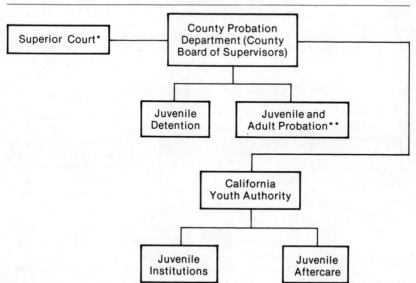

*Highest court of general trial jurisdiction.

**Two counties have separate juvenile probation departments.

Figure 2-3 Colorado Model

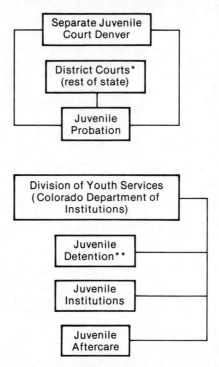

*Highest court of general trial jurisdiction. These courts and all juvenile probation are funded by the state judicial system.

**Detention administration was transferred from the judicial system to the Division of Youth Services on July 1, 1973.

Figure 2-4 Florida Model

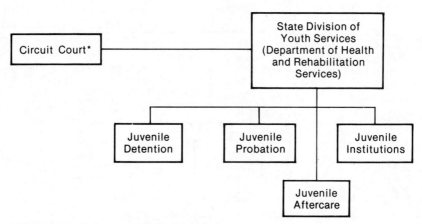

*Highest court of general trial jurisdiction.

Figure 2-5 **Massachusetts Model**

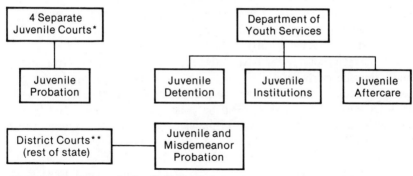

*Boston, Worcester, Springfield, Bristol.

**The Lower Court.

Note: Juvenile probation services are frequently organized into a regional probation district to serve up to five or six district courts within the same county.

Figure 2-6 **North Carolina Model**

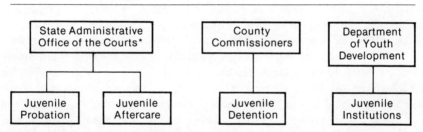

*Juvenile jurisdiction is within the District Court, the lower court. Chief District Court Counselors are appointed by the Administrative Director of Juvenile Services (Administrative Office of the Courts), with the concurrence of the Chief District Court Judge. Court Counselors are appointed by the Chief District Court Counselors, with the concurrence of the Administrative Director of Juvenile Services. The state funds the salaries and expenses of all court counselors (juvenile probation and aftercare workers).

Figure 2-7 **Utah Model**

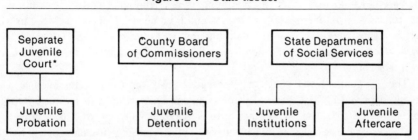

*This is a separately organized, statewide juvenile court. Its judges receive the same pay as judges of the highest court of general trial jurisdiction.

child in need of supervision (Section 601), the dependent or neglected child (Section 600), and the juvenile traffic offender. All juvenile courts handle the first three types of children and youth. Slightly more than one-third of our juvenile courts deal with the juvenile traffic offender. In the other states, this child is handled as an adult in the basic traffic court.

Utah juvenile courts also have jurisdiction over these four types of matters, although juvenile traffic offenders may be heard either in juvenile court or in the basic traffic court. However, the Utah Juvenile Court Act defines in-need-of-supervision types of offenses beyond the control of his parents, is labeled delinquent and is subject to commitment to the same delinquency institution to which a child who steals or robs may be sent. California appears to have been the first state to have legislatively separated from juvenile delinquency (Section 602), the juvenile status offenses of runaway, incorrigibility, and habitual truancy, to have categorized these separately (Section 601), and curtailed the power of the juvenile court judge to commit these youngsters to the California Youth Authority.

In 1962, the New York legislature adopted a similar reclassification, calling these children "persons in need of supervision" (PINS). While that legislature also restricted what a judge could do with this child, the absence of community service alternatives to receive or work with these children resulted in a subsequent amendment permitting New York family court judges to place these children in delinquency institutions. In 1965 Illinois adopted a similar provision, titled "minor in need of supervision (MINS), and in 1967 Colorado established the category "child in need of supervision" (CHINS). During the past fourteen of fifteen years more than half the states have created such a new category,[1] and concurrently have sought to restrict, if not prohibit, the capability of a judge to commit such a child to a state delinquency institution. Until this movement began, these children were known as delinquent children. Whether the child committed an armed robbery or simply ran away from home, the juvenile court judge had the power to place this child in a state delinquency institution. The creation of the "in need of supervision" category reflects the criticism that children are discriminated against by juvenile court legislation. Adults who run away, are incorrigible, or are habitually truant from the vocational or college training programs, are not subject to court intervention or restriction.

A major issue today is whether legislatures should take the next step and remove this type of offense from any sanction by the juvenile court. In the meantime, a child who runs away in Wyoming is a "delinquent child," but his cousin who runs away in New Mexico is a "child in need of supervision." In states such as New Mexico, juvenile delinquency is limited to a violation of a law which when committed by an adult would subject that adult to the jurisdiction of a criminal court.

The "dependent and neglected" category, also known in states such as Georgia as "deprived child," generally refers to the child who is abandoned, who has been subjected to abuse, who lacks proper parental care, or who is failing to receive necessary medical care. The battered child falls into this category. The child whose parents have died, are hospitalized, or are imprisoned, and for whom no suitable private care plan has been provided, is within this category. These children cannot be committed to delinquency institutions, and the judge is restricted to ordering social services, foster home or group home care, or medical or mental health services. Most juvenile courts hold the power to terminate parental rights to this child, involuntarily and permanently under circumstances of severe or ongoing neglect or abuse. Such termination of rights frees the child for adoption, and permits a subsequent application to adopt this child by other parties. However, only about one-fifth of juvenile courts have jurisdiction to hear adoption proceedings.[2] In the other states, the adoption proceeding is heard in a different court. Many states provide that juvenile courts may entertain the petition of a parent or parents who voluntarily seek to terminate their rights to their child. This proceeding is often referred to as "relinquishment." All states permit this proceeding, but generally it is not held in the juvenile court. Relinquishment also frees the child for adoption.

About one-fourth of juvenile courts have been granted jurisdiction to determine the paternity of a child;[3] and to issue support orders for the children. Further, some juvenile courts have jurisdiction over proceedings in connection with a child who is mentally ill or mentally retarded, and subject to commitment to mental health or retardation facilities. Many juvenile courts also hold jurisdiction over adults who may induce, aid, or encourage a child to violate a law. This is frequently known as "contributing to delinquency." Some juvenile courts may also be the center for the proceedings against parents who may neglect or abuse their children, and the court may take punitive action against such parents. This is different from the dependency or neglect jurisdiction referred to earlier, where the court's concern is whether or not the child has been neglected rather than whether the parents have neglected this child.

The Utah Juvenile Court Act grants juvenile court jurisdiction over juvenile violations of fish and game laws, but the Colorado statute places such juvenile violators in another court.

FAMILY COURTS

The concept of a family court embraces the juvenile jurisdiction plus a range of adult matters which relate to the family. The 1970 District of Columbia law sets forth perhaps the broadest range of family and juvenile matters subject to the jurisdiction of a single family court division. This court has jurisdiction over divorce and the range of divorce related matters such as custody, visitation, property settlement, alimony, and support of children. This court also has jurisdiction over intrafamily misdemeanor offenses, for example when a husband or wife injure each other or another family member. Its jurisdiction also includes paternity, child support (where there has been no divorce), mental illness and retardation as to children and adults, relinquishment and adoption, and delinquency, in-need-of-supervision, neglect, and additional miscellaneous matters. However, the Family Court for Jefferson County, Alabama (Birmingham), the Family Court in New York, and the Family Court in Delaware, are all entitled family courts, but their jurisdiction is less broad, and excludes divorce, for example. It is necessary to go beyond the title of a court to determine its jurisdiction.

The movement to unify courts and place juvenile courts within the court of highest general trial jurisdiction raises the question whether the new juvenile division of this court should really become a family court division. If so, what range of family-related matters should be tied together into one court division?

JURISDICTIONAL AGE

The question of what a juvenile court is also requires definition in terms of the age range for the court's original jurisdiction. Approximately thirty-four states including the District of Columbia assert jurisdiction over juvenile offenses until the eighteenth birthday.[4] Five states terminate this jurisdiction on the sixteenth birthday, and all other states on the seventeenth birthday. Until recently, three states had differing sex-age jurisdictional provisions. In Oklahoma juvenile court age went to the eighteenth birthday for girls, but to the sixteenth birthday for boys. Illinois and Texas juvenile courts went to the eighteenth birthday for girls, but to the seventeenth birthday for boys. Appellate court decisions in Oklahoma and Texas voided this age difference as unconstitutional. Illinois, in 1972, made a similar change by legislation. Subsequent legislation equalized the maximum jurisdictional age for boys and girls at seventeen years in Illinois and Texas, and at eighteen years in Oklahoma.

In New York State, where delinquency jurisdiction stops on the sixteenth birthday, but PINS jurisdiction continued until the eighteenth birthday for girls, an appellate court ruled that girls may no longer be subject to court sanctions for status offense behavior at age sixteen or seventeen years, since boys were not similarly subject to PINS jurisdiction after their sixteenth birthday.[5]

In recent years, a number of legislative efforts have attempted to drop the basic delinquency age by one or two years. Such attempts have generally been defeated, although some states have made changes so that within juvenile court age, but above a certain age, those who may have committed certain more serious offenses may be filed on directly in the criminal court and treated as an adult. While the criminal court judge, generally, has more severe sentences available to his disposition, this is not always true. Certain adult offenses are subject to maximum sentences of, for example, two years, whereas the same offense may subject a twelve-year-old youth to a statutory maximum of nine years probation or institutionalization. This is because many states place no restriction on the extent of juvenile probation or institutionalization other than, "to the twenty-first birthday unless sooner discharged." In reality, few youths serve such lengthy sentences, although they frequently serve more time on probation or in institutions and on parole than their adult counterparts.

Six states set minimum ages under which no child may be considered for a delinquency petition. Four states set such minimum age at ten years, two other at seven years.[6] One other age factor requires comment. Many juvenile court acts include provisions for what is known as a transfer or waiver hearing. These provide, generally, that if a child is over a certain age, such as sixteen years (although in some states this is either fourteen or fifteen years) and commits what would be a felony offense if committed by an adult (although some states fail to restrict these offenses to felonies), a special hearing may be held in the juvenile court where the judge considers whether to transfer this youth to the criminal court for consideration as an adult. Whether or not the youth is transferred hinges, usually, on the seriousness of the present offense, the past delinquency record, attempts to rehabilitate the youth, and the capability of the juvenile system to arrange rehabilitative programs which may be expected to achieve rehabilitation without further violation.

A decision to transfer a child to the criminal court should be seen as the most serious decision a juvenile court judge may make. While studies of what happens to transferred youngsters have shown that some are found innocent in criminal court and others are placed on probation, nonetheless the likelihood of an extensive sentence of penal incarceration looms for every youth transferred.[7] The next most serious decision a juvenile court judge makes is the commitment of a youth to a state delinquency institution, symbolic of a failure to achieve rehabilitation at the local level.

In Colorado, where the minimum delinquency age is ten years, Denver police have joked about holding a birthday party for certain children who are about to become ten years of age. The police, who have known these youngsters well from a variety of offenses, can then ask the court to file a delinquency petition. While the behavior of certain of these younsters could have been categorized as a status offense (CHINS) by court intake, legislative strategy had preferred noncourt assistance for such youthful law violators. . . .

EMERGING ISSUES IN JUVENILE JUSTICE

Juvenile court statutes set forth two major criteria which should govern decisions whether a child is detained, whether a child is handled formally, and the disposition a judge should make once he finds a delinquent act has been committed. These standards are: the best interests of the child, and the best interests of the community.

Obviously, these criteria are not clearly defined. Critics of the court have charged further that the court has been preoccupied with the best interests of the child and has slighted the best interest of the community. They point to the sometimes serious offenses committed by youths and the court's preference to retain youths in the community under probation status, or in conjunction with services provided by noncourt agencies. They point further to frequent repeat offenses by youths placed on probation or returned to their parents pending court consideration. In reality, we are only now beginning to gather reliable data as to recidivism and as to the effect of various interventive strategies in facilitating a juvenile's adjustment.

In part, our society has very mixed feelings about its children. Many recognize that adolescence is a period of experimentation, of searching to find out who one is, of emerging from a more dependent status into greater independence. On the other hand, we still wish to punish our children, or at least maintain a vehicle, such as as juvenile court, to threaten punishment when our children fail to conform to our expectations as to how they should behave. Schools still dump their "troublemakers" on the court. Parents turn to the court when their children rebel against parental expectations. And many believe the police more readily refer a child to court when his attitude is contentious than when he is subservient.[8]

Candidates and other politicians, in trumpeting their concern for mounting delinquency and crime rates, berate processing inadequacies as well as the policies of "soft headed judges." Prominent media attention to such utterances may result in a decision by a judge to detain a juvenile rather than not to detain him, or a decision to institutionalize rather than to continue with probation. While it is true that institutional alternatives remain underdeveloped, and that rehabilitative services are often ineffective, it is also true that many juvenile institutions contribute more to the destruction than the enhancement of the individual. It is important to recognize, however, that to urge improved rehabilitative services, and to veer away from unnecessary institutionalization, is not necessarily to ignore the principle of holding a youth responsible for his misdeeds. It can be said that both critics and friends of the court are dissatisfied with the rehabilitation services provided by or through the court.

Four major directions for juvenile justice now seem clear:
1. That the juvenile court is a court, and law and lawyers will play an increasingly more powerful role in the juvenile court of the future.
2. The movement to narrow the court's jurisdiction will continue. Concern for such victimless offenses as runaway, incorrigibility, and habitual truancy will lessen, while concern will focus more on youths who violate laws which if committed by adults would constitute crimes.
3. The court will rely even more on community-based alternatives to standard delinquency institutions.
4. The court will be increasingly professionalized, with better trained personnel, and with greater research and knowledge about the system utilized more extensively than ever before.

The Juvenile Court as a Court of Law

The Supreme Court's rulings have had marked effect upon the juvenile court. The 1967 *Gault* decision ruled not only that a child had the right to a lawyer and to a free lawyer if indigent, but also that written notice of the specifics of the offense must be provided the child and his parents, that the child must be advised by police officers of his right to silence and of this right to counsel during police interrogation, and finally that hearsay evidence was not admissible in the hearing which adjudicates whether or not an offense was committed.[9] A year earlier, the *Kent* decision ruled that in procedures concerning transfer from juvenile to criminal court due process fairness must attach, a hearing is required, counsel should represent the child at this hearing, and probation officer reports should be made available to the child's lawyer.[10] In 1970, the *Winship* decision ruled that the measure of proof in a delinquency trial must be beyond a reasonable doubt. The court reasoned that since one's freedom was at stake, due process required that the amount of testimony necessary for conviction be as high as the standard used in an adult criminal case.[11]

In 1971, in the *McKeiver* case, the court reverted to an early rationale in ruling that the federal Constitution did not compel that states provide the right of jury trial to an accused juvenile. The court majority stated that since the federal Constitution compelled jury trials only in criminal proceedings, juveniles were not constitutionally entitled to jury trials, although a state may legislate this opinion, or a state appellate court might determine that its state constitution compels a jury trial right within the state.[12] Eleven states allow jury trials for children charged with delinquency, either by statute or by case decision.[13] In many states which allow jury trials for juveniles, this right is infrequently invoked. The court opinion ruling against the right to a jury trial was also based in part on the majority's concern that jury trials might enormously expand court delays and confusion, increase formality and an adversary quality, and further disrupt this troubled institution.

The court resolved a further issue in 1975, deciding in *Breed* v. *Jones* that the double jeopardy clause of the Fifth Amendment applies, through the Fourteenth Amendment, to juveniles. In that case, a juvenile in California had been adjudicated on an armed robbery charge. Rather than receiving "sentence" on this offense, the juvenile court judge transferred his case to a criminal court where he was tried again and sentenced to an institution. The court held that it is the risk of duplicate trial and conviction, rather than the risk of duplicate punishment, which underpins the double jeopardy provision. This decision, then, announced an added constitutional protection for juvenile offenders.[14]

State appellate courts have been far busier than the U.S. Supreme Court in considering questions of juvenile law and procedure during recent years. It is probable that more appeals have been considered during the past five years than in the approximate seven decade prior history of the juvenile court. Legilatures have also been extremely busy in modernizing juvenile codes. Many juvenile codes had not received major revamping for forty years or more. A few states — California, New York, Illinois, Colorado, and several other — had approved major revisions prior to the *Gault* decision, but since then South and North Dakota, Texas, Georgia and Ohio, New Mexico and New Jersey and many other states have recast their juvenile courts acts.

The defense lawyer is probably more central to the legal renaissance in the juvenile court than is the judge. Also, the prosecuting attorney will play a far stronger role in this forum in the future than in the past. While annual reports of contemporary juvenile courts still show a limited number of contested juvenile trials, not unlike the criminal courts, lawyer activity in juvenile courts is quantitatively and qualitatively far stronger than in 1967. Law is a clearer priority.

The prosecutor's role is directed toward the community's interest. The defense attorney's objective is the child's interest. But these attorneys have broader concerns. Juvenile prosecutors regularly insist that police officers perform more skillful investigation, or that the practices of probation officers comply with legal requirements. Defense attorneys challenge the constitutionality of various juvenile code provisions and juvenile court practices, and ferret out community resources useful to their clients which may have escaped court attention. They have the adversary role at trial, but perform many other useful services. Yet acceptance and encouragement of attorneys is far from uniform among juvenile court judges, and the assignment of adequate numbers of prosecution staff is frequently of low priority to district attorneys.

A judge's interest in strengthening the legal component of his court depends on certain variables: the state juvenile code; the "cultural environment" of his court and community which encourages formalization or discourages legal representation; his relationship to the funding authority and whether he wishes to jeopardize this relationship by authorizing increased payments for expanded lawyer representation of indigent juveniles; the judge's own convictions, orientation, and background; his tolerance of legal challenges to his procedures and decisions.

Representation of juveniles by defense lawyers varies among the courts from perhaps 5 percent to 100 percent. Certainly the trend is toward greater representation, and there is increasing support for the view that no child should come before a juvenile court judge without legal counsel.

Narrowing the Jurisdiction of the Juvenile Court

The President's Commission on Law Enforcement and the Administration of Justice recommended in 1967 that "The conduct-illegal-only-for-children category of the court's jurisdiction, should be substantially circumscribed so that it ceases to include such acts as smoking, swearing, and disobedience to parents and comprehends only acts that entail a real risk of long-range harm to the child. . . .Serious consideration, at the least, should be given to complete elimination of the court's power over children for noncriminal conduct."[15]

While no state has thus far excised this conduct from juvenile court purview, legislatures have unsuccessfully tried to do this, at least in California and Massachusetts. In 1972 Pennsylvania shifted habitual truancy away from delinquency and into its "deprived child" (dependent/neglected) category, and in 1971 Utah removed the single act of runaway from its delinquency definition, permitting jurisdiction to apply only when this child may be beyond control of his or her parents. Consensus has developed that these children should be more substantially handled away from court, and countless communities have developed a variety of service alternatives to court.

Such a trend is not universal. This author studied one hundred youths referred for delinquency violations and ninety-seven youths referred for juvenile noncriminal conduct (status offenses) between April 1, 1971, and January 31, 1972, to the King County Juvenile Court in Seattle, Washington. Only nine of the former cases were formally filed, while nineteen of the ninety-seven status offense were filed. Eighteen of nineteen youngsters referred for "ungovernability" were formally filed, although none of the fourteen auto theft referrals and only two of nineteen burglary referrals were formally filed. Interestingly, and this is seen as a common pattern, girls are more commonly represented than boys among status offense referrals, and status offenses are not infrequently detained for longer periods of time in juvenile detention facilities than regular delinquency referrals.

A significant number of legal challenges have sought to invalidate court jurisdiction over status offenses on a number of grounds: as being "void for vagueness" (the statutory description of the banned behavior is not specific enough); as being punishment of a status rather than a criminal law violation; as unequal protection of the law (adults are not brought to court for similar activity). In general, these appeals have been denied by state appellate courts to date. Yet concern for elimination of this jurisdiction is gaining momentum. The National Council on Crime and Delinquency, in 1975 issued a policy statement, "Jurisdiction over Status Offenses Should be Removed from the Juvenile Court." NCCD has launched a major national program to remove such offenses from juvenile codes in all fifty states and the District of Columbia. A contra position was taken earlier by the National Council of Juvenile Court Judges, however.

The Juvenile Justice and Delinquency Prevention Act of 1974, enacted by the U.S. Congress, stipulates that eligibility for federal funding under this act requires a state plan within two years providing (1) that status offenders should no longer be held in locked pretrial detention centers, and (2) that status offenders should no longer be committed to state juvenile delinquency institutions. This latter provision will strengthen the implementation of Standard 14.1 *Courts,* National Advisory Commission of Criminal Justice Standards and Goals, which recommended a similar concept, and also urged that the definition of delinquency be limited to the violation of an act which would constitute a criminal offense if committed by an adult. The President's Crime Commission had also recommended, "Traffic violations by juveniles should be dealt with by traffic courts, except for serious offenses such as vehicular homicide and driving while under the influence of alcohol or drugs."[16] However, few of the eighteen states which included the basic juvenile traffic offenses within juvenile court jurisdiction have subsequently transferred this jurisdiction to the basic traffic court.[17]

The Increasing Reliance on Community Alternatives to Institutionalization

Despite the pressure from law and order advocates to mete out harsher sentences to juvenile offenders, a number of states in recent years have closed down juvenile institutions or significantly reduced institutional populations. California, through its probation subsidy law, has provided a financial incentive to county probation departments to intensify local probation services, provided commitments to both juvenile and adult state institutions are reduced. The consequence has been a number of closings of both juvenile and adult institutions, with significant cost savings.[17] Massachusetts has taken major steps in shutting down delinquency institutions and offering alternatives through small group home care and intensified community delinquency services. Washington state has shut down a delinquency institution, and Colorado has sharply reduced institutional populations. Monies made available to states and communities through funds from the Law Enforcement Assistance Administration and the U. S. Department of Health, Education, and Welfare have in recent years encouraged the development of a wide variety of community correctional alternatives, notably group homes and halfway houses, youth services bureaus, volunteer programs, decentralized probation services, and the addition of paraprofessional and ex-offender staff aides.

There has been recognition of the high cost of institutional care, the difficulties in effectively administering delinquency institutions, and the relatively high recidivism rate of institutional graduates. Such recognition supports the development of community alternatives. Further, the recognition of the stigma which attaches more significantly to youth the further they go in the juvenile justice system, is increasing the diversion of youth from police and court intake to alternative community services. Also, the increasing presence of defense counsel has placed added checks on the system. Lawyer advocates for children generally advocate against institutionalization and for reduced penetration.

A Heightened Professionalization of Juvenile Justice

Recent years have seen a dramatic expansion of training opportunities for the functionaries of the system. Judges, probation and detention staffs, prosecution and defense counsel, and staff members of a wide variety of related agencies, have taken advantage of increased in-service and out-service training programs to improve their knowledge, skills, and perceptions. Research has expanded, along with the development of more adequate information systems to provide more complete information on what is happening in juvenile courts and related agencies. A number of larger juvenile courts now have computer capability, and regular printouts permit managerial analysis of the system, and allow for greater utilization of this information to change and shift the ways courts and related agencies function. While many juvenile courts lack the managerial capability to utilize the information they gather, court management skills are improving.

THE JUVENILE JUSTICE CASEFLOW PROCESS

Juvenile processing is best understood by examining the decisions made at the different discretion points in the caseflow system: the offenses reported and not reported to the police; the juveniles apprehended by police officers, referred or not referred to the court; of juveniles taken by police officers to pretrial detention facilities, those detained and those released; of those detained, which are released one to three days later, following a "detention hearing"; which referred juveniles become the subject of formal court petition; for formal cases, where an offense is admitted to or found to be true, what dispositional alternatives are used by the judge, with which youth, for what reasons?

This process can be seen in the form of an inverted pyramid. At the top of the pyramid, somewhere between two and three million youngsters have police contacts during a year (this is not an unduplicated count: a given younster may have five or ten police contacts in a year). At the bottom of the pyramid is the number of youths committed to state delinquency institutions. This number has been approximated as 100,000 annually.[19]

Initial Discretion: The Police-Public Interface

Law enforcement agencies are the most frequent referral agents forwarding juveniles to juvenile courts. This is as it should be. Juvenile actions which have come to the attention of police officials should be the major focal point of society's concern for juvenile law violations. While remembering that juvenile arrest provisions are very broad in many states, and that not all offenses of juveniles, or of adults for that matter, can be proven at trial, annual reports of juvenile courts reflect that police referrals predominate, although there are differences in referral patterns. In 1973, in the Cook County Juvenile Court, Chicago, law enforcement agencies referred 99 percent of delinquency cases and 71 percent of status offense cases. In 1970 in Ft. Wayne, Indiana, law enforcement referrals constituted 79 percent of all juvenile court referrals. Interestingly, the probation department made 17 percent of these referrals, which suggests that probation officers enforced quite strictly violations of the terms of probation. In 1974, Tulsa, Oklahoma, police referred 88 percent of all delinquency and status offense referrals. During 1970, in the Juvenile Court of Memphis and Shelby County, Tennessee, law enforcement officials referred only 74 percent of all delinquency and in-need-of-supervision cases. Schools referred 14 percent, reflecting a substantial reliance by Memphis area schools on the authority of the court. Probation officers referred but 3 percent of such offenses, and parents referred 7 percent.

Many juvenile courts have urged that schools handle truancy matters and juvenile discipline problems without referral to the courts. Such a position has often irritated school officials who grew up with an earlier juvenile court model where courts were more receptive to school referrals. Courts in one southeastern state frequently committed habitual truants to state delinquency institutions, even though institutional school programs were often only one and one-half hours a day.

Major educational reform and the development of a wide array of educational alternatives is preferred to the ego destruction which may well be suffered by the truant child who finds that school is too difficult or conflictful, and also has a new problem, a court label.

Police decisions whether or not to refer to the court vary considerably from city to city. The chief of the Atlanta Police Department's detective division told this author during summer 1971, "Our policy has been to take everything to juvenile court."[20] The captain of the Salt Lake County Sheriff's Office, Juvenile Division, a month later, estimated that 75 percent of contacts with youngsters are referred to the court.[21] And a few days later the head of the Seattle Police Department Juvenile Bureau estimated that 45 to 50 percent of its juvenile cases were referred to the court. He added, "We know about how many the court can handle. If we referred a thousand more cases each year, probation would come unglued."[22]

Different factors seem to affect suburban and urban police decision-making. Suburban police seem more sensitive to cooperating with the parents of their community, who may well have the resources to obtain private programs to assist their children. Further, if a policeman has to make a 40-mile round trip to deliver a child to a detention center, he may well prefer to release the child to the parents and avoid such a drive. In urban centers, heavy court caseloads almost require extensive release by police officials. While such discretion may well favor the white middle class youth and disadvantage the urban minority youth, this is not universally true.

The more objective criteria utilized in police decision-making include the seriousness of the offense, the past record of the juvenile, the age of the juvenile. More subjective factors include the attitude of a juvenile, and possibly his color, ethnic background, and economic status. Parental availability and apparent parental resourcefulness are other factors assessed.

Growing concern over irregular exercise of discretion by police officials (as well as by probation intake officers, prosecutors, judges, and parole officials) has precipitated the recommendation for official guidelines to direct discretionary practices. The National Advisory Commission on Criminal Justice Standards and Goals recommended in 1973 that "Every police agency should establish in cooperation with courts written policies and procedures governing agency action in juvenile matters. These policies and procedures should stipulate at least . . . (c) the procedures for release of juveniles into parental custody; (d) the procedures for the detention of juveniles."[23]

Detention Admission

In some communities such as Houston and Wilmington, Delaware, an apprehended juvenile is taken before a local magistrate, advised of his rights, and then remanded to detention or released to his family. In Boston police officers bring the youth before the juvenile court judge during court hours. At other times a designated probation officer is contacted who, following telephone discussion with the policeman, decides whether or not the child should be taken to the detention facility. The more common approach, however, is for police officials who consider that detention is indicated to take the child directly to the detention center. Historically, most youngsters brought to the detention center have been admitted.

Few states provide a bail system for juveniles. Most statutes provide that a child should be released by police or by detention admitting officers unless his detention is necessary for his welfare or that of others. In 1972 a Pennsylvania statute set out additional admission criteria, such as that the child may abscond or be removed from the jurisdiction of the court, or that he has no parent or custodian able to provide supervision and care and return him to court when required.

Many statutes provide that children should not be detained in jail, except that above a certain age they may be detained separately from adults. But mounting evidence suggests that neither statutory constraints nor juvenile justice rhetoric has stanched the flow of youths into local jails. A 1970 survey of 4,037 locally administered jails discovered 7,800 juveniles detained on a single day.[24] Two years later a comparable study of 3,921 jails found 12,744 juvenile inmates under eighteen years of age.[25] A more recent assessment stated, '. . .it is probable that up to 500,000 juveniles are processed through local adult jails each year in the United States.'[26] Most of these youths were awaiting trial.

Most jails fall far below national standards of space, supervision, and medical care. While some children in recent years have hanged themselves in jails, and four youths perished in 1965 in a small jail in Arizona due to asphyxiation from a defective gas heater when the jail was left untended, two youths also hanged themselves in the Denver Juvenile Hall, one in 1970 and one in 1971. Such grim events need to be measured against the statutory instruction to the juvenile court, when it must remove a child from his family, to provide him with the care, guidance, and rehabilitative services he may need.

While a number of communities have developed quite effective juvenile detention facilities, frequently known as juvenile halls, detention centers in many urban communities are overcrowded and underprogrammed, and in more rural areas frequently do not even exist. In California juvenile halls are administered by county probation departments. In Tulsa, Oklahoma, as in many cities, the detention facility is administered by the juvenile court. In New Orleans, Louisiana, the welfare department administers this center. In Salt Lake County, Utah, the county commissioners have administered this program. In states such as Georgia, a regional detention structure has been created whereby, throughout the state, there is a designated facility in each region. This contrasts with other states where some areas are covered by detention facilities and other areas are not. A movement to a statewide detention administration is believed necessary to assure more uniform provision of facilities throughout the state.

It may be generalized that we have taken too many youngsters into our detention centers and we have kept them too long. In too many communities the police, in effect, determine detention admission. This author, in 1972, asked the superintendent of the Ft. Wayne, Indiana, detention facility how well he got along with the police department. He responded there were no problems at all. He was then asked whether he ever rejected for admission a child brought to the center by police officers. He answered to the negative.

More and more juvenile courts and probation departments are interposing screening staff to interview the child and his parents as immediately as possible, and to return home, without entry into the detention center, a substantially increased number of juvenile referrals. Improved communication between juvenile justice component agencies, together with increased agreement as to what types of youths should be detained, will reduce "overdetention," and result in more appropriate police referrals for detention.

The juvenile court in Salt Lake City maintains an eighteen-hour screening staff at the detention center, a staff member being "on call" the other six hours a day. Seattle and Atlanta provide screening staff twenty-four hours a day. Still, many courts do not provide such a service, and "overdetain," while others screen eight hours a day.

Overdetention may also be reduced by "detention alternatives." The Juvenile Court in the City of St. Louis maintains a corps of paraprofessional community workers, each to work daily with five youths who otherwise would be in detention pending court proceedings. Salt Lake County maintains more than fifty foster homes, and an open-group shelter adjacent to the detention center, to temporarily house youths who in the past had been detained in locked detention. The probation department in Sacramento, California, provides intensive crisis intervention counseling to referred youths and their families, and has significantly reduced detention admissions and the length of stay in detention.

Detention Hearings

Many courts hold daily detention hearings, generally presided over by a judge or referee, to provide judicial review of probation officer screening decisions at detention, and/or as a further check against overdetention or unnecessary detention, and for what may be a due process concern since few states provide bail procedures for juveniles. Parents are asked to attend these hearings, and some courts have legal counsel available for the child. The basic issue is whether or not his youngster needs to be detained further.

Statutes providing for detention hearings generally require them within forty-eight to seventy-two hours after admisison. Many courts hold these the day after admission, and it is likely that more courts will begin to hold Saturday detention hearings as well. A representative from the probation department is generally present to set forth his reasons in support of detention or release. Parental willingness to assume responsibility for the child is often a factor in whether a judge or referee releases the child to his parents.

The Court Intake Process

Whether or not a referred youth should become the subject of a formal petition, should have no further action taken against him, or should be handled through some informal procedure, is the next decision to be made. In most courts, this is made by the probation staff, particularly, the intake division of this department. There has been a decided move in the last decade to divide probation into an intake unit and a field supervision unit. In a number of California probation departments there is an in-between unit, the investigation division, which largely conducts social history studies of youths for use by the judge at the time of disposition. Variations in the delinquency intake process are illustrated in Figures 2-8 through 2-11. However, a number of courts still maintain probation staff

DELINQUENCY INTAKE PROCESS

Figure 2-8 **California**

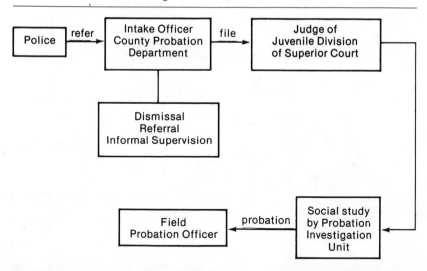

Note: County probation department administers juvenile detention, probation, ranches, special schools, and related community programs. Juvenile jurisdiction is in the Superior Court, the highest court of general trial jurisdiction.

Figure 2-9 **Denver, Colorado**

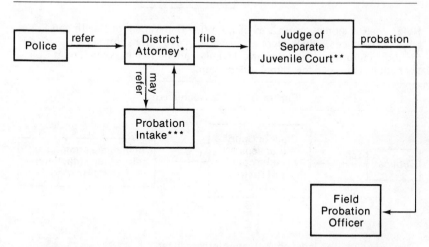

*A 1973 statute granted the prosecutor a decision-making role on delinquency referrals, and provided that the prosecutor *may* ask for intake investigation where further information is needed to make a final decision.

**Judges receive the same pay as judges of the highest court of general trial jurisdiction.

***Approximately sixteen paraprofessionals carry limited probation caseloads.

Figure 2-10 Florida

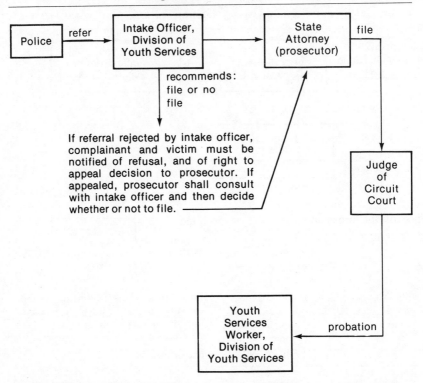

Note: The Division of Youth Services, Florida Department of Health and Rehabilitation Services, administers all juvenile intake, probation supervision, detention, institutions, and aftercare. Juvenile jurisdiction is in the Circuit Court, the highest court of general trial jurisdiction.

Figure 2-11 Massachusetts

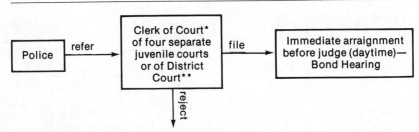

*Clerk of court is an independent, appointive officer.

**Lower court.

Note: On nights and weekends, police contact an on-call probation officer, who advises whether a child should be released or placed in detention. If detained, he is arraigned before a judge the next judicial morning. There is no probation intake and detention is administered by the Department of Youth Services; probation is a local or regional judicial function. The Clerk of Court prepares the petition.

who make intake decisions, conduct social studies, and provide field supervision for the same youth as he wends his way through the process. An advantage of the separate division system is greater attention to each function. The disadvantage is that the child and parents must adjust to two or three different probation staff members. The trend is, however, toward the former, a specialization of function.

There are other approaches to intake decision-making. In the Boston Juvenile Court the complaint is referred to the clerk of the court who scrutinizes the police report as to legal sufficiency. If the complaint is found sufficient a hearing is held with a judge or referee, who decides whether or not the case should go further. In some states or communities the district attorney is the decision-maker, and he may or may not have the advantage of a preliminary investigation by the probation intake division. By agreement with the Seattle prosecutor's office, the intake probation officer may adjust in-need-of-supervision cases, misdemeanors, and certain felonies, but may not dismiss or adjust other specified felonies without the concurence of the prosecutor. If there is disagreement, a hearing is held before a judge or referee to determine whether or not the case shall be filed. In Florida intake officers who decide against filing a referred case must advise complaining witnesses that they may appeal this decision to the prosecutor.

One national statistical source reports that for 1973, 1,143,700 delinquency and status offense cases were referred to American juvenile courts.[28] Of this number, 54 percent were handled "nonjudicially," 46 percent judicially. This means that somewhat more than four of each ten cases referred to juvenile courts were handled by formal petition. The remaining cases were handled by dismissal or informal adjustment. This report makes the following comment: "Even though it may be appropriate to handle as many cases as possible in this manner, it raises the question as to why so many that do not require judicial determination should even be referred to court."[29] A further breakdown on these figures reveals that 50 percent of juveniles referred to urban courts were handled nonjudicially, compared with 67 percent of those referred to semiurban courts, and 44 percent to rural courts.[30]

What is emerging is that the intake process has two major investigative areas: legal and social. Until recent years, intake departments had largely ignored careful scrutiny of the legal case against the child. Further, district attorneys were not particularly interested in assigning manpower to this court. The social investigation was stressed, although even this was often cursory.

Legal screening is best done by a prosecutor. Social screening is best done by an intake probation officer. If the legal foundation is sufficiently strong, and the social reasons justify a formal petition, then the petition should be filed. Factors influencing intake decision-making include the seriousness of the present offense, the past offense record, age, family resourcefulness, school adjustment, peer group associations, existing community alternatives to be used in lieu of the court, and, probably, attitude. Here, too, decision-making is irregular. The spirit of individualized justice is stronger than that of equal justice. The future should see more courts and intake officers develop written criteria as to what cases shall, might, or should not receive formal judicial consideration. Good administration suggests that these criteria be periodically reviewed in the light of experience and research, and adjustments made as indicated.

The case may be dismissed at this point. Or by legislation, court rule, or historical practice, the child may be placed under informal adjustment or supervision. For three to six months he is to counsel with a probation officer or work with a community agency, or just "keep out of trouble." If no further offense has occured, and the youth has complied with basic requirements, the offense is permanently dismissed.

Since 1967 some states have legislated a "consent decree" provision. This occurs, generally, subsequent to filing. In Pennsylvania and Tennessee, for example, an informal consent agreement is taken to a judge or referee to ratify. Upon successful completion of the approved requirements, the case is dismissed.

Disposition Hearings

When a case is filed, the child formally appears before a judge or referee, along with his parents. A probation officer generally attends. Defense and prosecution counsel may be present. The youth enters a plea to the complaints alleged in the petition. The general plea is an admission or denial to the allegations, juvenile court euphemisms for guilty and not guilty. While trials occur far more frequently today than ten or even five years ago, most juveniles still admit to the charges.

This author's study of referrals to three juvenile courts between April 1, 1971, and January 31, 1972, included 205 cases in Atlanta, 293 cases in Salt Lake City, and 197 cases in Seattle.[31] Approximately half of each sample were violations of the law, and the other half, juvenile status offenses. Atlanta formally filed 20 percent (42 cases), Salt Lake City 47 percent (138 cases), and Seattle 14 percent (28 cases). In Atlanta, 28 of these 42 cases went to trial, with the charge proven in 22 cases, and not proven in 6 cases. In Salt Lake City there were 13 trials among the 138 formal petitions, 6 resulting in the charge being proven, while 7 were not proven. In Seattle there were 5 trials among the 28 formal cases, 3 resulting in the charge being proven, 2 resulting in the charge not being proven. The number of innocent judgments suggests that the legal screening mechanisms in these courts may need to be tightened.

When a child admits to a petition or is found at trial to have committed an offense, a disposition hearing is held to determine what orders the judge should enter. In criminal court this is called a sentencing hearing, in juvenile court a disposition hearing. The disposition hearing may be held immediately following the plea of trial, or at a later date. A minority of juvenile courts calendar a two or three week delay between the adjudication and the disposition hearing. This affords more time for probation staff to complete a social investigation of the child's background and present adjustment, and to propose recommendations for judicial orders. The judge reviews this report prior to or at the time of the disposition hearing. Most states now permit defense counsel to review this report and question the probation officer at the hearing.

Many juvenile courts have achieved a certain distinction through broad-based disposition hearings, very careful deliberation, and strongly developed treatment plans. In general, juvenile court judges prefer to use community alternatives to institutionalization, and indeed this is what most juvenile court acts compel judges to favor. Close working relationships with mental health services, private and public community agencies, volunteer programs, and educational agencies, have frequently fulfilled a court's responsibility to enhance the future of a given child.

Violations of Probation

Probation is the most common disposition ordered by juvenile court judges. However, the extent of court utilization of probation depends upon the severity of delinquency offenses, the availability of alternative community services, public attitudes toward judicial use of probation and community services, judge and probation officer preferences, and other factors. The Cook County Juvenile Court, Chicago, during 1973, placed 2,416 youths on probation while committing 1,648 to state correctional centers. By contrast, Utah juvenile court judges in 1974 ordered probation status for 1,251 youths while committing but 75 to the state industrial school.

Trends in the delivery of probation services include more assistance from volunteers and from paraprofessional workers who are sometime ex-offenders; a greater use of group counseling and group activities programs; greater involvement of parents, including parent groups; a move to decentralize to branch probation offices in neighborhoods within a city or region; and growing evaluation of the effectiveness of probation services.

Youths on probation are required to follow certain rules prescribed by the judge. Certain of these rules are technical, such as reporting regularly to the probation officer, or being home at a given hour. Other rules broadly prohibit the youth from violating any further laws. When a violation of technical rules occurs the probation officer must decide whether to handle the matter informally, or bring it formally before a judge. When law violations are referred by the police they may be received by the youth's probation officer, or go through the court intake process with the decision to file either retained by intake staff or delegated to the youth's field probation officer. Here too, certain discretion is involved. While some courts expressly prohibit other than a formal consideration of a repeat offense, other courts leave this discretion to a probation officer without a clear directive. More than likely a technical violation is ignored or adjusted informally. A law violation is more often formally petitioned.

For youth institutionalized in state delinquency facilities, supervision may be assigned to a juvenile parole or aftercare worker upon release. This parole agent generally has discretion to adjust technical violations and minor repeat offenses. However, in some states, the repeat offense by a youth on parole goes back into the juvenile court intake process, and the decision whether formal action should be taken is make by juvenile court personnel rather than parole or aftercare workers.

THE JUVENILE COURT — INTERNAL ISSUES
AND STRUCTURAL RELATIONSHIPS

It is essential that the juvenile court become a well-coordinated, well-administered legal mechanism in which the more serious and more repeated juvenile offenders are processed and assisted. Its importance as a court has increased, due to the renaissance of law in this area, and to the enormous public attention riveted onto the court as a result of media publication of the extent of juvenile offenses, and, in certain cases, their seriousness.

While more states are structurally reorganizing the juvenile court into the court of highest general trial jurisdiction, the juvenile court division frequently retains a lower status than other divisions of the court. This is an historical inheritance, but it is also due to the fact that few cases are considered in other divisions where there are not lawyers on each side. Further, the stakes in a criminal trial or a civil suit often appear to be higher and of greater impact than the disposition of a juvenile offense. Yet, is this really valid?

One can obtain support for the proposition that it is better to more generously assign probation and community resources to juveniles, since they are often more pliable than adult offenders and their characters are less rigidly fixed. We can all agree that juvenile cases should be processed speedily, that the right decision should be made at the discretion points so that those who require it are moved along further into the system, while others are handled alternatively.

Juvenile court judges have been far too involved in administration, though they lack basic skills and training. But increased litigation in this court is keeping judges on the bench for longer periods, forcing them to rely more on their top staff. And this, in general, is good.

The current reform movement to organize all trial courts into a statewide court system, with a statewide court management relating to the local court management, and the new questions asked of the courts by state executive and legislative branches, is causing a positive discomfort to traditional juvenile courts.

Should juvenile courts continue to administer juvenile probation departments as they do in many states and localities? If so, what is the judge's role in hiring and firing? Is it rational that probation programs in some parts of a state approach adequacy, but are grossly inadequate elsewhere? Is it tolerable that some communities have pretrial detention centers for juveniles, but other areas of the state do not? What should be done when Court A takes 40 days from referral to disposition, but Court B takes 113 days? And what about Judge A. who committed 50 youths to the state last year, while Judge G. committed 200, and they both sit in the same juvenile court? While our goal remains individualized justice, there should be some uniformity of procedure and service throughout a state.

Juveniles are not afforded all the legal protections provided adults. Juveniles generally do get better probation and community rehabilitative service than adults. Yet many are made worse by the system. One of the most interesting legal challenge theories is called "right to treatment." Lawyers are arguing that if the court removes a child's freedom, effective treatment and rehabilitation must be added to the equation. Where juveniles have been institutionalized under custodial rather than rehabilitative conditions, then, it is argued, the state has failed in its obligation and the rationale for continuing institutionalization has been removed. Based on this theory a boys' delinquency school in Indiana has been ordered to significantly upgrade its program, two Texas juvenile institutions have ordered to close, the detention center in Chicago was ordered to take a deaf child daily from the center to a special school for the deaf, the juvenile section of the Baltimore jail was shut down, and a District of Columbia court ordered that a detention center must provide psychiatric assistance if one of its residents is in need of this assistance.[32]

A different argument is also developing, one which is less in contrast to the right to treatment than initially appears. Emanating from liberal sources, this view is termed the "right not to be treated," or the "right to punishment." It believes that rehabilitative efforts have been punitive, discriminatory, and ineffective. It urges that judges abandon treatment as a dispositional strategy, and argues that treatment services should be strictly voluntary. It contends there should be no discretion exercised by functionaries of the system, that humane punishment is an acceptable disposition, that institutional commitments should be for short and definite rather than for indeterminate terms, and that an institutionalized offender should be permitted to reject all service offerings without delaying his release date.[33]

Juvenile justice observers are carefully watching certain developments in states such as Florida, where juvenile probation and detention services have been transferred to the State Division of Youth Services, which also administers juvenile institutions, aftercare, and certain community services for juveniles. Will this state level executive branch agency be the model for the future, reducing the judge's powers over those social service workers who work with youngsters within or who have come through his jurisdiction?

Another significant issue is whether the movement to family courts, combining juvenile jurisdiction with divorce related matters, mental illness/retardation procedures, and criminal offenses within a family, will prove advantageous or whether the family will continue to be fragmented in these consolidated courts.

There is also the increased role of the prosecuting attorney, who has begun to challenge the intake powers traditionally held by probation staff. Concomitantly, some district attorneys have begun to ask for more repressive juvenile code amendments. A further development is the increased organization of probation and court staffs into unions, and the impact this may have on court processes and services.

Despite its certain chaos and conflicts, the juvenile court is now an improved and stronger court than a decade ago, somewhat better prepared to grapple with the complex issues and with the excessive demands and expectations which we have given it.

NOTES

1. Mark M. Levin and Rosemary C. Sarri, *Juvenile Delinquency: A Comparative Analysis of Legal Codes in the United States* (Ann Arbor: National Assessment of Juvenile Corrections, The University of Michigan, 1974), p. 12. This survey analyzed juvenile statutes through 1971, and reported twenty-five states had enacted such a separate legal category. Additional states subsequently created this legal category.

2. Ted Rubin, "The Structure and Jurisdiction of the Juvenile Court," preliminary report submitted to the Juvenile Justice Standards Project, Institute of Judicial Administration, New York, 1972 (mimeographed).

3. Ibid.

4. Levin and Sarri, *Juvenile Delinquency,* p. 13.

5. A. v. City of New York, 286 N.E. 2d 432 (1972).

6. Rubin, "Structure and Jurisdiction."

7. Ted Rubin, *Three Juvenile Courts: A Comparative Study* (Denver: Institute for Court Management, 1972) pp. 331 – 52.

8. See Irving Piliavin and Scott Briar, "Police Encounters with Juveniles," *American Journal of Sociology* 70 (September 1964): 206 – 14.

9. 387 1 U.S., (1967).

10. Kent v. U.S., 383 U.S. 541, 86 S.Ct. 1045 (1966).

11. In re Winship, 397 U.S. 358, 90 S. Ct. 1068 (1970).

12. McKeiver v. Pennsylvania, 402 U.S. 528, 91 S.Ct. 1976 (1971).

13. Levin and Sarri, *Juvenile Delinquency,* p.49.

14. Breed v. Jones, 95 S.Ct. 1779 (1975).

15. President's Commission on Law Enforcement and Administration of Justice, *The Challenge of Crime in a Free Society* (Washington, D.C.: Government Printing Office, 1967), p. 85.

16. Ibid.

17. Levin and Sarri, *Juvenile Delinquency,* pp. 23 – 24.

18. *California's Probation Subsidy Program: A Progress Report to the Legislature 1966–1973* (Sacramento: California Department of the Youth Authority, 1974).

19. U.S. Department of Health, Education, and Welfare, Social and Rehabilitation Service, *Statistics on Public Institutions for Delinquent Children, 1970,* National Center for Social Statistics (Washington, D.C.: Government Printing Office, 1971).

20. Rubin, *Three Juvenile Courts,* p. 233.

21. Ibid., p. 262.

22. Ibid., p. 284

23. National Advisory Commission on Criminal Justice Standards and Goals, *Police,* Standard 1.3.2. (Washington, D.C.: Government Printing Office, 1973).

24. U.S. Department of Justice, *National Jail Census, 1970,* Law Enforcement Assistance Administration, National Criminal Justice Information and Statistics Service (Washington, D.C.: Government Printing Office, 1973), pp. 10 – 15.

25. U.S. Department of Justice, *Survey of Inmates of Local Jails,* 1972, Law Enforcement Assistance Administration, National Criminal Justice Information and Statistics Service (Washington, D.C.: Government Printing Office, 1973).

26. Rosemary C. Sarri, *Under Lock and Key: Juveniles in Jail and Detention* (Ann Arbor: National Assessment of Juvenile Corrections, The University of Michigan, 1974), p. 5.

27. Roger Baron and Floyd Feeney, *Preventing Delinquency Through Diversion. The Sacramento County Probation Department 601 Diversion Project. A Second Year Report* (Davis: University of California, 1973).

28. U.S. Department of Health, Education, and Welfare, Social and Rehabilitation Service, *Juvenile Court Statistics, 1973,* Office of Human Development, Office of Youth Development, p. 7.

29. Ibid., p. 4.

30. Ibid., p. 7.

31. Rubin, *Three Juvenile Courts,* pp. 457–96.

32. See Donna E. Rehn, "The Right to Treatment and the Juvenile," *Crime and Delinquency* 19 (October 1973): 477; James D. Silbert and Alan Sussman, "The Rights of Juveniles Confined in Training Schools," *Crime and Delinquency* 20 (October 1974): Peter B. Sandmann, "The Juvenile's Right to Treatment," in *Proceedings of the Second Annual Management Seminar of State Juvenile Delinquency Program Administrators* (College Park, Md.: American Correctional Association, 1975), p. 77; Ted Rubin, "The Expectations of Juvenile Courts," in *Proceedings of Program Administrators,* p. 124.

33. Sanford J. Fox, "The Reform of Juvenile Justice: The Child's Right to Punishment," *Juvenile Justice* 25 (August 1974): 2; John Irwin, "The Right Not to Be Treated," in *Proceedings of Program Administrators,* p. 91.

3 PIMA COUNTY JUVENILE COURT CENTER, TUCSON, ARIZONA, 1977 ANNUAL REPORT

PIMA COUNTY

1977 was a year of progress towards our dual major goals of community treatment of juveniles and the deinstitutionalization of status offenders. This progress was a direct result of the unflagging efforts of the staff at the Pima County Juvenile Court, as well as many volunteers who gave thousands of hours of their time to put this Court in the vanguard of juvenile courts nationwide and, of course, the ceaseless efforts of rank and file "people participants" – too numerous to mention here and ever enforced by the "child oriented climate" fostered and maintained by our community at large.

In December, 1972 when I first came to the Pima County Juvenile Court my priority was to do something about children who were unnecessarily incarcerated. As a result of our receipt of the Deinstitutionalization of Status Offenders grant, we were able to demonstrate the techniques necessary to prevent this needless incarceration. Our task for 1978 and thereafter is to go beyond the decarceration of status offenders to removing them completely from the purview of the judicial system.

We at the Court are committed to the improvement of the juvenile justice system in our community. We believe that the citizens of Pima County are our partners in the endeavor. The time is long past for us to sit back smugly and congratulate ourselves for past successes. We must continually strive to hone our skills and seek breakthroughs in delinquency prevention and not wait vainly for others to show us what to do.

John P. Collins
Judge

The Pima County Juvenile Court serves a county of 9,240 square miles with an estimated population of 468,000 for 1977. Located in the southern part of Arizona, adjacent to Mexico and the 3 million acre Papago Indian Reservation, Pima County is a unique amalgam of cultures and customs. The population is ethnically 70 percent

From 1977 Annual Report, Superior Court of the State of Arizona, Pima County Juvenile Court Center, Tucson, Arizona. Reprinted by permission.

Anglo, 3 percent Black, 3 percent Indian and 24 percent Mexican-American. Approximately 148,000 citizens, or 31 percent, are juveniles under eighteen years of age. The average daily attendance at elementary and high schools for the academic year 1976–1977 was 89,495.

Pima County has been experiencing rapid growth for several decades; it is estimated that nearly 10 percent of Tucson's households have been in the county for less than a year.

Figure 3-1

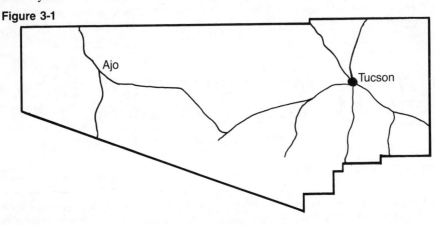

PIMA COUNTY JUVENILE COURT CENTER

The Pima County Juvenile Court is a full-fledged division of the Superior Court of Pima County with exclusive original jurisdiction of children under eighteen years of age alleged to be delinquent, dependent or incorrigible. The Juvenile Court Center cannot be considered simply a junior criminal court for youngsters because in addition to delinquent matters, its jurisdiction extends to dependency, adoptions and traffic, as well as the operation of the Pima County juvenile detention facility. The domain of status offenders or incorrigibles, children who are in violation of the law simply because they are under 18 years old, has historically been within the Court's purview but this Court has been striving to remove status offenders from the judicial arena. This issued notwithstanding, the Pima County Juvenile Court has been reexamining such traditional Juvenile Court assumptions as *parens patriae,* the Court as simply parent or sovereign over children. Much of the impetus for the reexaminiation of the Juvenile Court's philosophy stems from *In re Gault,* the landmark United States Supreme Court decision which articulates children's rights and has changed the face of juvenile justice significantly this past decade.

The backbone of the Pima County Juvenile Court's philosophy is the belief that the family is the institution of choice for the development and socialization of children. The use of surrogates for a stable family life, such as group homes or incarceration, rarely provides the continuity and nurturing necessary for optimum growth and socialization. When a child becomes a chronic behavioral problem, it often seems easier to place the child in an institution than deal with the day-to-day frustrations of trying to remedy the problem. However, such actions may only contribute to the further decline of a child since an institutional setting is but a crude imitation of a family. The Pima County Juvenile Court, therefore, looks to the family, its strengths and weaknesses, as the most appropriate setting for the remediation and socialization of delinquent children.

The unusually heterogeneous jurisdiction of the Juvenile Court — delinquents, dependents, status offenders and juvenile traffic offenders — diffuses the efforts the Court can make in any one area. The sheer volume of children referred in each of these categories is large.

TABLE 3-1   Number of Children Referred to Court in 1977.

Delinquent	5,994
Status Offense (Incorrigible)	1,325
Dependent	606
Traffic	5,776
TOTAL:	13,701

Many of the children referred as shown in the preceding chart were referred for more than one offense on a particular occasion or were referred on different occasions for different offenses. A referral for the purpose of this report is an officially registered allegation by law enforcement or others submitted to the Court for disposition. The referral may be for a solitary offense or multiple offenses.

The numbers of incidents for 1977 were:

TABLE 3-2   Number of Alleged Offenses

Delinquent	6,579
Status	2,930
Dependent	615
Traffic	7,365
TOTAL:	17,489

In 1977, 13,701 children were referred to the Juvenile Court for 15,369 referrals, comprising 17,489 offenses.

A child can be referred to the Juvenile Court for an alleged delinquent offense by the law enforcement officer either transporting the child to the Juvenile Court Center or releasing the child to the custody of his or her parents in exchange for their agreement to make an appointment at the Center. The former is called a *physical referral,* the latter, a *paper referral.*

The decision of which referral method to use is entirely within the discretion of the police. A child may be physically referred at any time, day or night, weekday, weekend, or holiday. Consequently, the Court provides at least one intake probation officer on duty around the clock to receive the child and decide whether or not the child should be detained at the detention home pending a Court detention hearing. In accordance with Arizona Supreme Court's *Rules of Procedure for the Juvenile Court* (as amended February 22, 1978),

> a child shall be detained only if there is probable cause to believe that the child committed the acts alleged in the petition, and there are reasonable grounds to believe:
> 1. That otherwise he will not be present at any hearing; or
> 2. That he is likely to commit an offense injurious to himself or others; or
> 3. That he must be held for another jurisdiction; or
> 4. That the interests of the child or the public require custodial protection.

Of the 7,398 referrals in 1977, 3,444 were referred on paper, while 3,954 were physically referred. The Intake receiving officers detained 1,461 children[1] in accordance with the *Rules of Procedure for the Juvenile Court*.

Figure 3-2   Referrals, Detentions, and Releases in 1977

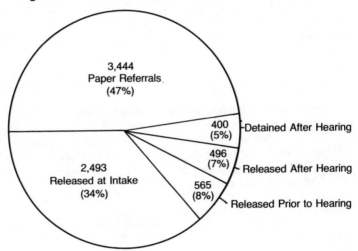

The decision to detain or release a child to parental custody may be of critical significance to the child and family. In the not too distant past, there was a tendency for Court personnel to detain children more readily and for longer periods of time in the

TABLE 3-3   Selected Detention Figures

YEAR	(FISCAL YEAR) 1953 – 1954	1960	1970	1973	1976	1977
Number of Children Admitted	904	2,517	1,634	2,127	1,539	1,461
Total Number of Detention Days	2,973	6,760	17,244	20,529	9,701	10,829
Average Stay Per Child (In Days)	3.28	2.69	10.55	9.65	6.30	7.41
Median Stay				2.89	1.93	2.16

(1976 and 1977 figures exclude federal detainees)

TABLE 3-4   Delinquent Offenses

Offenses	Number of Offenses		
	Male	Female	Total
Aggravated Assault	164	34	198
Arson	39	1	40
BB Gun/Slingshot/Fireworks	12	0	12
Burglary	981	69	1,050
Dangerous Drugs; Glue/Paint	37	3	40
Dangerous Drugs: Marijuana	614	112	726
Dangerous Drugs: Other	116	35	151
Disorderly Conduct	198	21	219
Disturbing the Peace	55	8	63
Fraud/Forgery/Embezzlement	50	23	73
Homicide	6	0	6
Kidnapping	3	0	3
Larceny:Shoplifting	804	611	1,415
Larceny: Other	420	31	451
Liquor (Non-Status)	20	5	25
Loitering/Vagrancy	43	6	49
Manslaughter	2	1	3
Miscellaneous	1,025	146	1,171
Obstruct Justice	14	5	19
Prostitution/Procuring	2	2	4
Rape/Sexual Assault	19	0	19
Robbery	68	3	71
Sex Offenses:Other	16	0	16
Simple Assault	248	53	301
Stolen Vehicle: GTA	266	27	293
Stolen Vehicle: Other	36	0	36
Trespassing	257	16	273
Vandalism	369	32	401
TOTAL:	5,884	1,244	7,128

hope that the detention experience would beneficial. This proved not to be the case, for detention quickly became overcrowded and fertile ground for unrest and disturbance. For the past four years, the Court has become increasingly circumspect about the decision to detain or release, electing to detain only when absolutely appropriate. The following chart indicates this trend.

What makes these figures even more dramatic in their impact is the comparable change in Pima County's population during this time. For example, in 1960, Pima County's population was 265,660; in 1970, 351,667; and in 1977, it is estimated that there were 475,000 people living in Pima County.

Within 24 hours[2] of the detention of a child, a petition setting forth the specific allegations of delinquency must be filed with the Clerk of the Court. Within 24 hours[3] of the filing of this petition, a hearing must be held to decide whether there is probable cause to believe the allegations in the petition, as well as whether or not the child should be detained any further. In 1977, 896 detention hearings were held; 496 children were released at the hearings, and 400 children were maintained in custody.

The decision to release or detain is independent of the subsequent court hearing which determines if a finding of delinquency can be made.

The following table displays a breakdown of selected delinquent offenses for 1977. The categories of offenses accord with those of the National Crime Information Center.

TABLE 3-5   Comparison of Selected Offenses

	NUMBER OF OFFENSES			
Offense	*1959*	*1965*	*1976*	*1977*
Shoplifting	20	482	1,490	1,415
Rape	8	6	20	19
Violation of Narcotic Code	7	3	897	917
Burglary	175	272	1,012	1,050
Aggravated Assault	31	18	148	202

Upon referral to the Pima County Juvenile Court, each case is assigned to a probation officer who evaluates the circumstances in order to recommend a course of action. If the referral is minor, the Court personnel are empowered by the Supreme Court, after the evaluation, to "adjust" the referral; that is, to resolve the matter without further legal procedure. If the officer believes that the referral is serious or that the child is on the verge of being a chronic delinquent, the case may be forwarded to the County Attorney's office for the issuance of a petition. All referrals that would be felonies in Adult Court are routinely forwarded to the County Attorney. The Deputy County Attorney decides whether the case has prosecutorial merit and if, indeed, that office will prosecute. If the Deputy County Attorney issues a petition, and it is filed, the matter will be set for an adjudicatory hearing, a trial wherein the allegations must be proved beyond a reasonable doubt for an adjudication to be made. If not, the petition is dismissed and the matter concluded.

Once the child is adjudicated a delinquent, the probation officer then investigates the factors that may have contributed to the delinquent conduct and proposes a plan to remedy the errant behavior. This plan may suggest that a child be placed on official probation for a period of time; that the child be placed in community treatment group home or foster home; that a child make restitution to a victim; that the child perform a certain community service for a period of time; that the child/family attend counseling; or that the child be committed to the Arizona State Department of Corrections. Sometimes, the probation officer will propose a combination of these prospective dispositions. However, the final decision regarding what disposition to order lies with the Presiding Juvenile Court Judge, although referees often are surrogate hearing officers who conduct formal hearings and make recommendations to the Judge.

The dispositions of delinquent and incorrigible referrals in 1977 are listed in Table 3-6.

Even a cursory glance at the above shows the Court's marked predisposition to keep children from unnecessarily becoming enmeshed in the Court processes. This predisposition is the concrete translation of the philosophy that formal Court processing may not have curative powers in and of itself.

Our departure from the traditional approach to children is our belief that it may not necessarily be in the child's best interest that the Court intervene in his or her life when the behavior is obviously transitory. Unnecessary contact with the Court may not be a salutary experience for some, or even most, children.

Perhaps the pivotal feature of the Court's philosophy is the notion that decisions about a child's future should be in accordance with the best interest of the child, as well as society; and this may be the most precarious of balances. If we err in one direction, we are too paternalistic; if we err in the other, we may inadvertently stigmatize a child as delinquent and make the label a self-fulfilling prophecy. Herein lies our dilemma.

Of the available dispositions for adjudicated delinquents, there has been a proliferation of alternatives during the past five years. A decade ago, virtually the only placement for children was a commitment to the State Department of Corrections. The development of placements and other resources within Pima County available for troubled children was a direct consequence of our reluctance to send children in large numbers to the State Department of Corrections. A brief glance at the rate this Court committed children to the Department of Corrections, compared to the rate children have been placed in noncorrectional settings, demonstrates this relationship.

The shift from correctional incarceration to residential placement within our community is an outgrowth of the Court's very firm belief in community-based

TABLE 3-6   Selected Dispositions

Adjustments	5,050
Petitions Filed	1,613
Adjudications	1,325
Found Guilty	103
Found Not Guilty	28
Pleaded Guilty	802
Dismissed in Court	309
Withdrawn by County Attorney	218
Official Probation	323
Placed Out-of-Home	
Residential	223
Foster Care	31
Committed to Department of Corrections	37

treatment. "Community-based treatment" is the view that if a child's delinquent problems originate within the community, then it is futile to seek remediation of those problems in isolation from the community. Through local group and foster homes, Pima County provides a wide range of treatment and placements. The fees for each placement are determined by the Arizona Department of Economic Security, in addition to regulating and funding these placements.

The Juvenile Court believes that Pima County citizens must form a partnership with the Juvenile Court in order to treat its delinquent children. Past experience with government run institutions has taught us that we bear the major responsibility for our errant children. To send children away from the community for treatment is treatment by proxy, if treatment at all. Eventually, each child committed to the State Department of Corrections will return to our community, its pressures and complexities. If this community — through the Court — has decided that a child's behavior is unacceptable, then this community bears the responsibility that efforts to remediate this behavior be performed within the community.

TABLE 3-7   Placements Out of the Home

YEAR	COMMITMENTS	CHILDREN PLACED IN NONCORRECTIONAL SETTINGS	TOTAL COMMITMENTS AND PLACEMENTS
1960	151		
1968	205		
1969	280		
1970	218	129	347
1971	176	161	337
1972	72	236	308
1973	20	278	298
1974	37	290	327
1975	18	360	378
1976	16	336	352
1977	37	254	291

The very incentives necessary for a child to change from a delinquent lifestyle are found within the community, not in the artificial environment of a reform school. It is practically impossible to marshall the entire range of social services necessary to assist a child in an institutional setting, geographically and, perhaps, culturally remote from the child's neighborhood.

The traditional community treatment instrument of the Court has been to place a child on "official probation" under the supervision of a court officer. Probation in the Pima County Juvenile Court is not the mere passive suspension of a more severe sentence for a period of time. Rather, probation is considered to be the active intervention of a probation officer as a broker of services with a child and his or her family in order to match the family to the relevant community services.

TABLE 3-8   Costs of Placements (Excluding D.O.C.)

YEAR	AMOUNT	% CHANGE FROM PREVIOUS YEAR
1970	$ 96,504	—
1971	$ 169,655	+ 75%
1972	$ 397,479	+134%
1973	$ 615,630	+ 55%
1974	$ 942,094	+ 53%
1975	$1,249,492	+ 33%
1976	$1,400,487	+ 12%
1977	$1,446,430	+ 3%

The belief that mere surveillance of the child in the community has curative powers has long since been debunked. Delinquency is not so much an act of individual deviancy as a pattern of behavior provided by a multitude of pervasive societal influences well beyond the reach of the actions of any judge, probation officer, correctional counselor or psychiatrist.[4]

The probation officer of the 1970s can no longer afford the luxury of being an ersatz policeman. Delinquent behavior rarely seems remediated by the simple threat of more dire consequences if errant behavior continues. Therefore, the modern juvenile probation officer must be an extremely deft practitioner. Among his or her other qualities, the juvenile probation officer is expected to be a peace officer, social worker, bailiff, bureaucrat, therapist, caseworker, supervisor, leader, follower and friend. We rarely achieve this amalgam of qualities, yet the public, in its various guises, holds us accountable for each.

Probation may be described as a plan of treatment individually tailored by the Court which aims at helping the child solve those problems that result in delinquent acts. Probation is an active partnership between Court and family in order to modify some specific bahavior. In accordance with this definition of probation services, caseloads, by necessity, are quite limited, enabling the probation officer to make maximum progress with each child.

The backbone of the Pima County Juvenile Court's strategy of handling status offenders[5] is Mobile Diversion, the unit providing crisis intervention services and referrals to nondelinquent children. Before 1975 and the commencement of Mobile Diversion, status offenders comprised 40 percent of all cases referred to the Court and these cases were treated in an identical fashion as delinquents. Though these children were not even accused of a criminal act, they were treated side by side with alleged delinquents.

Mobile Diversion can respond directly to a child's home in lieu of the police arresting and transporting the child to the Court Center. The Court worker meets the child where the crisis occurs and is better able to intervene and defuse the situation.

FIGURE 3-3   Number of Children Supervised on Probation

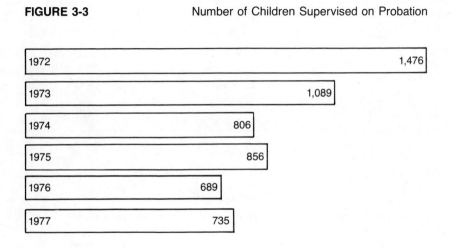

If a referral to another agency is required, the Mobile Diversion worker can recommend an agency, as well as transport the child there. Moreover, the worker can follow up the referral with further visits. There were 1,901 referrals handled by the Mobile Diversion Unit in 1977.

The following chart exhibits the very significant changes in the treatment of status offenders as a result of Mobile Diversion. In 1974 and 1975, when Juvenile Court Intake processed all status offenders, large numbers of children were detained and adjudicated incorrigible.

Foremost in the arsenal the Mobile Diversion Unit has at its disposal in the treatment of status offenders are shelter care homes. These homes, strategically located around Tucson, provided 562 children a respite for a total of 4,942 days for an average stay per child of 8.79 days. The shelter care option for status offenders is a radical departure from detention due largely to shelter care being totally voluntary on the child's part.

TABLE 3-9   Status Offenders

YEAR	REFERRALS	DETAINED	ADJUDICATED
1974	3,758	979	200
1975	3,524	792	232
1976*	2,117	52	13
1977	1,901	16	12

*Mobile Diversion Unit became operational.

Shelter care provides a child a surcease from personal or family crisis. In addition to food, shelter and custodial needs, shelter home workers are trained to assist the child and parents in trying to solve the problems that gave rise to the crisis. Rather than thrust the child and family into a Court setting, shelter care provides a neutral setting conducive to solving problems without resorting to the Court's authority. Thus, the Juvenile Court does not usurp the decision-making prerogative of the family nor does it lock a child up as the first step in grappling with internal family problems.

TREATMENT OF JUVENILES AND THE COURT

Were juvenile delinquency a specific social malady, easily diagnosed and curable by a particular treatment, then the Juvenile Court's task would be simple. Obviously, such is not the case; the state of the art of evaluation and treatment of juvenile delinquents is rudimentary at best. The Court cannot simply and arbitrarily adopt a solitary strategy, e.g., probation supervision, and expect to have wide-ranging success with children. We seem to need a multitude of strategies, for we are faced with children with a large variety of problems.

There are many agencies in Pima County which provide these strategies to the Court, from counseling to residential treatment to social welfare services to vocational preparation to educational remediation. This panoply of services effectively extends the Juvenile Court's treatment ability significantly which, in turn, makes the court very responsive and accountable to the community it serves.

INTENSIVE IN-HOME SOCIAL SERVICES

In July of 1977, the Juvenile Court inaugurated a new program designed for adjudicated delinquent children who would otherwise be candidates for residential placement and commitment to the State Department of Corrections. Intensive in-home social services, popularly known as the Street Program, provide home supervision by paraprofessionals and non-Court professionals in a nontraditional and innovative manner, with maximum caseloads of five children per staff member. These programs are an experiment designed to ascertain whether an unusually small caseload assigned to a person with a local community identity can be utilized in lieu of a residential placement. Intensive in-home social services cost about one-third that of residential placement and the programs are underwritten by the State of Arizona. Inasmuch as this program began in the middle of 1977, evaluative information is fragmentary. Ninety-two children were referred to the street programs during the first six months of operation, with an attrition of 30 children. Nevertheless, we believe that the very large majority of the remainder successfully completed the program and avoided the more costly and disruptive alternative of residential placement.

VOLUNTEER SERVICES

The Pima County Juvenile Court Volunteer Services is a direct link between the Court and the community. An outgrowth of a 1973 federal grant, this department has grown to be a mainstay of the Court Center. In 1977, volunteers functioned in virtually every Court unit, providing 9,634 hours of service. Volunteers served in the traditional one-to-one role of "big brother/big sister" type of assignment; volunteers worked in Intake, Diversion, Detention, Field Probation, Traffic and the Mobile Diversion Unit.

Through voluntarism, the Juvenile Court and interested citizens are brought together in a manner which enhances the Court's traditional dispositional techniques. Our volunteers bring a fresh perspective and boundless energy to a situation, often having a decisive effect with a troubled child. With an average of 55 active volunteers during 1977, the volunteer program has become a pillar of the Pima County Juvenile Court's services to families. Since its inception in 1973, over 600 Pima County citizens have served as active Court volunteers.

FAMILY COUNSELING

Arizona Revised Statutes 8–261 through 8–265, as amended, enable Arizona Juvenile Courts to contract with certified family counseling agencies or individuals to provide counseling at state expense for families unable to afford this service. Monies for the operation of this program are provided by the Arizona legislature and administered by the Arizona State Supreme Court.

The goal of the Family Counseling program is to divert delinquents and status offenders, as well as dependents, by providing counseling alternatives offered by private counselors. Each counselor in the program is thoroughly screened by the Court in accordance with criteria approved by the Supreme Court. Many of the families who enroll in this program are unable to afford the cost of counseling and would otherwise not be able to utilize this service. In addition to conventional counseling, this program also underwrites nontraditional services such as the Reading Clinic and vocational testing.

In 1977, 312 of the children referred to the Pima County Juvenile Court were, after a thorough evaluation, referred to local family counseling practitioners. These children attended 1,768 sessions for a cost of $26,520. The average number of sessions attended by a child was 5.6. Family counseling practiced in a professional non-Court setting is considered to be a valuable augmentation of Juvenile Court services.

TRAFFIC

The Traffic Court section of the Pima County Juvenile Court is responsible for all traffic violations for children under eighteen years of age. The burgeoning population of Pima County has resulted in ever growing traffic citations. In addition to fines, restrictions and suspensions, the traffic counselors refer children to Traffic Survival School, the Tucson City Traffic Driving While Intoxicated School and to voluntary agencies in order to perform volunteer services.

The principal aim of the Traffic Section is to educate children to become safer drivers. Many volunteer counselors from the community are used to assist this educational program.

TABLE 3-10   Traffic Referrals

	1953–54	1960	1965	1973	1975	1977
Number of Children	1,081	2,509	2,778	5,115	5,750	5,776
Number of Violations (Offenses)	1,449	4,067	4,190	7,703	8,864	7,365

Fines collected from juvenile traffic violators were $37,830.96 for 1977.

DEPENDENCY

The Juvenile Court's jurisdiction includes dependency, that is, where children are alleged to be abused, abandoned, neglected or without proper care and supervision. In addition, dependency also includes children under eight years of age who are alleged to have committed what would be a delinquent or incorrigible act for children older than eight. The statutes that delineate and define dependency are the laws that indicate when the State may intrude into the family and whether such intervention is warranted.

The investigation into the social circumstances of the family is provided by the Child Protective Services Unit of the Arizona State Department of Economic Security. If a child is adjudicated dependent, then the Department of Economic Security provides supervision of the case, with the exception of a few children who are under the "protective supervision" of the Juvenile Court.

TABLE 3-11   Dependency Hearings

	1971	1973	1975	1976	1977
Petitions Filed	203	348	344	417	613
Pre-Court Dismissals			92	141	329
Adjudications	131	150	173	213	231
Dismissals	76	78	60	26	41
Reviews	353	414	554	593	1,014

ADOPTIONS

The Pima County Juvenile Court, through the Adoptions Examiner's Office, investigates all potential adoptions except those arranged through agencies.[6] The Adoptions Unit prepares an extensive social study of the potential adoption in order to guide the court hearing officer in making a decision. In addition, this unit prepares social studies for those Court cases that are set for severence hearings, that is, termination of parental rights.

In 1977, 334 cases were set for Court hearings, which resulted in 261 decrees adopting 335 children. An additional 62 adoption cases were arranged through other agencies.[1]

DEINSTITUTIONALIZATION OF STATUS OFFENDERS GRANT

The year 1977 marked the end of the Deinstitutionalization of Status Offenders grant received by the Pima County Juvenile Court in December, 1975. The grant award of $1,480,090 by the Law Enforcement Assistance Administration and $166,600 in county "match" funding was a direct result of the Pima County Juvenile Court's philosophical posture in dealing with status offenders. Previously in our system, runaways, truants and incorrigibles were subject to the same harsh treatment accorded the delinquent offender more often than not. The Court was often right in the middle of feuding family members, with little to offer, yet expected to cure the "errant" child.

We sought the grant in order to evaluate the techniques necessary to provide status offenders service, yet at the same time, to keep them out of the possibly stigma-producing Court process. Although the data from the grant is still in the process of being gathered and interpreted, some conclusions may be tentatively drawn.

Treating status offenders away from the Court setting is not less effective than within the halls of the Court. In fact, it seems that the setting and lack of coercive outcome, such as detention, facilitates the effectiveness of crisis intervention. The removal of correctional consequences, coupled with a large increase in other community agencies for intervention services, does not result in a diminution of services. On the contrary, many outreach programs and alternative educational programs were developed because of the Juvenile Court's withdrawal from this area. Programs funded included shelter care, specialized advocacy for young women, alternative school approaches, a variety of outreach services, and job programs.

NOTES

1. Excluding federal detainees.
2. Exclusive of weekends and holidays.
3. Exclusive of weekends and holidays.
4. *President's Commission on Law Enforcement and Administration of Justice Report, 1967.*
5. Children subject to the Juvenile Court's correctional powers solely by virtue of their being less than 18 years of age.
6. Department of Economic Security, Arizona Children's Home, Catholic Social Services and Jewish Family Services.
7. Department of Economic Security, Arizona Children's Home, Catholic Social Services and Jewish Family Services.

4 Retain the Juvenile Court? Legislative Developments, Reform Directions, and the Call for Abolition

H. Ted Rubin

We are now beginning to hear a new call for the abolition of the juvenile court, this time from liberal theorist sources. Under the proposal, juvenile delinquency jurisdiction would be reorganized within the criminal courts. Before the abolition recommendation gains momentum, it should be reviewed in the context of current developments in the juvenile justice system and recently proposed reforms.

The 1967 *In re Gault*[1] decision placed a constitutional blanket upon the youngsters in the juvenile court, and it marked a turning point in juvenile court developments. At that time, those favoring abolition were typically in law enforcement: "If they have the same rights as adults, they should be treated as adults." However, neither *Gault* nor its progeny have yet accorded juveniles all the rights that adult defenders have. Although *Winship*[2] required that the state's evi-

From *Crime & Delinquency,* (July 1979) vol. 25: 281–98. Reprinted by permission.

dence, in the case of an offense that would be defined as a crime if committed by an adult, meet the adult standard of proof beyond a reasonable doubt, and *Breed* v. *Jones*[3] applied double jeopardy protection to prohibit a youth's adjudication both juvenile court and criminal court for the same offense, the Supreme Court rejected an interpretation that the federal Constitution mandated state juvenile courts to provide jury trials to youths as a matter of right.[4] While a dozen or so states authorize, by statute or constitutional interpretation, a jury trial for juveniles, the exercise of that right remains infrequent. In general, juveniles lack a right to bail and to a public hearing as well.

The new call for abolition rests on several assumptions:

1. Juvenile court judges and other agents repeatedly fail to apply the statutory and constitutional protections that have been mandated.
2. Criminal courts would provide wider protection of juvenile rights than do juvenile courts.
3. The proposed rationale for juvenile sanctions, which is a shift from treatment to proportionality and punishment, parallels the criminal court model more closely than it does the traditional juvenile court approach.
4. A juvenile court model based on proportionality and punishment is dysfunctional with other components of the juvenile court workload, such as the legal processing and court protective and service orders necessary for neglected and abused children.
5. The criminal justice process now accommodates the juvenile system practices of intake and diversion as well as more diversified sentencing alternatives.
6. A juvenile's criminal court defense attorney would be free to function in an adversarial role.

Before examining these assumptions, I will describe legislation recently passed by a number of state assemblies[5] and discuss certain pertinent reform proposals promulgated by the Institute of Judicial Administration-American Bar Association Juvenile Justice Standards Project and the Twentieth Century Fund Task Force on Sentencing Policy toward Young Offenders.

LEGISLATIVE DEVELOPMENTS

The Status Offender

Ancillary but pertinent to contemporary policy concern regarding strategies for dealing with juvenile law violators is the remarkable change in statutory provisions and juvenile justice practice concerning status offenders. Beginning with California in 1961, more than forty states have undertaken to separate conduct that is illegal for children only (e.g., running away from home, incorrigibility, and truancy) into a new legal category — denominated in the various states as section 601, PINS, CHINS, MINS, JINS, YINS, and Unruly. These assorted terms have done more than create a new language. They have helped many to recognize that the greatest harm caused by these actions has been to the youngsters themselves; it is delinquent youths, not status offenders, who have violated the criminal law.

The next stages of this development are being incorporated into law and practice: States are prohibiting or imposing substantial restrictions on the preadjudicatory secure detention of these youngsters as well as their incarceration in institutions housing adjudicated delinquents. Without doubt, the United States Juvenile Justice and Delinquency Prevention Act of 1974[6] accelerated and broadened the direction of this change. Further, recent amendments in Florida, Pennsylvania, Iowa, and Washington make status offenders subject to juvenile court jurisdiction only as dependent or neglected children. Youth service bureaus, detention alternatives (including shelter care facilities), a variety of residential and nonresidential community services, and public child welfare agencies have absorbed the primary responsibility for providing assistance to these youngsters in many jurisdictions. Diminished legal and social intervention by the juvenile court is altering the perception of this institution; its reduced workload and changing purpose reinforce abolitionist charges.

The Delinquent Offender

The status offense issue has not been the only impetus behind the state legislatures move to revise their juvenile codes. The most visible change has been an increasing severity in public policy concerning the handling of serious and repeated juvenile offenders — stimulated by the legislators' desire to protect the public from the apparently increased numbers of violent juveniles. The effects of the legislation have not yet been felt widely on the streets or in homes and businesses; however, the legislative process has resulted in the addition of strengthened legal protections for youngsters and in requirements that make it more difficult to restrict youths' freedom. An inflexible movement toward more predictable and lengthier juvenile sentences or toward forcing more youngsters into the criminal courts does not accurately describe recent laws. Enactments during 1978 in Wisconsin, Iowa, and Maine avoided harsher sanctioning authority. The new emphasis on protecting the best interests of the public has not canceled the decades-long preoccupation with the best interests of the child.

Purpose Clauses

During the past several years, legislation has been passed affecting the following principles underlying previous juvenile statutes: (1) The child should remain in the care of his family if possible, (2) the child should be removed only when necessary for his welfare or that of others, and (3) if removed, the child should receive the care, guidance, and discipline necessary for constructive citizenship. Again, the change has not been unidirectional.

In 1976, California added the following clause to its Welfare and Institutions Code:

> The purpose of this chapter . . . includes the protection of the public from the consequences of criminal activity, and to such purpose probation officers, peace officers, and juvenile courts shall take into account such protection of the public in their determinations under this chapter.[7]

The Virginia Juvenile and Domestic Relations enactment, in 1977, added:

> To protect the community against those acts of its citizens which are harmful to others and to reduce the incidence of delinquent behavior.[8]

That commonwealth's assembly inserted other provisions, however, to ensure fair hearings and to legitimate diversion:

> To provide judicial procedures through which the provisions of this law are executed and enforced and in which the parties are assured a fair hearing and their constitutional and other rights are recognized and enforced.[9]
> To divert from the juvenile justice system, to the extent possible, consistent with the protection of the public safety, those children who can be cared for or treated through alternative programs.[10]

The purpose clause revision of the 1977 Washington Juvenile Justice Act may be the most profound redefinition yet enacted. Cited are the following purposes of the act: to "protect the citizenry from criminal behavior"; to "make the juvenile offender accountable for his or her criminal behavior"; to "provide for punishment commensurate with the age, crime and criminal history of the juvenile offender"; to "provide due process for juveniles alleged to have committed an offense"; to "provide for the handling of juvenile offenders by communities whenever consistent with the public safety"; and to "provide for restitution to victims of crime."[11]

Direct Filings in Criminal Courts

In New York, prior to 1978, all cases of offending juveniles under sixteen years of age began and ended in the family court. Last year, however, New York authorized the criminal courts to process youths as young as thirteen years who had been charged with specified serious offenses. Today, a juvenile convicted of murder may receive life imprisonment. Maximum sentences for other Class A felonies are between four and fifteen years.[12] The punishment effect is obvious; the deterrent effect has yet to be shown.

In 1970, the Congress resolved not to lower the maximum age of eighteen years for juvenile court jurisdiction in the District of Columbia; instead, it empowered the United States Attorney to authorize that the criminal courts charge directly sixteen- and seventeen-year-old youths accused of such offenses as murder, forcible rape, first degree burglary, and armed robbery.[13]

Since 1967, Colorado has permitted the criminal courts to handle the charges facing sixteen and seventeen year olds who had allegedly committed an offense for which an adult might receive the death penalty or life imprisonment. One year later, in 1968, the minimum age was lowered to fourteen years. A later revision, in 1973, approved direct filings for sixteen and seventeen year olds charged with certain serious offenses who had been adjudicated for a prior felony within the previous two years.[14]

In contrast, states such as California and Washington, where transfer or certification has been the only bridge into the criminal court, have not yielded to pressures for eliminiation of the initial juvenile court process.

Certification or Transfer

All but a few states have long used certification or transfer to keep the basic juvenile courts jurisdictional age as high as it is (eighteen years in three-fourths of the states, sixteen years in four states, and seventeen years elsewhere). Under this approach, certain youths may be transferred from the juvenile to the criminal court. However, the states are authorizing increasing latitude in their provisions for discretionary transfer of juveniles. New Jersey's 1978 decision to lower the minimum transfer age from sixteen to fourteen years is one example.[15] Connecticut, which earlier had permitted transfer of fourteen and fifteen year olds charged with murder, expanded this provision in 1976 to permit transfer of those charged with a Class A or B felony who had previously committed a Class A or B felony.[16] Transfer was eased in 1977 in California: Today, if the charge is one of eleven specified offenses, the juvenile has the burden of proving his amenability to juvenile court disposition. In the past, the burden of proof rested with the prosecutor.[17] Virginia, as 1977, permits the court at the transfer hearing, to disregard the factor of amenability to rehabilitation in the cases of juveniles fifteen years and older charged with murder, rape, or armed robbery offenses.[18] And Washington now requires a transfer hearing, rather than leaving this optional, for sixteen and seventeen year olds charged with a Class A felony or attempted Class A felony and for seventeen year olds charged with any one of six specified offenses.[19]

Yet here, too, change has been in more than one direction. In the past, Alabama had authorized transfer of any youngster over fourteen years. Since 1977, Alabama has required a felony offense and sufficient evidence of the statutory waiver criteria.[20] New West Virginia transfer provisions designate more specifically the offenses for which transfer might be considered appropriate.[21] Idaho legislation in 1977 changed the transfer requirement from any criminal offense to felony.[22]

Dispositional Strictures

In addition to replacing the system of institutional commitment until the juvenile's eighteenth or twenty-first birthday with defined maximum terms, recent legislation in the states has tended to promote the following:

1. Minimum Institutional Stay. This is exemplified by legislation in New York. The minimum sentence for a youth between thirteen and fifteen years of age ordered into restrictive placement following conviction of a designated Class A felony is one year in a maximum security facility, followed by one year in a residential facility, followed by three years of intensive supervision.[23]

2. Proportionality.   The highly schematized Washington sentencing standards are the best example of the enactment of the doctrine of proportionality in juvenile sentences. A youth's age and current offense establish a base point number, which is multiplied by points received for criminal history; the resulting points establish the standard disposition. The point score is translated into a class ranking, which in turn determines the institutional stay and the security level of the institution to which the youth is initially sent. The legislation specifies minimum periods for any term of confinement: for example, confinement of no less than 80 percent of the maximum if the confinement term exceeds one year. The less serious or non-chronic juvenile offender may not be eligible for institutional confinement. Low point totals prohibit institutional confinement and mandate community service, supervision, or a fine.[24]

3. Mandatory Sentences.   In 1977, Colorado legislators used this strategy in mandating that judges must sentence a youth fifteen or older who has committed a designated crime of violence, or a child of any age who has committed a second felony offense, to a state institution or other out-of-home placement for not less than one year.[25]

4. Juvenile Institutional Stays Shall Not Exceed Adult Maximums.   The old guidepost that "we should be able to keep them until they are reformed" has now been dispensed with in California, West Virginia, Pennsylvania, and other states in which the maximum juvenile sentence may not exceed the maximum adult sentence for the same offense.

Restitution and Fines

Financial reimbursement to victims has long been used by juvenile probation intake officers (often without statutory authorization) and less frequently by judges. Currently, state after state is legitimating and extending both money and service hours restitution for juvenile offenders. This symbolizes increased concern for the "rights" of victims and dissatisfaction with unfettered counseling as a primary probation department response to a juvenile offense. Kentucky, Washington, and Maine are but three of the states deeming this good public and rehabilitation policy. The recent tendency of states such as Virginia and Colorado to increase the maximum fines judges may levy on juveniles seems to aim more at deterring recidivism than at swelling public coffers.

Enhanced Prosecution Role

If the entry of defense counsel into juvenile court proceedings best symbolized the impact of the *Gault* decision, perhaps the expanded role of the juvenile court prosecutor best exemplifies the "new" juvenile courts of the late

1970s. Today, the prosecutor is entering the juvenile court processing at its beginning. States in which change is less apparent still require only that the prosecutor present evidence upon judicial request; elsewhere, the debate centers on whether referral documents should proceed from police to prosecutor or whether the papers should flow from police to intake officer to prosecutor. While there are variations in this procedure, largely in the prosecutor's right to overrule an intake officer's rejection of a formal petition, prosecutor power is gaining momentum. "First level prosecutor screening" was adopted by Colorado in 1973, and by Washington and South Dakota in 1977. "Second level prosecutor screening," the so-called Florida model, is evident in California and Maine. With both approaches, the prosecutor is responsible for the preparation of the court petition.

The enlarged prosecutor role is consistent with a public protection stance, is acceptable to those supporting rankings of seriousness, and meets defense-based concerns that tests of legal sufficiency have been repeatedly disregarded at the intake stage.

THE REFORM PROPOSALS

The Institute of Judicial Administration-American Bar Association Juvenile Justice Standards Project

While the provisions outlined above diminish the juvenile court's long-standing romance with preventive intervention and the rehabilitative ideal, they leave extensive room for treatment intercession and experimentation at both the community and institutional levels.

A studied and comprehensive reconsideration of juvenile justice undertaken in 1971 by the Institute of Judicial Administration-American Bar Association Juvenile Justice Standards resulted in the publication of twenty-three volumes and commentary. Ten principles served as the foundation for this work:

1. Proportionality in sanctions.
2. Determinate sentences.
3. The least restrictive alternative for intervention.
4. The repeal of court jurisdiction over status offenses.
5. Visibility and accountability of decision making.
6. The right to counsel at all processing stages.
7. The right of juveniles to decide on actions affecting their freedom except where they are found incapable of making reasoned decisions.
8. A redefinition of the parental role with particular regard to conflicts of interest between parent and child.
9. Substantial restrictions on intervention before adjudication and disposition.

10. Strict criteria governing waiver of juvenile court jurisdiction and transfer of juveniles to criminal court.[26]

Items 1, 2, and 4 may be said to be the centerpiece of the IJA-ABA product. Proportionality legitimates punishment as an objective and relates its type and duration to the severity of the present offense and the offender's prior record (just deserts). These lead principles and certain other key provisions have been attacked bitterly by the National Council of Juvenile and Family Court Judges, which believes, perhaps accurately, that these directions will lead either to the end of the juvenile court or to the end of the juvenile court as its membership perceives it should be defined.

The IJA-ABA endorsement of proportionality also has been taken up by those attacking the juvenile court in their argument that the juvenile and adult court objectives are now so similiar that it is impractical to retain the former and beneficial to youngsters, in general, to embrace the latter. The IJA-ABA recommendation is that the specialized forum for youths be retained, but that the juvenile court be restructured into a family court division of the general trial court. The juvenile court jurisdiction over delinquency and neglect would be combined with the domestic relations jurisdiction and certain other family-related matters to form a single judicial center offering less fragmented legal and social intervention with different family members.

In addition, the IJA-ABA volumes contain the following provisions, critical to this discussion:

1. In urging initial juvenile court jurisdiction over all delinquent offenses committed by youngsters between ten and eighteen years of age, and in narrowly defining the cases that might be transferred to the criminal courts, the standards reaffirm the juvenile court's responsibility and importance. The published draft went so far as to restrict transfer consideration to youths charged with offenses punishable, if committed by adults, by minimum terms of at least twenty years.[27] The project executive committee later amended the published draft to allow transfer of other juveniles whose adult counterparts would face a sentence of more than five but not more than twenty years; the committee also lowered the minimum age for transfer from sixteen years to fifteen years.

2. Judicial administration of pretrial detention, intake, and all probation services, common in many states today, would be ended. The programs would be handled for the court by an executive agency. Thus, the full energies of the juvenile judge could be applied to primary judicial activities.[28]

3. Pretrial detention, which now affect hundreds of thousands of juveniles who have committed minor offenses, would not be permitted for those accused of misdemeanors; detention would be largely confined to violent felony offenders.[29]

4. Second-level prosecutor screening would occur, with the processing of cases from police to intake probation officer to prosecutor, and with the latter official granted the final determination regarding informal versus formal handling in all cases.[30]

5. The juvenile's right to counsel may not be waived. The child must be represented by counsel at every step in the process, including police interrogation, intake conferences, detention hearings, and all subsequent stages.[31] Were this standard implemented universally, and, assuming for the sake of argument that such representation were universally effective, the now valid contentions that juveniles suffer wholesale deprivation of their rights in juvenile justice processing would be muted tomorrow. Concurrently, however, an exacerbated adversarial process would add another parallel between the juvenile and criminal systems (at least the adult felony system) and possibly imspire still others to call for an end to the specialized juvenile court.

6. The essential information given to a judge at a dispositional hearing would be limited to the legal facts: age, the circumstances related to the offense, and any prior record of adjudicated delinquency and disposition. The social facts — information pertaining to the child's family, school performance, psychological makeup, and environmental background — "may be considered as relevant to a disposition." Preferably, judges would determine the duration and category of the sanction before receiving evidence as to the social facts — another instance of the orientation toward equal rather than individualized justice. Yet this directive is equivocal; it is difficult, so long as discretion is authorized, to decide on a community sanction as opposed to an institutional commitment without some individualization based on social facts. The least restrictive alternative is required, and judges would be mandated to indicate for the record the alternative dispositions considered and the reasons for their rejection.[32]

7. All delinquent offenses would fit into five sentencing categories for adults. The respective sentences are : Class 1, more than twenty years; Class 2, more than five but not more than twenty years; Class 3, more than one year but not more than five years; Class 4, more than six months but not more than one year; Class 5, six months or less. Juvenile sentences would be determinate, subject to no more than 5 percent reduction for "good time." The permissible duration of sanctions is correlated with three types of restraint: confinement in a secure facility, placement in a nonsecure facility, and conditional freedom. Accordingly, conviction of a Class 1 offense authorizes confinement in a secure or nonsecure facility for twenty-four months, or conditional freedom for thirty-six months. Conviction of a Class 4 offense authorizes secure confinement for three months (if there is a prior record), nonsecure placement for three months, or conditional freedom for twelve months.[33]

8. Correctional agencies are required to provide all services necessary to the normal growth and development of those adjudicated delinquent; however,

juveniles have the right to reject such proffered services as psychological counseling during their incapacitation.[34]

The Twentieth Century Fund Task Force on Sentencing Policy toward Young Offenders

This 1978 report confronted a critical but narrower concern, an idealized sentencing policy toward young offenders. While focusing on violent and chronic juvenile offenders, the task force did not ignore lesser offenders. It also reviewed the deficiencies in juvenile justice processing, juvenile correctional programs, and probation and community agencies serving juvenile offenders. The task force affirmed the continuation of the juvenile court and its serving as the initial processing point for all juveniles under eighteen years of age.[35] The four principles underpinning its youth crime policy were culpability, diminished responsibility resulting from immaturity, providing room for reform, and proportionality.[36] Transfer or waiver would be restricted to defendants past their early teens who were accused of serious criminal violence. Transfer would also be confined to those who, if found guilty, would merit punishment substantially more severe than that available to the juvenile court.[37]

Uniquely, the task force gave attention to sentencing policy for eighteen- to twenty-one-year-old defendants as well, applying a diminished responsibility principle and linking this with shorter sentences and age-segregated facilities for this group. All youths transferred to criminal courts would be sentenced within the framework of the policy specified for eighteen- to twenty-one-year-old offenders. Sentences of over five years for offenders under eighteen convicted of murder, and sentences exceeding ten years for those between eighteen and twenty-one would be limited to cases in which the offender was responsible for taking more than one life or had a substantial history of life-threatening violent offenses.[38]

The maximum confinement juvenile courts could authorize would be two and one-half years: "Cases calling for more fateful punishment decisions should be waived to criminal court, where procedural guarantees that juvenile court does not provide are available."[39] Unlike the IJA-ABA, the task force would authorize the correctional authority to select a release date short of the maximum.[40] Additional provisions included a presumption against formal juvenile court handling of first property offenses except burglary of a dwelling and a presumption favoring formal handling for a second serious property crime. Custodial confinement beyond one year would be prohibited for any property offense.[41] Restitution, including community service, and fines were advocated as noncustodial alternatives.[42]

THE ARGUMENTS FOR ABOLITION

The IJA-ABA commission never seriously considered elimination of specialized juvenile delinquency processing. The Twentieth Century Fund Task Force pondered this issue, but decided that the juvenile court was, on balance, the best alternative available. The abolitionists prefer to go farther.

Law professor Sanford Fox urges an end to the juvenile court; instead, serious and chronic offenders should be processed in the more legalistic criminal courts. The IJA-ABA endorsement of "the decline of prediction and treatment and the ascendancy of proportionality, culpability and other principles of criminal jurisprudence"[43] supports this direction. Judicial child rescuing should be discarded as conceptually flawed, and the valid humanitarian impulses which gave rise to the juvenile court should be transferred to community agencies and informal arbitration services in which status offenders and lesser delinquent youths can be assisted without coercion. In so doing, the concern for the welfare of such youngsters would be unmarred by legal threats and the help bestowed would be less ambiguous. Fox, a long-term advocate of rational classification of crime and sentencing based on graded severity, sees the IJA-ABA reforms as advancing the ultimate extinction of the juvenile court.

Law professor Francis McCarthy agrees with Fox that criminal courts would do a substantially better job of protecting the rights of juveniles than have juvenile courts. There, the rule of law would have primacy, and rehabilitative considerations would be subject to legal guidelines. McCarthy notes that most delinquencies are misdemeanors, and that the lower criminal courts would become the setting for processing the majority of juvenile offenders. Aware that these courts are "at the lowest level of the judicial hierarchy," he states, "Nevertheless, these are courts of law, in which legal principles are supposed to be adhered to as in any other court. If the quality of their judges is in question, that problem must be dealt with independently."[44] McCarthy observes that, in many states, particularly in rural areas, misdemeanor court judges also sit as juvenile court judges.

According to McCarthy, the death knell to juvenile court precepts has been signaled by the IJA-ABA's call to abolish status offense jurisdiction, its recommendation that the prosecutor should protect the public interest, and its provision that prosecutor advocacy should be heard at the dispositional hearing. Further, the curbing of a judge's broad discretion at disposition makes retention of the juvenile court still less desireable.

McCarthy goes on to contend that the expansion of adult diversion has removed another distinction between the two systems: Juvenile court intake had been "virtually unique," but, "to a large extent, this practice is now used in adult cases."[45] The individualized treatment of juveniles entering the adult system will be an accepted practice, since ABA criminal justice standards have directed prosecutors to explore noncriminal dispositions before pressing criminal charges.[46] Because dispositional procedures affecting youths would be so similar to those affecting adults, and because juvenile sanctions would be determined by reference to adult penalties, it would be more efficient to preserve the differences in adult and juvenile sentences by incorporating this distinction into criminal statutes rather than by "maintaining a separate judicial system."[47] Finally, McCarthy proposes that juvenile code provisions concerning confidentiality and protecting offenders against certain of the civil disabilities suffered by adult offenders following conviction can be handled alternatively in a new statute providing these protections for younger persons convicted of crimes.

Stephen Wizner and Mary F. Keller, supervising Attorneys in the Yale Law School Clinical Programs, express high regard for the IJA-ABA reform effort, but are critical of the fact that reforms do not go farther to end juvenile court jurisdiction over criminal acts. They contend that implementation of the reforms, particularly the elimination of status offense jurisdiction and the creation of five classes of offenses, will result in far more plea bargaining to lesser criminal offenses by juveniles rather than outright dismissal of delinquent charges or their reduction to sometimes less harmful status offense complaints. Wizner and Keller anticipate increased prosecutor overcharging of juveniles, and suggest that defense attorneys will more readily accept a bargain, be less willing to risk trials, and fail to achieve dismissals because of witness nonappearance. Implementation of the IJA-ABA standards will leave only briefer sanctions and such special defenses as immaturity or lack of criminal intent as the remaining distinctions between the systems. Like McCarthy, Wizner and Keller acknowledge adult diversion and criminal prosecutor dismissal of lesser cases. They note also that criminal courts do consider leniency and that certain states, such as Connecticut, provide a special youthful offender category for young adult offenders. Terming the IJA-ABA proposal a penal model, they would prefer adult court processing where "safeguards are taken for granted"[48] and where defense attorneys would not have "role strain" because of alleged juvenile court benevolence. They suggest a continuance of the juvenile court, but without the delinquency jurisdiction, in order to attend to "protection of abused, neglected, and emotionally disturbed children."[49]

As a final example, Martin Guggenheim, Director of the Juvenile Rights Clinic, New York University School of Law, contends that the juvenile justice system is unable to reform itself to adhere to the rule of law in practice or to ensure that youngsters subject to its jurisdiction receive the quality of care that should be provided. The specialized structure is inherently abusive of rights of juveniles, attorneys tend to abandon zealous representation in order to cooperate with the court to find suitable placements or treatment services for children, and the system is blinded by its own beneficient rhetoric to the significant harm it imposes on youths. While adult sentences may be harsher, Guggenheim believes the vast majority of children would be far better off if handled by an adult system that openly acknowledges punishment as a purpose. Status offenders would no longer be subject to judicial system intervention, and lesser delinquents would be differentiated from more serious delinquents and be liable only to minimal loss of liberty. Unique among the critics, he notes that states could, and seemingly should, maintain separate age-segregated facilities for juvenile offenders.[50]

AN ANALYSIS

Court abolition proposals, when they require another court to pick up the workload, have not been adopted speedily. The Wickersham Commission[51] in 1931, the President's Crime Commission[52] in 1967, and the National Advisory Commission[53] in 1973 recommended abolition of the lower criminal courts. This has been accomplished in fewer than ten states, and each has retained special divisions and a separate (lesser) class of judges to handle misdemeanor cases.[54]

While *Gault* exposed juvenile court pretensions, and legal writers and social scientists have since exposed still more shortcomings, there remains the real juvenile court system, which functions with substantial imperviousness to the scholars' assessments. Its conflicting roles — as both a helper and a punisher — are of very long standing[55] and it has accommodated, with great inconsistency, numerous procedural reforms. The juvenile court has enjoyed the exercise of broad discretion, but probably could adapt to an ameliorated determinacy and proportionality. While the position of the juvenile court judge remains an open temptation to superparent and clinician self-perceptions, since *Gault*, the judges are more often lawyers, and are more strongly wedded to legal procedure. Often, these judges have effectively advocated their beliefs, and no one should underestimate their energies or political skills in preserving their courts. Unlike the legal theorists, the judges do not perceive a change of rationale as occasioning an inquiry into what is the most rational public policy for structuring juvenile proceedings. They have fought vigorously to scuttle the IJA-ABA standards and are obviously prepared to take on the abolitionists.

While implementation of primary IJA-ABA reforms within a juvenile court or family court context would narrow the procedural and sentencing distinctions between juvenile and criminal courts, these national prescriptions will probably be adapted to a greater extent than they are adopted at state levels.

Still, the issue remains: Assuming a slow and partial incorporation of the standards into juvenile statutes, is specialized juvenile processing warranted? In this regard, one must assume that, regardless of structure, specialized pretrial detention, residential facilities, part-day programs, institutions, and somewhat specialized judges and probation officers will address the great majority of juvenile offenders.

Further, there would be need for a special body of statutory law for juveniles in the criminal courts, along with specialized rules of juvenile procedure. It would not be enough simply to provide that youths under a certain age would be entitled to specifically reduced sentences.

What is more practicable and less risky than abolition of separate juvenile processing is the elimination of separate juvenile courts, and the transfer of juvenile jurisdiction to a specialized division within the general trial court. Today, separately organized and administered juvenile courts are evident on a statewide basis in only a half dozen or so states, and within one or more districts in another half dozen. Far more common is the inclusion of separate juvenile processing and disposition within the trial courts, upper and lower.

The transfer of juvenile jurisdiction to a division of the general trial courts tends to be accompanied by a rotating assignment of judicial generalists from criminal, civil, or other courts to the division for limited tenures. The rule of law is more easily adhered to during juvenile division assignment since the general court's tone is one of legal precedent and adversarial practice.

What is noteworthy about the proposals to abolish the juvenile courts is the abolitionists' failure to assess the immense problems in the present criminal court process — problems which have long been taken for granted by criminal defendants and knowledgeable court watchers. Overcriminalization, ineffective defense representation, rehabilitation rhetoric, and severe punishments have characterized criminal courts as well as the juvenile courts.

The felony courts have been beset with processing delays, an insufficient number of judges, excessive public defender caseloads, poor administration by prosecutors, inadequate use of diversion, insufficient sentencing alternatives, ineffectual probation departments, and overreliance on plea sentence bargaining.[56]

The misdemeanor and ordinance violation courts are in substantially worse shape,[57] though processing may be too speedy rather than too slow. It is little exaggeration to suggest that, in these latter courts, defendants are dealt with more as numbers than as individuals by the jailers, prosecutors, defenders, judges, and probation personnel. The abolitionists tend to see as exemplary, at least in their legal procedures, the felony courts, which receive perhaps 10 percent of adult defendants, and fail to look critically at the lower courts, which remain the largest blight on American judicial administration. Yet those courts would receive the greatest share of juvenile offenders. In many such settings, the protections guaranteed in such decisions as *Argersinger,* which provides the right to counsel to persons who may be incarcerated for a misdemeanor or ordiance violation, are not granted routinely;[58] prosecutors screen only infrequently for legal sufficiency; the quality of the judiciary is substandard and a too-rapid processing of juveniles is predictable. Diversion, at present, does not affect more than 5 percent of the criminal caseflow.[59] Except where there are organized diversion programs, prosecutors tend to explore noncriminal dispositions modestly if at all. We cannot be sure that all ten-year-old misdemeanants will be diverted from the Los Angeles Municipal Court, nor can we predict how a Cleveland Municipal Court judge will sentence a fourteen-year-old petty thief after he has already disposed of thirty adult misdemeanants earlier that morning.

The abolitionists' criticism of present juvenile system shortcomings and assessment of what might follow implementation of the standards are valuable. Their dismay with the moralistic and overreaching stance of juvenile court judges is well founded. Their failure to project the more specific contours of what would happen following abolition is disappointing. A change in rationale need not necessitate a change in the structure and organization of the juvenile court, which still has some spirited concern and useful affection for those brought to its door.

REFORM, NOT ABOLITION

The early reformers who designed and enacted a specialized juvenile court system were motivated to a significant measure by the horrors of the adult system and the harms inherent in placing juveniles with adult offenders. Reformers today share many of these same concerns, and their proposals offer promise of a less ambitious but more rational response to juvenile law violators.

There can be no return to a pre-*Gault*, parens patriae scheme of juvenile justice. And today's tempo of legislative action augurs more than slow, evolutionary changes. But abolition, in court organizational terms, means more than passing off juvenile misdemeanants to misdemeanor courts and juvenile felons to adult felony courts. It is more likely to mean transferring neglected and abused children to the beleaguered divorce courts. In many states it would involve redistributing functions concerning the relinquishment and adoption of children, a change in proceedings in paternity suits and in dispute over the guardianship and support of children, a shift in handling juvenile traffic offenses, and changes in other related matters.

The IJA-ABA proposal to restructure the juvenile court into a family court division of the general trial court is attractive, but is should not be undertaken without rigorous analysis and careful planning. The particular difficulty of implementing it in metropolitan courts warrants incremental change before any wholesale modification is made. Yet it presents a reasonable organization of jurisdiction, and it could lessen the current fragmentation of issues related to the family by their distribution among different courts and different judges. It would mute the concerns of those who suggest that the elimination of status offense jurisdiction would leave the juvenile court with little to do. That court's inattention to its neglected-child caseload has been a serious omission; juvenile or family courts must attend to these youngsters with far more time and energy.

While it is hoped that the anticipated reduction in juvenile crime rates in the early 1980s, a result largely of the declining number of youths in the most crime-prone ages, should quell the outcries of the public for retribution and enable a more reasoned public policy debate, several changes would be beneficial today:

1. Repeal of the juvenile court's jurisdiction over status offenses.
2. Legislation prohibiting waiver of counsel at any stage of the process.
3. Final prosecutor control of intake determinations.
4. Requirements of accountability for the use of each more restrictive sanction.
5. Restriction of judicial and correctional system discretion to comport with proportionality, determinacy, and "equal handling of equals."

Helping youngsters who have violated legal norms remains an important societal undertaking. To retain separate juvenile proceedings is not to affirm the status quo. Reform, better than re-form, can advance the constitutional fairness, legal regularity, and judicial self-control that are in our enlightened best interest.

NOTES

1. In re Gault, 387 U.S. 1 (1967).
2. In re Winship, 397 U.S. 358 (1970).
3. Breed v. Jones, 421 U.S. 519 (1975).
4. McKeiver v. Pennsylvania, 402 U.S. 528 (1971).
5. See also Alan Susmann, "Practitioner's Guide to Changes in Juvenile Law and Procedure," *Criminal Law Bulletin,* July–August 1978, pp. 311–42.

6. Pub. L. No. 93–415, 93rd Cong. 1974.

7. *California Welfare and Institutions Code,* sec. 202.

8. *Virginia Juvenile and Domestic Relations District Court Law,* sec. 16.1–227.4.

9. Ibid., sec. 16.1–227.2

10. Ibid., sec. 16.1–227.1.

11. Washington Juvenile Justice Act of 1977, sec. 55.

12. New York Senate Bill 1–A, Cal. No. 1 (1978).

13. District of Columbia Court Reform and Criminal Procedure Act of 1970, sec. 16–2301(3).

14. *Colorado Revised Statues*, sec. 19–1–103 (9) (b).

15. New Jersey Assembly Bill No. 1641 (1978).

16. *Connecticut General Statutes Annotated,* sec. 17-60b.

17. *California Welfare and Institutions Code,* sec. 707d.

18. *Virginia Juvenile and Domestic Relations District Court Law,* sec. 16.1-296 (3) (b).

19. Washington Juvenile Justice Act of 1977, sec. 65 (1) (a) and (b).

20. *Alabama Juvenile Code,* art. 5, sec. 129.

21. West Virginia Senate Bill No. 364, sec. 49–5–10 (1978).

22. Idaho House Bill 188, sec. 16–1806 (1977).

23. New York Juvenile Justice Reform Act of 1976, Amendments to the Family Court Act, secs. 753–a, 515a, and 516.

24. State of Washington, Department of Social and Health Services, Bureau of Juvenile Rehabilitation, *Sentencing Standards* (1977).

25. *Colorado Revised Statutes,* Sec. 19–1–103.

26. Barbara D. Flicker, *Standards for Juvenile Justice: A Summary and Analysis, Institute of Judicial Administration*-American Bar Association Juvenile Justice Standards Project (Cambridge, Mass.: Ballinger, 1977). pp. 22–23. (Subsequent references to these standards will be cited as IJA-ABA Juvenile Justice Standards Project).

27. IJA-ABA Juvenile Justice Standards Project, *Standards Relating to Transfer Between Courts.*

28. IJA-ABA Juvenile Justice Standards Project, *Standards Relating to Court Organization and Administration* and *Standards Relating to Corrections Administration.*

29. IJA-ABA Juvenile Justice Standards Project, *Standards Relating to Interim Status.*

30. IJA-ABA Juvenile Justice Standards Project, *Standards Relating to Prosecution.*

31. IJA-ABA Juvenile Justice Standards Project, *Standards Relating to Pretrial Court Proceedings* and *Standards Relating to Counsel for Private Parties.*

32. IJA-ABA Juvenile Justice Standards Project, *Standards Relating to Dispositional Procedures* and *Standards Relating to Dispositions.*

33. IJA-ABA Juvenile Justice Standards Project, *Standards Relating to Juvenile Delinquency and Sanctions.*

34. IJA-ABA Juvenile Justice Standards Project, *Standards Relating to Dispositions.*

35. Twentieth Century Fund Task Force on Sentencing Policy toward Young Offenders, *Confronting Youth Crime* (New York: Holmes & Meier, 1978), pp. 8–9.

36. Ibid., pp. 6–6.

37. Ibid., pp. 10–11.

38. Ibid., pp. 15–17.

39. Ibid., p. 16.

40. Ibid., p. 11.

41. Ibid., p. 13.

42. Ibid., pp. 13–14.

43. Sanford J. Fox, "Abolishing the Juvenile Court," *Harvard Law School Bulletin,* vol. 28 (1977), pp. 22, 26.

44. Francis B. McCarthy, "Should Juvenile Delinquency Be Abolished?" *Crime & Delinquency,* April 1977, pp. 196, 202.

45. Francis B. McCarthy, "Delinquency Dispositions under the Juvenile Justice Standards: The Consequences of a Change of Rationale," *New York University Law Review,* November 1977, pp. 1093, 1116.

46. American Bar Association Project on Minimum Standards for Criminal Justice, *Standards Relating to the Prosecution Function and Defense Function,* Standard 3.8 (Chicago: American Bar Association, Approved Draft, 1971).

47. McCarthy, "Delinquency Dispositions." p. 1118.

48. Stephen Wizner and Mary F. Keller, "The Penal Model of Juvenile Justice: Is Juvenile Court Delinquency Jurisdiction Obsolete?" *New York University Law Review,* November 1977, pp. 1120, 1134.

49. Ibid., p. 1134.

50. Martin Guggenheim, *A Call to Abolish the Juvenile Justice System,* Children's Rights Report II (New York: American Civil Liberties Union Foundation, June 1978).

51. National Commission on Law Observance and Enforcement, *Report on Criminal Procedure* (1931; reprint ed., Montclair, N.J.: Patterson Smith, 1968).

52. President's Commission on Law Enforcement and Administration of Justice, *The Challenge of Crime in a Free Society* (Washington, D.C.: Govt. Printing Office, 1967), pp. 128–29.

53. National Advisory Commission on Criminal Justice Standards and Goals, *Courts,* Standard 8.1 (Washington D.C.: Govt. Printing Office, 1973).

54. The American Judicature Society and Institute for Court Management, *Misdemeanor Court Management Research Program,* Part I Report to the National Institute of Law Enforcement and Criminal Justice (June 1978), p.3.

55. Steven L. Schlossman, *Love and the American Delinquent* (Chicago: University of Chicago Press, 1977).

56. For a starting point to review felony courts shorcomings, see Russell R. Wheeler and Howard R. Whitcomb, *Judicial Administration: Text and Readings* (Englewood Cliffs, N.J.: Prentice-Hall, 1976), ch. 6.

57. See generally, John A. Robertson, *Rough Justice: Perspectives on Lower Criminal Courts* (Boston: Little, Brown, 1974).

58. See Sheldon Krantz et al., *Right to Counsel in Criminal Cases: The Mandate of Argersinger v. Hamlin* (Cambridge, Mass.: Ballinger, 1976).

59. Raymond T. Nimmer and Patricia Ann Krauthaus, "Pretrial Diversion: The Premature Quest for Recognition," *University of Michigan Journal of Law Reform,* Winter 1976, pp. 206–30; and Franklin E. Zimring, "Measuring the Impact of Pretrial Diversion," *University of Chicago Law Review,* Winter 1974, pp. 205–95.

The Differentiation of Offense Severity: Policy and Program Concerns

A. Serious and Repetitive Delinquency

INTRODUCTION

In the past, juvenile court judges were not restricted by law in meting out dispositional orders according to the type of juvenile offense. An armed robber could be placed on probation; an habitual truant could be sentenced to a state delinquency facility. While the severity or nonseverity of the offense did dominate a large number of judicial decisions, other criteria were influential: the number and quality of prior offenses, the intactness of the child's family, family strengths, school adjustment, socioeconomic status, race, and the attitudes of the victim, the child, and his parents, among other factors.

The advent of the status offense classification in the early 1960s led to the rather widescale prohibition on the institutionalization of status offenders in the mid- and late 1970s. This development, along with the embrace of labeling theory, the legitimation of informal probation supervision, the growth of diversion programs, and the apparent increase in more serious juvenile offenses, prompted a more sophisticated differentiation of offense severity via changes in legislation and juvenile justice practice. In part, the policy debate centers on resurrecting a "let the punishment fit the crime" theme. Another precipitant to policy review has been the increased questioning of rehabilitation effectiveness.

The Conrad article points out that serious offenses are but a small fraction of total juvenile offenses and cites the Philadelphia research finding that a small number of youths commit a disproportionate number of law violations. Although an indeterminate number of youngsters are transferred from juvenile to criminal courts because of offense patterns or intractability to juvenile rehabilitation, Conrad would prefer to see more youths retained within the juvenile system. He urges the juvenile system to develop better solutions with the more difficult delinquent youths.

He votes no confidence in present secure juvenile facilities, which too often are run more by the residents than by the staff. He opts for public subsidy of private resources which, less bound by bureaucratic concerns and constraints, can outperform public youth agencies. Conrad argues that neither the state nor the private agency should condone unlawful conduct by its clients, and describes certain positive values that the state should teach and insure.

Juvenile court judges and youth institution officials have relied on tests and evaluations by psychologists and psychiatrists in determining whether to institutionalize a youth or to release an institutionalized juvenile. The juvenile justice system has long expressed its concern for the "whole child" through its use of mental health professionals. From another perspective, the judge and the institutional release authority appear to prefer to share responsibility for their decisions with professionals who claim expertise in the area of emotions and the prediction of future behaviors. The Monahan review of the research into the predictability of future violent offenses finds the merits of these claims to be highly overrated.

Psychologically-based predictions of future violence are far more often false than true. The effect is to overinstitutionalize youngsters (and adults) and unnecessarily prolong their periods of institutionalization. Yet Monahan expects the preoccupation with childhood experience evaluation and psychological measurement to continue, partly because the juvenile justice system is so wedded to this approach, and also because the substitution of demographic or actuarial measures poses constitutional and ethical conflicts. He believes that such measures as age, sex, race, and socioeconomic status are more reliable predictors of future delinquency than psychological factors. Monahan contends that judges and institutional release authorities can ill afford to admit that they rely on these actuarial measures and therefore defer to clinical judgments which, while camouflaged, take into account these same measures. He would eliminate the clinical middleman, state candidly the actuarial bases of decisions, and then litigate their constitutionality.

The treatment rationale of the juvenile court, dominant in local practice, currently is under serious attack. Some criminologists and legal theorists would substitute the doctrine of proportionality, which correlates the severity of the sanction with the severity of the offense. This approach is founded on several principles: consistency, fairness, commensurability, predictabliity, and, probably, deterrence.

The report of the Twentieth Century Fund Task Force on Sentencing Policy Toward Young Offenders endorses proportionality as well as culpability. It affirms, with reservation, the juvenile court as the initial processing forum for all youths under eighteen years, but accepts the transfer of older juveniles to the criminal court when the mimimum punishment indicated is lengthier than that available through the juvenile system. Understandably, unanimity of opinion often is lacking among members of a task force. A dissenting opinion, for example, believes that the judge rather than the state youth agency or paroling authority should determine the release for a committed youth at the time of the sentencing hearing. This determinate sentence approach is consistent with proportionality; the task force, on the release issue, is inconsistent with its earlier premise and follows a rehabilitation and prediction model rather than its own offense-based principle. The report's summary analysis of juvenile offense data provides an important backdrop for its considerations.

5 *When the State Is the Teacher*
John P. Conrad

If the official behavior and public policies are reliable guides to our collective attitudes, Americans do not like other people's children, especially the children of the poor. We begrudge them support at a standard of living above mere survival. We educate them in generally old and dilapidated schools, and we prefer that poor children be kept separate from those who are born to more affluent families. The truth is that we are afraid of poor children, particularly those of other races. Like children of all classes, these children from time to time confirm our fears and our dislike of them by committing atrocious and frightening crimes.

The problem is old, but a new response is emerging. It is a hard line which justifies punishment as the only method for teaching good conduct to those children who do not learn virtue at home. Thus Ernest van den Haag, a leading exponent of the value severity:

> After the age of thirteen, juveniles should be treated as adults for indictment, trial, and sentencing purposes. Once they are in penal institutions or in confinement, they may be held separately and treated differently. . .To be sure, most juvenile offenders come from particularly trying backgrounds and home situations. However, there is no evidence that such home situations have become worse compared with what they were twenty years ago. Yet there are more offenders among juveniles. They are the product of the leniency of the law — of the privilege granted them — as much as anything else.[1]

Although I am not venturing here on a critique of this author, I cannot refrain from calling attention to the magnificent sample of *post hoc ergo propter hoc* reasoning embedded here in a paragraph written by a savant so widely extolled for the rigor of his logic. Many social changes have occurred in the past twenty years, among which the increased leniency of the courts which van den Haag presumes is only one. The inference of cause from effect is frail structure for the support of new social policy. Elsewhere van den Haag carries this line a little farther:

> . . .many offenders are classified as juvenile delinquents to be "reformed" rather than punished, and others — far too many — are excused as mentally incompetent. "Reform" — custody for juveniles have not been shown to be more effective than simple imprisonment. Incompetents referred to psychiatric institutions may be kept for life or for a few months, depending on utterly capricious psychiatric judgments.[2]

The essence of these quotations is the message of severity first. Like so many less articulate contemporaries, van den Haag truly believes that increasing severity will decrease crime like the operation of a pulley. The speculative quality of this conclusion does not deter him. He has heard from the statisticians that the rehabilitation of offenders has been tried and does not "work."[3] It takes a tough mind to face

From *The Serious Juvenile Offender,* Proceedings of a National Symposium, September 19 and 20, 1977, Minneapolis, Minnesota. Office of Juvenile Justice and Delinquency Prevention, Law Enforcement Assistance Administration, U.S. Department of Justice (Washington, D.C.: Government Printing Office, 1978), pp. 32–50. Reprinted by permission.

futility, and van den Haag, along with many others in the juvenile justice system itself, has decided that it is a futile effort to improve the behavior of delinquents by measures other than punitive intimidation. Concern about our inability to help the serious juvenile offender may be dismissed as the sentimentality of the incorrigible optimist. In van den Haag's world, realism is the recognition of the value of punishment without proving it.

The hard line has not yet prevailed everywhere, but its reception by ordinarily thoughtful reviewers show how seriously it must be taken. Its implications are ominous for the future management of children in the most serious kind of trouble. The view of human nature on which it rests does not reassure the optimist about the direction of the change of moral values in the society in which these children and law-abiding citizens confront each other.

The jeremiad which I have just delivered is a prelude to another. The conventional administration of juvenile justice against which van den Haag has inveighed has little cause for self-congratulation, particularly when we consider the problem of the serious juvenile offender with which we are concerned in this seminar. Because of the fragmentary nature of the data, a conclusive assessment of the system is impossible. Like the critics of whom I have been so critical, I must argue from a mostly nonempirical brief.

There are, however, some data, and I shall do what I can with them. Let us begin with the *Uniform Crime Reports* as a benchmark. In the 1975 edition of that annual compilation, we find that persons under eighteen were arrested for a total of 72,867 violent offenses — murder, forcible rape, robbery, and aggravated assault. That was an increase of 54.0 percent over the same figure for 1970. It was 24.5 percent of all the violent crimes for which arrests were made in 1975.[4] The FBI cautions that these figures measure law enforcement acitvity, not necessarily numbers of offenders. Two or more persons may be arrested for the same offense, and some individuals may be arrested more than once during a year. Still, there is some reason to think that violent crime committed by juveniles is a large share, perhaps a quarter of all the violent crime committed in our turbulent society.

But the same table also shows that juveniles committed 663,440 "index" offenses, of which the crimes against the person constituted only 11 percent. This fraction would diminish toward a vanishing point if all the nonindex and status offenses chargeable against juveniles could be added into the sum.

We can see that the imposing total of crimes against the person committed by juveniles becomes numerically trivial when compared with the total load of juvenile delinquency. But the FBI data cannot tell us how many serious juvenile offenders find their way into court, nor can we say how many of those who are brought to adjudication are placed under official control. These are difficult questions to answer, as my colleagues and I have been discovering in a study of violent juveniles conducted as a part of the Dangerous Offender Project.

Using police records of Columbus, our home town, as our source, we have traced the official fragments of the delinquent careers of 811 persons born in the years 1956–58 who were arrested in Columbus for the commission of a violent offense before reaching the age of eighteen. This is a total cohort comprising all persons born in those years who were arrested for crimes against the person. These

811 persons were arrested for 987 offenses which were classified as violent. They were also arrested for 2,386 nonviolent offenses in the course of their juvenile careers. Review of the records suggested that not all of the 987 violent offenses were really serious. Many of the assault and battery arrests were the results of trivial fights in which no damage was done. Limiting the definition of violent crime to those offenses which are index crimes against the person, as defined in the *Uniform Crime Reports,* we had 449 arrests which resulted in the disposition reflected in Table 5-1.

I do not know whether this response is as severe as Dr. van den Haag and like-minded critics would like. I cannot compare these data with those of any other city. My colleagues and I think that the juvenile justice system in Columbus is reasonably efficient. When nearly half of the juveniles who are found guilty of violent offenses receive a custodial disposition, something serious happens to a large number of serious violent offenders in our city. Indeed, if we can disregard the purse snatchers as no more than quasi-violent, the number of guilty individuals in this table who find their way into custody rise to 53 percent. We have not yet been able to compare the consequences of these dispositions; we shall not be surprised if recidivism rates are rather high across the board, and in this respect we believe Ohio will be found to be like most other states with large urban populations. . . .

But even if the workload is not as unmanageable as it is represented to be, even if we could be sure that in every city most serious juvenile offenders are picked up by the police and promptly placed under the court's control, the fundamental problem would remain. It is not an organizational problem to be solved by the improved training of the police or the selection of more and better juvenile court personnel. It is a conceptual problem of deciding on a constructive and effective response to the serious juvenile offender. In this respect, I contend that we are virtually bankrupt. Our ideas are threadbare and our programs are worse; all too often they continue the production of the "State-Raised Youth" so well described by John Irwin.

Irwin identifies four themes in the world of the state-raised youth. First, violence is the proper mode of settling an argument, and a man must be ready to inflict it and face it. Second, membership in cliques commands loyalties and defines values. Third, homosexuality defines an exploitative and often violent caste system, whereby sexual conduct is based on the ability to exercise force and the complementary deprivation of masculinity which results from subjugation. Fourth is the fantasy of the "streets" as a temporary sojourn for orgiastic pleasures, a place for holidays from the real world of the institution. Irwin sums up this product of the youth corrections system:

> The world view of these youths is distorted, stunted, or incoherent . . . . the youth prison is their only world, and they think almost entirely in the categories of this world. They tend not to be able to see beyond the walls. They do conceive of the streets, but only from the perspective of the prison. Furthermore, in prison it is a dog-eat-dog world where force or threat of force prevails. If one is willing to fight, to resort to assault with weapons . . . he succeeds in this world.[5]

No one wants to raise youths like this. Indeed, legislators, judges, and correctional officials will be unanimous that this is precisely the kind of result that they do not want to get. But this is a kind of young man that reform schools have

TABLE 5-1. Disposition of 449 Arrests for Index Crimes Against the Person Charged Against a Cohort of 811 Persons Born in 1956–58 Who were Arrested Once or More for Violent Offenses Committed in Columbus, Ohio, Before the Age of Eighteen*

| | OFFENSE | | | | | | | | | | | | |
| Disposition | Homicide | | Aggravated Assault | | Forcible Rape | | Aggravated Robbery | | Unarmed Robbery | | Purse Snatching | | Totals | |
	No.	%	No.	%	No.	%	No.	%	No.	%	No.	%	No.	%
State Institution	4	27	15	17	7	17.5	38	52.8	22	17.9	21	19.3	107	23.8
Detention/Jail	1	7	10	11	4	10.0	1	1.4	19	15.4	19	17.4	54	12.0
Other Placement	0	0	1	1	1	2.5	0	0	2	1.6	1	0.9	5	1.1
Probation	0	0	11	12	3	7.5	3	4.2	23	18.7	12	11.0	52	11.6
Reprimand & Release	0	0	25	28	4	10.0	1	1.4	16	13.0	9	8.3	55	12.2
Disposition Incomplete	4	27	4	4	4	10.0	13	18.1	9	7.3	15	13.8	62	13.8
Not Guilty	5	33	22	24	16	40.0	15	20.8	31	25.2	28	25.7	104	23.2
Unknown	1	7	2	2	1	2.5	1	1.4	1	0.8	4	3.7	10	2.2
TOTALS	15	101	90	99	40	100	72	100.1	123	99.9	109	100.1	449	99.9

*Table excludes all charges for violent crimes which were not index offenses.

been raising for many decades. Such young men are still being raised, mainly because the state is not sure what else to do with them once it gets them.

The absence of ideas and the inappropriateness of programs for the management of the serious juvenile offender as a separate class is a familiar state of affairs. The inadequacies of youth correctional facilities are staple items for reformist rhetoric. The traditional reform school has been denounced, and roundly, for many decades. Modifications of architecture, program activities, and staff orientation have indeed taken place. But the more it changes, the more it is the same. The hideous old battlements, which our nineteenth century forebearers built with the apparent intention of scaring kids into better behavior, have been demolished or at least remodeled. The occasional survival of this legacy of oppression is unanimously deplored and its use justified on account of the absence of funds to replace it. Discipline by "cadet officers" which was once the mainstay of order in the reformatory has gone for good, and so has the unsightly and humiliating lockstep. The vestiges of military programming which remain are the harmless elements of a noxious tradition. Generally, it is accepted that such facilities should be quite small, and that staff should be qualified to administer a resocializing program.

The new dilemmas confronting state agencies in planning residential treatment for youth have only recently become matters of general recognition. The title of our seminar, "The Serious Juvenile Offender," is novel. We have not been accustomed to differentiating this or any other class in the workload of juvenile delinquency. For years, enlightened judges and probation officers have operated on the principle that it is desirable to limit the penetration of the juvenile corrections system so far as possible in considering the disposition of any delinquent boy or girl. Therefore, some kids went on probation, and only those who seemed to be unmanageable in the community went into training schools. The nature of the offense obviously had something to do with the disposition, but the ideology prevailed, and still does, that the nature of the child's difficulty rather than the nature of his/her offense should determine his/her treatment. The population mixture in the institutions includes delinquents of an extremely serious order and others whose infractions of the law have been close to insignificant. But once arrived at the institution, treatment tends to be undifferentiated except as to its duration. Its content depends on present behavior rather than on the events which brought the youth into the custody of the state. Considering our uncertainty about measures which can be expected to prepare people in custody for a return to the community, this lack of differentiation is entirely understandable. So far, our experiments in differential treatment have been inconclusive for the formulation of new policy.

The need for change is in the air. Perhaps we may attribute its recognition to Professor Wolfgang and his colleagues, who first called attention to the momentous potential for harm contained in a small group within the Philadelphia Birth Cohort designated as chronic offenders.[6] Perhaps it was the alarm of a number of juvenile court judges who have been critical of the ineffectiveness of youth corrections but have not had any alternative disposition available. Certainly the fascination of the media for the youthful mugger and rapist has put the entire juvenile justice system on the defensive. Whatever the sources, we now have a consensus that there is a Serious Juvenile Offender, and that the state's response to him/her is inadequate for the protection of the public. . . .

At this point, we need to consider the directions in which our thought about the Serious Juvenile Offender is taking us. It certainly cannot be said that our anxieties about him/her have propelled us far into the realms of innovation. Public discourse seems to be limited to four major themes for the modification of the official response to the problem of violent crime when committed by children. I think it will be useful to discuss these options as specifically as I can because each of them illustrates the obstacles to constructive change.

First, there is the response of the juvenile court to the exceptionally serious offense, ordinarily committed by a minor whose maturity in criminal behavior is all too apparent to everyone in contact with him/her. Such a case can be, and often is, declared inappropriate for adjudication in the juvenile court. It would be interesting to know how many cases are handled this way, of what types, and with what consequences. Unfortunately, the statistical picture is murky. The *Uniform Crime Reports* have for many years published a table entitled, "Juvenile Offenders taken into custody, by type of disposition and size of place." Inspection of the column headed, "Referred to criminal or adult court" for the years 1972–75 reveals that for the country as a whole, in 1972 there were 16,439 such referrals, accounting for 1.3 percent of the total dispositions. In 1973, the corresponding figures were 18,767 and 1.5 percent. But in 1974, the total number of reporting agencies doubled and the number of bind-overs increased to 63,527 or 3.7 percent of all dispositions. In 1975, the total number of reporting agencies increased from 8,649 to 9,684 covering a population coverage which increased from 160 million to 180 million. Yet, the number of bind-overs decreased from 63,527 in 1974 to 38,958 in 1975, representing 2.3 percent of all dispositions.[7] I have gone into this detail because I have not thought of a way to account for the apparent reversal of this trend, except to charge it off as an artifact of criminal justice bookkeeping. I think it is an obligation of the social scientist who makes discoveries of this kind to call them to public attention in the interest of reminding a credulous world of the difficulties inherent in making sense out of official statistics. We can only say that in the universe of juvenile dispositions the referral to an adult court occupies an inconspicuous space. Whether they amount to 40,000 or 60,000 they are not proportionately a large part of the solution to juvenile delinquency. We are unable to say what fraction of the universe of serious· juvenile offenders is bound over for the supposedly sterner adult procedures. The population bases in the *Uniform Crime Reports* vary so widely from table to table that it is impossible to go into one table with data from an adjoining table to make such estimates with any confidence at all. I ask you to keep this example in mind because it illustrates the statistical confusion which the nation faces in defining and understanding juvenile justice policy problems after all these years of the *Uniform Crime Reports* and the earnest efforts of the Law Enforcement Assistance Administration to create a usable data base for criminal justice policy makers.

In our cohort of 811, there were thirteen boys bound over to the adult court for a total of fifteen offenses. Two were sixteen; the rest were well past their seventeenth birthday. Except for two burglaries, the offenses were extremely serious crimes against the person, including three murders. It is impossible to say how typical of other cities these data are, but certainly recourse to the bind-over has so far been minimal in the data now available to us.

Still, we have a firm data on the number of bind-overs which occur or even whether there is a trend to use this option more frequently. That says nothing of the types of cases bound over, the actions taken by the adult criminal court, or the consequences of those actions for the individual, for the correctional system to which he is committed, or to the community at large for the supposed protection of which the juvenile is converted into an adult. We shall have to wait patiently until some future year for data which can facilitate an informed discussion of these issues.

Although we cannot measure, we can inspect the logic of the waiver of juvenile court jurisdiction and consider where it will lead us. In the days of the pre-*Gault* court (which, we must remind ourselves, still prevails in philosophy if not in some precedures), the rationale is logical. The custodial facilities which the juvenile court can command are juvenile institutions. Jurisdiction over any ward is limited to the duration of his/her minority — with some adjustments in the law of some states. If the court has to consider the case of a seventeen-year-old chronic recidivist charged with a heinous crime, it is understandable that it would wish to assure control beyond the maximum of four years to which its jurisdiction is limited.

The commitment of an experienced young violent offender with previous commitments to juvenile institutions to yet another such facility is difficult to defend, as in either the boy's interests or in society's. The institution for older deliquents is balanced on an opposition between a staff culture and a criminal culture which is easily tipped. The contribution of the boy to the criminal culture is likely to outweigh the positive benefits he may gain from the commitment. The court has every reason to ask, Why on earth continue the pretense that this young thug is child in trouble? Why should he not be counted as a young adult in the prison system rather than an old child in the youth corrections system?

The answer to these questions is anything but obvious. For the boy himself, the advantage of yet another youth commitment is less time to serve — although in states which are experimenting with mandatory sentences for juveniles, the advantage will be narrower than it used to be. For the state, the value of more time served by an adult commitment is increased incapacitation of a young man of whom the community is afraid. There is also the popular belief that an adult commitment will be more effective in achieving the goals of general deterrence and intimidation. This belief has yet to be convincingly verified, but skeptical critics of the sytem have not yet shaken it with data. Whatever the truth may be about these issues, the chances that the offender himself will be better for the experience of incarceration in either system are negligible. The bind-over will accomplish a longer incapacitation and a more vigorous expression of community outrage. These are negative accomplishments, and their value is impossible to verify.

The bind-over is an option available to the juvenile court, and it is exercised in different ways by different judges. Indeed, we hear that in some communities minors ask to be bound over, evidently believing that the chances for leniency are greater in adult than in the juvenile courts. But the uncertainty about the propriety of the bind-over hides a conceptual vacuum. We don't know what to do with this apparently dangerous youth, so we put him away for as long as we can. The most we can hope for is that the experience will be so unpleasant that he will do whatever he can to avoid repetition.

I do not know of any evidence on the effectiveness of incarceration in the intimidation of any offenders from the commission of further crime. The data on recidivism available to me appear to show that a majority of the people released from prison — perhaps as many as 60 percent — do not recidivate.[8] I doubt that they have been rehabilitated, so I will tentatively conclude that intimidation has motivated them to keep out of trouble. But we are talking about a Serious Juvenile Offender. He is usually a chronic recidivist for whom incarceration holds few unacceptable terrors. Even if intimidation is effective for many prisoners, it is least effective for him.

Is this all we can do? Is it reasonable to concede so much to the prevailing pessimism? The worse aspect of the consensus that "nothing works" is the corollary to which it leads: nothing can work. As logical as the bind-over seems to the judge and the public, the consignment of the young aggressive recidivist to prison is an admission of defeat. The record of youth training facilities with such young men is discouraging, but the structural and programmatic faults in most of them glare at us so obiously that it is clear that improvements must be possible if we have the will to undertake them. To excuse the juvenile justice system from the effort on the ground that "nothing works" is to admit that society is indifferent about results. Against the occasional bind-over of the truly exceptional delinquent as an individual case I will not complain. But to define a class of offenders who may be bound over is to create a policy which closes out the prospect of change. There must be continuing pressure on administrators, clinicians, and researchers to generate a better solution for this troublesome fraction of the delinquent population than the Deep Six to which the tough-minded "realists" are willing to consign them.

The reverse of the bind-over strategy is the mandatory sentence for the Serious Juvenile Offender. Instead of sending him/her off to an adult prison, he/she is to be kept in the juvenile justice system two to three years. I do not hear from advocates of this policy any suggested activities to fill up those years. That would not matter if the professionals who are responsible for the design of programs appeared to have any treatment innovations in mind. They don't. We are asked to make the same act of faith in the usefulness of a mixture of incapacitation and intimidation implied by advocates of more bind-overs.

The emerging solution — as the category of the Serious Juvenile Offender takes form as a class for which there are criteria for selection — is the secure facility, usually rather small, usually well provided with staff positions, and usually quite expensive to operate. If dollars were the only measure of our concern, it would be clear that despite my jeremiads, our society has not given up on these young people. But again, we have a conceptual vacuum.

Two examples will illustrate the point. The publication last year of *Juvenile Victimization* by my diligent colleagues, Bartollas, Miller, and Dinitz, provides us with an account of how things go in a well-designed, fairly new (1961), and generously staffed (145 staff for 192 residents) facility for aggressive older boys in Ohio.[9] Although most of the problems in maintaining control are recognized by the staff, the culture is exploitative and criminal. Many of the staff are so fearful of their charges that they hide in the security of their offices. A constant testing of the courage and resourcefulness of the others seems to go on. When residents are out of the sight of staff, there is considerable violence and sexual imposition, following, as if by prescription, the theoretical analysis which I have quoted from Irwin. In the air is a climate of intimidation with all the roles which result from that kind of interaction. The program itself consists of the usual mixture of counseling, remedial education, and vocational training. It is supported in the institutional program statements by such language as "[Our goals are] to promote positive attitudinal and behavioral change within an atmosphere of mutual respect and personal dignity; to provide a resident with opportunities to gain an increased understanding of himself, others, and his enviornment; and to learn to meet his needs in socially acceptable ways."[10]

The institution which is described in the Bartollas-Miller-Dinitz study is not atypical, except that the discrepancies between intentions and performance have been documented with painful thoroughness. This is a situation in which the staff still has the last word, but the dominant boys among the residents enjoy most of the control. Those familiar with the literature of youth training schools or who have access to oral accounts of how things have been for the last half-century will recognize this facility as the legitimate heir of an old and disgusting tradition. One can account for the persistence of the tradition: staff idealism erodes in the incessant backwash of unrealized expectations, training is insufficient to prepare recruits for the interactions ahead, leadership by seniors is perfunctory and rhetorical — the list can go on. To my mind, the primary failing to which this dismal list of failings its attributable is the compromise with residents over lawful conduct. Once that compromise has been made and unlawfulness has been overlooked, the hope for creating a civic culture is gone. As the authors of this powerful book put it, "instead of modeling themselves after other professional staff, the professional staff is subverted and adopts the style and values of the residents. . .[A]s long as personnel are in the institution, they must react and respond in resident terms. The turf belongs to the inmates. . ."[11]

. . . I said that there seem to be four approaches to the problem of the Serious Juvenile Offender. Binding over the older ones converts them into adults. To require a mandatory sentence of two or three years is tantamount to changing part of the juvenile justice system into an essentially adult system in which incapacitation is the primary goal. To modify the existing system by developing specialized secure units constitutes an act of continuing faith in the state as a vehicle for treatment. Each approach calls for the state to continue raising youth.

These three propositions contain within them the foundations of doubt. As to the first two, we back down on our national commitment to a fair start for children. Perhaps we can give up on the adult offenders, or some of them, as too scarred, too damaged to be accessible to help. I don not think we are yet willing to give up on the sixteen- or seventeen-year-old kid who has foundered in delinquency because of the mismanagement of his/her early years by the adults in his/her life. As to the third proposition, the placement of these minors in small state institutions, we have only too much reason to believe that state agencies for the extension of help to people needing help will become bureaucratized, impersonal, and preoccupied with procedures. There are many things that only the state can do well, but the management of human relationships is not one of them.

So the fourth policy option is the regeneration of the private sector. In a sense, this choice has always been available. Children of the upper classes who get out of control have for many years been sent away to military academies or similar residential schools for attention and discipline which they could not get at home. Some of these facilities may be well managed; some are certainly frauds against distracted parents. We don't really know much that is objective about these places, but there are suspicions that in keeping the bad rich boy out of a reform school, his parents may not be getting a much better bargain from the boarding school which is willing to take him in.

The state as *parens patriae* has money to spend, too. Nobody really knows anything definite about the traffic in difficult children — often across state lines — which gets them out of institutions in which they are unmanageable and places them into group homes, camps, or private institutional situations which are willing to manage them for a price and which are able to make a profit from that price. Obviously, there should be much more known about this situation, and it may well be that it is one of those many entrepreneurial activities of modern times which needs a federal regulatory agency to assure the maintenance of standards.

All that is by way of recognition is that the private sector is not necessarily an avenue toward the conversion of the Serious Juvenile Offender into an inoffensive but productive citizen. Nevertheless, I think there are a number of reasons for supposing that most of the future progress to be made in improving the state's response to this figure of our concern may lie in this direction. I would like to wind up my contribution to this discussion by outlining my reasons for believing that enlightened policy should go as far as it can in the encouragement of the private sector to care for these kids and to create programs for their socialization.

First, as I have indicated earlier, the state is not well adapted to the helping role. I think that is as it should be. The state should prevent avoidable misery, but it has no business making individuals happy or morally better. Its tools are those of management and order; its procedures are bureacratic; its agents cannot express the state's love or concern because the state is not an entity capable of love and concern. Impersonality, fairness, and rationality are what we expect from the state. It is not to take risks, and although it may and does experiment, the experiments it conducts are directed at the improvement of state services, which sets a special boundary to the possibilities for improvement.

Second, the kinds of services which Serious Juvenile Offenders need do not lend themselves to the kinds of careers for which civil servants are recruited and around which they build their lives. The pattern of thirty or so years in the same service, with promotion by seniority, civil service and union rules about hours, duties, privileges, rights, and training is workable for a fire department or for highway construction and maintenance. It is much less appropriate when the work to be done is in the influencing of others by example, counseling, and control. It is even less appropriate for the special tasks which those assigned to the Serious Juvenile Offender must carry out.

All of us know in our bones what the problem is. The best of intentions and the highest of motivations will erode with emotional fatigue. It is a rare man or woman who can confront hostility professionally and constructively for the duration of a normal civil service career. Some day, some salty young resident will sling a stereo speaker at the staff member and the response will be inappropriate, not because the counselor is new and untrained, but rather because he/she is too experienced and burnt out. I suggest that ways have to be found to enlist energetic and well disposed young people to work for a few years only in facilities of this kind. I don't think that such a way can be found in the civil service.

The third problem is one of leadership. It has been my observation that the best programs revolve around the personality of a manager or director who possesses that attribute which we call, for want of a better word, charisma. Examples come readily to my mind, and probably to the mind of anyone else who has watched schools, counseling services, group therapy, and even prisons, and I won't labor my examples now. We should make it easier for people of this kind to build programs that fit their potential contributions. I don't think that conventional state procedures lend themselves to the kind of voluntarism which the charismatic leader requires for scope, happy accidents to the contrary notwithstanding.

Fourth, a private employee is much more easily hired or fired than a civil servant. Although it is untrue that civil servants cannot be fired (I have seen it done) the difficulties will daunt all but the most determined manager and will certainly detain him/her from more profitable uses of his/her energies.

Finally, as Dr. [Jerome] Miller has frequently pointed out, it is a lot easier to get rid of an unsatisfactory program which is on a service contract to the state than it is to phase out a budgeted state program. In either case, the Commissioner of Corrections, or whoever is in charge, does not have an easy task. Other arrangements have to be made for service, pressures to continue the program in spite of poor performance will usually be heavy, and the Commissioner is in the politically undesirable position of making a considerable number of enemies and few, if any, friends. But it is easier to refuse a new contract than to close down a bad state program, and failure is a contingency for which provision must be made.

I cannot prove that the private sector is the best hope in this unpromising challenge to the state's competence. Obviously, if we are to choose this route, we cannot expect an overnight transformation. Legions of young men and women are not out there eagerly waiting for their chance to show what they can do with these troubled and sometimes frightening young offenders. Nor is there an obvious category of people-serving organizations who can channel their energies into constructive service.

And even more obviously, once we have state funds transferred to private organizations for the provision of services, there will be abuses and shortcomings and failures which could have been prevented had adequate precautions been taken. The state will still have standards to set and practices to regulate. It will, however, be out of the business of regulating itself, but it will still be the teacher.

Many years ago, Mr. Justice Brandeis wrote, "Our government is the potent, the omnipresent teacher. For good or ill, it teaches the whole people by example. Crime is contagious. If the government becomes a law breaker, it breeds contempt for the law; it invites every man to become a law unto himself; it invites anarchy."

He was not writing about the operation of facilities for the management of the Serious Juvenile Offender, but his point extends to our problem. What the state finds itself doing in even fairly well run juvenile facilities is condoning unlawful conduct by allowing a criminal culture to control the turf. This is exactly the example which cannot be permitted in residential facilities. It may be possible to avoid it in a state facility, but I suggest that we will all be a little safer if we turn the task over to the concerned entrepreneur who is willing to comply with the state's guidelines and to do as the state requires, but not as the state itself has so commonly done in the past.

What do we want the state to teach? I think that whatever else is taught — from welding to the primal scream — the lessons have to take place in a lawful community, one in which violations of the criminal law do not occur, or, if they do, they result in immediate adverse consequences. Obviously, life outside is not like that. The Serious Juvenile Offender usually comes from a nearly lawless society and will return to it. That cannot excuse the state from its duty to assure that while he/she is in custody, he/she is safe and prevented from unlawful conduct. We don't know what good observance of this principle will do, but we know all too well what harm will be done by not observing it.

NOTES

1. Ernest van den Haag, *Punishing Criminals; Concerning a Very Old and Painful Question* (New York: Basic Books, 1975), p. 249.

2. Ibid., p. 164.

3. *Uniform Crime Reports*, 1974, Table 31, p. 183.

4. Robert Martinson,"What Works? — Questions and Answers About Prison Reform," in *The Public Interest* 36 (Spring 1974): pp. 22-54.

5. John Irwin, *The Felon* (Englewood Cliffs, New Jersey: Prentice-Hall, 1970) pp. 26-29. See also for another and confirming account, Malcolm Braly, *False Starts* (Boston: Little Brown, 1976), pp. 36-60.

6. Marvin E. Wolfgang, Robert Figlio, and Thorsten Sellin, *Delinquency in a Birth Cohort* (Chicago: University of Chicago Press, 1972).

7. *Uniform Crime Reports*, 1972, Table 21, p. 116; 1973, Table 21, p. 119; 1974, Table 25, p. 177; 1975, Table 25, p. 177.

8. See *Uniform Parole Reports,* December, 1976, published by the National Council on Crime and Delinquency, for the most optimistic estimate of prison recidivism.

9. Clemens Bartollas, Stuart J. Miller, Simon Dinitz, *Juvenile Victimization, The Institutional Paradox* (New York: The Halsted Press, 1976).

10. Ibid., p. 31.

11. Ibid., p. 273.

6 *The Prediction of Violent Behavior in Juveniles*
JOHN MONAHAN

Despite William James' admonition that we cannot hope to write biographies in advance, the juvenile justice system expends a great deal of energy attempting to identify today the child who tomorrow will be violent. Decisions regarding who should be processed by the juvenile justice system rather than diverted from it, who should be waived to the adult courts, and when juvenile detention should end, often are based on explicitly or implicitly held beliefs about future violent behavior. While the predictive/preventive approach to the adult justice system has fallen on hard times with the rise of the "just deserts" model of sentencing, no comparable waning of interest in prediction can be found in the juvenile system. The prediction of future behavior is an integral part of the "rehabilitative ideal," and the "rehabilitative ideal" is the essence of juvenile justice.

This paper will selectively review the most important research on the prediction of violent behavior in juveniles as well as supporting research done with adults, and will discuss several findings relevant to the accuracy of those predictions and their use in juvenile justice.[1]

There are two overlapping but clearly distinct perspectives on the prediction of violent behavior in juveniles. The first focuses upon the childhood precursors of adult violence. It asks the question, What factors in the upbringing or development of a child lead to his/her adopting a violent life style as an adult?

The second perspective uses a more telescoped time frame. It does not ask what factors or characteristics of a juvenile predict his/her adult crime, but rather what predicts future crime as a juvenile. The question addressed from this point of view is whether or not a given juvenile, if released from detention, or if not detained at all, will commit a violent act next month or next year, rather than farther down the path of life.

While it is this latter, time limited perspective which I believe has the most important implications for public policies at this time in history, most psychological and sociological research has focused on the life span development approach, and it is this that we shall look at first.

It is one of the more established pieces of psychiatric folklore that the childhood triad of pyromania (fire setting), enuresis (bed-wetting), and cruelty to animals is clinically predictive of adult violence.[2] While the child who awakes from his/her bed to set fire to the cat is indeed a problem, there exists no research to support the belief that he/she will later turn to murder as an avocation.

One survey reviewed 1,500 references to violence in psychiatric literature, interviewed over 750 professionals who dealt with violent persons, and retrospectively analyzed over 1,000 clinical cases to ascertain the best childhood predictors of adult violence.[3] The authors reported that the four "early warning signs" most frequently mentioned in the literature, the interviews, and the case studies were fighting, temper

From *The Serious Juvenile Offender,* Proceedings of a National Symposium, September 19 and 20, 1977, Minneapolis, Minnesota. Office of Juvenile Justice and Delinquency Prevention, Law Enforcement Assistance Administration, U.S. Department of Justice (Washington, D.C.: Government Printing Office, 1978), pp. 148–60. Reprinted by permission.

tantrums, school problems, and an inability to get along with others. The child, in other words, is indeed father or mother to the grown-up.

Plainly, the most influential study assessing the childhood correlates of later criminal behavior — most influential until the Wolfgang, Figlio and Sellin cohort study [4] — was *Unraveling Juvenile Delinquency*, published by Sheldon and Eleanor Glueck in 1950.[5] While not concerned specifically with violent criminality, the Gluecks claimed that three factors — supervision by the mother, discipline by the mother, and cohesiveness of the family — were predictive of later crime in young adolescent boys. This research is among the most methodologically criticized in all of criminology, and there appears to be a consensus that the practical utility of the Glueck factors is marginal at best.

Earlier this year [1977], Lefkowitz, Eron, Walder and Huesman published the results of a longitudinal study entitled, *Growing Up To Be Violent*.[6] This research followed a sample of over 400 males and females in Columbia County, New York from the time they were eight until they were nineteen. They used peer ratings, parent ratings, self-report, and a personality test to measure violent aggression. Lefkowitz and his coworkers found that "aggression at age 8 is the best predictor we have of aggression at age 19 irrespective of IQ, social class, or parents' aggressiveness" (p. 192). Several other variables, among them the father's upward social mobility, low identification of the child with his/her parents, and a preference on the part of boys for watching violent television programs, were significantly predictive of aggression at age nineteen. Boys who, in the third grade, preferred television programs such as "Gunsmoke" or "Have Gun, Will Travel" were rated by their peers ten years later as three times as aggressive as boys who, in the third grade, preferred "Ozzie and Harriet," "I Love Lucy," or "Lawrence Welk."

The authors suggest government intervention to restrict violent television programs to being shown only after 11:00 p.m. and to enforce "the rights of the public not to be taught (by the "news media") that violence pays" (p. 209). They do not consider whether this prevention program would require repeal of the First Amendment.

Research on the prediction of more immediate violence in juveniles is more difficult to come by. The most comprehensive study was reported by Wenk et al. in 1972.[7] These researchers studied violent recidivism in over 4,000 California Youth Authority wards. Attention was directed to the record of violence in the youth's past, and an extensive background investigation was conducted, including psychiatric diagnoses and a psychological test battery. Subjects were followed for fifteen months after release, and data on 100 variables were analyzed retrospectively to see which items predicted a violent act of recidivism. The authors concluded that the parole decision-maker who used a history of actual violence as his sole predictor of future violence would have nineteen false positives in every twenty predictions, and yet "there is no other form of simple classification available thus far that would enable him to improve on this level of efficiency" (p. 399). Several multivariate regression equations were developed from the data, but none was even hypothetically capable of doing better than attaining an 8 to 1 false to true positive ratio.

This finding — that violent behavior is drastically overpredicted — is paralleled in the research on the prediction of violent behavior in adults. Wenk et al. reported two studies undertaken in the California Department of Corrections. In the first study, a violence prediction scale which included variables such as commitment offense, number of prior commitments, opiate use, and length of imprisonment, was able to isolate a small group of offenders who were three times more like to commit a violent act than parolees in general. However, 86 percent of those identified as violent did not in fact commit a violent act while on parole.

In the second study, over 7,000 parolees were assigned to various categories keyed to their potential aggressiveness on the basis of their case histories and psychiatric reports. One in five parolees was assigned to a "potentially aggressive" category, and the rest to a "less aggressive" category. During a one-year follow-up, however, the rate of crimes involving actual violence for the potentially aggressive group was only 3.1 per 1,000 compared with 2.8 per 1,000 among the less aggressive group. Thus, for every correct identification of a potentially aggressive individual, there were 326 incorrect ones.

Kozol, Boucher, and Garofalo[8] have reported a ten-year study involving almost 600 offenders. Each offender was examined independently by at least two psychiatrists, two psychologists, and a social worker. A full psychological test battery was administered and a complete case history compiled. During a five-year follow-up period in the community, 8 percent of those predicted not to be dangerous became recidivists by committing a serious assaultive act, and 34.7 percent of those predicted to be dangerous committed such an act. While the assessment of dangerousness by Kozol and his colleagues appears to have some validity, the problem of false positives stands out. Sixty-five percent of the individuals identified as dangerous did not in fact commit a dangerous act. Despite the extensive examining, testing, and data gathering they undertook, Kozol et al. were wrong in two out of every three predictions of dangerousness.

Data from an institution very similar to that used in the Kozol et al. study have been released by the Patuxent Institution.[9] Four hundred and twenty-one patients, each of whom recieved at least three years of treatment at Patuxent were considered. Of the 421 patients released by the court, the psychiatric staff opposed the release of 286 of these patients on the grounds that they were still dangerous and recommended the release of 135 patients as safe. The criterion measure was any new offense (not necessarily violent) appearing on FBI reports during the first three years after release. Of those patients released by the court against staff advice, the recidivism rate was 46 percent if the patients had been released directly from the hospital, and 39 percent if a "conditional release experience" had been imposed. Of those patients released on the staff's recommendation and continued for outpatient treatment on parole, 7 recidivated. Thus, after three years of observation and treatment, between 54 and 61 percent of the patients predicted by the psychiatric staff to be dangerous were not discovered to have committed a criminally act.

In 1966, the U.S. Supreme Court held that Johnnie Baxstrom had been denied equal protection of the law by being detained beyond his maximum sentence in an institution for the criminally insane without the benefit of a new hearing to determine his current dangerousness (*Baxstrom v. Herold*, 1966). The ruling resulted in the transfer of nearly 1,000 persons "reputed to be some of the most dangerous mental patients in the state [of New York]" from hospitals for the criminally insane to civil mental hospitals. It also provided an excellent opportunity for naturalistic research on the validity of the psychiatric predictions of dangerous upon which the extended detention was based.

There has been an extensive follow-up program on the Baxstrom patients.[10] Researchers find that the level of violence experienced in the civil mental hospitals was much less than had been feared, that the civil hospitals adapted well to the massive transfer of patients, and that the Baxstrom patients were being treated the same as the civil patients. The precautions that the civil hospitals had undertaken in anticipation of the supposedly dangerous patients — the setting up of secure wards and provision of judo training to the staff — were largely for naught. Only 20 percent of the Baxstrom patients were assaultive to persons in the civil hospitals or the community at any time during the four-year follow-up of their transfer. Further, only 3 percent of the Baxstrom patients were sufficiently dangerous to be returned to hospital for the criminally insane during the four years after the decision. Steadman and Keveles followed 121 Baxstrom patients who had been released into the community (i.e., discharged from both the criminal and civil mental hospitals). During an average of two and one-half years of freedom, only nine of the 121 patients (8 percent) were convicted of a crime and only one of those convictions was for a violent act. The researchers found that a Legal Dangerousness Scale (LDS) was most predictive of violent behavior. The scale was composed of four items: presence of juvenile record, number of previous arrests, presence of convictions for violent crimes, and severity of the original Baxstrom offense. In subsequent analyses, Cocozza and Steadman found that the only other variable highly related to subsequent criminal activity was age (under fifty years old). In one study, seventeen of twenty Baxstrom patients who were arrested for a violent crime when released into the community were under fifty and had a score of five or above on the fifteen-point Legal Dangerousness Scale. Yet the authors conclude:

> For every one patient who was under 50 years old and who had an LDS score of 5 or more and who was dangerous, there were at least 2 who were not. Thus, using these variables we get a false positive ratio of 2 to 1. . . .Despite the significant relationship between the two variables of age and LDS score and dangerous behavior if we were to attempt to use this information for statistically predicting dangerous behavior our best strategy would still be to predict that none of the patients would be dangerous.[11]

The Supreme Cour's Baxstrom decision promoted a similar group of "mentally disordered offenders" in Pennsylvania to petition successfully for release in *Dixon v. Pennsylvania,* 1971. The results of the release of 438 patients have been reported by Thornberry and Jacoby,[12] and are remarkably similar to those reported by Steadman. Only 14 percent of the former patients were discovered to have engaged in behavior injurious to another person within four years after their release.

Finally, Cocozza and Steadman[13] followed 257 indicted felony defendants found incompetent to stand trial in New York State in 1971 and 1972. All defendants were examined for a determination of dangerousness by two psychiatrists, with 60 percent being predicted to be dangerous and 40 percent not so. Subjects were followed in the hospital and in the community (if they were eventually released) during a three-year follow-up. While those predicted to be dangerous were slightly but insignificantly more likely to be assaultive during their initial incompetency hospitalization than those predicted not to be dangerous (42 percent compared with 36 percent), this relationship was reversed for those rearrested for a crime after their release, with 49 percent of the dangerous group and 54 percent of the not-dangerous group arrested. Predictive accuracy was poorest in the case of rearrest for a violent crime, "perhaps the single most important indicator of the success of the psychiatric predictions." Only 15 percent of the dangerous group, compared with 16 percent of the not-dangerous group, were rearrested for violent offense. While these data are susceptible to alternative interpretations,[14] the authors believe that they consitute "the most definitive evidence available on the lack of expertise and accuracy of psychiatric predictions of dangerousness" and indeed, represent "*clear and convincing evidence* of the inability of psychiatrists or of anyone else to accurately predict dangerousness."

The conclusion to emerge most strikingly from these studies is the great degree to which violence is overpredicted. Of those predicted to be dangerous, between 54 and 99 percent are false positives — people who will not in fact be found to have committed a dangerous act. Violence, it would appear, is vastly overpredicted, whether simple behavior indicators or sophisticated multivariate analyses are employed, and whether psychological tests or thorough psychiatric examinations are performed.

Several factors have been suggested which might account for the great degree of overprediction found in the research.[15]

1. Lack of Corrective Feedback to the Predictor.   The individual is usually incarcerated on the basis of the prediction and so it is impossible to know whether or not he/she actually would have been violent.

2. Differential Consequences to the Predictor of Overpredicting and Underpredicting Violence.   False negatives lead to much adverse publicity, while false positives have little effect on the predictor.

3. Differential Consequences to the Individual Whose Behavior Is Being Predicted.   A prediction of violence may be necessary to insure involuntary treatment.

4. Illusory Correlations Between Predictor Variables and Violent Behavior.   The often cited correlation between violent behavior and mental illness, for example, appears to be illusory.

5. Unreliability of Violence as a Criterion Event.   There is little consensus as to the definition of violence, and great unreliability in verifying its occurrence.

6. Low Base-Rates of Violence.   The prediction of any low base-rate event is extremely difficult.

7. Low Social Status of Those Subjected to Prediction Efforts.   Overprediction may be tolerated in part because of class biases in the criminal justice and mental health systems.

What are we to make of all this? Several points seem germane to current policy debates.

1. The Ability to Predict Which Juveniles Will Engage in Violent Crime, Either as Adolescents or as Adults, Is Very Poor.   The conclusion of Wenk and his colleagues that "there has been no successful attempt to identify within. . .offender groups, a subclass whose members have a greater than even chance of engaging again in an assaultive act" is as true for juveniles as it is for adults. It holds regardless of how well trained the person making the prediction is — or how well programmed the computer — and how much information on the individual is provided. More money or more resources will not help. Our crystal balls are simply very murky, and no one knows how they can be polished.

2. It Is Possible to Identify Juveniles Who Have Higher than Average (But Still Less Than Even) Chances of Committing Violent Crime.   While our ability to predict violent acts in juveniles is not very good, neither is it completely nonexistent. The research discussed earlier provides us with several factors which, if present in a given juvenile, would raise his or her probability of committing a violent act above the base-rate or norm. It should be remembered that if one out of one hundred juveniles commits a violent act in a given year, a given juvenile could be forty-nine times more likely than average to commit a violent crime, and still have less than a fifty-fifty chance of being violent.

Chief among those characteristics, from the Wolfgang study[17] and other sources, which would affect the probability of a juvenile's committing a violent crime, are his/her age, sex, race, and socioeconomic status. Also relevant would be educational achievement, IQ, and residential mobility.

3. The Best Predictor of Future Violent Behavior in a Juvenile Is His or Her Record of Past Violent Behavior.   If there is any consistency in the research, it is this: The probability of future violence increases with the frequency of past violence. It is certainly true that "not every child who commits an offense is teetering on the brink of a criminal career."[18] Wenk, for example, found that nineteen out of twenty juveniles with a violent act in their history did not commit another violent act, at least in the first fifteen months after release.[19] It is not that past violence is a good predictor of future violence, it is merely the best predictor available. And, if the research suggests that prediction is problematic even in the case of individuals with a history of a violent act, it is emphatic that prediction is foolhardy for those juveniles or adults without violence in their backgrounds. In the words of one psychiatrist who believes that violence can be predicted: "The difficulty involved in predicting dangerousness is immeasurably increased when the subject has never actually performed an assaultive act. . .No one can predict dangerous behavior in an individual with no history of dangerous acting out."[20] This point can hardly be overemphasized in discussions of public policies to control violent crime by juveniles.

4. The Poorest Predictors of Violent Behavior in Juveniles Are Those That Relate to Psychological Functioning.   With the possible exception of IQ, psychological variables have not proven to be particularly useful as prognosticators of violent behavior in juveniles. While Lefkowitz et al.[21] did find positive correlations between a child's lack of identification with his/her parents, preference for violent television programs, and father's upward social mobility, and later violence, these correlations explained only about 10 percent of the variance of adult aggression.

As Mischel noted in his classic review of psychological prediction, "A person's relevant past behaviors tend to be the best predictors of his future behavior in similar situations. It is increasingly obvious that even simple, crude, demographic indices of an individual's past behaviors and social competence predict his future behavior at least as well as, and sometimes better than, either the best test-based personality statements or clinical judgments."[22]

No psychological test has been developed which can *post*dict, let alone *pre*dict, violence in either juveniles or adults.[23]

5. Actuarial Tables May Be Superior to Clinical Judgments in Predicting Violent Behavior in Juveniles.   The two generic methods by which violent behavior (or any other kind of event) may be anticipated are known as clinical and actuarial prediction. In clinical prediction, a psychologist, psychiatrist, parole board member, or other person acting as a "clinician," considers what he or she believes to be the relevant factors predictive of violence, and renders an opinion accordingly. This was the method used in the Kozol, Steadman, Thornberry and Jacoby, and Patuxent studies reviewed earlier. The clinician may rely in part upon actuarial data in forming the prediction, but the final product is the result of an intuitive weighting of the data in the form of a professional judgment. Actuarial (or statistical) prediction refers to the establishment of statistical relationships between given predictor variables such as age, number of prior offenses, etc., and the criterion of violent behavior. This method was used in the Wenk et al. series of studies and the Glueck research. The prediction variables may include clinical diagnoses or scores on psychological tests, but these are statistically weighed in a prediction formula.

One of the "great debates" in the field of psychology has revolved around the relative superiority of clinical versus actuarial methods. It is one of the few such debates to emerge with a clear-cut victor. With the publication of Paul Meehl's classic work in 1954[24] and its many subsequent confirmations,[25] actuarial methods have come to be recognized as the generally superior way of predicting behavior.

While actuarial tables have not yet proven their superiority in predicting violent behavior in juveniles, the impression persists that clinicians have "taken their best shot" at prediction and that it has been so wide of the mark that the future lies with actuarial methods, especially those building on the work of Wolfgang, Lefkowitz, and others.

6. One Reason Clinical Prediction Persists in Juvenile Justice Is That It Allows Socially Sensitive Predictor Variables to Be Hidden.   If, after the commission of a violent act, the best predictors of future violence are simple demographic characteristics of the juvenile, and if actuarial tables may be more accurate than expert judgments, then why is there still such reliance upon psychiatric or psychological assessments of violence potential in the juvenile justice system? Surely a judge is as capable as a psychologist to check off whether a youth is male or female, black or white, thirteen or seventeen, rich or poor, or how many times his/her parents have moved. Why doesn't he or she just make explicit the variables being considered in the prediction and eliminate the psychiatric middleman? In all likelihood, the judge's prediction would be as good — or as bad — as the "expert's."

The reason that the predictive factors are not made explicit seems clear. They are too socially "hot" to handle.

Assume for a moment that the four best predictors of violent behavior in juveniles, *after* a violent act has been committed, are age, sex, race, and SES [socioeconomic status]. Assume that is, that these four factors, which do show up consistently in the research, are not merely artifacts of racist, sexist, ageist, or capitalistic biases in the juvenile and criminal justice systems — although such biases undoubtedly do exist to some extent and to that extent attenuate the strength of the correlation. Assume that, for whatever reason, the relationships still exist when the biases of the system partialled out.

Can one imagine a juvenile court judge, presented with two youths, one black and one white, who have committed the same violent act and who are comparable in all other respects, sentencing the black child to a longer period of detention than the white one, and admitting publicly that he or she was doing it because blacks have a higher actuarial risk of violent recidivism than whites? The Supreme Court would be quick to overrule such an appallingly "suspect" and unconstitutional prediction system, even if it could be shown to be statistically accurate. The same, one hopes, would be true if the prediction were made on the basis of socioeconomic status, with the poorer juvenile dealt with more harshly precisely because he/she is poor, and poverty is statistically associated with violence.

The case is less clear with sex and age. If two youths, comparable in all but their sex, came before a juvenile court judge, could the judge explicitly give more lenient treatment to the female because the actuarial table, like the insurance company tables, says that females are much less likely to recidivate than males? Or that thirteen-year-olds are less likely to commit another violent crime than seventeen-year-olds?

The "virtue" of clinical prediction is that a judge or youth authority board does not have to deal with these highly sensitive social questions, but can camouflage the issues by deferring to clinical expertise. The clinician is then free to take all these variables into account — indeed, *must* take these variables into account if the prediction is to be any good — and no one will be the wiser. The sensitive issues will never be raised because they are hidden in the depths of "professional judgment," while in fact that judgment is made on the basis of the same factors that might be unconstitutional if used in open court. In this sense, clinical prediction represents a "laundering" of actuarial prediction, so that the sensitive nature of the predictor variables cannot be traced.

A related reason for not putting our actuarial cards on the table is that it is unclear which way the deck should be cut. Some of the factors which lead to an increase in predictive accuracy also imply a decrease in moral culpability. If one used poverty or race as variables in a predictive/preventive scheme, for example, one would deal more harshly with the poor and the nonwhite. If, on the other hand, one was attempting to match the sanction — not to a utilitarian calculus but rather to the moral desert or culpability of the offender — it could be argued that a history of adversity and discrimination should attenuate rather than exacerbate the sanction. One cannot, in other words, maximize public safety and moral justice at the same time. The juvenile court itself is a good example of this. We deal more leniently with a sixteen-year-old violent offender than with a fifty-year-old one, on the moral ground that the older man should know better and is more "deserving" of punishment, while, in fact, the chances of violent recidivism are much higher in the sixteen-year-old. If our primary purpose was to prevent violent acts, it is the juvenile, rather than the adult, we would subject to lengthy incarceration.

7. Despite Its Primitive State of Development, It is Highly Unlikely That Prediction Will Cease to Play a Major Role in Juvenile Justice.   One cannot attempt to rehabilitate juvenile offenders without first predicting which of them is in need of rehabilitation — which is to say, which of them will be violent if not rehabilitated — and one desists with rehabilitation primarily on the basis of a prediction that the risk of violence has decreased. To cease prediction is to cease rehabilitation, and to cease rehabilitation is to cease the juvenile justice system. The alternative to prediction and the rehabilitative ideal is a system of sanctions based upon moral desert, and that is how we sanction adult offenders.

I would suggest that the next step in the reform of juvenile justice is an increased honesty in how predictive decisions are made. Let us cease to sweep the troublesome issues under the psychologist's rug, and be open about the value issues which confront us. Let us publish our actuarial tables and have the legitimacy of each predictor item litigated both in courts of law and in the court of public opinion. I do not know which way the decision would fall. I do not even know which way I would vote. But, I do believe that the outcome of this legal and social debate would clarify what it is we wish to accomplish in juvenile justice, and the price we are willing to pay for it.

NOTES

1. For a more detailed discussion of some of the issues raised in this paper, the reader is referred to D. Gottfredson, "Assessment and Prediction Methods in Crime and Delinquency," in *Task Force Report: Juvenile Delinquency and Youth Crime* (Washington, D.C.: President's Commission on Law Enforcement & Administration of Justice, 1967); J. Monahan, "The Prevention of Violence,," in J. Monahan (ed.), *Community Mental Health and the Criminal Justice System* (New York: Pergamon Press, 1976), pp. 13–34; and J. Monahan, "The Prediction of Violent Criminal Behavior: A Methodological Critique and Prospectus," in National Research Council (ed.), *Deterrence and Incapacitation: Estimating the Effects of Criminal Sanctions on Crime Rates* (Washington, D.C.: National Academy of Sciences, 1978), pp. 244–69.

2. D. Hellman and N. Blackman, "Enuresis, Firesetting, and Cruelty to Animals: A Triad Predictive of Adult Crime," *American Journal of Psychiatry,* 122 (1966): 1431–1435.

3. B. Justice, R. Justice, and J. Kraft, "Early Warning Signs of Violence: Is a Triad Enough?" *American Journal of Psychiatry,* (1974): 457–459.

4. M. Wolfgang, R. Figlio, and T. Sellin, *Delinquency in a Birth Cohort* (Chicago: University of Chicago Press, 1972).

5. S. Glueck and E. Glueck, *Unraveling Juvenile Delinquency* (New York: The Commonwealth Fund, 1950).

6. M. Lefkowitz et al., *Growing Up To Be Violent* (New York: Pergamon, 1977).

7. E. Wenk, J. Robison, and G.Smith, "Can Violence Be Predicted?" *Crime and Delinquency* 18 (1972): 393–402.

8. H. Kozol, R. Boucher, and R. Garofalo, "The Diagnosis and Treatment of Dangerousness," *Crime and Delinquency* 18 (1972): 371–392.

9. Department of Public Safety and Correctional Services, State of Maryland, "Maryland's Defective Delinquency Statute — A Progress Report" (Manuscript, 1973).

10. H. Steadman and J. Cocozza, *Careers of the Criminally Insane* (Lexington, Mass.: Lexington Books, 1974); H. Steadman and A. Halfon, "The Baxstrom Patients: Backgrounds and Outcome," *Seminars in Psychiatry* 3 (1971): 376–386; H. Steadman and G. Keveles, "The Community Adjustment and Criminal Activity of the Baxstrom Patients: 1966–1970," *American Journal of Psychiatry,* 129 (1972): 304–310.

11. J. Cocozza and H. Steadman, "Some Refinements in the Measurement and Prediction of Dangerous Behavior," *American Journal of Psychiatry,* 131 (1974): 1012–1020.

12. T. Thornberry and J. Jacoby, "The Uses of Discretion in a Maximum Security Mental Hospital: The 'Dixon Case" (Manuscript, 1974).

13. J. Cocozza and H. Steadman, *The Failure of Psychiatric Predictions of Dangerousness: Clear and Convincing Evidence,* 29 Rutgers L. Rev. 1084–1101 (1976).

14. J. Monahan, "Prediction Research and the Emergency Commitment of Dangerous Mentally Ill Persons," *American Journal of Psychiatry,* 135 (1978): 198-201.

15. Monahan, "Prevention of Violence" (1976).

16. Wenk, Robinson and Smith, "Can Violence Be Predicted?"

17. Wolfgang, Figlio and Sellin, *Delinquency in a Birth Cohort.*

18. S. Fox, "Prediction Devices and the Reform of Juvenile Justice," in S. Glueck and E. Glueck (eds.), *Identification of Predlinquents (New York:* Intercontinental Medical Book Corporation, 1972) pp. 107-114.

19. Wenk, Robinson and Smith, "Can Violence Be Predicted?"

20. Kozol, Boucher and Garofalo, "The Diagnosis and Treatment of Dangerousness," p. 384.

21. Lefkowitz et al., *Growing Up To Be Violent.*

22. W. Mischel, *Personality and Assessment* (New York: Wiley, 1968).

23. E. Megargee, "The Prediction of Violence with Psychological Tests," in C. Spielberger (ed.), *Current Topics in Clinical and Community Psychology* (New York: Academic Press, 1970).

24. P. Meehl, *Clinical Versus Statistical Prediction* (Minneapolis: University of Minnesota Press, 1954).

25. J. Sawyer, "Measurement and Prediction, Clinical and Statistical," *Psychological Bulletin,* 66 (1966): 178–200.

7 *Confronting Youth Crime*

Twentieth Century Fund Task Force on Sentencing Policy Toward Young Offenders

INTRODUCTION

. . . Youth crime has always been the subject of public concern; in recent years, it has become a matter of public alarm. Unfortunately, the media and the public tend to focus on sensational cases. Misinformation and emotional rhetoric often substitute for fact in the public debate over crime.

From *Confronting Youth Crime,* Report of the Twentieth Century Fund Task Force on Sentencing Policy Toward Young Offenders (New York: Holmes & Meier Publishers, Inc., 1978), pp. 3–20. Reprinted by permission.

Some basic facts:

- Most young persons violate the law at some point during adolescence; relatively few young persons are repetitive, serious criminals.
- Most youth crime is not violent crime; offenses involving property outnumber violent crimes by more than ten to one; yet violent crime by the young has increased and is a substantial social and public health problem.
- Most violent crime by the young is committed against young victims; a substantial amount of violence also spills over to other age groups, and about 10 percent of all robbery by young offenders involves elderly victims.
- Most young persons who commit serious offenses will outgrow the propensity to commit crime in the transition to adulthood; a significant minority of serious young offenders will persist in criminal careers.
- Most young offenders who commit acts of extreme violence and pursue criminal careers come from minority ghettos and poverty backgrounds; so do their victims.
- Youth crime has increased dramatically over the past fifteen years, in part because of the growth of the youth population in large urban areas that have been incubators of crime; in the next few years, youth crime rates will probably not continue to grow at the pace of recent years because the total youth population will decline and the minority youth population in most major cities will remain relatively stable.[1]

This Task Force is concerned with sentencing policy toward the large number and great variety of young offenders arrested each year. Our mission is broader than the reform of juvenile justice in the sense that it encompasses all adolescents accused of crimes — both those youths who are sent to criminal court and those who are sent to juvenile court.

Too often, efforts to reform juvenile justice have ignored the treatment of young offenders in criminal courts. The boundary between the juvenile court — whose task, in theory, is to provide help and guidance for those who come under its jurisdiction — and criminal court — where the young offender is usually subject to the full range of criminal sanctions but also is entitled to a jury trial and the full range of appeals — is both arbitrary and subject to abrupt change. The maximum age of juvenile court jurisdiction varies in the United States from under sixteen to under nineteen. In the past five years, no fewer than ten of the fifty states have changed the maximum — some raising it and others lowering it. The Task Force is convinced that no single age during mid-adolescence should be used as a sharp dividing line for sentencing policies. We have considered sentencing policy toward young offenders in both juvenile and criminal courts and recommend coordinating the policies of these two institutions so that public policy toward young offenders is based on consistent and coherent premises.

The mission of this Task Force is also narrower than that of some other recent law reform study commissions, which have dealt with the entire range of behavior that is currently under the jurisdiction of the juvenile court.[2] This Report focuses on youth crimes with discernible victims — crimes against property and personal safety — and on the sanctioning decision rather than on the reform of procedures for fact-finding and court organization. . . .

FOUNDATIONS FOR A SPECIAL YOUTH CRIME POLICY

In fashioning and justifying a discrete policy toward youth crime, the Task Force has been guided by four principles:

- culpability
- diminished responsibility resulting from immaturity
- providing room to reform
- proportionality.

Culpability

When six-year-olds steal or set fires, the legal system correctly recognizes that extreme immaturity should operate as a complete defense to criminal responsibility. In its deliberations, the Task Force did not consider the appropriate minimum age at which children should become partially responsible for threatening social behavior. The Task Force did decide that at age thirteen or fourteen, an individual may appropriately be considered responsible, at least to a degree, for the criminal harms that he or she causes.

The moral universe of early adolescence is complicated, but a basic sense of right and wrong is a part of that stage of development. We feel that most young offenders of that age are aware of the severity of the criminal harms they inflict and that, much as they fall short of maturity or self-control, they are morally and should be legally responsible for intentionally destructive behavior. The older the adolescent, the greater the degree of responsibility the law should presume. Whether criminal behavior on the part of adolescents should be called delinquency or crime is of little consequence to this conclusion and was not a subject on which the Task Force took a position.

Diminished Responsibility

In reaching the conclusion that young offenders should be legally responsible for intentional criminal harms, the Task Force relied on its opinion that adolescent offenders have moral judgment and varying degrees of capacity for self-control. At the same time, the Task Force recognizes that adolescents, particularly in the early and middle teen years, are more vulnerable, more impulsive, and less self-disciplined than adults. Crimes committed by youths may be just as harmful to victims as those committed by older persons, but they deserve less punishment because adolescents may have less capacity to control their conduct and to think in long-range terms than adults. Moreover, youth crime as such is not exclusively the offender's fault; offenses by the young also represent a failure of family, school, and the social system, which share responsibility for the development of America's youth.

The Task Force believes that a balanced sentencing policy toward young offenders must recognize both culpability and its limits. It is unrealistic to view a sixteen-year-old as completely devoid of judgment and control; it is equally unrealistic to treat young offenders as if they have fully mature judgment and control.

Providing Room to Reform

The Task Force believes that protecting young offenders from the full force of the criminal law is prudent social policy. Many forms of youth crime are a product of the special pressures and vulnerability of adolescence. This is why adolescent rates of crime are high and why persons who have violated the law in their youth usually desist from criminality as they grow up. The Task Force assigns a high priority to providing young offenders with the opportunity to pass through this crime-prone stage of development with their life chances intact.

Providing room to reform simply means using procedures that minimize stigma, custodial confinement, and exile from society. In advocating such a policy, the Task Force does not mean to imply that young criminal recidivists should go unpunished. The treatment encountered by young offenders inevitably serves an educational function, and the last thing the Task Force would wish young people to learn is that criminal behavior goes unpunished. In some cases (fewer than many suppose), protecting the young offender from being scarred by severe punishment is inappropriate. But in general, giving young offenders a chance to reform is intelligent social policy. Such a policy involves risks and costs; a considerable minority of young offenders may not outgrow their propensity to crime. But there is no evidence that secure confinement is more effective than lesser measures in dissuading young offenders from pursuing criminal careers.

Proportionality

No coherent theory of criminal justice that acknowledges punishment as an appropriate response to crime can treat bank robbers and bicycle thieves as equal for the purpose of punishment. "Proportionality" is not a magic slogan that automatically produces consensus on appropriate punishment. But the Task Force believes that the degree of punishment available for youth crime should be proportional to the seriousness of the offense.[3] The point seems obvious, but proportionality is not an integral part of the present jurisprudence of juvenile justice. We believe it should be.

THE DUAL SYSTEM OF JUSTICE — ABOLITION OR REFORM?

At present, an adolescent accused of a crime may be processed in one of two court systems: younger adolescents are tried in juvenile court and older adolescents in criminal court. The Task Force debated the issue of whether a child-centered court is appropriate for processing serious criminal charges against fifteen- to seventeen-year-olds. The alternative to this "dual" system would be the abolition of juvenile court jurisdiction for felony charges and the referral of such charges to either the criminal court or a special court for young offenders. We concluded that, although the principles and processes of the juvenile court require rethinking and reform, juvenile court jurisdiction over individuals in their mid-teens is preferable to alternatives.[4]

Shifting jurisdiction to a special "court for young offenders" would simply apply a new label to an institution quite similar to the contemporary juvenile court.

For the purpose of processing accused youths, juvenile court has two advantages over criminal court: the judge before whom the accused appears is likely to have a special concern for and some experience with young persons and, if detained, the accused is likely to be placed in age-segregated facilities.

Although a juvenile detention facility is typically not a satisfactory place to house a young person accused of an offense, it is far more satisfactory than a jail. And for those convicted, although "training schools" neither train nor school, they are less destructive than the crowded and dangerous mega-prisons used to warehouse older offenders. A separate court should not be needed to assure diverse correctional treatment. Indeed, the Task Force recommends that even those young offenders who are convicted in criminal courts should be placed in age-segregated facilities. But separate, specialized, and decent facilities are more easily achieved with the juvenile court than without it.

JURISDICTIONAL AGE AND WAIVER

If the juvenile court is to continue, some boundary line must be established between those who will be processed by the juvenile court and those who will be processed by the criminal court. For most arrested young persons, this line is the maximum age of juvenile court jurisdiction; a few persons still young enough to go to the juvenile court but accused of serious offenses may stand trial in the criminal court, depending on the waiver policies of the state in which they are tried.

The Task Force recommends that juvenile court jurisdiction extend to all criminal acts committed before an accused's eighteenth birthday.[5] Eighteen is not the end of adolescence (it may be a rough boundary between middle and late adolescence), and it should not mark the end of a special sentencing policy toward youth crime. Hence, although eighteen- to twenty-one-year-old defendants should be tried in criminal courts and eligible for higher maximum sanctions than those in juvenile court, the sanctions available for individuals in this age group should be lower than those for adults. Thus, the passage from juvenile to adult court would be a transition from one youth crime policy to another — somewhat less lenient — youth crime policy.

Any large jurisdiction that retains young offenders until age eighteen will encounter a few extremely serious offenses that will seem, to the court and the community, to demand more substantial punishment than is normally available to the juvenile justice system. State law can provide for these "deep-end" cases in three ways: by lowering the maximum age of juvenile court jurisdiction (typically to under sixteen or seventeen), by increasing the sentencing authority of the juvenile court, or by providing for the transfer of cases to the criminal court.

The minimum age for criminal court jurisdiction might be lowered either for all crimes or for specific offenses such as murder and rape. Generally lowering the jurisdictional age would burden the adult system with thousands of cases in order to cope with the problems posed by a few. Offense-specific reduction of jurisdictional age would be less objectionable, but it would require categorical judgments regarding accessories as well as principal offenders. Moreover, the publicizing of atypical, sensational cases may result in amendments to a legislative list of heinous crimes, lengthening it to include crimes that are generally less serious.

Expanding the punishment power of the juvenile court also has disadvantages. First, it bases the punitive outer limits of the court on a few exceptional cases, virtually letting the tail wag the dog in setting sentencing policy. Second, it puts too great a burden on the procedural structure of the juvenile court. A court that does not provide access to jury trial should not be able to impose five- or ten-year sentences. Juvenile court is unlikely to establish a full array of procedural formalities for all cases; attempts to make it do so would be another instance of letting the few exceptional cases set policy for the bulk of the court's work.

The Task Force believes that the least harmful method of dealing with extremely serious cases is to transfer them to the criminal court. The process we recommend differs from the present practice of waiver in two respects. First, under current practice in most states, the judge makes the decision to waive at his discretion, without any explicit standard for guidance. We would confine waiver to cases where the judge finds probable cause to believe that a serious, violent crime has been committed and further determines that, should the defendant be found guilty, the minimum punishment necessary is substantially larger than that available to the juvenile court. The waiver decision would be automatically reviewed by an appellate tribunal (unless the defendant and his counsel elected to give up this right), which could nullify the decision to transfer to criminal court if the basis for the juvenile court's finding were not clear and convincing.

A second distinction between present practice and our proposal concerns the consequences of transfer to the criminal court. At present, waiver to criminal court means eligibility for the full range of maximum adult sentences, including life in prison or the death penalty. Under our proposal, the juvenile transferred to criminal court would have the same status that we propose for young offenders eighteen to twenty-one. Juveniles in the criminal court would thus face increased maximum sanctions, but the legal system would not totally ignore their youth in setting punishment.

The Task Force also recommends that waiver be restricted to defendants who are accused of serious criminal violence and who have passed their early teens. We are unanimous in recommending that very young adolescents should not be eligible for transfer to criminal court. A majority of the Task Force favors a bar on the transfer to criminal court of any child under age fifteen.[6]

THE SENTENCING STRUCTURE

The Task Force considered a variety of models of sentencing structure. We recommend a system of sentencing in which *the legislature* fixes the maximum period of loss of liberty and supervision, *the judge* retains discretion to determine whether or not the offender should be subjected to loss of liberty and to fix the maximum duration of social control in each individual case, and *a centralized correctional authority* retains the power to select a release date short of the maximum.[7] Some members of the Task Force who endorse this system believe that an early release decision of the correctional authority should be subject to the approval of the sentencing judge.

In our deliberations, we considered and rejected presumptive, or legislatively fixed, sentences as inappropriate to most young offenders in both juvenile and criminal courts.[8] The Task Force also considered and rejected indeterminate sentences, in which a young offender's confinement ends only when a correctional authority feels that the offender has been reformed. Although rehabilitation and helping services are a necessary part of any rational scheme of dealing with young offenders, the Task Force believes that the need for services should not be used to justify placing a young offender in custodial confinement or continuing such confinement until an administrative agency considers him "cured."

In recommending an allocation of sentencing authority that retains a substantial amount of discretion for judges and correctional authorities, the Task Force recognizes that this discretion carries with it the danger of disparity in sentences. Some of the policy recommendations and the maximum sentences suggested later in the report are designed to reduce the risk of disparity. The sharing of power between the sentencing judge and a central correctional authority can lead toward less variation in sentences for similar offenders. Unfortunately, the flexibility that is the virtue of a discretionary policy can still result in abuses. But in the sentencing policy we propose, we have sought to minimize the use of secure confinement, to retain discretion, and to provide mechanisms for reducing disparity.[9]

SENTENCES FOR YOUNG PROPERTY OFFENDERS

At present, there are no legislative or administrative guidelines to govern the hundreds of thousands of property offenders who are referred to the juvenile court and few principles to guide criminal courts in dealing with the adolescent property offender. In its deliberations, the Task Force reached a substantial consensus on appropriate policy toward these high-volume, youth-dominated crimes.

Property Offenders in Juvenile Court

The Task Force concluded (with one dissent) that the juvenile court should retain jurisdiction over all defendants accused of nonviolent offenses. For all property offenses except burglary of a dwelling, the Task Force favors an administrative presumption that juveniles who have not previously been arrested for a serious offense should be handled informally. The shock of arrest, a stern admonition by judge or intake worker, and referral to helping services are regarded as an adequate response to the first-arrested vandal, shoplifter, thief, or joyrider, although formal handling of a case may be thought necessary in some instances.

The Task Force considers burglarizing a dwelling too serious an incident to justify a presumption of informal handling. Other forms of burglary and vandalism that involve substantial fear or property loss may also merit formal handling.

If an offender is arrested a second time for a serious property crime, the Task Force recommends that the presumption should shift; most cases should proceed to a formal hearing on the defendant's guilt and to a subsequent dispositional hearing. If the defendant is found guilty, the Task Force favors a presumption against custodial confinement for young persons first convicted on property charges. The Task Force also supports a one-year limit on custodial confinement and a two-year limit on total state-imposed power as the maximum sanction for property offenders in juvenile court.

The Task Force considers repetitive property crime by juveniles a serious matter. Limiting the use of secure confinement generates a need to find other less drastic means of censuring such offenders. A wide variety of such alternatives is available in many juvenile justice systems, and the Task Force recommends the expanded use of sanctions that impress on the offender the seriousness of his conduct but do less harm than detention homes and training schools. Among promising intermediate sanctions, the Task Force identified the following:

- restitution programs, in which the young offender's efforts or resources are used to offset at least a part of the losses he caused
- community service orders, in which young offenders work for public agencies to atone for offenses that violate social norms
- fines that are geared to an offender's ability to pay, so that the offender rather than his family will bear the financial burden[10]
- loss of privileges, such as driving, which young people value highly
- participation in remedial educational, drug treatment, or alcohol treatment programs in appropriate cases.[11]

Many of these approaches are intended to help improve a young offender's life chances. All are coercive exercises of state power that are imposed because the juvenile has committed serious offenses. The Task Force feels that it is appropriate for the offender and the community to recognize that these measures are imposed, in part, as punishment. Open recognition of the punitive function of assigned participation in such a program seems preferable to a policy in which the rhetoric of rehabilitation is used to explain decisions that inevitably (and properly) spring in part from punitive motives.

These proposals are a radical departure from present theory but are closer to present practices than the public might believe. In one study of a major urban area, it was found that fewer than one out of fifty auto theft arrests resulted in secure confinement after trial; the odds for an accused burglar were one in twenty-five. A much larger proportion of accused property offenders were detained prior to the adjudication of their charges.[12] Pretrial detention appears to be widely used as punishment for young property offenders in both juvenile and criminal courts. The Task Force urges the abolition of punitive pretrial detention for juvenile property offenders.

Young Property Offenders in Criminal Court

The Task Force believes that it is necessary to coordinate treatment of property offenders in late adolescence with the policies proposed for juveniles. Specifically, we recommend a presumption against incarceration for first offenders in criminal court, the extensive use of alternative sanctions, and a two-and-a-half-year maximum sentence in custodial confinement for any property offense committed before the defendant's twenty-first birthday. This scale of punishment includes sentences longer than those available to the juvenile court because older adolescents are more mature and should be held more accountable for criminal conduct. But the proposed maximum penalties are lower than those available for adults because the reasons for a separate youth policy do not disappear on an offender's eighteenth birthday.

SENTENCING POLICY TOWARD THE VIOLENT YOUNG OFFENDER

Youth arrests for police-classified "violent" offenses are less than 10 percent of total youth arrests. These offenses range from fistfights to murder, from schoolyard extortion to life-threatening armed robbery. Most violent crimes that lead to youth arrests are less serious than media coverage suggests, but young offenders are all too frequently involved in armed robbery, life-threatening assaults with deadly weapons, rape, and murder, in that order. Serious violent offenses are the hardest cases for social policy that seeks to protect both young offenders and the community.

In considering sentencing policy toward offenses against the person, the Task Force found it necessary to define three classes of violent offenders. First and most numerous are those who have committed assaults that did not involve serious threats to life or robberies in which the defendant did not personally use a deadly weapon or inflict grave bodily harm. Second are offenses that threaten life or person more directly:

- robbery where the defendant personally used a deadly weapon or inflicted grievous bodily harm
- battery, for which an offender is personally responsible, that involved a firearm, dangerous wounding with a knife, or force that required hospitalization
- voluntary manslaughter
- attempted rape
- accessorial responsibility for class 3 offenses
- arson of a dwelling or of an occupied building.

Third are those offenders personally responsible for:

- murder and attempted murder
- forcible rape
- arson with intent to commit bodily harm.

Violent Offenses in Juvenile Court

The Task Force recommends a presumption favoring formal processing of all but the most trivial of offenses against the person. Even within the lowest grade of crimes against the person, only fistfights, schoolyard extortions, and episodes of limited self-defense (overreaction to provocation) may merit less than formal processing.

For the first and least serious class of offenses against the person, the Task Force recommends no minimum sanction and a maximum sentence of eighteen months of custodial confinement or a longer but limited maximum period of noncustodial social control.

For the second and more serious class of offenses against the person, the Task Force believes that minimum sentences of custodial confinement are worthy of serious consideration and that the maximum sentence should be two years of custodial confinement. The Task Force also favors a presumption of waiver to the criminal court for those once convicted of a class 2 offense who are again arrested and are probably guilty of a second such offense.

For class 3 (the most serious) offenses, the Task Force recommends minimum sentences of some custodial confinement and maximum sentences of two-and-a-half years of custodial confinement. The Task Force favors this relatively low maximum because of the procedural frailty of the juvenile court. We believe that cases calling for more fateful punishment decisions should be waived to criminal court, where procedural guarantees that juvenile court does not provide are available.

Youth Violence in Criminal Court

Crimes against the person test the limits of a separate social policy toward youth crime in the criminal court. The Task Force is unanimous in suggesting that the maximum sentencing options be significantly lower for violent young offenders than those for adults convicted of comparable crimes. We also agree that the case for minimum punishment is stronger for young offenders (and transferred juveniles) in criminal court than for those in the juvenile court.

The Task Force is divided on the question of whether offenders under twenty-one should ever be subject to sentences of over five years for any crime short of murder. This division is not a sign of disarray. Our deliberations on this topic reflected both the difficulty of moving from general principles to specific guidelines and the arbitrary nature of any specific numerical guideline. The debate specifically concerned defendants convicted of repeated instances of class 2 or class 3 violence. Those members of the Task Force who oppose the five-year limit are themselves divided; some favor prescribing some increase in the maximum sentence (e.g., 7½ years);

others advocate providing for discretionary waiver to the full range of adult sanctions for repetitive offenders between eighteen and twenty-one. Thus, this division of the Task Force is limited to the issue of whether repetitive, violent young offenders should be subject to a five-year maximum, exempted from a youth crime policy, or subject to longer sentences as part of a youth crime policy.

Murder remains the hardest of the hard cases. The young offender who dominates or commits an intentional killing is the ultimate test of the limits of diminished responsibility. The Task Force agreed that maximum sanctions for young offenders should be lower than those for adults. The principle of diminished responsibility makes life imprisonment and death penalties inappropriate in such cases. The Task Force recommends substantial presumptive minimum sanctions as appropriate because of the gravity of the offense; eighteen months of custodial confinement for offenders under eighteen and three years of custodial confinement for offenders between eighteen and twenty-one. The Task Force recommends that sentences of over five years for offenders under eighteen convicted of murder and sentences exceeding ten years for offenders between eighteen and twenty-one be confined to cases where the offender is responsible for taking more than one life or has a substantial history of life-threatening violent offenses.

PUNITIVE DETENTION

Ten times as many juveniles are in secure confinement before trial as after trial, and the purpose of this confinement is, in many cases, punitive. Of course, in criminal courts, too, far more defendants are in jail before trial than after adjudication of charges. The Task Force considers punitive pretrial detention inappropriate and unjust.

Any unjust but prevalent practice may be difficult to abolish. The Task Force favors a variety of devices as alternatives to the present high rate of secure detention before trial. Specifically, we favor community supervision rather than detention to assure that young defendants appear at trial, nonsecure pretrial housing where necessary, and judicial and administrative monitoring of information on detention. These practices are needed in both branches of the dual system of criminal justice but are particularly necessary in the juvenile court. . . .

CONCLUDING REFLECTIONS

The Task Force, like many other study groups that have preceded its work, is saddened by the low quality of the courts, community facilities, and residential institutions that process and house young offenders in most jurisdictions. In many rural areas, the judge who presides over juvenile court cases is more like a justice of the peace than a specialist in sentencing policy toward young offenders. In many cities, the juvenile court often resembles the local traffic court, and the professional prestige of judges charged with dealing with young offenders is low. These conditions must change.

Most detention, probation, and correctional facilities for young offenders are evidence of social and governmental indifference. The observation that youth correctional facilities are better than their adult counterparts is valid, but small praise. Currently, confinement in age-segregated facilities is necessary but insufficient to assure even decent processing and acceptable housing, let alone appropriate program options.

The need to reform both the principles and the institutions that confront the young offender is particularly acute because juvenile and criminal courts are an important source of the image of justice perceived by young offenders. They learn from their experience in courts and correctional institutions. They are influenced most by what actually happens to them and how it happens; by what is done rather than by what is supposed to be done; by the attitudes and actions of the police, corrections officers, and magistrates, not by ringing declarations about justice or by leatherbound statute books.

In most juvenile and criminal courts, young offenders learn the hypocrisy of punishment in the name of rehabilitation, of disparity in the cloak of individualized justice, and of assembly line treatment in the guise of informality. Young offenders are not easy to trick. Candor and consistency in sentencing policy are a first and fundamental step toward instilling respect for law and legal institutions in young persons whose respect for law is a critical element of their personal futures and the safety of our communities.[13]

NOTES

1. The sources on which these conclusions are based, and the difficulties inherent in the confident use of existing sources of data are discussed in Chapter I of the background paper.

2. See, for example, Institute of Judicial Administration/American Bar Association, Juvenile Justice Standards Project, Tentative Draft volumes (Cambridge Mass.: Ballinger Publishing Company, 1977). See also American Justice Institute, *A Comparative Analysis of Standards and State Practices* (nine volumes), National Institute for Juvenile Justice and Delinquency Prevention, Office of Juvenile Justice and Delinquency Prevention, Law Enforcement Assistance Administration, U.S. Department of Justice (Washington, D.C.: Government Printing Office, 1977).

3. Peter Edelman comments: While I agree that the concept of proportionality should be applied to youth sentencing policy, I want to state explicitly that I am opposed to the full-fledged "miniaturization" of the adult system, as represented by some recent proposals. Differentiation is certainly appropriate as between violent acts and property crime, and perhaps between repeated serious property crime and other property crime, but further distinctions at the sentencing level, given the relatively short time frames that are appropriate for young offenders, seem to me highly artificial.
   Justine Wise Polier wishes to associate with this comment.

4. Marvin Wolfgang comments: However, for *serious* offenders, at least, the sanctioning process should be the same as that used for adults.

5. Marvin Wolfgang dissents: If the juvenile court is kept, jurisdiction should not extend beyond, at most, age sixteen.

6. Sister M. Isolina Ferre, M.S.B.T., dissents: I oppose waiver of juveniles to the adult criminal justice system under any conditions because, given the chaotic state of the criminal courts, neither the public nor the individual youth can benefit more from criminal court processing than from juvenile court processing.

Moreover, any use of waiver subjects juveniles to a system of justice based on "category of offense" rather than on concern with the individual and with the social and cultural aspects of the case. Such concern is the principal virtue of the juvenile justice system.

7. Peter Edelman comments: While I endorse this distribution of responsibility, I also would stress that what the correctional authority should retain is the power to select a facility or program for the offender as well as a release date short of the maximum. In cases of serious violent acts, I believe that judges should have the power to require a minimum period of secure confinement; otherwise, I think the nature of the loss of liberty should be up to the correctional authority. Especially where youth are concerned, "custody," "loss of liberty," and "social control" should not be equated with institutionalization or incarceration. I take these terms to encompass placement in group homes or other community-based residences, in family foster care, or even in a youth's own home with adequate professional supervision.

   Aryeh Neier dissents: I believe that the length of a sentence should depend on the underlying crime. The trial judge is best informed about that crime and, accordingly, should fix the length of the sentence. Correctional authorities, such as parole boards, currently base decisions regarding early release on predictions about the individual inmate's future behavior. Such predictions are unreliable and unfair. Elsewhere, the report rejects rehabilitation as a purpose of confinement (although it favors providing opportunities for rehabilitation to people in confinement). Allowing a correctional authority to alter release dates on the basis of a subjective judgment as to the psychological state of the inmate implies that rehabilitation is a valid objective of confinement.

8. I do not mean to preclude prison officials from modifying sentences slightly in recognition of good behavior. The availability of this incentive may aid correctional authorities in exercising their managerial responsibilities. The distinction I am drawing is between the subjective judgment that a person is rehabilitated and will not commit crimes if released and a more objective evaluation of past behavior as, in itself, justifying early release.

   Marvin Wolfgang dissents: I am not prepared to reject presumptive sentences as strong guides for all offenders.

9. Marvin Wolfgang comments: I am troubled by the degree to which the sentencing structure proposed by the Task Force retains discretion. Such discretion invites sentencing disparity in both juvenile and criminal courts. Recently, mechanisms, such as sentencing guidelines and — for some cases — presumptive sanctions, have been proposed for the criminal court. As I read this Task Force Report, it does not foreclose the use of these promising reform mechanisms. But I would go further and suggest that presumptive sanctions or greatly narrowed sentencing discretion should be a major objective of sentencing reform in both juvenile and criminal justice.

10. Cruz Reynoso dissents: I object to the inclusion of fines as an "intermediate sanction." While the theory that fines should be levied only in terms of the offender's ability to pay is a good one, experience suggests that fines can seldom be levied in a manner that does not "punish" the parents.

11. Peter Edelman comments: The key word in this context is "sanction." The enumeration in the text is not intended to exclude use of community-based group care and family foster care as available dispositions. The Task Force took the view that they might be coupled with sanctions but would not be themselves imposed for punitive purposes.

12. Data provided by June Dorn, Illinois Law Enforcement Commission.

13. Sister M. Isolina Ferre, M.S.B.T., dissents: The administration of the criminal and juvenile justice systems is largely in the hands of the white community. Those most affected by these systems are black and Hispanic. The Task Force has failed to consider this issue or to recommend measures to bring black and Hispanic people into the criminal justice system so that they can participate in decisions that affect their own people. This omission leaves the Task Force Report open to criticism as a racist document.

The Differentiation of Offense Severity: Policy and Program Concerns

B. Juvenile Noncriminal Offenses

INTRODUCTION

The section which follows reports certain noteworthy developments and policy re-directions as to society's response to juvenile misbehaviors. Previously called delin-quency, this wide range of juvenile misconduct is now referred to more generically as status offenses. Other descriptors are "conduct illegal only for children" and "juvenile noncriminal misbehavior." Different statutes refer to these youngsters as persons in need of supervision (PINS), children in need of supervision (CHINS), the unruly child, and other names. The most common status offenses have been run-away, ungovernability or incorrigibility, and habitual truancy. Another subtype involves the violation of specific statutes or ordinances applicable only to children, such as curfew violations, and possession or use of alcohol or tobacco. A further grouping includes such anachronistic or ill-defined misbehaviors as deporting oneself so as to injure or endanger the morals or health of the actor or any other person; in danger of leading an idle, dissolute, lewd, or immoral existence; using vile, obscene, vulgar, profane, or indecent language; and sexual misconduct.

Laws regulating such behaviors arose in Puritan New England and carried into many parts of the country prior to the 1899 enactment of the first juvenile court act in Illinois. The juvenile court's involvement with such youngsters and their confine-ment in jails, pretrial detention facilities, and state level institutions went largely un-questioned until two decades ago. Reappraisal of the public policies concerning status offenders has led many to recognize that what these youngsters have done or not done must be classified at the low end of any seriousness scale which ranks the severity of offenses according to the harm done to others. These youths may have emotional adjustments ranging from normal to highly disturbed, have family re-lationships ranging from good to poor, may trouble their parents and teachers to a substantial degree, and may do things that threaten their own health and well-being. But the overriding present issues are whether and under what circumstances courts should intervene with status offense youths, and if so, what remedies and sanctions may be utilized.

The argument is highly charged. On one side is the National Council of Juvenile and Family Court Judges, a group dedicated to retaining this jurisdiction for the court and for the utilization of judicial orders when voluntary efforts fail. Schools, probation and social agencies, mental health clinics, and parents, tend to align themselves with the judges. Urging jurisdictional repeal are the National Council on Crime and Delinquency, American Civil Liberties Union, academic scholars, public defenders and even prosecutors, and the Institute of Judicial Administration-American Bar Association Juvenile Justice Standards Project.

The reporter for that project's volume on Noncriminal Misbehavior, Aidan R. Gough, authors the first article in this section. His analysis reflects his legal discipline and incorporates data and theory from the social sciences in reaching the conclusion that current legislation which authorizes juvenile court intervention with these youngsters should be repealed, and the responsibility for assisting such youths transferred to community agencies which lack coercive authority. He sketches several court alternatives which report promising results and lists others which could be instituted or adapted by schools and community agencies, but recognizes that "hands off" and voluntary approaches will fail in certain cases. He reasons that the social costs are too severe to afford retaining jurisdiction in order to sanction the small percentage of cases that fail to respond to voluntary community efforts. The rationale for the Standards Project's resolution to dejudicialize status offenses is richly described.

Conflicts between policy makers and policy implementers are illustrated in the next reading, a case study of a New York Court of Appeals decision which interpreted that state's Family Court Act to prohibit confinement of status offenders (PINS) in state delinquency institutions. This decision was oppositional to the New York Division for Youth's preference for development of institutional programs based on the nature of individual children's problems rather than on the legal labels they carried. The decision, however, resulted in "little meaningful change" with institutional programming except for the basic reshuffling of youths into institutional facilities segregated by the legal classification of the particular residents. A subsequent decision of the New York Court of Appeals, in 1974, removed the ambiguity from the *Ellery C.* decision by approving separate institutional facilities for PINS rather than prohibiting their confinement in any state institution. Still later, under the impetus of the United States Juvenile Justice and Delinquency Prevention Act of 1974 which emphasized deinstitutionalizing status offenders, the Division for Youth dramatically expanded noninstitutional programs for these youngsters through a variety of community-based alternatives.

A Supreme Court of Appeals of West Virginia ruling utilized constitutional standards, rather than a statutory interpretation that occurred in New York, in holding that the incarceration of status offense youths in delinquency institutions violated guarantees of equal protection, due process, and protection against cruel and unusual punishment. The decision set forth dispositional guidelines prohibiting the confinement of status offenders in a "secure, prison-like facility," housing delinquent youths convicted of law violations. The 1977 West Virginia case which is reported here arose at a time when status offenders were included within that state's delinquency definition; the youth in point had been adjudged delinquent due to absence from school for fifty days. The court unmasked the inherent discrepancy between the statutory purpose to help these children and the statutory sanction authorizing incarceration. Their commitment to a segregated, secure institution devoted solely to the rehabilitation of status offenders would be permitted following findings that no other alternative was available or could reasonably be made available, and that a child's incorrigibility was not amenable to treatment or restraint short of incarceration. Those holdings were subsequently enacted into statutory form. It is also noteworthy that the concluding section of the decision ordered copies of the ruling to be posted in delinquency facilities, to encourage other confined status offenders to bring habeas corpus actions requesting their releases.

8   *Beyond-Control Youth in the Juvenile Court – The Climate for Change**
Aidan R. Gough

The juvenile court's jurisdiction over children's noncriminal misbehavior has long been seen as a cornerstone of its mission. Indeed, assertions of state power over unruly children far antedate juvenile courts themselves; the laws conferring court jurisdiction over unruly children have their roots in "early colonial concerns with the child's key role as a source of labor for the family economic unit" and some early statutes punished filial disobedience with death.[1]

This jurisdiction over noncriminal misbehavior is both widespread and widely invoked. Every American juvenile court law has some ground or grounds extending the court's power of intervention to cases involving antisocial but noncriminal behavior. Such cases probably comprise — though firm figures are not available — no less than one-third and probably close to one-half the workload of America's juvenile courts.[2] While the labels vary from state to state — Person/Child/Minor/Juvenile in Need of Supervision (commonly abbreviated PINS, CHINS, MINS, JINS); Beyond-Control Child; Ungovernable Child; Incorrigible Child; Unruly Child; Wayward Child; Miscreant Child — the jurisdictional thrust is essentially the same, allowing coercive judicial intervention in cases of juvenile misbehavior that would not be criminal if committed by an adult.

Because the laws conferring this jurisdiction are typically couched in terms of the child's condition rather than in terms of the commission of specific acts — for example, a child's being "habitually beyond the control of his parents," or being "an habitual truant" — cases brought under such statutes are frequently (albeit a bit ineptly) referred to as "status offenses." Though there are many variations among the states, the status offense jurisdiction typically and essentially comprehends a wide spectrum of behavior, such as disobedience to a parent or guardian or school authorities, being truant, running away from home, being sexually promiscuous or otherwise "endangering morals," or acting in a manner "injurious to self or others." A majority of states include status offenders within the category of "delinquents." The remainder attempt in various ways to "break out" status offenses by creating a separate category in addition to the traditional classifications of neglect and delinquency. As will be seen, however, the treatment has not followed the label, and status offenders are generally subjected to the same modes of disposition as are juveniles

---

* Substantial portions of this chapter are taken from the introduction and commentary to *Juvenile Justice Standards: Non-Criminal Misbehavior,* for which the author served as Reporter. Reprinted with permission from BEYOND CONTROL: STATUS OFFENDERS IN THE JUVENILE COURT, Copyright 1976, Ballinger Publishing Company.

who violate the criminal law. Additionally, they likely bear the same burdens of stigma as do delinquents.[3]

The juvenile court's jurisdiction over unruly children is based on assumptions — most often implicit — that parents are reasonable persons seeking proper ends; that youthful independence is malign; that the social good requires judicial power to backstop parental command; that the juvenile justice system can identify noncriminal misbehavior which is predictive of future criminality; and that its coercive intervention will effectively remedy family-based problems and deter further offense.[4]

On the available evidence, these haruspical assumptions and pretensions do not prove out; it simply cannot be established that the behavior encompassed by the status offense jurisdiction is accurately "proto-criminal."[5] Indeed, as the California legislature noted, "Not a single shred of evidence exists to indicate that any significant number of [beyond control children] have benefited [by juvenile court intervention]. In fact, what evidence does exist points to the contrary."[6]

Most parental defiance and other forms of noncriminal misbehavior — troublesome though they are — represent a youthful push for independence and are both endemic and transitory. They are at worst "transitional deviance" which is outgrown.[7] It is widely conceded that unruly child cases are usually the most intractable and difficult matters with which the juvenile court has to deal; perhaps this is in part so precisely because the court is not the place to deal with them. The judicial system is simply an inept instrument for resolving intrafamily conflicts, and dealing with these cases in it results in a vast and disproportionate draining of time and resources, to the detriment of cases of neglect, abuse or delinquency which are properly there and represent threats to safety which the court must address. Erik Erickson has written:

> Youth after youth, bewildered by the incapacity to assume a role forced on him by the inexorable standardization of American adolescence, runs away in one form or another, dropping out of school, leaving jobs, staying out all night, or withdrawing into bizarre and inaccessible moods. Once "delinquent," his greatest need and often his only salvation is the refusal on the part of older friends, advisors and judciary personnel to type him further by pat diagnoses and social judgments which ignore the special dynamic conditions of adolescence.[8]

A study done of PINS cases in New York City in 1973 revealed not only a wide range of conduct alleged to demonstrate a need for official intervention, but also the fact that the status offense jurisdiction was used in many cases of violation of the criminal law, supporting the conclusion that it masks cases which are properly delinquency or neglect matters and should be dealt with on that basis. "Short runaway" was the allegation in 51 percent of the cases; "refusal to obey" in 47 percent; truancy in 43 percent; late hours in 36 percent; possession of drugs in 23 percent; staying out overnight in 19 percent; undesirable boyfriends in 19 percent; and undesirable companions in 14 percent. Assault was alleged in 9 percent of the cases; larceny in 5 percent; possession of drugs for sale and possession of a dangerous weapon in 2 percent. Twenty-one percent of the cases involved "other" allegations, including refusal to bathe regularly; having an abortion against parental wishes; sleeping all day; refusal to do household chores; being "selfish and self-centered"; banging a door in reaction to a parental command; wanting to get married; suicide attempts, and "being an invertebrate (*sic*) liar."[9] All studies encountered suggest that the range of family-centered problems is immense and that these allegations are typical of those in status offense cases elsewhere.

To address the operation of the status offense jurisdiction with some particularity, clearly the greatest vice is our treatment of noncriminal but ungovernable children in essentially the same way as we treat youthful violators of the criminal law, with maximum impetus (and opportunity for tutelage) given the former to become the latter. In the great majority of American jurisdictions, status offenders are subject to exactly the same dispositions as minors who commit crimes, including commitment to state training schools. Only a handful of states have followed New York in prohibiting the commitment of PINS to state schools which house delinquent youth, and even in the few states where intermixing is prohibited, status offenders are likely to be treated similarly to delinquents.[10] Furthermore, very few states have prohibited the temporary detention of ungovernable youth with delinquents pending adjudication; in the remainder, they are held in the same secure institutions as serious law violators.

A system which allows the same sanctions for parental defiance as for armed robbery — often with only the barest glance at the reasonableness of parental conduct — can only be seen as inept and unfair. Moreover, secure institutions housing youthful violators of the criminal law are necessarily geared to the custodial demands of the worst of their inmates, and the "treatment" for which the unruly child was committed is very often nonexistent. Some such institutions are both illegal and inhumane.[11]

Accurate national data are simply not available, but the number of unruly children inducted into the juvenile justice system under ungovernability statutes, and subjected as a consequence of that induction to the same dispositions as youth whose behavior has been criminal, is substantial indeed. The National Council on Crime and Delinquency estimates that more than 66,000 youth are confined in state training schools or their equivalents, and that between 45 and 55 percent of them are status offenders.[12] One study of probation officers' recommendations showed that juveniles referred for law violations had an eight times greater chance of having the probation officer recommend discharge or probation than did children referred for being ungovernable and "offending against parents."[13] Roughly a dozen states have prohibitions against direct commitment of status offenders to state training schools, but a number of these states appear to allow an unruly child to be so committed on a second status offense, on the rationale that that juvenile has then violated a court order and thus becomes a delinquent.[14]

Though the "labeling theory" of criminal causation — that a young person who has not committed a criminal act but is treated as and stigmatized as a delinquent is likely to become one — has been under recent attack, there is also some recent evidence to the contrary. A study of 222 inmates of the Indiana Boys Training School showed a "significant and linear decrease" in self-concept in the cases of boys not previously incarcerated. Conversely, minors showing an increase in self-concept had become increasingly involved in criminal behavior. The study found a correlation between incarceration and the internalization of delinquent values and self-concept. Put another way, it demonstrated that the minors had become what they were labeled to be.[15] On commonsense grounds *vice* the lack of conclusive empirical data, it seems likely that (1) coercive judicial intervention in unruly child cases produces some degree of labeling and stigmatization; and (2) whatever effect this has on the child's self-perception and future behavior will be adverse.

Even in cases where there is no order of institutional commitment, the juvenile court's status offense jurisdiction is not apt. A fourteen-year-old's being lazy, failing to do assigned chores, buying a sandwich at a place her mother had told her not to go, and "being a disruptive influence" should not support secure interim custody, judicial intervention, or official probation supervision.[16] These are significant consequences — as indeed, any juvenile court disposition is — and not only are they inept to resolve the problems presented by the unruly child, they are often imposed by a process that denies to the unruly youth before the court procedural rights which must be afforded to juveniles accused of delinquent acts. In some jurisdictions, status offenders may be denied the right to counsel.[17]

It is the rule rather than the exception that the status of "being beyond control" is established by a preponderance of the evidence, rather than by the rigorous standard of proof beyond a reasonable doubt required by the U.S. Supreme Court in a delinquency adjudication.[18] Moreover, it is likely that evidence may be admissible at a PINS hearing which would not be admissible in the trial of a delinquency petition, and some statutes expressly authorize this.[19] This, together with the lower standard of proof commonly required, may explain in part why criminal offenses are not infrequently dealt with under the PINS or other unruly child rubric.

They may also be dealt with there because juvenile courts and their personnel believe a PINS adjudication to be less stigmatizing than an adjudication of delinquency. This reasoning seems perverse. It is probable that a greater stigmatizing effect will result from an adjudication of incorrigibility, based on a pattern of behavior, than from an adjudication of a single act. Furthermore, proof of unruliness is, in the words of one judge, "easy to present and usually impossible to controvert successfully."[20] As a result, and because of the inherently greater power of the complainant parent, contests of PINS cases appear to be rare, at least in many courts. The New York study indicated that in New York County 69 percent of the youths appearing on PINS petitions admitted all the allegations: 24 percent made partial admissions, i.e., to some of the allegations; and only 7 percent denied all allegations and went to trial. In Rockland County, 94 percent of the cases involved a full admission and 7 percent a partial admission; there were no denials in the sample studied.[21]

Parenthetically, it would appear that the existence of the status offense jurisdiction may be an important element in perpetuating plea bargaining in the juvenile court; it has been described as "a kid's way of copping a plea."[22]

A further problem is that almost invariably the ungovernability statutes are impermissibly vague in wording and overbroad in scope. Such language as that extending jurisdiction over a child "who is in danger, from any cause, of leading an idle, dissolute or immoral life" or who is "ungovernable" or who is "growing up in idleness and crime" falls far short of the specificity that would allow a minor to determine what behavior fell within the prohibitions of the statute and what lay without.[23] Given the overbreadth of these statutes, every child in the United States could theoretically be made out to be a status offender. How many children have not disobeyed their parents at least twice?

The last few years have seen sharply mounting attacks — in the literature, in the legislatures, and in the courts — on the statutes conferring the status offense jurisdiction, for their vagueness and their overbreadth, as well as on the dispositions that attend their use.[24]

However, it must be said that attacks on such statutes based on the void-for-vagueness doctrine have thus far largely been turned back by the upper courts, and the Supreme Court of the United States has not closed with the issue, despite its striking down of a classic adult vagrancy (status) statute in *Papachristou v. City of Jacksonville*[25] on vagueness grounds, and its affirmance without opinion of a three-judge federal court's decision invalidating New York's youthful offender statute, which extended court jurisdiction (as a wayward minor) to one who was "morally depraved or . . . in danger of becoming morally depraved."[26] In *Mercado v. Carey*,[27] the Supreme Court summarily dismissed for want of a substantial federal question a challenge on void-for-vagueness grounds to New York's PINS law, N.Y. Family Court Act Sec. 712(b) and in *Mailliard v. Gonzalez*,[28] the Court vacated and remanded a decision by a three-judge federal court striking down that portion of the California beyond-control statute which extended the juvenile court's jurisdiction to minors leading or in danger of leading an "idle, dissolute, lewd, or immoral life."[29]

One cannot properly conclude, however, that juvenile status offense statutes have therefore been certified as constitutionally valid. In *Gonzalez,* the high court vacated and remanded for reconsideration of the lower court's grant of injunctive relief; the sparse memorandum decision suggests that the issuance of an injunction was deemed improvident. The Court's directions on remand indicate that the declaratory aspect of the lower court's opinion is still valid. One may surmise that the Court was moved by the factual mootness of the case at bar, the youngest petitioner in the case presumably having reached eighteen years of age and passed beyond the jurisdiction of the juvenile court when the Supreme Court's decision was handed down. Further, it is not unlikely that the Court recoiled from the prospect of facing the innumerable challenges to the status offense laws of the various states, and to commitments made under them, which would result if the lower court were upheld on the merits. One suspects, also, that state courts have been moved by similar considerations.[30]

In summary, federal courts at the level of the "firing line" have thus far generally concluded (in the comparatively few cases that have posed the question) that juvenile status offense statutes at issue before them were void because of vagueness, and deprived youth of due process of law. Upper courts seem to have concluded, at least by implication, that reformation of the status offense jurisdiction of the juvenile court must be a legislative rather than a judicial task, perhaps because the sheer volume of cases of children affected would swamp the courts.

The statutes conferring juvenile court jurisdiction over ungovernable youth are arguably infected with constitutional infirmity on yet another basis: infringement of the Equal Protection clause. Virtually without exception, the defined class — children — is underinclusive and hence suspect, because the child is subject to sanction and the parent, who shares responsibility for the child's behavior, is untouched by the law.[31]

Finally, the Supreme Court of the United States has ruled that it is constitutionally impermissible to impose sanctions on a status in the case of an adult.[32] Yet, as was discussed above, that is what the juvenile court's status offense jurisdiction does with respect to unruly children.

The jurisdiction over unruly children is thus a kind of moral thumbscrew by which we seek to demand of our communities' children a greater and more exacting adherence to desired norms than we are willing to impose upon ourselves. And infirmities of constitutional law aside, the jurisdiction in operation is otherwise maladroit in several major respects.

First, far more than in matters involving allegations of child abuse or delinquency, ungovernability cases present for resolution issues which are peculiarly ill suited for, and unbenefited by, legal analysis and judicial fact finding. The judicial system can decide quite well whether or not a person committed a given act; it is "incapable, however, of effectively managing, except in a very gross sense, so delicate and complex a relationship as that between parent and child."[33] The law is simply inept as a corrective of the kinds of family dysfunction these cases most frequently involve, which are "of vastly greater duration, intimacy, complexity and (frequently) emotional intensity" than other cases in the justice system.[34] Using legal compulsion to restore (or provide) parent-child understanding and tolerance, and to build up mechanisms for conflict resolution within the family unit, is akin to doing surgery with a trowel.

Further, allowing formalized coercive intervention (which is coercive only on one side — the child's) in unruly child cases undermines family autonomy, isolates the child, polarizes parents and children, encourages parents to abdicate their functions and roles to the court, may blunt the effectiveness of any ameliorative services that are provided, and cuts against the development of controls and means within the family for the resolution of conflicts. It thus may impede the child's maturation into an adult who possesses effective ways of handling and adjusting problems of interpersonal relationships because it misplaces the focus of service onto the child as a person with problems, rather than upon the family complex.[35] Relinquishment by a parent of his or her child to court control is probably the ultimate rejection. As the President's Commission on Law Enforcement and Administration of Justice observed, "It is within the family that the child must learn to curb his desires and to accept rules that define the time, place and circumstances under which highly personal needs may be satisfied in socially acceptable ways."[36]

The juvenile court's status offense jurisdiction may actually retard the range of services available to the unruly child and the family, and their chances of getting effective help, in two different ways. First, many community agencies of service may be leary of "court-associated" youth and be reticent to take a youth who has been processed by the juvenile justice system. Second, the existence of the ungovernability jurisdiction in the juvenile court may have provided an unfortunate incentive to schools and other community resources to avoid developing mechanisms for handling family problems, which are basically not susceptible of forced solution. So long as the juvenile court must take and deal with the problems, they need not; no matter that the judicial system is not the place for solution.

Finally, and at least as importantly, it is likely that the existence of the juvenile status offender jurisdiction furthers racial, sexual, and economic discrimination, particularly in urban centers.[37] Because very little national information is available and one must extrapolate from the few studies that have been done, it is difficult to estimate the degree to which this occurs; the literature is very thin. The Juvenile Justice Standards Project's study of PINS cases in the New York City courts showed that a majority of the youth involved were nonwhite (assuming a definition, as the study did, of "white" as including Hispanic ethnicity): Black youths comprised 40 percent of the cases, white youths 31 percent, and Hispanic youths 28 percent. Sixty-eight percent of the youths were over fourteen years of age, 44 percent over fifteen, and the cases predominantly involved girls (62 percent).[38]

A study done for the New York Judicial Conference indicated a predominance of boys among PINS cases (57 percent); black youths constituted 48 percent of the sample; Puerto Rican youths, 25 percent; and white youths, 24 percent. It also disclosed a sharp disparity between the levels of service afforded the three groups. Placement in a residential treatment center was recommended for 116 children in the sample; it was actually secured for 28. Black children for whom residential treatment was recommended were so placed in 10 percent of the cases, Puerto Rican children in 9 percent, and white children in 62.5 percent.[39]

A number of states have had different age levels for the assertion of ungovernability (and sometimes delinquent and neglect) jurisdiction as between boys and girls. Where challenged, these definitions of the susceptible class based on the gender of the child have quite uniformly been struck down as denying equal protection of the laws.[40] It is probable, however, that the status offense jurisdiction is in fact more often invoked for girls than for boys, as the New York study found.[41] As American society has traditionally been more concerned over the preservation of the sexual virtue of girls than of boys, so this concern is reflected in the invocation of the ungovernability jurisdiction. The Juvenile Justice Standards Project's New York City study found that although girls only accounted for 62 percent of the total PINS sample, they accounted for 100 percent of the cases involving allegations of prostitution, promiscuity, "cohabiting," and "general sex innuendo" (whatever in God's world that may mean, if anything).[42]

For these reasons, the juvenile court's status offense jurisdiction has been under increasing scrutiny for some time, with consequent and mounting pressure for its abridgement. In 1967, the President's Commission on Law Enforcement and Administration of Justice recommended that "serious consideration" should be given to completely eliminating from the juvenile court's jurisdiction conduct illegal only for children.[43] The National Council on Crime and Delinquency adopted a policy in 1974 that all status offenses — those acts of youthful misbehavior which would not be crimes if committed by adults — should be removed from court jurisdiction.[44] This position conforms to its proposed Model Juvenile Court Statute, the commentary to which states "This is the arch-instance by which courts confirm that children are not people; that they are the property of their parents and other custodians such as schools."[45] A similar position was taken by the California Assembly Committee on Criminal Procedure in 1971,[46] and a Select Committee of the same body later observed that "the court functions in a world of definite alternatives; not situations that are ambivalent, changing and little understood. . . . Not only is the court not able to cope with the real, underlying problems of youth brought before it on [a status offense petition], it is hardly able to cope with the symptoms."[47] Similar conclusions have been reached by legislative committees in other states.[48]

On the federal level, there have been two recent developments of considerable significance. In 1974, the Department of Health, Education and Welfare recommended the elimination of juvenile court jurisdiction over status offenses,[49] and in the same year, the Juvenile Justice and Delinquency Prevention Act of 1974 was enacted by the Congress and signed into law, providing in pertinent part that a state must, within two years from the date of submission of a plan for funding, treat "juveniles who who are charged with or who have committed offenses that would not be criminal if committed by an adult" in shelter facilities and cease placing them in juvenile correctional or detention facilities.[50] The Act expresses the "clear legislative intent that states be offered the incentive to move toward minimizing contact between law enforcement personnel and non-criminal juvenile 'offenders', especially runaways."[51]

JUVENILE JUSTICE STANDARDS PROJECT

The *Standards* promulgated by the Juvenile Justice Standards Project eliminate the general juvenile court jurisdiction over status offenses and non-criminal juvenile misbehavior.[52] They recognize, however, that the problems presented by such youth are very real and very complex, and that there will have to be established varieties of innovative services, both crisis-oriented and longer term, to offer help in resolving them. The *Standards* adopt the general principle that, although there must be tightly drawn possibilities of limited coercive intervention — "coercive exposure," if you will — in situations where the youth is in immediate jeopardy, services to youth and their families for the amelioration and resolution of family problems should be community-based, voluntarily sought, and readily accessible. They permit limited coercive intervention in their provisions for limited custody; for dealing with runaway youth; for court approval of substitute residential placement; and for emergency medical services to minors in crisis. Even in these limited instances, the least detrimental alternative consonant with the youth's needs is stressed.

It is the position of the *Standards* that the dejudicialization of status offenses and reliance on voluntarily based services will make those services more appropriate to the needs of the youth and his or her family; it is both true and a truism that help which a person selects to receive and in which he or she willingly participates has a better likelihood of success than services imposed at the end of a writ. Removal of the status offense jurisdiction will, it is submitted, encourage more people to get more effective help; stimulate the creation and extension of a wider range of voluntary services than is presently available; end the corrosive effects of treating noncriminal youth as though they had committed crimes; and free up a substantial part of the resources of the juvenile justice system to deal with the cases of delinquency and of abused and neglected children which belong in it.

The critical question is, of course, will it work? And the short answer is, we will not know until we have tried it, but it is quite plain that what we are doing now with status offenders does not work. Two pilot programs underway in California offer both interest and some hope. Both are aimed at the diversion of the juvenile status offender from the judicial process, but each adopts a different model.

In the first program, that of Sacramento County, beyond-control youth are referred by law enforcement agencies or parents to the probation department in the usual way, and are then deflected from the usual procedures of intake and petition by referral to a team of probation officers specially trained in crisis intervention techniques and family counseling. A two-year study demonstrated that beyond-control youths handled by diversion recidivated noticeably less frequently than did a control group of such children handled by the usual processes of intake and petition.[53] It also reflected impressive savings in terms of cost and resources freed up for other purposes: The average beyond-control case handled in the usual way consumed 23.7 work hours from initial booking to informal settlement or adjudication (not counting any aftercare or informal supervision) and cost $561.63 to handle, while the average diversion case required 14.2 work hours for conclusion and cost $274.01.

In the second pilot program, in Santa Clara County, a different process of diverting status offenders was adopted: Rather than involving the probation staff in the mechanics of diversion, on the belief that diversion before a youth got into the juvenile court system was preferable to induction into and deflection out of it, that responsibility was placed on the local law enforcement agencies. Each police department in the county (which has a population of roughly 1,400,000 and twelve local law enforcement agencies) cooperated with the program and received a share of grant monies, based on population and volume of cases, for additional personnel and the development of local resources. Under this program, the police attempted to resolve the problem at the local level without referral to the probation department or the juvenile court. Youth and families were assisted by officers specially assigned to the program who arranged referrals to community agencies, developed alternative voluntary placements where necessary, and rendered other assistance as required. The program's goal in the first two years of operation was to reduce by two-thirds the number of youth referred to the juvenile court and probation department for beyond-control behavior; in fact, a reduction of 67.2 percent in the number of beyond-control referrals was achieved.[54]

Both in terms of the frequency of reinvolvement with the juvenile justice system and in terms of the severity of that reinvolvement, youth handled by this program showed a distinctly better track record than a one-year sample of preproject youth. A total of 21 percent of all diverted youth became reinvolved on a new offense, while 48.5 percent of the preproject sample of status offenders handled by the usual processes, tracked for a one-year period, committed a new offense. Of that sample, 22 percent had reentered the juvenile justice system for a *third* time within one year.[55]

It was found that 70.8 percent of the youths in a sample of cases handled by the diversion project made contact with the agencies recommended to them by the police, and 62.9 percent actually received services. A sample of parents, on the other hand, followed police recommendations in 51.2 percent of the cases and received help in 44 percent. Roughly 49 percent of the youths and parents indicated that the services were helpful; one-third of the parents, however, felt the services were of little help. Service agency and resource records indicated that the police initiated the contact in more than half the cases, while clients were the initiating party in 35.5 percent of the cases.[56] Twenty percent of a sample of parents felt the handling was too lenient and stated they thought the youth should have been booked into the juvenile hall; 73 percent of those parents said booking "would have impressed upon the child the seriousness of the pre-delinquent behavior."[57]

Perhaps most impressive, a countywide preprogram survey revealed that prior to the diversion project, the county's law enforcement agencies used a total of 15 community resources of various kinds, public and private, in attempts to obtain services for unruly children. During the first two years of the program, the number of community resources utilized by police in handling beyond-control cases had grown to 110, about equally divided between public and private resource agencies in frequency of use.[58] It is not known how many of these were in existence before the project began; it seems safe, however, to assume that some of the resources were created or developed because of the demand created by diversion and referral for help on a voluntary basis.

Without the diversion program, to handle the beyond-control referrals in the first two years of the project would have cost the probation department and the juvenile court not less than $1,785,319 and 51,645 work hours in delivering services. With the program in operation, servicing beyond-control cases during this period cost approximately $744,756 and consumed 23,930 work hours, a savings of approximately $1,040,563 and 27,715 work hours. The cost of providing police services during the two-year period was $346,401, with such project expenses as consultation by probation personnel, supplies, transportation, and research and evaluation making up the balance.[59]

These studies certainly provide no final answers. They do suggest, however, that abridgement of the status offense jurisdiction and reliance on services outside the juvenile justice system, for the most part voluntarily utilized, may be a feasible and realistic approach to the handling of noncriminal misbehavior. It appears not unlikely that as the juvenile court's possibility of intervention is removed, the responsiveness and efficacy of the resources in handling unruly youth and their families will increase, as will the satisfaction of the clients. It also seems reasonable to suppose that some resources, at least, hitherto have not brought to bear the full measure of effort they might have given had the court not always been there as a last resort.

In particular, the studies appear to support the following points which underscore the feasibility of curtailing the juvenile court's status offense jurisdiction:

1. Runaway, beyond-parental-control, and other forms of noncriminal misbehavior can be successfully dealt with outside the juvenile justice system.
2. Formalized detention in such cases can be avoided through counseling services and alternative residential placements that are nonsecure, temporary and voluntary.
3. Youths involved in noncriminal misbehavior who are handled in this way, rather than by induction into the intake and adjudication processes, are likely to have fewer subsequent brushes with the law and to have a better general adjustment to life and its problems than those drawn into the juvenile justice system.
4. Though many resources which do not now exist will have to be created, and many of those extant will have to be strengthened and redirected, a start on handling noncriminal misbehavior cases outside the juvenile justice system can

feasibly be made, in most cases, with resources now available. And at least to some notable extent, the services now lacking may be created when the demand is created.

One of the principal reasons for the present retention of the status offense jurisdiction is, one assumes, that it provides something of a base from which the court can respond to a youth's presented needs by directing appropriate orders to school authorities and other social agencies. It should be noted that elimination of that jurisdiction should not hinder the ability of courts to so respond. Enabling statutes and orders issued pursuant to the court's inherent powers can provide the basis of judicial leverage and assistance without the need to sweep in the youth under the status-offense jurisdiction.[60] It is a perversion of basic fairness and the system of justice when coercive jurisdiction over a child is the only way to reach a recalcitrant official in breach of his or her duty to the child.

The *Standards* posit the elimination of the status offense jurisdiction of the juvenile court and the substitution of services outside the formal justice system, largely voluntarily based, on the assumptions that (1) noncriminal misbehavior cases will benefit from the immediate intensive handling which this will allow, rather than the piecemeal investigation, adjudication, and referral which is now more the rule than the exception; (2) the majority of service and helping time should be at the onset of the problem, when the family confronts a crisis, rather than weeks or months later after attitudes and positions have hardened with the passage of time; and (3) such services will be of greater help if they are not coerced. Our experience with the divorce law has demonstrated that the legal system is too blunt an instrument to resolve the complexities of family dysfunction, and that the legal system cannot by compulsion order personal relationships.[61] When, as an example, a sixteen-year-old girl must petition the juvenile court to declare her incorrigible as the only way out of a home she finds intolerable, the ineptitude of the present mechanisms for resolving the intrafamily conflicts which status offenses represent is apparent.[62] The old saw is perfectly true and hard cases do indeed make bad law; in respect of status offense cases, it is not beyond the mark to conclude that they are all hard.

As has been noted, virtually all existing status offense laws comprehend an extremely wide range of behavior, typically including disobedience to the orders of a parent or custodian; truancy; disobedience to the orders of school authorities; sexual misconduct; behaving in a manner allegedly injurious to the minor or others; absence from home without parental or custodial permission; the presence of circumstances constituting immediate jeopardy to the minor; and so forth. It may be useful to consider the status offense jurisdiction with respect to some of these specific behaviors.

DISOBEDIENCE TO PARENT OR CUSTODIAN

State intervention has proven a poor buttress of parental authority and family harmony in handling the problems of rebellious children. As American society moves toward granting young persons greater rights at an earlier age, it is increasingly less adroit to give the weight of legal authority to what is frequently rigid and arbitrary parentage.[63] Furthermore, there appears to be no evidence that "the viability of the family will be jeopardized by more freedom for the children,'' or that the present possibilities of judicial intervention as a parent surrogate, under the status offense jurisdiction, help to restore harmony to the dysfunctional family or benefit the child.[64]

Again, to apply to behavior that is not criminal, no matter how vexing, the same sanctions that obtain in cases of behavior that is criminal is fundamentally perverse. There is evidence that children develop the capacity and perception for intricate moral judgments much earlier than is commonly supposed.[65] A young person who is incarcerated for parental defiance in the same place and program as a youth who has committed five armed robberies is not likely to perceive as fair the legal process that put him or her there, nor internalize its values, nor through normal developmental processes come to see delinquent behavior as inconsistent with, and adverse to, his or her self-concept. In short, justice will not be seen to be done.

Judicial intervention in beyond-parental-control cases would appear to encourage parents to resign their parental roles to the court. The studies discussed above suggest that parents of ungovernable children regard the juvenile court and detention facilities as there to provide the ''control'' they cannot; they also demonstrate that the court has been visibly unsuccessful as a substitute parent in such cases.

Moreover, the family problems encountered in the exercise of the status offense jurisdiction range from seemingly trivial matters to complicated and many-faceted dilemmas which virtually defy solution. All represent, to a greater or lesser degree, failures of communication within the family unit which are likely to be worsened by judicial intervention, and which in most cases will be better served by noncoerced assistance. Many status offense cases are in reality cases of neglect, abuse or delinquency and should be dealt with on that ground. The line is often exceedingly thin, and decisions to invoke the status offense jurisdiction in a particular case may be based on such fragile considerations as having no evidence to proceed on another ground (but thinking that the youth's situation requires that *something* be done, however unlikely of success), or for convenience (e.g., that the youth in question presents an age and level of independence with which the dependent shelter is unsuited to deal).

The *Standards* take the position that conduct which infringes the criminal law should be dealt with under the procedures for handling youth crime. Cases of parental or custodial defiance which evince neither culpable parental neglect or abuse (which should of course also be dealt with under that jurisdictional rubric) nor criminal conduct on the part of the youth should not have the possibility of resulting in coercive judicial intervention, but should be channeled to services outside the justice system.

TRUANCY

School attendance is properly the business of the schools, not the courts. Judicial coercion can at best (and that very seldom, short of twenty-four-hour confinement) dragoon the physical presence of the youth's body, with strong indications that the ''heart and mind'' will not only not follow, but will be strongly repelled. Truancy represents a highly complex set of problems. The failure of a child to attend school may stem from parental disinterest or other neglect; from disability; from a fear of violence, at or enroute to school; from a defeat of motivation for learning by wooden and insensitive school programs which utterly fail to respond to the child's needs; and from a host of other factors.

The typical American response to failure to attend school has long been for the school to suspend the child for nonattendance and to refer the problem to the juvenile court in order that the latter may compel attendance. It could hardly be more disserving. The ultimate sanction for failing to obey the court's order, in most jurisdictions, is commitment to the same system of state facilities charged with the maintenance and treatment of the most violent and depredatory youthful offenders.[66]

Whatever the causes of truancy, in the aggregate or in the particular case, the existence of the truancy jurisdiction in the juvenile court cuts against the school's assumption of its own responsibilities and the improvement of its programs. As long as that jurisdiction remains, the schools have a ready dumping ground for their problem children. As with the other areas of noncriminal misbehavior, the problems of school attendance are best met by noncoercive services based outside the juvenile justice system. The court's forcing a child back into school is likely to have malignant consequences for all. As one court observed, "Forcing [the student] into classical schoolrooms introduces a disruptive element which is not good for the school, the teachers, the other students and likewise is not good for [him]."[67]

Providing for the excision of juvenile court intervention in truancy cases in no sense denigrates the importance of a decent education, nor the devastating impact of a child's not having one. It reflects, rather, the conviction that coercive judicial intervention has not proven demonstrably effective in securing that education, and in many cases has worked positive mischief by treating truant youth in the same way as if they had committed criminal acts.

Finally, withdrawal of the court's truancy jurisdiction is not antagonistic (though at first glance it may seem logically impure) to maintaining a requirement of compulsory education. A variety of other means and sanctions may be invoked to promote attendance, such as proper educational counseling suited to the child's circumstances and needs; realistic alternative curricula and special programs of education; "escort" services to school provided by the school or by community groups or agencies; even curtailment of the youth's franchise to attend when all other avenues of promoting attendance have been tried; and various programs involving the parents.

DISOBEDIENCE TO SCHOOL AUTHORITIES

As in the case of the truancy jurisdiction in the juvenile court, the existence of the "school insubordination" jurisdiction encourages the off-loading of problems which ought to be handled by the schools, and dampens the school's responsibility and ability to develop means of doing so.

In the case of violent or threatening behavior or other conduct which significantly disrupts the school and endangers or disturbs others, the responsible youths can and should be handled under the appropriate laws relating to juvenile crimes. If the behavior does not rise to that level of gravity, it should not be susceptible of being dealt with by the juvenile court.

SEXUAL MISCONDUCT

In virtually every case, the status offense statutes of the several states extend the jurisdiction of the juvenile court on the basis of ungovernability to youthful sexual promiscuity, which is essentially to say whenever any sexual activity is shown. The available evidence indicates that the "morals jurisdiction" is much more frequently invoked with respect to girls than boys.[68]

Constitutional issues of due process and equal protection aside, in cases of sexual misconduct as in cases of other noncriminal misbehavior, judicial intervention rarely reaches root causes and too often exacerbates problems rather than having its intended effect. Adolescent sexual activity is certainly of grave concern to parents, and it is perfectly true that in many cases the youth will need help. It is submitted, however, that the juvenile justice system is neither the place to get it nor to be referred from for it. While the aphorism is that morality cannot be legislated, the equal reality is that it cannot be worked even upon the young by adjudication and judicial decree — even if there were general agreement as to what it was. One person's deviance is another person's pluralism.[69]

If the sexual behavior is such as to threaten harm to another, it should be dealt with as a violation of the applicable criminal law. If it is not, and is not proscribed by the criminal code, it should not be the subject of juvenile court handling unless it evidences child abuse or neglect, in which case it should be dealt with under the abuse and neglect jurisdiction.

ACTING IN A MANNER ALLEGEDLY INJURIOUS TO SELF OR OTHERS

It is recognized that some children will be found to be in need of immediate help and treatment. Most of these problems are essentially medical — drug or alcohol intoxication or overdose and severe mental disturbance are perhaps the most obvious. The status offense jurisdiction is frequently used at present to cover such cases because the law provides no firmer ground for court intervention and possible mental health commitment.[70] The *Standards* envision procedures for the provision of help in crises of this sort which do not entail the assertion of the juvenile court's ungovernability jurisdiction over the affected youth. Establishing a form of emergency short-term civil commitment, they define crisis intervention services and impose requirements of informed consent, when the youth's medical condition permits, and limits on invasive therapy.[71]

RUNAWAYS

Nationally, juvenile court control over runaway youth — excepting those who have fled from court-ordered placements — is almost invariably imposed by reliance upon the ungovernability and status offense statutes. The problem is an increasing one: In 1968, FBI statistics reported more than 100,000 arrests of youth for running away; in 1972, more than 260,000.[72] It is widely agreed that such figures in no way reflect the true dimensions of the problem; informal estimates for 1973 and 1974 run to better than one million runaways each year.

The status offense laws of the several states commonly do not define runaways in terms of a specific period of time away from home, though specific law enforcement departments, youth corrections agencies and juvenile courts may have particular rules of thumb. However, it appears that short runaways are quite common and frequently result in parents seeking judicial intervention. It will be recalled that "short runaway" was the single most frequently alleged ground of noncriminal misbehavior in the Juvenile Justice Standards Project's study of New York PINS cases, comprising 51 percent of PINS cases.[73] A study made of 1664 cases received in the first three and a half months of the DHEW-funded National Runaway Switchboard indicated that 35 percent had been away from home less than five days, and 52.8 percent had been away less than ten days.[74] Better than 73 percent of the youth had run away one, two, or three times before, suggesting that although a majority of runaway youth do not stay away for extended periods of time, they are likely to leave again if the family situation has not significantly changed. Nearly 64 percent of the youth were reported as being in their home state when they called. Seventeen and one-half percent of the calls were from potential or prerunaways. Three and one-half percent of the calls were from "kick-outs," youth who had left home because they were forced to.[75] Sixty-four percent of the young people calling were girls; the callers' average age was 16.5 years.

The available evidence — though it must be said that the surface of the runaway problem is only just beginning to be scratched by research — indicates that runaway youth are no more likely to violate the criminal law than youth who remain at home.[76] Like other forms of noncriminal misbehavior, running away from home should not be treated as, nor subjected to the same sanctions as, behavior which violates the criminal law. The family may be in greater disharmony in the cases of runaways than in perhaps any other single class of status offense behavior, and juvenile court intervention is perhaps least likely to be helpful. This is at least partly because the juvenile justice system affords precious few resources short of secure confinement for children with histories of flight. Yet, there is some evidence that these cases are especially susceptible to family and communication therapy.[77]

From whatever perspective the act of running away is viewed, it "cannot be seen solely as a negative, unbalanced and impulsive response."[78] Indeed, in some cases it may be the most rational, mature and adaptive response to an intolerable situation, "a sign of health seeking surface."[79]

On the federal level, the Juvenile Justice and Delinquency Prevention Act of 1974,[80] which contains as Title III the Runaway Youth Act of 1974,[81] makes clear the congressional intent that runaway youth should not be subjected to juvenile court jurisdiction and treated within the juvenile justice system. The Act states it to be the finding of the Congress that "the problem of locating, detaining and returning runaway children should not be the responsibility of already overburdened police departments and juvenile justice authorities."[82] It posits instead locally controlled runaway houses to provide temporary shelter and counseling. To receive federal funding, the runaway house must be located in an area which is "demonstrably frequented by or easily reachable by" runaway youth; must have a maximum capacity of no more than twenty youth, with an appropriate children-to-staff ratio to assure adequate supervision and treatment; and "shall develop adequate plans for contacting the child's parents or relatives [if required by state law] and assuring the safe return of the child according to the best interests of the child."[83]

To comport with the requirements of the Act, the *Standards* provide that runaway houses should not be secure facilities, should be state licensed, but not necessarily state run (indeed, local management is desirable), and place responsibility for parental notification, child and parent counseling and arrangements for return or alternative living arrangements upon the house's staff.[84] As nearly as may be determined, the evidence available suggests that runaway youths do seek out noncoercive runaway shelters, and that the great majority of runaways may be expected to avail themselves of such facilities. The DHEW-sponsored Switchboard study discussed above indicated that many runaways had as a principal fear the possibility that they might be forced home against their will. It also found that 68.2 percent of all its runaway calls were made to have a message delivered to the youth's parents, which may suggest that runaways are not, in most cases, so implacably hostile or headstrong as to wish to cut all ties with their families.[85]

It is inevitable that there will be some hard cases where the juvenile refuses to go home, and refuses to agree to any acceptable alternative living arrangements, or refuses to stay in the temporary facility. The *Standards* do not provide coercive sanctions to keep the juvenile there, on the conviction that the existence of such sanctions will inevitably lead back to a status offense jurisdiction. It is the stated intent of Congress that the immediate needs of runaway youth who have violated no criminal law should be dealt with "in a manner which is outside the law enforcement structure and juvenile justice system."[86] While it seems reasonable to expect that the vast majority of runaway youth will be amenable to acceptable alternative living arrangements if they are not ordered to accept them and are not ordered to return home, some will not. Some juveniles will simply flee, and keep fleeing, and some will commit crimes while in flight. If they do, they will be subject to and should be dealt with under the delinquency jurisdiction. As with the rest of the status offense jurisdiction, it is submitted that the social costs of retaining it to provide for secure detention or other sanctions in what is expected to be a relatively small number of cases, are too great.

If the juvenile and the family are in intractable conflict and cannot agree upon mutually acceptable living arrangements, the *Standards* provide an additional instance of restricted official intervention, in the form of the juvenile court's approval or disapproval of alternative residential placement.[87] This is to be done upon motion, without the possibility of wardship or other jurisdiction over the child. The court should approve the placement of the juvenile's choice unless it finds, upon a prepon-

derance of the evidence, that the placement imperils the juvenile and that it is probable that the juvenile's living conditions will be improved by available alternatives.
When practicable, the court should provide an opportunity for the chosen placement
to correct defects before final disapproval. The court may remove the child from a
placement that imperils him or her, but may not compel a return to the parents'
residence. A placement is considered to imperil a juvenile if it fails to provide physical protection, adequate shelter or nutrition; seriously and unconscionably obstructs
the juvenile's medical care, education or development; or exposes the juvenile to
unconscionable exploitation. The *Standards* provide that no placement should be
made in a secure facility, and that services should be provided to juveniles and their
families during such placements to facilitate their reunion.

PRESENCE OF CIRCUMSTANCES CONSTITUTING
IMMEDIATE JEOPARDY

Realistically, there must be some means of dealing with youth who have committed
no crime but are in circumstances of immediate jeopardy, such as the twelve-year-old
who is prowling the subways at midnight. At present, that is frequently accomplished
by invoking the ungovernable child jurisdiction. While the *Standards* abridge that
jurisdiction, they provide for limited coercive intervention by law enforcement officers when a juvenile is in circumstances amounting to a substantial and immediate
danger to his or her physical safety, by empowering the officer to take the minor into
"Limited Custody." Such custody should not include holding in a secure detention
facility; should be terminated as soon as practicable; and cannot in any event extend
beyond six hours from the time of initial contact by the law enforcement officer.[88] In
so providing, the *Standards* attempt to strike the difficult balance of preserving a
means of necessary official action, while at the same time sufficiently circumscribing
that intervention and its consequences to prevent the court's status offense jurisdiction from regenerating itself.

　　In all instances, the *Standards* call for the least restrictive course of action consistent with the minor's immediate safety, and caution the avoidance of ethnic
stereotypes in determining whether or not danger exists. It is to be recognized that the
particular focus of societal concern about juvenile behavior will vary, depending
upon the particular local community. However, all of the component behaviors that
constitute the present status offense jurisdiction are prevalent, and concern over them
all transcends minority community, urban-rural and affluence lines.

SUMMARY

Thus, the *Standards* posit a structure of services to juveniles in conflict with their
families, who are not victims of abuse or neglect and have not violated the criminal
law, which would for the most part be voluntarily based and which would not lead to

juvenile court wardship. The court is given limited and special jurisdiction to approve or disapprove alternative residential placements for minors who cannot come to agreement with their parents or custodians as to where, how and with whom they will live. Additionally, restricted powers of official intervention are given where the minor is at substantial risk from his or her condition or circumstances.

The sources of assistive services should be convenient, well publicized, decentralized in most cases, aligned to the needs of the people they serve, and so set up and run that their function does not become submerged in their form.

This scheme is grounded upon the conviction that assistance which lets the youth have a say in what happens to him or her will far more likely result in the youth's developing mature and socially acceptable means of resolving conflicts than will help by court order, which in these sorts of cases is too often no help at all.[89] It is also more likely to promote family harmony, if that can be achieved, and it follows the concept that the court should properly be concerned only with securing the least invasive alternative that will afford help. Many resources now exist to help families and children, some effective and some feeble indeed. Many more need to be developed, and many of those extant must be greatly strengthened or radically and imaginatively changed. However, in many instances services exist which could provide at least the starting point for appropriate voluntarily based help to the child and family, if properly used on that basis without judicial compulsion.

I am under no illusion that the proposals provide firm solutions, and I am aware that in some individual courts, the status offense jurisdiction is wisely and humanely used, at least most of the time, which is perhaps all we can reasonably demand of our juridical systems. Viewed nationally, however, the picture is catastrophic and the juvenile justice system is clotted with cases that do not belong there. The *Standards* seek to provide a starting point to correct that, from which to proceed to a rigorous evaluation of how they work, and the scrutiny of regular review once the proposals are tried.

Inevitably, if the status offense jurisdiction is removed, some cases will be lost to help and some youths will go unassisted who might have been aided if the formal scheme of coercive intervention in cases of noncriminal misbehavior were kept. It is believed, however, that their numbers will be relatively few, and that the social costs of retaining the status offense jurisdiction as it now exists far outweigh the relatively small benefits. In the great majority of cases, it is to be expected that voluntarily based services will be accepted, and will prove far more effective than wardship and court-ordered commitment. And the removal of beyond-control cases from the juvenile court's jurisdiction should allow the vigorous application of its now taxed resources to cases of abuse and criminal conduct, to the benefit of all.

Many years ago, the British legal historian Sir Henry Maine wrote that the progress of civilized society was marked by the transition from status to contract.[90] It is time we took that transitional step in our response to family-rooted problems centered on the noncriminal misbehavior of children, and the *Standards* attempt to provide the basis for it.

NOTES

1. Note, "Ungovernability: The Unjustifiable Jurisdiction," 83 *Yale L.J.* 1383 at note 5 (1974); *cf. Mass. Provincial Stats.* 1699–1700, c.8 §§2–6, in *Mass. Colonial Laws* 27 (1887 ed.), in which the court was invested with criminal jurisdiction over "stubborn servants or children"; Commonwealth v. Brasher, 359 Mass. 550, 270 N.E.2d 389 (1970); Katz and Schroeder, "Disobeying A Father's Voice: A commentary on *Commonwealth v. Brasher,*" 57 *Mass. L.Q.* 43 (1972); Kleinfeld, "The Balance of Power Among Infants, Their Parents and the State," 4 *Fam. L.Q.* 319 (1970), 4 *Fam. L.Q.* 410 (1970), 5 *Fam. L.Q.* 63 (1971).

2. In one California county of better than 500,000 population, a thorough study done in preparation for a diversion program revealed that noncriminal misbehavior cases accounted for 40 percent of all minors detained in juvenile hall and 72 percent of court-ordered out-of-home placements and commitments. *R. Baron* and *F. Feeney, The Sacramento Diversion Project: A Preliminary Report* (Sacramento Co. Probation Dept./Center for Admin. of Criminal Justice, Univ. of California, at Davis, 1971).

3. Stiller and Elder, "PINS: A Concept in Need of Supervision," 12 *Am. Crim. L. Rev.* 33 (1974).

4. *Cf.* Bazelon, "Beyond Control of the Juvenile Court," 21 *Juv. Ct. Judges J.* 42 (1970); Glen, "Juvenile Court Reform: Procedural Process and Substantive Stasis," [1970] *Wis. L. Rev.* 431, 444 (1970); Fox, "Juvenile Justice Reform: An Historical Perspective," 22 *Stanford L. Rev.* 1187, 1192, 1233; Lemert, "The Juvenile Court — Quest and Realities," in President's Commission on Law Enforcement and Administration of Justice, *Report of the Task Force on Juvenile Delinquency: Delinquency and Youth Crime* at 91, 93 (1967) [hereinafter cited as *Task Force Report*].

5. *See generally E. Schur, Radical Non-Intervention: Rethinking the Delinquency Problem* 46–51 (1973); Bureau of Social Science Research Legal Action Support Project, *Research Memorandum on Status Offenders* 3, 22 (1973); *Task Force Report.*

6. *Report of the California Assembly Interim Committee on Criminal Procedure: Juvenile Court Processes* 7 (1971).

7. Rosenheim, "Notes on 'Helping': Normalizing Juvenile Nuisances," 50 *Soc. Serv. Rev.* 177 (1976); Rosenheim, "Youth Service Bureau: A Concept in Search of a Definition," 20 *Juv. Ct. Judges' J.* 69 (1969).

8. *E. Erickson, Identity: Youth and Crisis* 132 (1968).

9. Note, "Ungovernability: The Unjustifiable Jurisdiction," 83 *Yale L.J.* 1383, 1387–8 at note 33, 1408 (1974).

10. Lavette M. v. City of N.Y., 35 N.Y.2d 136, 316 N.E.2d 314, 359 N.Y.S.2d 20 (1974), *In the Matter of Ellery C.* 32 N.Y.2d 588, 300 N.E.2d 424, 347 N.Y.S.2d 51 (1973). Blondheim v. State, 84 Wash.2d 874, 529 P.2d 1096 (1975) ("incorrigible dependents" not to be committed for treatment or confinement in same area of institution where they may associate with delinquent youth); *cf. The Ellery C. Decision: A Case Study of Judicial Regulation of Juvenile Status Offenders* (I.J.A. 1975).

11. *See, e.g.,* Nelson v. Heyne, 355 F. Supp. 451 (N.D. Ind. 1972), supp. opin. 355 F. Supp. 458, *aff'd.* 491 F.2d 352 (7th Cir. 1974); Morales v. Turman, 364 F. Supp. 166 (E.D. Tex. 1973); Martarella v. Kelley, 349 F. Supp. 575 (S.D.N.Y. 1972); *In the Matter of Ilone I.,* 64 Misc. 2d 878, 316 N.Y.S.2d 356 (Fam. Ct., 1970); Note, "Persons in Need of Supervision: Is There a Constitutional Right to Treatment?", 39 *Brooklyn L. Rev.* 624 (1973); Gough, "The Beyond-Control Child and The Right to Treatment: An Exercise in the Synthesis of Paradox," 16 *St. Louis U.L.J.* 182 (1971).

12. *M. Rector, PINS: An American Scandal* (Nat'l Council on Crime and Delinquency, 1974). In Nelson v. Heyne, *supra* note 11, the court observed that nearly one-third of the inmates of the Indiana Boys Training School — which it described as a medium-security prison for boys twelve to eighteen years of age — had committed no criminal offense whatever, but were incarcerated for being truants or beyond parental control.

13. Cohn, "Criteria for the Probation Officer's Recommendations to the Juvenile Court Judge," 9 *Crime and Del.* 262 (1963).

14. L.A.M. v. State, 547 P.2d 827 (Alaska 1976); *J. Dineen, Juvenile Court Organization and Status Offenses: A Statutory Profile* 43 Nat'l. Center for Juvenile Justice (monograph, 1974).

15. Culbertson, "The Effect of Institutionalization on the Delinquent Inmate's Self-Concept," 66 *J. Crim. L. and C.* 88 (1975); for a contrary view, *see* Mahoney, "The Effect of Labelling on Youths in the Juvenile Justice System: A Review of the Evidence," 8 *Law and Soc. Rev.* 583 (1974).

16. *See In re* Walker, 14 N.C. App. 356, 188 S.E.2d 731 (1972), *aff'd.* 282 N.C.28, 191 S.E.2d 702 (1972).

17. *See, e.g., In re* Spaulding, 273 Md. 690, 332 A.2d 246 (1975); *In re* Walker, *supra* note 16.

18. *In re* Winship, 397 U.S. 358 (1970). It appears that only one-fourth of the states require adjudication of a need for supervision to be based upon proof beyond a reasonable doubt. *Compare In re* E., 327 N.Y.S.2d 84 (1971) *with In Interest of Potter,* 237 N.W. 2d 461 (Iowa 1976); *In re* Henderson, 199 N.W.2d 111 (Iowa 1972), and *In re* Waters, 13 Md. App. 95, 281 A.2d 560 (1971).

19. *See, e.g., Calif. Welf. and Instn's. Code* §701 (West Supp. 1976), providing that the admissibility of evidence at the trial of beyond-control cases is governed by the rules of evidence applicable to civil cases, rather than by the stricter rules applicable in cases of criminal law violation.

20. *M. Midonick* and *D. Besharov, Children, Parents and the Courts; Juvenile Delinquency, Ungovernability and Neglect* 92 (1972).

21. Note, "Ungovernability: The Unjustifiable Jurisdiction," 83 *Yale L.J.* 1383, 1389 at note 50 (1974).

22. Office of Children's Services, Judicial Conference of the State of New York, *The PINS Child: A Plethora of Problems* 17 (1973).

23. *See, e.g., Del Code Ann.* title 10 §901 (1974); *D.C. Code Ann.* §16–2301 (Supp. 1975); *Hawaii Rev. Stat.* §571–11 (B) (Supp. 1975); *Mich. Comp. Law Ann.* §712 A.2 (Supp. 1976); *Wash. Rev. Code Ann.* §13.04.010 (1962); *Wyo. Stats. Ann.* §14–41 (Supp. 1975).

24. *See generally* Wald, "The Rights of Youth," 4 *Human Rights* 13, 21 (1974); Note, "Parens Patriae and Statutory Vagueness in the Juvenile Court," 82 *Yale L.J.* 745 (1972); Comment, "Juvenile Statutes and Non-Criminal Delinquents: Applying the Void-for-Vagueness Doctrine," 4 *Seton Hall L. Rev.* 184 (1972); McNulty, "The Right to Be Left Alone," 11 *Am. Crim. L. Rev.* 141 (1972); Comment, "Delinquent Child: A Legal Term Without Meaning." 21 *Baylor L. Rev.* 352 (1969).

25. 405 U.S. 156 (1972).

26. Gesicki v. Oswald, 336 F. Supp. 371 (S.D.N.Y. 1971), *aff'd.* Oswald v. Gesicki, 406 U.S. 913 (1972).

27. 420 U.S. 925 (1974).

28. 416 U.S. 918 (1974).

29. *Cal. Welf. and Instn's. Code* §601 (West Supp. 1975); that portion of the statute was stricken by A.B. 432, 1975 Cal. Legis. Reg. Sess., effective 1/1/76.

30. *See, e.g., In re* Napier, 532 P.2d 423 (Okla. 1975); *In re* L.N., 109 N.J. Super. 278, 263 A.2d 150 (App. Div.), *aff'd.* 57 N.J. 165, 270 A.2d 409 (1970), *cert. den. sub. nom.* Norman v. New Jersey, 402 U.S. 1009 (1971); E.S.G. v. State, 447 S.W.2d 225 (Tex. Civ. App., 1969), *cert. den.* 398 U.S. 956 (1970); *cf.* District of Columbia v. B.J.R., 332 A.2d 58 (D.C. App. 1975).

31. Sidman, "The Massachusetts Stubborn Child Law: Law and Order in the Home," 6 *Fam L.Q.* 33, 49–56 (1972); *see also* State v. In Interest of S.M.G., 313 So.2d 761 (Fla. S.Ct., 1975) (juvenile court lacks jurisdiction to order the parent of a delinquent child to participate in the child's rehabilitative program).

32. Robinson v. California, 370 U.S. 660 (1972).

33. *J. Goldstein, A. Freud,* and *A. Solnit, Beyond the Best Interests of the Child* 8 (1973).

34. Note, "Ungovernability: The Unjustifiable Jurisdiction," 83 *Yale L.J.* 1383, 1402 at note 119 (1974).

35. *Cf. V. Satir, Conjoint Family Therapy* 2 (1967).

36. *Task Force Report, supra* note 4, at 45 (1967).

37. *See* Paulsen, "Juvenile Courts, Family Courts and the Poor Man," 54 *Calif. L. Rev.* 694 (1966).

38. *Supra* note 34 at 1387, notes 26 and 27.

39. Office of Children's Services, Judicial Conference of the State of New York, *The PINS Child: A Plethora of Problems* 21–22 (1973).

40. *See, e.g.,* People v. Ellis, 57 Ill.2d 127, 311 N.E.2d 98 (1974); *In the Matter of Patricia A.,* 31 N.Y.2d 83, 286 N.E.2d 432, 31 N.Y.S.2d 83 (1972); *cf.* Stanton v. Stanton, 421 U.S.F. (1975).

41. *Accord, R. Baron* and *F. Feeney, Preventing Delinquency Through Diversion, A Second Year Report* at Appendix A (Sacramento Co. Probation Dept./Center for Admin. of Criminal Justice, Univ. of California at Davis, 1973); American Justice Institute, *Research and Evaluation Study of the Santa Clara County, Calif., Pre-Delinquent Diversion Program* 61 (1974).

42. *Supra* note 34 at 1388–1389; note 41; *see generally* Green and Esselstyn, "The Beyond-Control Girl," 23 *Juv. Justice* 13 (Nov. 1972).

43. *Task Force Report, supra* note 4 at 27.

44. Nat'l. Council on Crime and Delinquency, "Jurisdiction Over Status Offenses Should Be Removed from the Juvenile Court," 21 *Crime and Del.* 97 (1975).

45. Nat'l. Council on Crime and Delinquency, *A Model Juvenile Court Statute* 7 (draft submitted to the N.C.C.D. Council of Judges, Oct. 1973).

46. *Report of the California Assembly Interim Committee on Criminal Procedure: Juvenile Court Processes* (1971).

47. *Report of the California Assembly Select Committee on Juvenile Violence: Juvenile Violence* 56–7 (1974).

48. *See, e.g., Report of the Virginia Advisory Legislative Council,* 1 *Fam. L. Reporter* 2515–6 (1975). It may be noted that the director of Youth Services in the Virginia Department of Corrections, speaking in support of the proposal to remove the status offense jurisdiction, stated that the removal of such minors from state institutions would reduce the number of girls in state care by 80 percent and the number of boys in state care by 50 percent.

49. Office of Youth Development, DHEW, *Model Acts for Family Courts and State-Local Children's Programs* 14–15 (1974).

50. Juv. Justice and Delinquency Prevention Act of 1974, 88 Stat. 1109–43 (codified in widely scattered sections of Titles 18 and 42 U.S.C.A.), at §223 (a) (12) *et seq.*

51. Note, "California Runaways," 26 *Hastings L.J.* 1013, 1043 (1975).

52. Juvenile Justice Standards Project (I.J.A.-A.B.A.), *Juvenile Justice Standards: Non-Criminal Misbehavior* (1976).

53. The study and its results are discussed in Feeney, "The PINS Problem — A No Fault Approach," *supra* pp. 249–269, and hence are not detailed here. See also *R. Baron* and *F. Feeney, Preventing Delinquency Through Diversion, A Second-Year Report* (Sacramento County Probation Department/Center for Administration of Justice, Univ. of California at Davis, 1973).

54. American Justice Institute, *Research and Evaluation Study of the Santa Clara County, California Pre-Delinquent Diversion Program* v (1974).

55. *Id.* at v, 20, 26.

56. *Id.* at vii, 46–52.

57. *Id.* at 50.

58. *Id.* at 37.

59. *Id.* at v, 57.

60. *See, e.g., N.Y. Fam. Ct. Act* §255; Janet D. v. Carros, Ct. Common Pleas, (Allegheny Co.) No. 1079–73 (unreptd.), 6 *Juv. Ct. Dig.* 139 (Pa. 1974; director of county child welfare services cited for contempt for failure to obtain care as directed for runaway girl); Carrigan, "Inherent Powers of the Courts," 24 *Juv. Justice* 38 (May 1973); State ex rel. Weinstein v. St. Louis Co., 451 S.W.2d 99 (Mo. 1970); State on inf. of Anderson v. St. Louis Co., 421 S.W.2d 249 (Mo. 1967).

61. *Cf.* Uniform Marriage and Divorce Act; *Report of the California Governor's Commission on the Family* (1966).

62. *See In re* Snyder, 85 Wash.2d, 182, 532 P.2d 278 (1975); *cf.* Wald, "The Rights of Youth," 4 *Human Rights* 13, 21 (1974).

63. *See* Wald, *supra* note 62 at 13; *M. Paulsen* and *C. Whitebread, Juvenile Law and Procedure* 44 (1974); *J. Holt, Escape from Childhood* 45–53 (1974).

64. Wald, *supra* note 62 at 24.

65. *See, e.g.,* Juvenile Justice Standards Project, *Summary of Symposium on Moral Development and Juvenile Justice* (Oct. 13–15, 1974); Konopka, "Formation of Values in the Developing Person," 43 *Am. J. Orthopsychiatry* 86 (1973); Kleinfeld, "The Balance of Power Among Infants, Their Parents and the State," 5 *Fam L. Q.* 64, 69 at note 29 (1971); *J. Piaget, The Moral Judgment of the Child* (Gabain transl. 1965).

66. *See, e.g.,* Nelson v. Heyne, 355 F. Supp. 451 (N.D. Ind. 1972), *Supp. opin.* 355 F. Supp. 458, *aff'd.* 491 F.2d 352 (7th Cir. 1974); *In the Matter of* Mario, 317 N.Y.S.2d 659 (Fam. Ct. 1971); *but cf. In re* Shinn, 195 C.A.2d 683, 16 Cal. Reptr. 165 (1961); State ex rel. Pulakis v. Superior Ct., 128 P.2d 649 (Wash. 1942).

67. *In re* Peters, 14 N.C. App. 426, 430–31, 188 S.E.2d 619, 621–22, *aff'd.* 288 N.C. 28, 191 S.E.2d 702 (1972).

68. *Supra* note 42; *cf.* E.S.G. v. State, 447 S.W.2d 225 (Tex. Civ. App. 1970), *cert. den.* 398 U.S. 956 (1970).

69. *See H. Packer, The Limits of the Criminal Sanction* (1968).

70. *See, e.g.,* Office of Children's Services, Judicial Conference of the State of New York, *The PINS Child: A Plethora of Problems* 48–50 (1973). (Eighteen children of a sample of 254 PINS cases or 7 percent, were diagnosed as schizophrenic; fifty-five, or 22 percent, were diagnosed as having a "personality disorder.")

71. *Juvenile Justice Standards: Non-Criminal Misbehavior,* Part VI, Emergency Services to Juveniles in Crisis (1976).

72. Federal Bureau of Investigation, *Uniform Crime Reports 1968* and *1972; cf. Hearing on the Runaway Child Before the California Senate Select Committee on Children and Youth, 1973–74, Reg. Sess.* 10, 111. In 1970, the last year for which figures were separately reported, there were 25,012 youths admitted to California juvenile halls for running away. *State of California, Dept. of the Youth Authority, Annual Report: 1970* at 100.

73. Note, "Ungovernability: The Unjustifiable Jurisdiction," 83 *Yale L.J.* 1383, 1408 (App. A) (1974).

74. Palmer, "A Profile of Runaway Youth," *D.H.E.W. Youth Reporter* (March 1975) at 5,6.

75. *Cf.* Cornfield, "Emancipation by Eviction: The Problem of the Domestic Push-Out," 1 *Fam. L. Reptr.* 4021 (1975).

76. *See Hearings on Runaway Youth Before the Subcommittee to Investigate Juvenile Delinquency of the U.S. Senate Committee on Judiciary,* 92d Cong., 1st Sess. (1972) [hereinafter cited as *U.S. Senate Hearings*]; Shellow et al., "Suburban Runaways of the 1960's," 32 *Monographs of the Society of Research in Child Development* (1967), reprinted in U.S. Senate Hearings, *supra,* at 201.

77. *See generally* Suddick, "Runaways: A Review of the Literature," 24 *Juv. Justice* 47 (1973).

78. Note, "California Runaways," 26 *Hastings L.J.* 1013, 1016 (1975).

79. *L. Ambrosino, Runaways* (1971), quoted in *U.S. Senate Hearings, supra* note 76, at 238.

80. 88 Stat. 1109–43 (1974).

81. 42 U.S.C.A. §5701–5751, (Supp. 1976).

82. 42 U.S.C.A. §5701 (4) (Supp. 1976).

83. 42 U.S.C.A. §5712 (Supp. 1976).

84. *Juvenile Justice Standards: Non-Criminal Misbehavior,* Part III (Runaway Youth).

85. Palmer, *supra* note 74 at 5–7.

86. 42 U.S.C.A. §5711 (Supp. 1976).

87. *Juvenile Justice Standards: Non-Criminal Misbehavior,* Part V (Alternative Residential Placement for Juveniles in Family Conflict).

88. *Id.,* Part II (Juveniles in Circumstances Endangering Safety: Limited Custody).

89. Youth should be the time, Ambrose Bierce reminds us, when "Justice never is heard to snore." *A. Bierce, The Devil's Dictionary* 144 (Dover ed. 1958).

90. *H. Maine, Ancient Law* 182 (Pollock ed. 1906).

9 The Ellery C. Decision: A Case Study of Judicial Regulation of Juvenile Status Offenders

Institute of Judicial Administration

INTRODUCTION

The present study is an examination of the impact of a decision by the New York State Court of Appeals on Young persons legally characterized as "Persons in Need of Supervision" (PINS). PINS respondents are before the court because they are charged with such behavior as staying out late, disobeying their parents, or truanting — behavior which is illegal only for persons under a designated age.[1] Juvenile delinquency statutes had long failed to differentiate such misbehavior from criminal conduct until New York revised its Family Court Act in 1962.[2] The new law distinguished between the noncriminal and criminal offenses of youths and gave the family court jurisdiction over any female less than eighteen years of age or any male less then sixteen years of age "who does not attend school in accord with the provisions of part one of article sixty-five of the education law or who is incorrigible, ungovernable, or habitually disobedient and beyond the lawful control of parent or other lawful authority."[3]

Central to this division of criminal and noncriminal conduct and the change in nomenclature was the hope that the juvenile justice system could deliver treatment and services to young persons with the stigma of "delinquency" eliminated.

When a youth is found to be a PINS the law mandates that the family court hold a dispositional hearing to determine whether he or she requires "supervision or treatment."[4] As originally enacted, the Family Court Act of 1962 prohibited training school placements for PINS.[5] This reflected the legislature's belief that the custodial orientation of training schools was not the proper environment in which to provide supervision or treatment to PINS and that PINS ought not be forced to reside with youngsters who had committed criminal offenses. This moratorium proved to be short-lived. In 1963, the legislature enacted the first of a series of "temporary" measures allowing for the incarceration of PINS in training schools.[6] Similarly "temporary" one-year extensions of the amendment were passed in successive years until 1968 when the legislature made the provision permanent.[7] A PINS adjudicationn presently makes a youngster liable to a wide variety of dispositional alternatives ranging from "informal supervision" to placement in a state training school.

Implicit in the legislature's differentiation of PINS from juvenile delinquents is an assumption that the treatment modalities to which youngsters will successfully respond and the arena in which treatment should occur vary according to the conduct which underlies the legal designation of PINS or delinquent. On the other hand, the

From The Ellery C. Decision: A Case Study of Judicial Regulation of Juvenile Status Offenders (New York; The Institute of Judicial Administration, Inc., 1975), pp. 1-13 and 52-62. Reprinted by permission.

treatment philosophy officially propounded by the New York State Division for Youth (DFY), which is responsible for the provision of care and services to a substantial portion of PINS and delinquent children, including all those in the state training schools,[8] approximates the antithesis of this assumption. It is the Division's position that:

> it is more appropriate and effective to develop programs that are based on the nature of the problems confronting each youngster rather than to develop programs based on the legal label that has been assigned to them by the courts. This position has led the Division to develop differential programs for youngsters based on the social and psychological problems of children rather than a program based on legal designation.[9]

DFY contends that all youngsters whose misbehavior is sufficiently serious to warrant training school placement face similar problems, regardless of official designations as PINS or delinquents.[10] To substantiate this position the Division had conducted studies of the populations of two training schools, verifying that there were no statistically significant psychological differences between those youngsters labelled as PINS and those labelled delinquent.[11]

DFY attributes these similarities to a blurring in practice of the legal distinction between PINS and delinquents. The "true" PINS child, the Division maintains, is diverted to the probation department, a private agency or state job corps camps and youth development and work training programs.[12] The PINS cases that are placed in training schools are generally "youngsters who have been involved in antisocial behavior for a considerable period of time, or who have committed a serious offense but for a variety of reasons, have not been designated as Juvenile Delinquents."[13] The Division therefore favors abandonment of the present breakdown between PINS and delinquents (but without removal of status offenses from family court jurisdiction) with replacement by a single category, such as "children in need."[14] The administration of services to juveniles in custody of the family court isn New York State has thus been confounded in recent years by DFY's rejection of the legislature's assumption that the legal categories of PINS and delinquent necessarily reflect differentiated diagnostic categories of treatment needs.

For several years the Legal Aid Society, providing law guardians for PINS in New York City, has sought to obtain reversals of training school placements for PINS. The key issues presented in these appeals, beginning with *In re Jeanette P.*[15] and *In re Arlene H.*[16] have been: (1) the individual's right to treatment, and (2) that the individual receive the least restrictive placement consistent with this right, as an alternative to the training school. The training school is viewed by the Legal Aid Society as the functional equivalent of a prison, lacking adequate treatment programs and detrimental to the client's welfare.

In *In re Ellery C.*[17] the Legal Aid Society appealed to the New York Court of Appeals seeking to reverse a decision by a trial court which was upheld by a closely divided Appellate Division, requiring the appellant, a PINS, to remain confined at Otisville State Training School. The Appellate Division had upheld the 1971 family court disposition of a "training school placement," accepting the probation department's recommendations concerning the inefficacy of other dispositional options.[18]

In its brief, the Legal Aid Society maintained that PINS have both a statutory and constitutional right to treatment and that PINS incarcerated in New York State training schools are denied this right because training schools are totally unfit to provide such children adequate supervision and treatment. The Legal Aid Society therefore requested the Court of Appeals to hold that "[c]onfinement of PINS in training schools which fail to provide minimally adequate care and treatment is a violation of their statutory and constitutional rights and should be forbidden per se."[19]

In its decision, the court addressed itself to the issue of whether confinement of status offenders (PINS) to the same facilities as juvenile delinquents was consistent with the proper supervision and treatment to which PINS were entitled. In developing this line of analysis, Chief Judge Fuld emphasized the "vital distinction" between the PINS child and the delinquent child which had been acknowledged in the PINS statute of 1962 and in litigation concerning PINS placements preceding *Ellery C.*, observing:

> Until 1962 a child who committed acts which now warrant his adjudication as a person in need of supervision was treated as a juvenile delinquent. . . .The new PINS statute "represents enlightened legislative recognition of the difference between youngsters who commit criminal acts (juvenile delinquents) and those who merely misbehave in ways which, frequently, would not be objectionable save for the fact that the actor is a minor (e.g. running away from home, keeping late hours, truancy)."[20]

The court concluded that the appellant's confinement at Otisville Training School along with juveniles convicted of committing criminal acts "could not in any realistic sense be considered appropriate supervision and treatment."[21] The court mandated that "[p]roper facilities must be made available to provide adequate supervision and treatment for children found to be persons in need of supervision."[22] In the absence of adequate treatment alternatives for PINS, the distinction between them and delinquents was judged to be useless.

The Court of Appeals' findings did not include a clear mandate to DFY on how PINS should be supervised, treated or otherwise cared for. The opinion was little more than a statement of the court's interpretation of the legislature's intent in the passage of the PINS provisions of the Family Court Act.[23] The court determined that since the act did not prescribe "confinement" as a suitable disposition for PINS, PINS should not be confined.[24] The decision went on to interpret the training schools as places of confinement which were "contaminated" by the presence of juvenile delinquents who required confinement, thereby rendering such institutions unsuitable for housing PINS. The court did not specify an institutional configuration that would provide appropriate supervision and treatment to PINS.

The omission of an explicit statement of the type of facilities or treatment programs which would satisfactorily fulfill DFY's obligations to PINS created a situation in which several different interpretations could be given to the court's mandate. Depending upon one's viewpoint, the decision could be read as necessitating fundamental and widespread transformation of the state's juvenile care mechanisms or requiring little change in existing procedures and systems. . . .

The ambiguity of the language of *Ellery C.* contributed significantly to the decision's impact. Perhaps even more significant to the changes ultimately effected by the decision was the substance of the holding itself. The principal issues of dispute in the *Ellery C.* litigation were the PINS' right to treatment and their placement in the least restrictive alternative available to the court.[25] The commingling of juvenile delinquents and PINS, while referred to in the appellant's brief, was not considered to be of primary import prior to the court's ruling. The court's emphasis on this particular aspect of the several points at issue was unanticipated by all the parties involved or affected by the decision. Most notably surprised was DFY. . . .the ultimate effect of the decision was undeniably affected by its unexpectedness.

A factor which may have contributed to the holding was DFY's nonparticipation in the suit. At the time *Ellery C.* was litigated, DFY was not a party to appeals of placements of children in its facilities.[26] The court's findings of fact in this matter were therefore determined without the benefit of the understanding of DFY's treatment philosophy, especially with reference to "mixed" PINS-delinquent juvenile institutions and "label-oriented" treatment in general. *Ellery C.* was decided in a relative vacuum with regard to first-hand knowledge of training school programs or the effects of the mingling of PINS and delinquents in these institutions. . . .[27]

CONCLUSIONS

At the time it was decided, *Ellery C.* was expected to be a milestone along the road to winning additional legal rights for juveniles, especially those accused of noncriminal offenses. Given the nature of the petitioner's grievances — i.e., denial of the right to treatment and the inability of New York's training schools to provide that right — virtually any affirmative relief would be expected to have important consequences for the juvenile justice system and the youngsters processed through it. We have seen little, if any, evidence that the decision did in fact stimulate any significant changes in the treatment and services provided to juveniles.

For *Ellery C.* personally, the immediate result of the decision was supervised release. For PINS children and the juvenile justice system however, the immediate future was not what *Ellery C.*'s advocates had hoped. After a brief period of administrative uncertainty, a flurry of memoranda, some institutional reshuffling, and even some early discharges, little meaningful change occurred.

Undeniably, the ruling had some impact on the state's handling of juveniles. Some PINS were paroled from training schools earlier than would have been expected. With one exception,[28] PINS and delinquents no longer reside in the same training scchools. However, it has been demonstrated that the reorganization of the institutions has in no way reflected the "vital distinction" between PINS and delinquents. Rather, these institutions offer little or nothing different in the way of services, supervision or treatment to each of the now discrete PINS or delinquent populations.

It is not our contention that we have proved the new institutions, undifferentiated with regard to treatment, supervision, etc. among themselves, do not offer different services than the mixed PINS-juvenile delinquent pre-*Ellery C.* training schools. Such a proof is beyond the scope of this report. It should be noted that DFY regarded the *Ellery C.* decision as requiring significant upgrading of the treatment and services offered to PINS in training schools if commitment of these youngsters to such facilities was to be permitted. However DFY does not assert that it has succeeded in improving the quality of care afforded PINS in its reorganized institutions. Rather, the Division maintains that in order to comply with *Ellery C.* it lost ground in its attempt to assure adequate care and treatment for all youngsters in its custody. DFY argues that in fulfilling its mandate to offer "label-oriented" rather than "need-oriented" treatment facilities, there was a loss in terms of flexibility of programs it was able to offer clients.

In the family court system, our investigators found that *Ellery C.* stimulated no modifications of policies or procedures. Aside from some temporary disruption of routines, occurring immediately after the decision, the courts and allied agencies were unaffected by *Ellery C.* The expectation that the decision might cause youngsters charged with PINS offenses to be diverted from the family courts was not fulfilled. Taken as a whole, the prospect raised by *Ellery C.* of new patterns of judicial commitments and of distinctly different programs for PINS have not been realized. . . .

Ambiguity can provide a range of discretion to those who must act in response to a judicial directive. Lacking a clear statement of what the court expected in fulfillment of its decree, DFY was given a relatively free hand in complying with the decision (as long as PINS and delinquents were no longer mixed in facilities). Given DFY's philosophy of treatment and its negative feelings toward "label-oriented" care,[29] it is not surprising that the decision had as little impact as it did on the youngsters in the Division's custody. Similarly the failure of the Court of Appeals to provide any directives to the family courts with regard to differential handling of PINS and delinquency respondents permitted these lower courts to view the effects of the decision as falling outside their jurisdiction.

In re Lavette M.

It has often been the case that judicial "victories" do not immediately realign social and/or legal structures in the manner envisioned by litigants when they initiated the litigation. Recognizing this to hold true for the decision presently under discussion, *Ellery C.'s* advocates, the Legal Aid Society, continued to attempt to gain the reforms originally sought. Not only did they work in conjunction with DFY to reach a satisfactory interpretation of *Ellery C.*, but they pressed new litigation through the courts to gain clarification of the mandate. In this way at least one of the textual ambiguities of the *Ellery C.* decision was resolved by the Court of Appeals.

In *In re Lavette M.*[30] the court was urged to intrepret *Ellery C.* as holding that placement of a PINS child in a training school is unlawful *per se.* A unanimous court refused to do so, stating that "it is confinement of PINS children in a prison atmosphere along with juveniles convicted of committing criminal acts that is proscribed, and not the fact alone of placement in a training school."[31]

Whatever "right to treatment" implications existed in *Ellery C.* were severely restricted by a now more cautious Court of Appeals. The *Lavette M.* decision acknowledged a commendable start toward upgrading the PINS child's right to care and treatment at DFY training schools. Apparently in reaching this conclusion the court relied upon information provided by DFY in its *amicus curiae* brief and attached appendices. since this study finds no hard evidence to support that conclusion.[32]

The decision in *Lavette M.* goes on to recognize the difficulties of a court attempting to measure the adequacy and effectiveness of treatment afforded PINS children. Faced with this difficult task, the court announced that its role is to assure the presence of a *bona fide* individualized treatment program. It specified that the right to treatment encompassed a right to an initial diagnosis and of periodic assessment of the child's needs. But the court was unwilling to go further in defining the requirements of a "right to treatment.". . .[33]

Those who viewed *Ellery C.* as a springboard-type decision saw its elasticity sapped by the rather restrained decision in *Lavette M.*. However, the *Lavette M.* court did indicate that failure to provide adequate treatment cannot be justified by lack of staff or facilities and further indicated that a serious question of due process would be raised by depriving a child of liberty as a PINS and then failing to deliver the promised treatment.[34] Thus, future challenges to DFY programs are not foreclosed, and are in fact invited. But success in such challenges will be more difficultly wrought given the wording of *Lavette M.*. The court might have placed the burden more clearly on the State to affirmatively show that a PINS child can be confined only when a *bona fide* and possibly, reasonably effective treatment system actually is operative. However, the language of the opinion could be interpreted to indicate that those who would challenge the adequacy of treatment programs have the burden of coming forward with the evidence and the burden of proving inadequacy. The court said "[A]bsent a clear showing that the treatment provided at a training school is significantly inadequate to the task, the current experiment with training school placement for PINS children, as authorized by statute (Family Ct. Act, 756), should be permitted."[35]

NOTES

1. *See* Comment, *Delinquent Child: A Legal Term Without Meaning,* 21 BAYLOR L. REV. 352 (1969), for a survey of state laws in this field. Such offenders are often referred to as "status offenders."

2. N.Y. LAWS ch. 686 (1962).

3. N.Y. FAMILY CT. ACT §712 (b) (McKinney Supp. 1974). That portion of this section which provides for a maximum age of sixteen for males and a maximum age of eighteen for females for applicability of procedures was held to unconstitutionally discriminate against females without any justification for the age sex distinction. *A. v. City of New York,* 31 N.Y.2d 83, 286 N.E.2d 432, 335 N.Y.S.2d 33 (1972).

4. N.Y. FAMILY CT. ACT §743 (McKinney 1963).

5. N.Y. LAWS, Ch. 686, §756 (1962).

6. N.Y. LAWS ch. 809, §10 (1963), *as amended* N.Y. LAWS ch. 811, §4 (1968).

7. N.Y. LAWS ch. 874, §3 (1968).

8. Responsibility for maintaining the training schools was transferred to DFY from the State Department of Social Services in 1971. N.Y. EXEC. LAW Art. 19-G (McKinney 1972).

9. DFY document, "Responses to Questions from the Governor's Office Regarding the Division for Youth's Proposal for Separating Juvenile Delinquents and PINS." August 14, 1973.

10. *Id.* at 5. The document also states that "it is reasonable to assume that PINS cases that do not get to the training schools are probably less delinquent than those that do, and in settings other than the training schools, programs for PINS may be distinctly different."

11. *Id.* Statement by Malcolm Goddard to the New York State Assembly Judiciary Committee, March 28, 1974.

12. *See* DFY document, *supra* note 9, at 6.

13. *Id.* at 5.

14. *Id.* at 6. Goddard, Statement to New York State Assembly Judiciary Committee, March 28, 1974.

15. 34 A.D.2d 661, 310 N.Y.S.2d 125 (2d Dept. 1970).

16. 38 A.D.2d 570, 328 N.Y.S.2d 251 (2d Dept. (1971).

17. 32 N.Y.2d 588, 300 N.E.2d 424, 347 N.Y.S.2d 51 (1973).

18. *In re Ellery C.,* 40 A.D.2d 862, 337 N.Y.S.2d 936, (2d Dept. 1972). It should be noted that the training school placement actually occurred in the context of a probation revocation proceeding.

19. 32 N.Y.2d at 589.

20. *Id.* at 590–91.

21. *Id.* at 591.

22. *Id.*

23. NEW YORK LAWS ch. 686 (1962).

24. Family Court Act § 743 (McKinney 1963) reads:
    When used in this article, "dispositional hearing" means in the case of a petition to determine delinquency, a hearing to determine whether the respondent requires supervision, treatment or confinement. In the case of a petition to determine need for supervision, "dispositional hearing" means a hearing to determine whether the respondent requires supervision or treatment.

25. 32 N.Y.2d at 589–90.

26. However, DFY could have sought leave of the court to file an *amicus curiae* brief. Legislation passed on May 30, 1974 amended executive law to allow the Division to intervene, as a matter of right, in any appeal from any court of New York State which relates to programs, conditions or services provided by the Division.

27. The contention that the court's unfamiliarity with the Division's programs and treatment philosophy contributed to its holding as it did is supported by the circumstances surrounding the findings in a related case, *In re Lavette M.,* 35 N.Y.2d 136, 359 N.Y.S.2d 41 (1974). In that case the Court of Appeals clarified some of the language of *Ellery C.,* clearly allowing training school placements for PINS. In its finding, the court relied heavily on information contained in an *amicus curiae* brief filed by the Division. Had DFY not participated in *Lavette M.* there is a strong possibility the court's decision would have been quite different.

28. The Brookwood institution houses both PINS and DC, but maintains them in segregated programs.

29. *See* footnote 9 and accompanying text.

30. 35 N.Y.2d 136, 359 N.Y.S.2d 41 (1974).

31. *Id.* at 141.

32. *See* note 27 *supra.*

33. This is not the occasion to attempt the complex task of defining treatment. However, whatever the nuances and disputes over the term, at its core is an intervention designed to improve or cure a given condition. Naming the condition (diagnosis) and reassessing the intervention — the *Lavette M.* criteria — thus fall on both sides of treatment *per se.*

34. *Id.* at 142.

35. *Id.* at 141.

10 *State ex rel. Harris v. Calendine*

Supreme Court of Appeals of West Virginia. March 22, 1977. 233 S.E.2d 318

NEELY, Justice.

This habeas corpus proceeding calls into question the constitutional validity of West Virginia's classification and disposition of juvenile offenders. The Court does not find unconstitutional *W. Va. Code,* 49–1–4 [1941], which defines a "delinquent child," or *W. Va. Code,* 49–5–11 [1975], which authorizes certain methods of disposition for children adjudged delinquent; nevertheless, we find that definite guidelines are needed to prevent these statutes from being unconstitutionally applied in violation of *W. Va. Const.,* art III, sec. 10, the due process clause, and *W.. Va. Const.,* art III, sec. 5, the cruel and unusual punishment clause.

The petitioner, Gilbert Harris, is a sixteen-year-old boy now confined in the Davis Center, a forestry camp for boys, pursuant to an order of the Calhoun County Juvenile Court adjudging the petitioner delinquent because he had been absent from school for 50 days.

On April 9, 1976, the Director of Supportive Services for the Calhoun County Board of Education petitioned the juvenile court to find Mr. Harris either neglected or delinquent because of his irregular school attendance. A summons was served on petitioner's mother and stepfather stating that they were required to appear before the Calhoun County Juvenile Court, and after several continuances a hearing was finally held on May 17, 1976 at which the petitioner, his attorney, and petitioner's mother appeared. At the hearing the petitioner did not deny the allegations against him and was adjudicated a delinquent child. The juvenile court committed the petitioner to the care, custody, and control of the Commissioner of Public Institutions for the State of West Virginia for assignment to the Industrial School for Boys at Pruntytown until the petitioner became sixteen years old in July 1976. Upon reaching age sixteen, petitioner was to be reassigned to a Youth Center for the balance of a one-year period, after which he was to be remanded to the custody of the Calhoun County Juvenile Court. Petitioner had never been charged with a delinquent act before the bringing of the petition now under review and had never previously appeared before the juvenile court. Furthermore, petitioner was nearly sixteen at the time he was adjudged delinquent for truancy, and he was ordered incarcerated for almost a year past the legal age when school attendance is required. *W. Va. Code,* 18–8–1 [1951].

Petitioner lived in a remote, rural section of Calhoun County and had some difficulty getting to school during the winter months. More importantly, however, it appears that the petitioner was ridiculed and shunned by his classmates because he suffered from a facial disfigurement and was mildly retarded. Petitioner had been

From *State of West Virginia ex rel. Harris v. Calendine,* 233 S.E.2d 318, Supreme Court of Appeals of West Virginia, No. 13815, March 22, 1977.

enrolled in a special education class during junior high school and high school, but the record does not disclose any details about those classes in the local schools or the programs offered by either the industrial school at Pruntytown or the Forestry Camp at Davis.

In support of his petition, petitioner alleges that he was not afforded adequate and sufficient notice of the charges against him; that the commitment is null and void because the petition filed against him was fatally defective for failing to set forth specific facts constituting neglect or delinquency; that the proceeding in the juvenile court was void because his parents did not have legal counsel at the hearing; that the trial judge abused his discretion in committing him to incarceration beyond the period during which he was required to attend school; and, that the entire juvenile commitment procedure violates the due process clauses, and the cruel and unusual punishment clauses of the State and Federal constitutions. The Attorney Genereral of West Virginia confessed error in this proceeding and, consequently, there is no record before us.

The absence of a detailed record necessarily limits our review of the alleged procedural irregularities. Accordingly we confine ourselves in this opinion to reaffirming that a juvenile defendant in a delinquency proceeding is entitled to counsel who will represent and defend him both at trial and on appeal, and that his parents, guardians or other custodians are entitled to be informed that their child has a right to counsel. *W. Va. Code*, 49–5–10 [1975]. An indigent defendant has a right to court appointed counsel, *Code*, 49–5–10 [1975], and all parties, particularly parents, guardians, or other custodians must be fully and meaningfully informed of their rights and must be accorded a reasonable time to confer with counsel and prepare a defense. Furthermore, any delinquency petition must allege sufficiently specific underlying facts to give the defendant and his parents, guardians, or other custodians fair notice of the charges against the defendant. *State ex rel. Wilson v. Bambrick*, W.Va., 195 S.E.2d 721 (1973); *Crow v. Coiner*, 323 F.Supp. 555 (N.D.E.Va.1971); *In re Gault*, 387 U.S. 1, S.Ct. 1428, 18 L.Ed.2d 527 (1967).

As we decide this case on the basis of the Constitutional issues fairly raised in the petition, we need not reach the question of whether the trial judge abused his discretion in confining petitioner beyond the age at which school attendance is required.

I

The primary question presented by this proceeding is whether *W. Va. Code*, 49–1–4 [1941] and *W. Va. Code*, 49–5–11 [1975] establish methods for handling juvenile offenders which are inherently unconstitutional. These West Virginia statutes, which indiscriminately combine status offenders[1] with criminal offenders, present an enormous potential for abuse and unconstitutional application. Nonetheless, under the doctrine of the least obtrusive remedy, this Court will avoid striking down legislation whenever ". . . there is an adequate remedy to prevent such legislation from being unconstitutionally applied." Point 4, Syllabus, *State ex rel. Alsop v. McCartney*, W.Va., 228 S.E.2d 278 (1976). To save these statutes from constitutional infirmity and to assure that they will be constitutionally applied, this Court will discuss the perimeters dictated by the *Constitution of the State of West Virginia* which circumscribe their application.

W. Va. Code, 49–1–4 [1941] establishes the conditions under which a child may be adjudicated delinquent. That Section provides:

'Delinquent child' means a person under the age of eighteen years who:

1. Violates a law or municipal ordinance;

2. Commits an act which if committed by an adult would be a crime not punishable by death or life imprisonment;

3. Is incorrigible, ungovernable, or habitually disobedient and beyond the control of his parent, guardian, or other custodian;

4. Is habitually truant;

5. Without just cause and without the consent of his parent, guardian, or other custodian, repeatedly deserts his home or place of abode;

6. Engages in an occupation which is in violation of law;

7. Associates with immoral or vicious persons;

8. Frequents a place the existence of which is in violation of law;

9. Deports himself so as to willfully injure or endanger the morals or health of himself or others.[2]

Once a child has been adjudicated delinquent the methods of court disposition are set forth by W. Va. Code, 49–5–11 [1975] which provides as follows:

With a view to the welfare and interest of the child and of the State, the court or judge may, after the proceedings, make any of the following dispositions:

1. Treat the child as a neglected child, in which case the provisions of article six [Sec. 49–6–1 *et seq.*] of this chapter shall apply;

2. Order the child placed under the supervision of a probation officer;

3. If the child be over sixteen years of age at the time of the commission of the offense the court may, if the proceedings originated as a criminal proceeding, enter an order showing its refusal to take jurisdiction as a juvenile proceeding and permit the child to be proceeded against in accordance with the laws of the State governing the commission of crimes or violation of municipal ordinances;

4. Commit the child to an industrial home or correctonal institution for minors;

5. Commit the child to any public or private institution or agency permitted by law to care for children;

6. Commit the child to the care and custody of some suitable person who shall be appointed guardian of the person and custodian of the child;

7. Enter any other order which seems to the court to be in the best interest of the child.

Both of these statutes must be interpreted and applied in conformity with *W. Va. Const.,* art. III, sec. 10, which provides "No person shall be deprived of life, liberty, or property, without due process of law, and the judgment of his peers" and *W. Va. Const.,* art. III, sec. 5, which provides in part, "Excessive bail shall not be required, nor excessive fines impossed, not cruel and unusual punishment inflicted. . ."

Inherent in the due process clause of the State Constitution are both the concept of substantive due process and the concept of equal protection of the laws.[3] I order for the statutory scheme concerning juvenile delinquents to withstand constitutional scrutiny under the substantive due process standard, it must appear that the means chosen by the Legislature to achieve a proper legislative purpose bear a rational relationship to that purpose and are not arbitrary or discriminatory.[4] Furthermore, under the equal protection standard it must appear that the statutes do not invite invidious discrimination based on race, color, creed, sex, national origin, or social class.

The cruel and unusual punishment standard requires that no person be punished unless he has done something which is generally recognized as deserving of punishment. Furthermore, as we implied in *State ex rel. Hawks v. Lazaro*, W.Va., 202 S.E.2d 109 (1974), the state cannot punish a person in fact while alleging to rehabilitate or otherwise help him.

The statutes under consideration, in the absence of guidelines for their application, fail to meet the equal protection, sustantive due process, and the cruel and unusual punishment standards because they permit the classification and treatment of status offenders in the same manner as criminal offenders.

II

We are not concerned with whether a child may be committed to a state correctional facility such as Pruntytown or the Davis Center when, in the language of subsections 1 and 2 of *Code,* 49–1–4 [1941], the child either violates a law or municipal ordinance or commits an act which if committed by an adult would be a crime not punishable by death or life imprisonment. These subsections provide for both punishment and rehabilitation of those children who commit criminal acts which have long been recognized at common law.

We are, however, concerned with incarceration of children for status offenses. Particularly in the language of subsections 3 through 6 and subsection 8 of *Code,* 49–1–4 [1941] we are concerned with a child who is incorrigible, ungovernable, habitually disobedient and beyond the control of his parents, truant, repeatedly deserts his home or place of abode, engages in an occupation which is in violation of law, or frequents a place the existence of which is in violation of law. The Legislature has vested the juvenile court with jurisdiction over children who commit these status offenses so that the court may enforce order, safety, morality, and family discipline within the community. The intention of the law is laudable; however, the means employed to accomplish these ends are unconstitutional insofar as they result in the commitment of status offenders to secure, prison-like facilities which also house children guilty of criminal conduct, or needlessly subject status offenders to the degradation and physical abuse of incarceration.

At the outset the Court should make clear that we are not impressed with euphemistic titles used to disguise what are in fact secure, prison-like facilities.[5] We define a secure, prison-like facility, regardless of whether it be called a "home for girls," "industrial school," "forestry camp," "children's shelter," "orphanage," or other imaginative name, as a place which relies for control of children upon locked rooms, locked buildings, guards, physical restraint, regimentation, and corporal punishment. Somehow, it appears to us that if the State's purpose is to develop a society characterized by peace and love, that our institutions for children should reflect those qualities and not their opposite. In fact, as we shall develop shortly, the status offender has a constitutional right, if not to love, at least to the absence of hate.

W. Va. Code, 49–5–11 [1975] provides a number of methods of disposition for juvenile offenders, including placing the delinquent child under supervised probation, committing the child to a public or private institution or agency, committing the child to the care and custody of some suitable person, entering any other order which would appear to be in the best interest of the child, and then finally committing the child to an industrial home or correctional institution for minors, i.e., a secure, prison-like facility. It is parsimony which circumscribes our courts' ability to treat status offenders constitutionally, not the absence of statutory authority.

The Equal Protection Standard

We find that with regard to the status offender the procedure for disposition set forth in *Code,* 49–5–11 [1975] can be applied in a manner repugnant to the basic principles of equal protection because it discriminates invidiously against children based upon social class, sex, and geographic location. It is obvious that a child from a family with financial resources will have an opportunity to use private institutional facilities which are far less restrictive, less dangerous, and less degrading than public correctional institutions. What would have happened to the petitioner in the case before us if he had come from an upper middle-class family in a city such as Charleston or Wheeling? He certainly would have had an opportunity to go to a private school. In the case before us we may reasonably infer that the Calhoun County Juvenile Court committed petitioner to a reform school because of the lack of a reasonable alternative which would have existed if petitioner had been from a different area or belonged to a different socioeconomic class.

Furthermore, the status offender is inherently in a different class from the criminal offender. The Legislature could choose to punish children guilty of criminal conduct in the same manner as it punishes adults, but as a matter of public policy the Legislature provided instead for a comprehensive system of child welfare. The aim of this system is to protect and rehabilitate children, not to punish them. *See State ex rel. Slatton v. Boles,* 147 W.Va. 674, 130 S.E.2d 192 (1963); *State ex rel. Browning v. Boles,* 147 W.Va. 878, 132 S.E.2d 505(1963). It has always been assumed that the Legislature can at any time withdraw some or all the benefits of this system from children guilty of criminal conduct. There is no such prospect for status offenders, however, since without the child welfare legislation they are guilty of no crimes cognizable and punishable by courts. This explains why status offenders have a special position within the current system, despite the fact that technically they are not distinguished from children guilty of actual criminal conduct. Since the class to which status offenders belong has been created under authority of the State's inherent and sovereign *parens patriae* power, *Warner Bros. Pictures v. Brodel,* 179 P.2d 57 (Cal.App. 1947); *Johnson v. State,* 18 N.J. 422, 114 A.2d 1 (1955), and not under the plenary powers of the State to control criminal activity and punish criminals, *Barker v. People,* 3 Cow. (N.Y.) 686 (1824), status offenders must be treated in a fashion consistent with the *parens patriae* power, namely, they must be helped and not punished, *State ex rel. Slatton v. Boles, supra;* otherwise their classification becomes invidious, and accordingly, unconstitutional.

Finally, it should be noted that status offender legislation discriminates invidiously against females. It is apparent that status offense petitions can easily be used to bring under control young women suspected by their parents or by other authorities of promiscuous behavior. Our society tends to condemn female promiscuity more severely than male promiscuity, and this tendency may explain why females often are unfairly classified and treated as status offenders. This Court offers no explanation for this phenomenon, nor do we make any normative judgments regarding the wisdom of such a distinction; however, we recognize its existence and its discriminatory effect on female status offenders.[6] The control of sexual behavior may be accomplished by other means.

The Substantive Due Process Standard

Furthermore the Court finds no rational connection between the legitimate legislative purposes of enforcing family discipline, protecting children, and protecting society from uncontrolled children, and the means by which the State is permitted to accomplish these purposes, namely incarceration of children in secure, prison-like facilities. . . .

In view of the foregoing, and in view of the fact that there are numerous alternatives to incarceration for status offenders[7] we hold that the State must exhaust every reasonable alternative to incarceration before committing a status offender to a secure, prison-like facility. Furthermore, for those extreme cases in which commitment of status offenders to a secure, prison-like facility cannot be avoided, the receiving facility must be devoted solely to the custody and rehabilitation of status offenders. In this manner status offenders can be spared contact under degrading and harmful conditions with delinquents who are guilty of criminal conduct and experienced in the ways of crime.

However, this does not limit the authority of the juvenile court to house and educate status offenders and criminal offenders together in shelter homes, residential treatment centers, and other modern facilities staffed by well trained, attentive, and dedicated people, where the atmosphere is characterized by love and concern rather than physical violence, corporal punishment and physical restraint of liberty, provided the court determines there is no danger to the physical safety or emotional health of the status offender.

The Cruel and Unusual Punishment Standard

In the case before us we are confronted with a child who was obviously in need of help, and yet the State chose to degrade him, to humiliate him, and to punish him by sending him to institutions which fail to meet his needs and cannot help him.

At the outset this Court acknowledges that the cruel and unusual punishment standard cannot easily be defined and certainly is not fixed; consequently, we feel the standard tends to broaden as society becomes more enlightened and humane. *See State ex rel. Pingley v. Coiner,* 155 W.Va. 591, 186 S.E.2d 220 (1972). The standard ought to be especially broad in its application to status offenders, whom the State has pledged *not* to punish at all, but rather, to protect and rehabilitate. Furthermore, status offenders are not guilty of the criminal conduct which ordinarily serves to make society's exercise of the penal sanction legitimate.

A good starting point for applying the cruel and unusual punishment standard to West Virginia's treatment of status offenders is the concept of disproportionality. This concept is explicitly recognized in *W. Va. Const.*, art III, sec. 5, "Penalties shall be proportioned to the character and degree of the offence" and is implicit in the Eighth Amendment to the *United States Constitution,* which originates in the same tradition as our own constitutional provision. *See Weems v. United States,* 217 U.S. 349, 30 S.Ct. 544, 54 L.Ed. 793 (1910), and *Ralph v. Warden,* 438 F.2d 786 (4th Cir. 1970).[8] A recent federal case, overturning the application of West Virginia's habitual offender law to a particular defendant, discussed the concept of disproportionality and identified three objective factors which can be used in determining whether certain punishment is constitutionally disproportionate. These factors are: (1) the nature of the offense itself; (2) the legislative purpose behind the punishment; and (3) what punishment would have been applied in other jurisdictions. *Hart v. Coiner,* 483 F.2d 136 (4th Cir. 1973).

As the preceding sections of this opinion have made clear, this Court is concerned with the class of offenders known as status offenders. By definition, the nature of the class of offenses committed by status offenders is noncriminal. Accordingly, the status offender is located on the extreme end of a spectrum of juvenile misconduct running from most serious to least serious offenses. The nature of their offenses thus tends to indicate that status offenders incarcerated in secure, prison-like facilities, along with children guilty of criminal conduct, are suffering a constitutionally disproportionate penalty.

The second consideration, the legislative purpose behind the punishment, has already been discussed at length in the substantive due process section of this opinion. To reiterate, this Court is unable to discern any rational connection between the legitimate legislative purposes of enforcing family discipline, protecting children, and protecting society from uncontrolled children and the incarceration of status offenders in secure, prison-like facilities along with children guilty of criminal conduct. We, like the court in *Hart v. Coiner, supra,* are in accord with Mr. Justice Brennan's observations: "If there is a significantly less severe punishment to achieve the purposes for which the punishment is inflicted, the punishment inflicted is unnecessary and therefore excessive." *Hart v. Coiner, supra* at 141.

Finally, we perceive that a "better rule" is emerging in other progressive jurisdictions, which eliminates or significantly limits the juvenile court's power to commit status offenders to secure, prison-like facilities along with children guilty of criminal conduct. . . .Other jurisdictions, typical of those which do not incarcerate status offenders in secure, prison-like facilities along with children guilty of criminal conduct, include Massachusetts and Maryland. *See Massachusetts General Laws Annotated,* 119 § 39G [1973] and *Annotated Code of Maryland* § 3–832 [1973]."[9] The nature of status offender punishment in other jurisdictions, which is by no means uniform, cannot, of course, control the outcome of this case. Nevertheless, in deciding in what direction an enlightened and humane society should move, this Court is entitled under *W. Va. Const.*, art III, sec. 5 to consider the response of other jurisdictions to the common problem which is presented here.

For all of the foregoing reasons, we conclude that the incarceration of status offenders in secure, prison-like facilities along with children guilty of criminal conduct inflicts a constitutionally disproportionate penalty upon status offenders, and as such, violates *W. Va. Const.*, art III, sec. 5.

III

Accordingly, we hold that a status offender may still be adjudged delinquent under *W. Va. Code,* 49–1–4 [1941]; however, before he may be committed to a penal institution pursuant to the provisions of *W. Va. Code,* 49–5–11 (4) [1975], there must be evidence on the record which clearly supports the conclusion, and the juvenile court must specifically find as a matter of fact, that no other reasonable alternative either is available or could with due diligence and financial commitment on the part of the State be made available to help the child, and that the child is so totally unmanageable, ungovernable, and antisocial that he or she is amenable to no treatment or restraint short of incarceration in a secure prison-like facility. Furthermore, to reiterate in this context what we said above, no status offender in any event, regardless of incorrigibility, may be incarcerated in a secure, prison-like facility which is not devoted exclusively to the custody and rehabilitation of status offenders. We emphasize here that State parsimony is no defense to an allegation of deprivation of constitutional rights. The State may not punish a person not deserving of punishment merely because such action serves the State's interest in convenience of frugality. *See Lavett M. v. Corporation Counsel of City of N. Y.,* 35 N.Y.2d 136, 359 N.Y.S.2d 20, 316 N.E.2d 314 (1974) and *Rouse v. Cameron,* 125 U.S.App.D.C. 366, 373 F.2d 451 (1966).

Consequently, the standard which the juvenile court must apply is not a standard of what facilities are *actually* available in the State of West Virginia for the treatment of juvenile status offenders, but rather a standard which looks to what facilities *could reasonably be made* available in an enlightened and humane state solicitous of the welfare of its children but also mindful of other demands upon the State budget for humanitarian purposes. We recognize that problems may arise, as for example, when a court is located in a rural part of West Virginia which lacks child-care facilities, and the court has no place to send a status offender except a correctional facility. Nevertheless, in such cases, if rehabilitation of the status offender could be accomplished by his committment to a well-run, centralized state residential treatment center, or a local shelter facility where a small number of children live with professionally trained house parents, or by any other reasonable method, then the juvenile judge, as a matter of state constitutional law, must make a disposition under *Code* 49–5–11 [1975] which does not involve commitment to a secure, prison-like facility, or he must discharge the defendant.

For the foregoing reasons the writ of habeas corpus for which the petitioner prays is awarded and it is ordered that the petitioner be discharged forthwith from custody and restored to his liberty. Children currently committed to State facilities in violation of the guidelines enunciated in this opinion may bring actions in habeas corpus in the local circuit courts. It is further ordered that the Clerk of this Court shall send three copies of this opinion to the superintendents of each and every correctional facility in which juvenile offenders are committed together with an order of this court that those copies be posted in conspicuous places.

Writ awarded.

NOTES

1. A status offender, for the purposes of this opinion, may be defined as a child who "is beyond the control of his parents or is engaging in non-criminal conduct thought to be harmful to himself. . . ." M. Paulsen and C. Whitebread, *Juvenile Law and Procedure* 32 (1974), or who commits acts, which if committed by an adult, would not be crimes.

2. "Subsections 7 and 9 of *Code*, 1931, 49–1–4, as amended, defining a delinquent child as one who '[a]ssociates with immoral or vicious persons' and as one who '[d]eports himself so as to wilfully injure or endanger the morals or health of himself or others' are void as violative of the Due Process Clauses of Article III, Section 10 of the *Constitution of West Virginia* and the Fourteenth Amendment of the *Constitution of the United States*." Point 6, Syllabus, *State v. Flinn,* W.Va., 208 S.E.2d 538 (1974).

3. In the continuously evolving tradition of Anglo-American common law there can be no fixed definition of due process of law, which is an inherently elusive concept; nevertheless, it is apparent that due process of law under the *West Virginia Constitution* contains an equal protection component the scope and application of which are coextensive or broader than the equal protection clause of the Fourteenth Amendment to the *United States Constitution. See Johnson v. Robinson,* 415 U.S. 361, 94 S.Ct. 1160, 39 L.Ed.2d 389 (1974) which imports the equal protection clause of the Fourteenth Amendment into the Fifth Amendment to the *United States Constitution,* the due process language of which is nearly identical to that found in W. Va. Const., art III, sec. 10. *See also Linger v. Jennings,* 143 W.Va. 57, 99 S.E.2d 740 (1957), which strongly suggests that *W. Va. Const.,* art III, sec. 10 affords West Virginia citizens a guarantee of equal protection of the laws as a matter of State constitutional doctrine.

4. While the substantive due process requirements of the *United States Constitution* have been subject to some erosion, *see Ferguson v. Skrupa,* 372 U.S. 726, 83 S.Ct. 1028, 10 L.Ed.2d 93 (1963), the concept of substantive due process within the *United States Constitution* is still alive. *See Roe v. Wade,* 410 U.S. 113, 93 S.Ct. 705, 35 L.E.d.2d 147 (Stewart, J. concurring) (1973); *Rouse v. Cameron,* 125 U.S.App.D.C. 366, 373 F.2d 451 (1966); *Wyatt v. Stickney,* 325 F. Supp. 781 (D.C.Ala. 1971). In any event, substantive due process remains a viable concept under *W. Va. Const.,* art. III, sec. 10, and in evaluating whether statutes meet substantive due process requirements, a West Virginia court must adhere to the following basic standard: ". . . to satisfy the requirements of due process of law, legislative acts must bear a reasonable relationship to a proper legislative purpose and be neither arbitrary or discriminatory." Point 1, Syllabus, *State v. Wender,* 149 W.Va. 413, 141 S.E.2d 359 (1965). *See also State ex rel. Hawks v. Lazaro,* W.Va., 202 S.E.2d 109 (1974).

5. Shakespeare instructs us well that merely changing the name of an object does not change its true character: "What's in a name? that which we call a rose By any other name would smell as sweet;" *Romeo and Juliet,* Act II, Sc. ii.

6. A recent study (December 1976) by the Division of Corrections, West Virginia Department of Public Institutions, indicates that female status offenders comprise a much larger percentage of the total number of their sex committed to secure, prison-like facilities than male status offenders comprise of theirs. This study identified 138 status offenders out of the total number of 477 children committed at that time to West Virginia's secure, prison-like facilities. Overall then, 29 percent of the children committed were status offenders.

There were 404 males in the sample population, of whom 72 were status offenders, or approximately 18 percent. On the other hand there were 73 females in the sample population, of whom 66 were status offenders, or approximately 90 percent.

The study provides additional evidence of the uneven treatment of females. Of the 72 males committed for status offenses, 41, or about 57 percent, had a prior history of criminal conduct. Although this prior history by itself would be insufficient, under the guidelines of this opinion, to justify the commitment of these male status offenders to secure, prison-like facilities, the figures do suggest that juvenile courts are giving some attention to the severity of male status offenders' behavioral problems before committing them to secure, prison-like facilities. On the other hand, only 12, or about 18 percent of the 66 females committed for status offenses had a history of prior criminal conduct.

The inequities of the present commitment process are all the more alarming because male and female status offenders are being referred to juvenile courts in approximately equal numbers. According to the West Virginia Department of Welfare statistics, 1974 referrals for status offenses were divided 48 percent males, 52 percent females; 1975 referrals for status offenses were divided 47 percent males, 53 percent females; and 1976 referrals were 49.7 percent males, 50.3 percent females. Therefore, it appears that the present system manifests its sexual bias not in the mere referral of status offenders to the authorities, but rather in the failure to accord evenhanded treatment at the stage where a determination is made to commit status offenders to secure, prison-like facilities.

7. Such alternatives include, but are not limited to, supervised probation; specialized foster care arranged through the Department of Welfare; nonsecure, adequately supervised residential shelter facilities similar to the Children's Home Society, Wheeling and "Patchwork" in Charleston; a group home program, with structured live-in treatment, and access to counseling and psychiatric care, similar to the Davis-Stuart group homes in Bluefield, Princeton, Beckley and Fayetteville; residential treatment in a hospital setting for status offenders with psychological or emotional problems, similar to Opportunity Hall at Spencer State Hospital; and a residential center for intensive treatment outside the hospital setting, staffed by psychologists and medical professionals. Other satisfactory alternatives to incarceration could also be developed by a society solicitous of the welfare of its children and dedicated to treating the special problems of status offenders.

8. Indeed, the concept of disproportionality can be traced back to the Magna Carta, Chapter 14 of which stipulated: "A free man shall not be amerced for a trivial offence, except in accordance with the degree of the offence; and for a serious offence he shall be amerced according to its gravity. . ." This limitation on excessive and oppressive penalties was very likely the Magna Carta's most significant impact on the mass of the people at that time. *See Furman v. Georgia,* 408 U.S. 238 at 243, 92 S.Ct. 2726, 2729, 33 L.Ed.2d 346 (1972).

9 .Of similar import are the recommendations of the National Conference of Commissioners on Uniform Laws. They propose that as to status offenders "the court may make any disposition authorized for a delinquent child except commitment to the state department or state institution to which commitment of delinquent children may be made." *Uniform Juvenile Court Act,* sec. 32. Alternatively, sec. 32 would permit commitment of status offenders along with delinquent children only when the status offender is found in a separate hearing not to be otherwise amenable to treatment and rehabilitation. *Id.*

The Front End of the Juvenile Justice System

A.   Police Practices with Juveniles

Introduction

Public interest in juvenile delinquency, as well as scholarly commentaries and critiques, have focused less on police practices with juveniles than on the juvenile court process itself. Yet law enforcement agents serve as the primary referral source for any juvenile court's workload of law violation cases. The three articles included here describe and evaluate police practices with juveniles from the earliest processing point, the arrival at the scene of the alleged offense, through the interrogation stage. Police exercise of discretion as to whether to arrest a youth and whether an arrested youth should be diverted to a community agency or referred to court is reviewed also, in combination with a critique of police interrogation of juveniles in the absence of an attorney or the youth's parents.

The initial article involves on-site observation and recording of police activities with juveniles. The approach used is especially valuable because it goes beyond official police statistics to examine the particular circumstances surrounding police decision making, and because it replicates and fundamentally confirms earlier, similar research in other cities. It is significant to learn, among other findings, that the "great bulk" of the offenses were less than felony level; only 16 percent of the youths were arrested; offense severity influenced the arrest rate; citizen presence and preference strongly influenced an arrest decision; and the higher arrest rate for black youths was due to the presence and preference of black complainants.

While other studies suggest that police dispositions are more severe for minority than for majority youths when the offense is held constant, the replication research and its forerunner exonerate police prejudice for the higher arrest rate for black youths.

The second article reviews police diversion practices. Diversion removes a youth from the juvenile justice system prior to formal judicial consideration, redirecting the youngster to a service agency, governmental or private, at an early stage of the juvenile justice process. Typically, a coercive condition accompanies diversion. "True diversion," the rejection of formal processing accompanied by a voluntary suggestion that external services be obtained, but without any strings attached, is believed to be a rare practice. Lecture and release, used by police agencies daily in terminating law enforcement interest in a case, is not diversion; it is classed as a dismissal since no alternative servicing agency is involved.

A concern expressed in the literature is that the type of youngster who used to be dismissed by police agents or probation intake officials prior to the advent of formal diversion programs may now experience diversion: "Either go there or go to court." The Klein and Teilmann report of police diversion practices in Los Angeles County reveals that this practice, known as "widening the net," is common there. The absence of strong police commitment to diversion agencies is also revealed. But an expansion of police diversion practices, influenced by federal funding and changed juvenile justice processing expectations, is noted.

In reviewing the constitutional requirements of police interrogation of juveniles, the United States Supreme Court has held that 1.) law enforcement agents must advise juveniles of their rights to silence and to counsel and free counsel if indigent, and that interrogation must terminate upon invocation of one of these rights (*In re Gault*, 387 U.S.1, (1967)) and 2.) interrogation may lawfully proceed when a youth on probation, suspected of murder, asks to consult not with an attorney but with his probation officer, and this request is denied by police officers (*Fare v. Michael C.*, 78-334 (June 20, 1979)). The concluding article, written prior to the *Fare* decision, and, inferentially, in opposition to this holding, considers the constitutionality of juvenile waiver of rights prior to interrogation.

Police attempts to obtain confessions from juvenile as well as adult suspects have been standard operating procedures. A few states have enacted statutes requiring that parents be present during interrogation and that they be advised of their child's rights to silence and counsel. The failure to involve parents in this way results, as in Colorado and Oklahoma statutes, in the inadmissibility of the confession at trial.

In the absence of this type of statute, most appellate courts have adopted the "totality of the circumstances" rule as to police-juvenile interrogation, holding confessions admissible if the juvenile is viewed as mature enough or sophisticated enough from prior contact with the police or court system to be able to intelligently waive his constitutional protections and enter an admission to the offense. A small number of states have held otherwise, concluding that a minor, regardless of maturity or sophistication, lacks the legal capacity to forgo his constitutional protections.

This latter view is discussed in the final article. Drawing on the recommendations of the Institute of Judicial Administration-American Bar Association Juvenile Justice Standards Project, the author concludes that it is constitutionally necessary to involve parents and counsel to safeguard a juvenile's rights both as to police questioning and police searches. Present police practices would require radical change if this policy were instituted.

11 *Police Control of Juveniles: A Replication*
Richard J. Lundman, Richard E. Sykes, John P. Clark

In 1970, Donald Black and Albert J. Reiss, Jr. presented a series of eight propositions which they suggested provided "the beginning of an empirical portrait of the policing of juveniles" (Black and Reiss, 1970:76). The propositions were as follows:

Reprinted, with permission of the National Council on Crime and Delinquency, from Richard J. Lundman, Richard E. Sykes, and John P. Clark, "Police Control of Juveniles: A Replication," *Journal of Research in Crime and Delinquency,* January 1978, pp. 74–91.

1. Most police encounters with juveniles arise in direct response to citizens who take the initiative to mobilize the police to action.
2. The great bulk of police encounters with juveniles pertain to matters of minor legal significance.
3. The probability of sanction by arrest is very low for juveniles who have encounters with the police.
4. The probability of arrest increases with the legal seriousness of alleged juvenile offenses, as that legal seriousness is defined in criminal law for adults.
5. Police sanctioning of juveniles strongly reflects the manifest preferences of citizen complainants in field encounters.
6. The arrest rate for Negro juveniles is higher than that for white juveveniles, but evidence that the police behaviorally orient themselves to race as such is absent.
7. The presence of situational evidence linking a juvenile to a deviant act is an important factor in the probability of arrest.
8. The probability of arrest is higher for juveniles who are unusually respectful toward the police and for those who are unusually disrespectful.

Black and Reiss also noted that these propositions adumbrate a general theory of social control.

As compared to other studies of this type (Goldman, 1963; Piliavin and Briar, 1964; Werthman and Piliavin, 1967; Terry, 1967; Wilson, 1968), Black and Reiss studied police work with juveniles in three large metropolitan areas[1] and utilized qualitative as well as quantitative data collection techniques. As a consequence, their sample was comparatively large and representative and their analysis extensive. Moreover, the impact of their findings was increased by their publication in one of the more prestigious and widely read of the sociological journals. Finally, study of the Social Science Citation Index reveals that their article received the greatest number of independent citations. Thus, in the four years following publication, Black and Reiss were cited three times more frequently than Piliavin and Briar (1964) and six times more frequently than Terry (1967).

As is true of all studies, however, a fundamental question which must be asked is to what extent are the data and interpretations advanced by Black and Reiss generalizable? That is, to what extent do their findings apply to police-juvenile encounters occurring in cities other than Boston, Chicago, and Washington, D.C., and to periods other than the summer of 1966?

To answer these and other questions, replication data are necessary. Replication increases confidence in research findings and furthers the cumulative nature of sociology (Selltiz et al, 1965; Denzin, 1970). Specifically, only with replication data can we be confident that Black and Reiss have, in fact, sketched the beginning of an empirical portrait of the policing of juveniles and adumbrated a general theory of social control.

The central aim of the present study, therefore, is to examine the extent to which the Black and Reiss findings hold for police-juvenile encounters occurring in a large midwestern city, 1970–71.

METHOD

During a fifteen-month period beginning in June 1970, we conducted a participant-as-observer study of police-citizen encounters in a midwestern city of more than 500,000 located in a SMSA [Standard Metropolitan Statistical Area] of over 2,000,000. A group of seven observers, trained over three months, traveled with police on a random-time sample basis, using portable electronic coding equipment and an interaction process code. Without prior notice, observers appeared at a precinct station to ride in a randomly selected patrol car for a full shift. Which car they were to ride in was not known to the police in advance.

The data base consists of 2,835 *potential* police-citizen contacts. When such contacts involved police-citizen interaction, they were defined as encounters (n = 1,978 involving about 9,000 citizens), and the interaction was simultaneously and sequentially content analyzed and coded using the portable equipment. Among the situational factors coded were whether the encounter was initiated by the police or the citizen, the purpose of the call, the kind of space in which the activity occurred, and whether there was conflict between citizens when the officers arrived. The nature of the interaction was measured by a variety of action and interaction codes pertaining to civility and incivility, giving and following orders, and displays of anger; and codes relating to specific kinds of violence, aggressive threats, or acts. The specific outcome of the encounter was also coded. Demographic data were collected from visual and audial observation and coded for complainant, victim, alleged violator, participants, and bystanders. Interobserver reliability was calculated utilizing Scott's II (Scott, 1955; Krippendorf, 1970), and the coefficient for codes reported herein ranged between .70 and .80.

To isolate police-juvenile encounters from other activities, the calls selected for analysis in this study met the following two criteria: (1) An alleged violator was present, and (2) the alleged violator was under eighteen years of age. Of the 1,978 encounters, 200 or approximately 10 percent met these criteria.

ANALYSIS AND RESULTS

In order to facilitate comparison of our findings with those of Black and Reiss, we will follow the format established in the earlier paper. Consequently, we will compare our results with the earlier findings in the following areas: (1) detection of juvenile deviance, (2) seriousness of juvenile deviance, (3) arrest rates, (4) legal seriousness and arrest, (5) citizen preference and arrest, (6) race and arrest, (7) evidence and arrest, and (8) demeanor and arrest.

DETECTION OF JUVENILE DEVIANCE

Of the 281 encounters observed by Black and Reiss, 72 percent were citizen initiated and 28 percent were initiated by the police while in patrol. Excluding traffic violations, the proportions become 78 percent and 22 percent, respectively. As a consequence, Black and Reiss concluded that most deviant acts by juveniles are detected by citizens rather than the police.

Of the 200 encounters we observed, 52 percent were *police* initiated and 48 percent were initiated by citizens. Excluding traffic violations, the proportions become 34 percent and 66 percent respectively. What accounts for these differences is that the police department of the city we studied maintained a monthly traffic ticket quota system for patrol officers, thereby forcing patrol officers to become more proactive.[2]

It is necessary, therefore, to modify Black's and Reiss's conclusion since departmental policy, as well as the moral standards of the citizens, (Black and Reiss, 1970:66), determines the detection of juvenile deviance. This modification is as follows: *(1) Police have the capacity to change the ratios of police-and citizen-initiated encounters by becoming more proactive; (2) therefore, the ratios of police- and citizen-initiated encounters are dependent upon departmental policy.*

SERIOUSNESS OF JUVENILE DEVIANCE

The Black and Reiss data reveal that only a minority of police-juvenile transactions involved alleged felonies. For both black and white juveniles, nearly two-thirds of the encounters observed involved nothing more serious than juvenile rowdiness. They note, however, that, compared to white juveniles, there was a greater tendency for black juveniles to be involved in alleged felonies. Finally, they note that their data do not contain evidence of differential police selection by reference to race.

Our data are essentially supportive of these findings. First, only a minority of the juveniles we observed were involved in alleged felony encounters. Although more of our encounters revolved around alleged felonies than those observed by Black and Reiss, it remains that the great bulk of police encounters with juveniles pertain to matters of minor legal significance.

Second, our data are also supportive of the earlier finding that black juveniles are more frequently involved in alleged felony encounters than white juveniles. Specifically, our data, as compared to those of Black and Reiss, show an even greater rate of involvement of minority juveniles in alleged felony transactions. This is the case for both citizen- and police-initiated encounters, but the differences between the two data bases is especially clear when one examines citizen-initiated encounters.

Finally, there is also support for the earlier observation that there is no evidence of police selection of juveniles for involvement in encounters by reference to race. Based upon our data, it is clear that involvement of minority juveniles is much more frequent in citizen- than police-initiated encounters. Although these data do not speak directly to the issue of racial discrimination by the police, it does appear that Black's and Reiss's conclusion of an absence of evidence of discrimination is warranted.

Because of the essentially supportive nature of our data, it appears appropriate to suggest two subpropositions descriptive of the seriousness of juvenile deviance. They are: *(1) As compared to white juveniles, black juveniles are more frequently involved in alleged felony encounters; and (2) the greater involvement of black juveniles in alleged felony encounters does not appear to be attributable to police discrimination.*

ARREST RATES

Of the encounters observed by Black and Reiss, only 15 percent ended in arrest. They note that the remaining 85 percent of the cases typically are not included in official delinquency statistics. And, since many juvenile offenses are never detected by citizens (see Williams and Gold, 1972), and of those which are detected, only a minority are reported to the police (Ennis, 1967), it is clear that police statistics significantly underestimate the total volume of juvenile deviance.

Of the 200 encounters we observed, only 16 percent ended in arrest. The juveniles involved in the 84 percent of the encounters which ended without an arrest were, in effect, diverted from the juvenile justice system. Therefore, it seems reasonable to note: *Police diversion of juveniles from the juvenile justice system is a common practice.*

LEGAL SERIOUSNESS AND ARREST

Black and Reiss note that since only 15 percent of the encounters they observed ended in arrest, a "high level of selectivity enters into the arrest of juveniles" (1970:68). As a consequence, they undertake an extended analysis of the factors which influence police exercise of discretion.

The first of the variables they examined in relation to arrest was the legal seriousness of the alleged offense. They found that nearly three-fourths of the alleged felony encounters ended in an arrest, as compared to less than 15 percent of the rowdiness encounters and none of the noncriminal dispute encounters. They concluded that the probability of arrest increases with the legal seriousness of the alleged offense.

Our replication data are supportive of this conclusion. Thus, all of the alleged felony encounters we observed ended in an attempted or actual arrest, as compared to less than 5 percent of the rowdiness encounters and none of the noncriminal dispute encounters. Thus, the Black and Reiss conclusion that legal seriousness is among the factors which influence police exercise of arrest discretion is supported.

CITIZEN PREFERENCE AND ARREST

A second set of factors examined by Black and Reiss was the relationship between the presence of citizen complainants and police exercise of arrest discretion. Black and Reiss reasoned that citizen complainants exert an important influence on police officers by their mere presence. Moreover, they reasoned that certain complainants may prefer arrest and that this preference increases the probability that the encounter will end in arrest.

Their data were supportive of both observations. Thus, encounters where only a suspect was present ended in arrest less frequently than encounters where a suspect and complainant were both present. And, in those encounters where it was possible to determine citizen preference, it was clear that when complainants preferred arrest, the probability of arrest was significantly greater than when complainants preferred an informal disposition.

Our data confirm these earlier findings. Thus, encounters where a suspect and complainant were both present ended more frequently in arrest than encounters where only a suspect was present. And, in those encounters where it was possible to determine citizen preference, the officers we observed complied with citizen preferences in every situation in which preference was made manifest. As a consequence, there is no reason to modify the basic Black and Reiss conclusion that police exercise of arrest discretion is influenced by complainant preferences.

It does appear reasonable, however, to add to this conclusion. As Black and Reiss indicate (1970:72), these data suggest that citizens, rather than the police, determine the total volume of official delinquency. In addition to citizens' exercise of discretion in the context of calling the police about a delinquent act they have witnessed, in their roles as complainants, citizens influence arrest rates by their willingness to remain at the scene of an offense until the police arrive and by making thier dispositional preferences manifest. We would add the following subproposition: *Citizens, therefore, largely determine official delinquency rates.*

RACE AND ARREST

A number of studies both before and after the Black and Reiss study have considered the relationship between race and arrest. Piliavin and Briar (1964), for example, reported that with offense held constant, black juveniles were arrested more frequently than white juveniles. Wilson (1968) reached an essentially similar conclusion for the eastern city he examined. In one sense, then, the Black and Reiss conclusion of an absence of evidence of discrimination in the context of arrests stands as something of an exception when compared to other studies.

Black and Reiss base their conclusion on a number of interrelated observations. They note, first, that encounters involving black suspects more frequently contained (black) complainants than encounters involving white suspects. Second, they note that black complainants more frequently lobby for arrest of black suspects than white complainants involved in encounters with white suspects. Finally, they note that the police officers they observed complied more frequently with the arrest preferences of black complainants. Put simply, it is their argument that black complainants account for the higher rate of arrest of black juveniles.

Our data are supportive of these observations. Thus, in the encounters we observed, more of the black suspect than white suspect encounters involved complainants. Moreover, it was also the case that more black than white complainants lobbied for formal police action. Finally, police compliance with the arrest preferences of black complainants was also perfect. For these reasons, we concur with the Black and Reiss conclusion that there is no evidence that the police are behaviorally oriented to the race of juvenile subjects. *Instead it would appear that the higher rate of arrest for black juveniles is attributable to black complainants who lobby for formal police action.*

SITUATIONAL EVIDENCE AND ARREST

Black and Reiss note that another variable that should affect the probability of arrest is the nature of the evidence present in the situation. They examined the impact of evidence on arrest decision; . . . encounters wherein a citizen linked a juvenile to an offense ended in arrest most frequently. Police-witness encounters occupied an intermediate position, while only one of the no-evidence encounters ended in an arrest. As a consequence, Black and Reiss emphasize the importance of situational evidence in police arrest decisions.

Our data, with the exception of no-evidence encounters, are essentially similar. Citizen testimony encounters ended in arrest more frequently than police witness encounters. Therefore, our data are supportive of the emphasis given the importance of situational evidence.

Our data, however, do not support the finding of a low rate of arrest in no-evidence encounters. Specifically, white suspect, no-evidence encounters ended in arrest more frequently than comparable citizen testimony or police witness encounters. Additional analysis revealed an explanation: A minority of the white suspects involved in these encounters were unusually respectful or disrespectful in their interactions with the police.

As a consequence, it appears necessary to offer the following by way of clarification: *In no-evidence encounters, the demeanor of the juvenile is the most important determinant of whether or not formal action is taken.*

DEMEANOR AND ARREST

A number of studies both before (Piliavin and Briar, 1964) and after (Lundman, 1974) the one being replicated here have considered the relationships between citizen demeanor and police arrest decisions. And, as in the case with the Black and Reiss study, most have discovered that the probability of arrest increases with level of disrespect. Once again, though, Black and Reiss are unique in reporting higher rates of arrest for unusually respectful juveniles.

Our data are supportive of *both* observations. Thus, black and white juveniles who were antagonistic were arrested more frequently than juveniles who were civil. However, for white juveniles, the bipolar pattern reported by Black and Reiss holds for our data also. Thus, white suspects who were very deferential in their interaction with the police were also arrested more frequently than antagonistic juveniles. The small number of very deferential black suspects precludes meaningful comparison.

We would also agree with the explanation by Black and Reiss of this phenomenon. As the data from both studies make clear, the majority of police encounters with juveniles are civil. Only a minority of these juveniles are antagonistic in their interaction with the police and an even smaller group are very deferential. In one sense, deferential juveniles are suspicious because their demeanor is so clearly different from that of their colleagues. In another sense, their extreme deference is illogical or inappropriate given the circumstances in which it is expressed. Therefore: *The higher rate of arrest of very deferential juveniles may be explainable by reference to the suspicions their demeanor arouses among police patrol officers.* We agree with Black and Reiss however, that "a good deal more research is needed pertaining to the relations between situational etiquette and sanctioning" (1970:75).

OVERVIEW

We have in this paper replicated the research of Donald Black and Albert J. Reiss in the area of police control of juveniles. Based upon comparative data separated by four years and many miles, we found, in general, that our data were supportive of their earlier conclusions. We have, however, also offered a number of subpropositions, clarifications, and extensions of their basic findings. They, along with the propositions advanced by Black and Reiss and supported by us, can be summarized as follows:

1. Most police encounters with juveniles arise in direct response to citizens who take the initiative to mobilize the police to action.
   a. However, police have the capacity to change the ratios of police- and citizen-initiated encounters by becoming more proactive.
   b. Therefore, the ratios of police- and citizen-initiated encounters are dependent upon departmental policy.
2. The great bulk of police encounters with juveniles pertain to matters of minor legal significance.
   a. As compared to white juveniles, black juveniles are more frequently involved in alleged felony encounters.
   b. The greater involvement of black juveniles in alleged felony encounters does not appear to be attributable to police discrimination.
3. The probability of sanction by arrest is very low for juveniles who have encounters with the police.
   a. Police diversion of juveniles from the juvenile justice system is a common practice.
4. The probability of arrest increases with the legal seriousness of alleged juvenile offenses, as that legal seriousness is defined in criminal law for adults.
5. Police sanctioning of juveniles strongly reflects the manifest preferences of citizen complainants in field encounters.
   a. Citizens, therefore, largely determine official delinquency rates.
6. The arrest rate for Negro juveniles is higher than that for white juveniles, but evidence that the police behaviorly orient themselves to race as such is absent.

    a. Instead, it would appear that the higher arrest rate of black juveniles is attributable to the more frequent presence of black complainants who lobby for formal police action.

7. The presence of situational evidence linking a juvenile to a deviant act is an important factor in the probability of arrest.

    a. In encounters where there is no evidence linking a juvenile to an offense, the demeanor of the juvenile is the most important determinant of whether or not formal action is taken.

8. The probability of arrest is higher for juveniles who are unusually respectful toward the police and for those who are unusually disrespectful.

    a. The higher rate of arrest of very deferential juveniles may be explainable by reference to the suspicions their demeanor arouses among police patrol officers.

We would draw a number of implications from these findings.

First, it would appear that we now have more than the beginning of an empirical portrait of police control of juveniles. Although additional research would clearly be beneficial, the essentially supportive nature of our efforts suggests a remarkable uniformity insofar as police control of juveniles is concerned. It appears to us, therefore, that we now have a relatively clear understanding of the factors which determine police actions toward juvenile suspects.

Second, we would also agree with Black and Reiss that at some point empirical research must inform theory. And, we see these researches as speaking most directly to the labeling perspective. At the time Black and Reiss wrote, this perspective was still in the ascendency and their data were supportive of basis labeling assertions, including Becker's that "deviant behavior is behavior that people so label" (1963:9).

Since 1970, however, many students of social deviance have become disenchanted with labeling theory. Liazos (1972), for example, suggested that proponents of the labeling perspective have ignored overt institutional violence, while Thio (1973) asserted that labeling theorists are biased in favor of elites. Moreover, recent research has indicated that labeling may not be as consequential as originally indicated. Specifically, there are now reasons to believe that deviant careers do not necessarily nor even frequently follow the labeling (Foster et al., 1972; Fisher, 1972). As a consequence, some have asserted that the labeling perspective has exhausted its initial promise (Manning, 1973).

We believe, as did Black and Reiss, that our data point to a fundamental contribution of the labeling perspective. Namely, that professional labeling is at least as much a function of the situational contingencies surrounding a rule-violative act as the act itself. Thus, whether or not a juvenile is sanctioned for a delinquent act depends at least as much on who detected the act, whether a complainant is present, the complainant's preference, and the demeanor of the alleged violator as on the nature of the alleged offense. To ignore this labeling insight in favor of a return to more traditional perspectives (Manning, 1973) or an exclusive focus on elites (Taylor et al., 1973) is to ignore a fundamental contribution of the labeling perspective.

Finally, we, as was the case with Black and Reiss, are unable to precisely determine the extent to which these specific findings might apply to other instances of lay and professional labeling. Paraphrasing Black and Reiss, we are uncertain as to the ways in which these findings might apply to transactions between a mate and a residually deviant spouse or physician and an addicted colleague.

However, evidence from other sources suggests that the situational contingencies surrounding a rule-violative act play an important role in many instances of lay and professional labeling.[3] Study of the process whereby persons become mental patients, for instance, suggests that acquisition of patient status is a "socially structured event" rather than the "direct outcome of mental illness" (Sampson et al., 1962:88). Additionally, comparison of the experiences of skid-row excessive drinkers (Spradley, 1970) with those elite excessive drinkers (Roman, 1974) indicates that the probabilities of labeling, arrest, or involuntary treatment vary directly with resources and power of the drinker. Similar differences exist when one compares the experiences of street-level drug addicts (Waldorf, 1973), with those of physician addicts (Hessler, 1974).

Therefore, the studies cited along with our replication of the Black and Reiss data yield a single general conclusion: *Labeling as deviant is at least as much a function of the circumstances surrounding a rule-violative act as the act itself.*

REFERENCES

BECKER, H. S.   1963, *Outsiders: Studies in the Sociology of Deviance*. New York: Free Press.

BLACK, D., and A. J. REISS, JR.   1970, "Police Control of Juveniles." *American Sociological Review* 35 (February): 63–77.

DENZIN, N.   1970, *The Research Act*. Chicago: Aldine.

ELLIS, P.   1967, *"Crime, Victims, and the Police."* Trans-Action (June): 36–44.

FISHER, S.   1972, "Stigma and Deviant Careers in School." *Social Problems* (Summer): 78–83.

FOSTER, J. D., S. DINITZ, and W. C. RECKLESS   1972, "Perceptions of Stigma Following Public Intervention for Delinquent Behavior." *Social Problems* (Fall): 202–209.

GOLDMAN, N.   1963, *The Differential Selection of Juvenile Offenders for Court Appearance*. Washington, D.C.: National Council on Crime and Delinquency.

HESSLER, R. M.   1974, "Junkies in White: Drug Addiction among Physicians." In *Deviant Behavior*, Clifton D. Bryant, ed. Chicago: Rand McNally.

KRIPPENDORF, K.   1970, "Bivariate Agreement Coefficients for Reliability of Data." In *Sociological Methodology*, Ernest Borgotta and George Bornsted, eds. San Francisco: Jossey-Bass.

LIAZOS, A.   1972, "The Poverty of the Sociology of Deviance: Nuts, Sluts, and 'Preverts.'" *Social Problems* (Summer): 103–120.

LUNDMAN, R. J.   1974, "Routine Police Arrest Practices: A Commonweal Perspective." *Social Problems* (Fall): 127–141.

————   1979, "Police Work with Traffic Law Violators." In *Police Behavior: A Sociological Perspective*, Richard J. Lundman, ed. Chicago: Rand McNally.

MANNING, P. K.   1973, "Survey Essay on Deviance." *Contemporary Sociology* (March): 123–128.

PILIAVIN, I., and S. BRIAR 1964, "Police Encounters with Juveniles." *American Journal of Sociology* (September): 206–214.

ROMAN, P. R. 1974, "Settings for Successful Deviance: Drinking and Deviant Drinking among Middle- and Upper-Level Employees." In *Deviant Behavior.* Clifton Bryant, ed. Chicago: Rand McNally.

SAMPSON, H., S. L. MESSINGER, and R. D. TOWNE 1962, "Family Process and Becoming a Mental Patient." *American Journal of Sociology* (July): 88–98.

SCOTT, W. A. 1955, "Reliability of Content Analysis: The Case of Nominal Scale Coding." *Public Opinion Quarterly* (Fall): 321–325.

SELLTIZ, C., M. JOHODA, M. DEUTSCH, and S. COOK 1965, *Research Methods in Social Relations.* New York: Holt.

SPRADLEY, J. 1970, *You Owe Yourself a Drunk.* Boston: Little, Brown.

TAYLOR, I., P. WALTON, and J. YOUNG 1973, *The New Criminology.* New York: Harper and Row.

TERRY, R. 1967, "The Screening of Juvenile Offenders." *Journal of Criminal Law, Criminology and Police Science* 58: 173–181.

THIO, A. 1973, "Class Bias in the Sociology of Deviance." *American Sociologist* (February): 1–12.

WALDORF, D. 1973, *Careers in Dope.* Englewood Cliffs, N.J.: Prentice-Hall.

WERTHMAN, C. and I. PILIAVIN 1967, "Gang Members and the Police." In *The Police,* David J. Bordua, ed. New York: John Wiley.

WILLIAMS, J. R., and M. GOLD 1972, "From Delinquent Behavior to Official Delinquency." *Social Problems* (Fall): 209–229.

WILSON, J. Q. 1968, "The Police and the Delinquent in Two Cities." In *Controlling Delinquents,* Stanton Wheeler, ed. New York: John Wiley.

NOTES

1. The sites were Boston, Chicago, and Washington, D.C.
2. For a discussion of the traffic ticket quota system in operation, see Lundman (1979).
3. The authors are grateful to an anonymous reviewer for suggesting this point.

12 Pivotal Ingredients of Police Juvenile Diversion Programs

Malcolm W. Klein and Kathie S. Teilmann

As part of an extensive program of research on police diversion of juvenile offenders, the "Pivotal Ingredients" project was formulated to provide information not otherwise being gathered on the enforcement end of the diversion process. Our other

National Institute for Juvenile Justice and Delinquency Prevention, Office of Juvenile Justice and Delinquency Prevention, Law Enforcement Assistance Administration, U.S. Department of Justice (Washington, D.C. Government Printing Office, 1977). Reprinted by permission.

research support has concentrated more on the diverted offenders and on the community agencies to which many offenders are referred for treatment. The importance of quickly gathering data on the impact of these programs lies in the rapidity with which they are literally exploding in numbers across the nation, with minimal proof of their utility.

In a paper prepared during the project year, it was suggested that between 150 and 200 diversion projects are currently active in California alone and that they are annually increasing in numbers in a straight, linear fashion. Yet there is still limited evidence concerning diversion impacts on the justice systems agencies, and the various offender populations.

The "Pivotal Ingredients" project intended to raise four major questions:

1. How do police diversion programs develop, and how do the several patterns of development relate to success in program establishment and changes in police roles and organizational structures;
2. How can we best interpret *reported* referral rates from diversion programs and distinguish between their various components so as to derive more comparable cross-program criteria for impact evaluation;
3. What are the relationships between departmental diversion rates and referral rates, and what are the recorded characteristics of diverted vs. referred youngsters; and
4. What modifications in recommendations derived from evaluated diversion projects must be suggested because of the very nature of *evaluated* (and therefore atypical) projects?

The relevant data were gathered in two major phases and were buttressed via numerous informal conversations and observations in police departments and community agencies. The first major phase involved an interview with the juvenile officer or other individual charged with diversion/referral responsibilities in each of 35 police departments, as well as in eight divisions of the Los Angeles Police Department (LAPD). These interviews were pertinent primarily to aims one and four above. Predetermined, open-ended questions were asked in eight areas:

1. Structure of the program (who does what, where, and why?);
2. Police perception of referral agencies in the community (choice criteria, contacts, complaints, etc.);
3. Goals and purposes of the program;
4. Historical development of program (where initiated and developed, funding sources, conflicts);
5. Changes in police department structure;
6. Community involvement (past, present, and changes);
7. Impact of evaluators on program;
8. Involvement of administration in the program (closed-end questions — importance of success, pressure, time spent, etc.)

Each interview was coded twice. The two coded versions were checked for discrepancies that were resolved in group meetings. The data were then key-punched for computer analysis.

The second major phase involved the collection of data from 100 randomly selected case files in 33 of the above 35 cities (the two omitted cities had information systems not capable, at the time, of yielding the case samples). The data from these three thousand or so case files were extracted, coded, and prepared for computer handling to deal with issues raised under aims two and three above. A few of the cities yielded less than 100 arrest cases during the three month data collection period.

AIM ONE: DEVELOPMENT

The processes by which police diversion projects developed were complex and almost irretrievable as historical events. There are two reasons for this: first, diversion projects range from highly structured, formal arrangements to very informal operations, and these latter in particular tend to be natural outgrowths of prior activities with no clear point of differentiation; second, current project personnel often were hired or transferred into the project after its initiation and cannot serve as adequate sources of historical data.

As an example, the current status of diversion in the Los Angeles Police Department properly should be referred to administrative changes in the Juvenile Bureau in the late 1960s, changes whose reverberations are still traceable today. Each of these reverberations since the abandonment of the large, centralized operation of the 1960s could be cited as the initiator of the current program; the choice would be arbitrary.

By way of contrast, the extensive diversion program in the Los Angeles Sheriff's Department (LASD) has clear points of progress. These include a particular discussion between an initiating outside agency and an Assistant Sheriff, a decision to launch a one-station pilot program in 1970, a decision following that pilot program to expand to other stations and add a central staffing capability, and a plan (later successful) to obtain a major grant to evaluate diversion by establishing a controlled field experiment in nine stations.

As it happens, the contrast between the situations in these two very large departments mirrors that in the others involved in this research, in that the source of initiation (inside or outside the department) is one of several important, interacting variables. Also, it happens that the pattern illustrated above is reversed in the other departments, as we shall report.

In addition to time spent in various ways with the LAPD and LASD, we interviewed diversion personnel in 35 suburban departments which were confirmed as having diversion programs. One of these interviews yielded no usable information. In the other 34, we found eight unfunded programs being run informally on deparmental budgets, 15 programs funded by LEAA money via the regional criminal justice planning agency, and 11 others funded either by the California Youth Authority with "probation subsidy" money or by the city budget in a special appropriation. In other words, federal money is behind almost half of these programs, state money behind about a half dozen others, city money behind a few more and, in eight cases, no special money at all. So far as the departments are concerned, most are doing diversion because someone else wants them to.

In the course of the interviewing, it became clear that there are a number of different structural types of diversion programs.[1] The most basic difference between them, both philosophically and structurally, was the distinction between *inhouse programs* and *outside referral programs.* That is, some departments took on an inhouse counseling staff while others used community-based agencies as referral resources. On both sides of this dimension there were departments which felt strongly that their approach was the more appropriate. This development, in addition to our original intention to explore the interrelations among historical, structural, and attitudinal factors, led us to make a series of cross-tabulations among all variables judged to fall under each of these categories. The results were clear and strong.

First, as might be expected, inhouse programs are positively associated with the structural additions of new divisions or details and new staff. Not so obviously, inhouse programs are positively associated with initiation of the program from inside the department. Conversely, programs using outside referrals were more likely to have remained structurally unchanged and were more likely to have been initiated from the outside — usually by a state planning agency.

Second, inside initiation and inside development of the program are associated with structural changes and with having a period of civic funding, or no funding at all, at some point in in the program's history. . . .

The composite picture so far, then, is one set of programs that were self-initiated and developed, that were operating without funds or with civic funding for a period of time, that have added staff, and that have an inhouse counseling arrangement. Another set of programs, initiated and developed with the help of outside agencies (usually the state planning agency), have always operated on outside government funding, have made no structural changes, and refer offenders to outside counseling agencies.

Perhaps more interesting, these historical and structural variables were found to be closely associated with certain attitudinal variables [which] seem to represent a dimension of optimism versus pessimism about the program and its effects, including prospects for changing the crime rate, confidence in counselors, and possible effects on public relations. Clearly, optimism is associated with the inhouse programs and pessimism with the outside referral programs.

Although there are some departments that have self-initiated, self-developed, self-funded programs that have resulted in structural changes in the department — in short, a group of "committed" practitioners of diversion and referral — there are more who cannot be so described. This latter group, making up a substantial proportion of the recent "explosion," has been induced from the outside to begin programs about which they are not especially optimistic. From our informal contacts and from data inferences, it is clear that the inducement is government money. The question immediately arises: what happens when federal money is withdrawn, as it inevitably will be? Does diversion become a thing of the past? Probably not for the self-initiated programs that are clearly operated by juvenile officers committed to diversion. However, it is just as clear at this point that the government-initiated programs will probably die unless something is done to change the attitudes of those officers.

In line with this last remark, it is appropriate to note that, in general, the government-funded projects started more recently than the self-initiated ones. It is possible that there has not been time for the officers in these programs to see positive results and therefore become convinced of the merits of diversion. The opposite possibility is, of course, equally possible. It might be advisable for the state planners to turn their attention to this problem. Succinctly put, funders must face the fact that rationales and commitment behind funding and planning at an administrative level do not necessarily filter down to the operating level of the juvenile officer.

AIM FOUR: EVALUATION

Although out of numbered sequence here, the materials on Aim Four appropriately follow those of Aim One. The basic question is whether or not the presence of an evaluation component in a diversion project sufficiently alters the project to invalidate generalizations derived from the results of that project. The question was to be approached in two ways, through interviews with police personnel and through interviews with independent project evaluators.

That an evaluation can have some impact is clear from the experience with the experimental diversion project in the Los Angeles Sheriff's Department. The use of an experimental design and an independent university evaluator in that project led to unusual care in designating referrable youngsters, a slight increase in paper work, and greater attention to referral follow-ups. On the other hand, data collected during the project revealed that the offenders selected did not differ very appreciably from offenders referred prior to the project. That is, internal or procedural impacts seemed to have little effect on the offender selection process (Klein, 1975).

Turning to the interviews in 34 other cities, we find that seven of our police respondents had *no* knowlege of any evaluation while 10 had detailed knowledge. The other 17 could be classified as being aware of the existence of some evaluation but not particularly knowledgeable about its nature or impact. On this score, the research team turned out to be more knowledgeable than the respondents, for we were able to document some formal or informal evaluation component in 31 of the 34 cities. Thus our original question, does the presence or absence of an evaluation make a difference, became moot. Most programs *were* being evaluated in some fashion.

However, when we recall that only 10 of our respondents were really clear on the nature of the evaluation and seven (one-fifth of the total) knew of no evaluation, we must question how much impact these evaluations are having. After all, our respondents were carrying out the daily procedures of their diversion programs, and could be expected to be aware of changes occasioned by the imposition of evaluation mandates.

If the evaluation/no evaluation contrast is lost to us, we can still investigate the relative impact of *types* of evaluation. We found that 16 of the projects were being evaluated by outside, independent researchers or research teams. In most cases, these projects were funded by LEAA or California Youth Authority funds. Of the 15 inside evaluations — that is evaluations being carried out be department personnel — eight could be characterized as formal, and seven as quite informal. The basic distinction between formal and informal evaluations was whether or not *any* sort of written records on the program were being maintained. This is certainly a minimal statement of evaluation formality and reinforces the impression that these inside evaluations were not likely to have much program impact.

Data from the police interviews were prepared for computer analysis, and comparisons made between ''inside'' and ''outside'' evaluation sites on all interview items thought likely to reflect the impact of evaluation. It was expected that the outside or independent evaluations would have the greater impact on program procedures. But with one exception, we found absolutely no differences between projects with inside and outside evaluations.

The locus of evaluation made no difference in level of supervision, selection criteria, feedback procedures, or any other of the 21 variables investigated in the interview responses. The one exception was the tendency for projects with outside evaluators to select offenders who had one or two prior offenses rather than none. But other than this, no differences emerged.

Anyone experienced in action research knows that there is an intimate relationship that develops between the program and evaluation components of a project, each being affected by the other, occasionally quite profoundly. Not so in these diversion projects. Here, the salience of the evaluations has been low, their contribution to the projects quite negligible, and the financial and professional investment in them seemingly equally low.

This does not speak well for the evaluations, nor for the seriousness with which they have been solicited. It does not augur well for what we may learn from these projects. On the other hand, from the point of view of *our* question, it does suggest that fair generalizations from these 30 or more projects *can* be made without concern for their having been ''contaminated'' by obtrusive research procedures. We seem to be reviewing ''natural'' projects, relatively unaffected by the requirements of research evaluation.

Having reached this conclusion some time prior to the writing of this report and during the time when we were expanding the data collection for Aims Two and Three, we questioned whether interviews with the independent evaluators would be a profitable use of our funds. A pilot interview with one evaluator was carried out, but yielded an unsatisfactory level of information; our procedures clearly were not eliciting what we thought might be available. It was decided *not* to commit ourselves to a series of further extensive interviews without first testing further their likely utility.

Accordingly, phone calls were made to two of the potential interviewees. The first reported that while the impact of his evaluation was great on the resource agencies in the community, it was to all intents and purposes nonexistent on the several police departments with which it was concerned. There were no changes in attitude, structure, paperwork, or selection criteria.

The second phone call revealed that the "independent evaluator" had in fact been a graduate student whose dissertation was the diversion project. He initiated the program, did the referring, and evaluated his own success. When the dissertation was completed, so was the diversion. Again, we have a low-impact case.

Given these experiences and our conclusions that the various evaluations were of such little impact to our police respondents, we abandoned the plans for further interviews with evaluators. They could only have confirmed further the lack of connection between the diversion projects and efforts at evaluation. As noted, in an earlier progress report, the bulk — though not all — of the evaluations we encountered were not well formulated, were minimal and often self-serving for the department, and were not designed to reveal possible negative results. Consequently, the evaluation which *could* make a difference would have to be exceptional.

AIMS TWO AND THREE: DISPOSITION RATES

During the course of the project, some minor modifications of Aims Two and Three were made, so that these concerns were narrowed to two basic questions:

1. What proportions of arrested juveniles are given certain post-arrest dispositions by the police an how do these vary across departments? Obviously our main interest here is in the proportions of offenders referred to community agencies.
2. What characteristics of the juveniles and of their offense charges are related to the major disposition categories? This second question, for policy-related purposes, might be recast to ascertain whether referred juveniles are coming more from a pool of youngsters ordinarily counseled and released or more from a pool of youngsters ordinarily subject to the filing of petitions with the court.

Table 12-1 presents the overall data on 3,025 case dispositions of juveniles arrested in 33 cities in January, February, and March 1975. The proportion released (with or without referral) approximates the oft-cited national average of around 50 percent. The referral rate of about eight percent is far greater than it was in 1970 when an estimate greater than one percent might have been generous. Referral, in this instance, definitely means a referral to a community agency, usually private, and corresponds to what is mistakenly called "diversion" by many of the programs involved. Thus, two corollary conclusions might be drawn thus far: (a) *over the past five years, referral rates have increased substantially and (b) due to the low initial rates, the current increase has not substantially affected release or petition rates* over all departments.

Table 12-2 presents the disposition data for the 33 departments separately. To simplify reading, only the percentages are reported, and these only for the four dispositions of major interest in this report.

Table 12-2 reveals a good bit of variability in departmental practices. Counsel and release rates vary from a low of 11 percent to a high of 74 percent. Referral rates

TABLE 12-1   Disposition Rates Over 33 Cities

	n	%
Counsel and Release	1,384	45.8
Community Referral	246	8.1
Other J.J. System Referral *	259	8.6
Nondetain Petition	574	19.0
Detain Petition	334	11.0
Other	228	7.5
Total	3,025	100%

*Usually other police departments, or probation or parole officers

TABLE 12-2   Disposition Rates for Each Department

DEPT.*	COUNSEL & RELEASE	REFERRAL	NONDETAIN PETITION	DETAIN PETITION
01	49.0	7.0	16.0	9.0
02	62.2	10.2	10.2	6.1
05	48.0	6.0	5.0	4.0
06	11.0	24.0	32.0	17.0
07	40.2	2.3	20.7	20.7
08	40.2	13.0	19.6	10.9
09	49.1	0.0	5.3	3.5
11	48.0	4.0	13.0	17.0
14	46.0	6.0	17.0	17.0
15	34.3	0.0	53.5	11.1
16	27.2	3.0	0.0	17.0
17	57.8	3.1	12.5	23.4
18	43.0	0.0	21.0	14.0
19	33.7	13.3	32.7	13.3
20	26.0	8.0	44.0	6.0
21	74.0	3.0	8.0	9.0
22	68.1	0.0	5.8	7.2
23	49.0	0.0	21.0	16.0
24	48.0	16.0	15.0	14.0
26	25.0	22.8	2.2	6.5
27	59.0	2.0	18.0	9.0
29	59.0	0.0	24.0	9.0
31	55.6	9.1	11.1	11.1
32	34.0	18.0	27.0	2.0
33	37.0	12.0	29.0	14.0
34	64.7	5.9	20.6	2.9
35	34.0	14.4	17.5	2.4
37	59.0	9.0	12.0	10.0
38	57.0	1.0	19.0	14.0
39	39.5	18.4	26.3	10.5
41	37.6	26.7	7.9	5.9
46	70.0	8.0	14.0	2.0
49	42.0	0.0	38.0	14.0

*Project code numbers for 33 of the 49 departments in L.A. County involved in this report.

(in departments self-labeled as doing referrals) range from zero (seven cases) to 26.7 percent. Nondetain petition rates fall between zero and 53.5 percent, while detain petition rates — those applied to the most serious cases — range from two to 23.4 percent. Earlier attempts to explain such variabilities (Sundeen, 1974; Klein, 1974) have proven fruitless. It is clear, however, that *practice varies widely and this fact itself belies the notion that there is clarity on what should be done with juvenile offenders.*

The question of whether referrals are coming more from the petition pool or from the release pool of offenders can now be addressed, although only tentatively. Looking at the seven departments with *no* referrals, we find that they have a mean counsel and release rate of 49.2 percent, while the middle 19 departments have a release rate of 50.8 percent and the seven departments with the highest referral rates have a mean counsel and release rate of only 32.7 percent. Since the corresponding differences in nondetain petition rates are negligible (19.7, 17.0 and 24.1 percent), *it seems likely that the referrals are primarily being taken from the release pool.*

This finding fits well with what we learned from interviews with the juvenile officers. Their criteria for referral cases, they said, included less serious offenses, cases with few or no prior arrests, younger rather than older offenders, and offenders with a lower estimated probability of rearrest. These are precisely the kinds of cases that commonly receive counsel and release dispositions. If this pattern is continued and confirmed, it would suggest that "true" diversion — turning offenders away from the justice system who would otherwise be inserted into it — has been displaced by the provision of referral and treatment for offenders who otherwise would have been simply released. This latter may or may not be a justifiable activity, but it is not what federal funds were supposed to promote.

To approach this question more directly, we can compare characteristics of referred offenders with those of both released and petitioned offenders. The model for this analysis is presented in Table 12-3 which employs fabricated data as an illustration. Using age as a descriptive variable, the table shows in Column A the case in which 75 percent of released offenders are younger than the median age and 25 percent are over the median age. Similarly, Column C shows percentages for those receiving nondetain petitions, in this case with the percentages reversed because we would expect fewer younger and more older offenders to have petitions filed. We ignore detain-petition offenders in this analysis because these are the most serious cases and would seldom be considered for referral by the police.

TABLE 12-3   Analysis Model

Factor: Age	A Counsel & Release	B_1	B Referred	B_2	C Nondetain Petition
Below Median	75	70		30	25
Above Median	25	30		70	75

The critical question in such a table is whether the data in Column B would resemble those in B_1 or B_2 . Column B_1 shows ages of referred offenders far more similar to those of released offenders suggesting that referral is used as an alternative for ordinarily released offenders; Column B_2 shows ages of referred offenders far more similar to petitioned offenders, suggesting that referral is used as an alternative to insertion further into the justice system. We will apply the model to four factors already known to distinguish consistently between released and inserted offenders: age, sex, number of prior offenses, and seriousness of the instant offense. Hopefully, the four factors will yield a consistent pattern in one direction or the other.

With respect to age, the released and petitioned cases show reversed but not very different patterns (see Table 12-4).[2] However, rather than falling in between these two patterns, the age difference in the referred condition actually exaggerates the release pattern; a higher proportion of referred offenders — five out of eight — are below the median age than is true not only of petitioned offenders but even of released offenders. Referrals are most commonly made among younger offenders.

TABLE 12-4.   Age Patterns in Three Dispositions: Percentages

	COUNSEL & RELEASE	REFERRED	NONDETAIN PETITION
Below Median*	53	63	47
Above Median*	47	37	53

*Median age is 15.4

In all cases, there are more male offenders (see Table 12-5). However, once again the proportions among the referred cases resemble the release proportions more than the petitioned proportions, in fact exceeding the pattern by showing two percent more females, the group generally accorded the more lenient treatment. So far, then, we can say that referred youngsters not only resemble the released ones more, but in fact are even more likely to be young and female.

TABLE 12-5.   Sex Patterns in Three Dispositions: Percentages

	COUNSEL & RELEASE	REFERRED	NONDETAIN PETITION
Female	24	26	11
Male	76	74	89

Regarding the number of prior arrests (see Table 12-6), the referred pattern does fall between the other two as it surprisingly did not in Tables 12-6 and 12-5. However, once again the pattern for referred offenders is more like that of the released than that of the petitioned offenders. Five out of eight referred offenders have no prior record. The trend across the three tables is thus very consistent.

Offense seriousness was measured by use of the Rossi scale (Rossi et. al., 1975), reflecting general popular views of criminal activity. The pattern here is like that for prior records: the referred pattern falls in between the other two but is far closer to that of the release group (see Table 12-7). Thus we can now conclude that *with respect to age, sex, prior record, and seriousness of instant offense, referred offend-*

ers resemble released rather than petitioned offenders and are in all likelihood drawn consistently from the former pool rather than from the latter.

Another way of demonstrating this pattern is to look at it among the seven cities with the highest referral rates (ranging from 14.4 to 26.7 percent). With *four* variables — age, sex, priors, and seriousness — in *seven* cities, we have 28 opportunities to ask whether the referral pattern more closely approximates the release or petition pattern.

TABLE 12-6. Number of Prior Arrests in Three Dispositions: Percentages

	COUNSEL & RELEASE	REFERRED	NONDETAIN PETITION
No Priors	68	63	47
Priors	32	37	53

Of these 28, tied data or unexpected distributions prevent the comparison in nine cases.[3] In the remaining 19 instances, there are 17 in which the referrals approximate or even *exceed* the release pattern, and only two in which they approximate or exceed the petition pattern. In other words, the overall patterns we described above are explicitly and almost uniformly to be found precisely where they should be, in the departments putting out the greatest level of referral effort. It seems clear that to make this effort, the departments are turning to their normally released offenders.

TABLE 12-7. Seriousness of Instant Offense in Three Dispositions: Percentages

	COUNSEL & RELEASE	REFERRED	NONDETAIN PETITION
Below Median	79	71	49
Above Median	21	29	51

As consistent as this pattern is, the strength of the conclusion can be increased by means of a further consideration. The reader may recall that the most serious offenders, those receiving detain petitions, were excluded from this analysis because they are so seldom even considered eligible for community referral. On the other end of the scale there is a similar group of *very* minor cases — sometimes called "Mickey Mouse" cases — that police officers are equally reticent to refer. A stereotype of such a case would be the ten-year-old daughter of a physician arrested for the first time by a patrol officer who spotted her on school grounds after curfew.

If cases like these were to be excluded from the release data as were the most serious from the petition data, then it would be even more clear that referrals are usually made as alternatives to release rather than as alternatives to system insertion. Obviously, the same effect could be created by including the detain petition cases in the analysis.

This analysis does not tell us why *these* particular offenders were referred rather than released; a different sort of investigation would be required to deal with that question. However, it does deal directly with the question originally posed about the characteristics of diverted versus referred youngsters. It suggests that there are indeed few differences and that these diversion programs are referring for treatment a group of offenders who have *not* been diverted from the juvenile justice system. For such *referral* to mean *diversion,* we would have to be able to predict with some certainty that these referred youngsters would have eventually received petitions for future delinquent acts. Currently, there is no way to make such a prediction. In fact, most data analyses in the past would suggest that the bulk of these offenders would never be arrested again.

Having reached this stage in the analysis and its implications, we can now attempt to connect our concerns under Aim One with those under Aims Two and Three. Specifically, we turn our attention finally to two questions.

First, are the high referral departments more highly committed to referral as defined earlier; i.e. were they self-initiated, self or city funded, optimistic, and characterized by inhouse counseling programs? Second, is this commitment variable, as so described, related to the tendencies to refer disproportionately with respect to age, sex, prior record, and seriousness of instant offense? More broadly, of course, we are using these two questions to ascertain whether there are relationships between structural characteristics of police diversion programs and the referral practices associated with those programs.

With respect to the first question, we expected high referral rates to predict positively to high departmental commitment to the program. Data trends surprisingly suggest just the opposite. Of the seven high referral departments, five are among the lower commitment group. In direct contrast, five of the seven departments with no referrals in 100 arrest cases were among the high commitment group. We can only speculate on the reasons for this, but our suspicion is that the major acting variable here is the source of funding. We believe that a program, even one which is quite inactive, which was initiated and sustained primarily through local funding, reaches a level of activity satisfactory to itself. This includes low levels of activity.

By contrast, it may well be that outside funding — LEAA or CYA — "buys" a far greater rate of referral, but not a greater rate of personal commitment or enthusiasm. Further, since such funds are often used to purchase services from (and benefit for) outside agencies, there is little material gain for the police in this arrangement. Cognitive dissonance theory has spawned numerous studies showing an inverse relationship between size of reward as an incentive and satisfaction with task.

Another implication is that committed departments would refer more cases if they were given the outside funds to do so. Of course, funds usually go to the departments which do not, of their own accord, have referral programs.

Finally, what about the "committed" versus the "uncommitted" departments; do they tend to refer different types of offenders? Source of funding seems·to be a pivotal variable and was central to the cluster of variables that characterized departments as more committed or as less committed to referral. Therefore, we undertook a comparison on the age, sex, prior record, and seriousness variables between departments which relied more on municipal funds and departments which responded to the availability of federal or state funds.

We have suggested as a result of the previous analyses that the latter group — the less committed — were doing far more referring and reaching further into the counsel and release pool of offenders to accomplish their end. Thus it is likely that the less committed departments will refer more of the young, female, less serious offenders with no prior record than will more committed departments.

However, the data with respect to released, referred, and nondetain petitioned offenders do not show major differences, with two exceptions. Less committed departments tend to refer a smaller proportion of less serious cases — contrary to our prediction. The figures are 67 percent versus 79 percent. The less committed departments also refer a higher proportion of offenders with no prior arrests — in accordance with our prediction. This time the figures are 70 percent versus 49 percent.

But these were the largest differences to emerge. Age and sex ratios do not differ among referrals, and none of the four variables differ when comparing more committed versus less committed departments on released or petitioned offenders. Why should this be the case, given the strong pattern reported earlier?

The answer may lie in the approaches to analysis. When comparing extremes — the seven highest referring departments and the seven nonreferring departments — the dependent variable was commitment. In reversing this order, we have now built in the seven departments — five of them being high commitment cases — where there are *no* referrals. Thus we are now dealing with a truncated distribution which works against the emergence of differences. Some of the prior analyses used all 33 departments with equal weight. This reverse analysis does not. Further, the earlier analysis, using the two sets of seven departments only, took advantage of the extremes of the distribution while this last analysis dichotomizes the distribution with the attendant "watering down" of effects occasioned by inclusion of middle range cases.

It will be well to remember that our conclusions work best in predicting from referral rates to characteristics of offenders, that they work reasonably well in predicting from referral rates to structural variables, but that they do not work in predicting from structural variables to characteristics of offenders. The causal connections in the latter direction may have become too diffused by intervening variables and processes (cf. Sundeen, 1974).

REFERENCES

Klein, Malcolm W., *Alternative Dispositions for Juvenile Offenders*. Social Science Research Institute, University of Soutthern California, 1975 (mimeo).
—, "Labeling, Deterrence, and Recidivism: A Study of Police Dispositions of Juvenile Offenders." *Social Problems, 22* (December, 1974), pp. 292–303.
—, Kathie S. Teilmann, Joseph A. Styles, Suzanne Bugas Lincoln, and Susan Labin-Rosensweig, "The Explosion in Police Diversion Programs," Chapter IV in Malcolm W. Klein (ed.), *The Juvenile Justice System*, Beverly Hills, SAGE Publications, 1976.
Rossi, Peter H., Emily Waite, Christine E. Bose and Richard E. Berk, "The Seriousness of Crimes: Normative Structure and Individual Differences." *American Sociological Review, 39* (April, 1974) pp. 224–237.
Sundeen, Richard A. Jr., "Police Professionalization and Community Attachments and Diversion of Juveniles." *Criminology, 11* (February, 1974) pp. 570–580.

NOTES

1. The following remarks were originally made at the 1975 meetings of the Pacific Sociological Association in Victoria, British Columbia and have been incorporated in edited form in a chapter manuscript prepared for the SAGE Publications volume, *The Juvenile Justice System,* edited by Malcolm W. Klein, 1976.

2. Differences in Tables 4 through 7 are all statistically significant beyond the .01 level; N's are over 2,000.

3. An example of the latter is the city in which below-median serious offenses lead to petitions twice as often as above-median serious offenses.

13 *Preadjudicatory Confessions and Consent Searches: Placing the Juvenile on the Same Constitutional Footing as an Adult*
Joseph Adnoff Levitt

INTRODUCTION

In the last decade, the Supreme Court has revolutionized the juvenile justice system by extending to juveniles[1] certain constitutional rights at trial.[2] Many lower courts have followed the Supreme Court lead by also granting juveniles constitutional protection during preadjudicatory stages. These courts accord juveniles the same procedural safeguards given adults in connection with confessions and consent searches.[3] The Juvenile Justice Standards Project, in its volume entitled *Police Handling of Juvenile Problems* (Standards),[4] suggests that, because of juveniles' greater vulnerability, such protection is inadequate. It recommends that juveniles receive the assistance of both parents and counsel during custodial interrogation in order to prevent confessions that are not voluntarily or intelligently made. Moreover, it suggests that prior to a police search based on consent, juveniles should receive certain warnings not now available to adults. . . .[5]

Constitutional Analysis of the Standards' Fifth Amendment Recommendation

A. The Recommendation

At present, most courts determine the validity of juvenile waivers of the privilege against self-incrimination according to the same principles applicable to adults. With-

From Boston University Law Review, 57 (July 1977): 778-95. Reprinted by permission.

out the *Miranda* warnings, no waiver of the privilege is valid; once the warnings are given, the court examines the "totality of the circumstances" to determine whether the waiver was "voluntarily, knowingly and intelligently" made.[6] In applying this standard, courts consider such factors as the defendant's education, intelligence and prior experience with police, as well as the interrogation's length, time of day and coercive nature.[7] In the case of juvenile waivers, special scrutiny is required.[8] Thus, juvenile courts also consider both a defendant's age[9] and whether he consulted with a parent or other friendly adult.[10]

Although the vast majority of states employ this case-by-case approach,[11] the Standards favor a per se rule requiring parental presence during custodial interrogation. Under this proposal, both the juvenile and parent must receive the *Miranda* warnings and have time to consult privately before making the waiver decision.[12] This parental presence test is currently followed in two states by judicial decision. The Standards also provide that, when the juvenile and parent decide to waive the fifth amendment privilege, a defense attorney must be consulted before the actual interrogation commences.[14] This proposal is based on certain problems that inhere in having parents present during police questioning. The parent may force the child to confess or may be hostile to the child's best interests. Other problems derive from parents' own limitations. A parent may not understand the warnings or may himself be intimidated by police pressures. In none of these cases is the parent likely to provide much assistance to the accused juvenile.[15]

B. The Parental Presence Requirement

The primary difficulty in evaluating juvenile waivers of the privilege against self-incrimination is the greater vulnerability of juveniles during police interrogation. This vulnerability arises from two distinct shortcomings associated with youth: (1) insufficient emotional maturity to withstand normal police pressures and (2) inadequate mental capacity to understand the nature of one's rights and the consequences of one's confession. The Supreme Court has repeatedly recognized the relevance of these characteristics in the context of juvenile waivers. In *Haley v. Ohio*,[16] a fifteen-year-old boy was interrogated through the night until he finally confessed to first degree murder. In invalidating the confession on due process grounds,[17] the Court noted that juveniles are more susceptible than adults to police pressures: "Mature men possibly might stand the ordeal from midnight until 5 a.m. But we cannot believe that a lad of tender years is a match for the police in such a contest."[18] Several years later, the Court went on to indicate that juveniles lack a fully developed sense of insight. In *Gallegos v. Colorado*,[19] involving substantially similar facts, the Court stated that "a fourteen year old boy, no matter how sophisticated . . . is unable to know how to protect his own interests or how to get the benefit of his constitutional rights."[20]

The Court reiterated these positions more recently in *Gault* when it recognized that a juvenile's waiver of the right to silence, even in the more open atmosphere of the courtroom, creates "special problems." The Court warned that the "greatest care" must be taken to ensure that the waiver is neither the "product of ignorance" nor of "adolescent fantasy, fright or despair."[21]

Virtually all lower courts recognize this problem of vulnerability. They disagree, however, over the appropriate method for evaluating juvenile waivers of the privilege against self-incrimination to ensure that this factor is fully considered. As was noted above, most courts adopt a case-by-case approach that considers all the surrounding circumstances and the characteristics of the particular juvenile defendant.[22] The strength of this totality-of-the-circumstances test is that it allows each case to stand or fall on its own facts. Thus, a particularly sophisticated youth of fourteen might be permitted to waive his fifth amendment privilege whereas a seventeen-year-old with significantly less experience might not. The major problem with this approach is that it forces police to consider a myriad of factors without providing adequate guidelines for reaching a decision. As a result, the test is often arbitrarily applied, as illustrated by the vast number of juvenile waivers invalidated by courts.[23]

Although this problem of arbitrariness has been discussed in the context of juvenile waivers of the fifth amendment privilege, it is instructive to observe that *Miranda* itself addressed many of these same considerations in an analogous context. There, the Court saw the potential for arbitrariness in case-by-case determinations of the admissibility of adult confessions made without the benefit of prescribed warnings. In an examination of police procedures utilized in custodial interrogation, *Miranda* established a new standard for adult waivers of the fifth amendment privilege. The Court rejected the existing standard of voluntariness,[24] as determined from the surrounding circumstances, in favor of a broader "voluntary, knowing and intelligent" requirement. In implementing this new standard, the Court refused to extend the totality-of-the-circumstances approach to the knowledge component. Because of the subjective nature of the inquiry under this approach, courts could only speculate as to whether a defendant actually knew of his rights. In order to make this inquiry objective, the Court therefore established the requirement[25] that the accused be advised of his right to silence. This eliminated the possibility of arbitrariness by ensuring that every adult waiver is in fact a knowing decision.[26]

In essence, the *Miranda* decision rejects a case-by-case analysis and adopts a per se rule. Once the accused receives the warnings, the knowledge component is presumed to exist. Similarly, a waiver is ordinarily assumed to be intelligently made if the accused has been advised both that what he says may be used against him in court and that he is entitled to counsel.[27] Moreover, because the aggregate effect of the warnings is to lessen the coercive nature of the interrogation process, voluntariness may also be inferred from the administration of the warnings.[28]

Although *Miranda* warnings are now administered without regard to age, the assumptions made in connection with their intended effect do not hold true for children. Juveniles lack the emotional maturity of adults and thus are more susceptible to police pressures and less likely to believe in their right to silence. As a result, the voluntariness component cannot simply be assumed from the administration of the warnings. Similarly, because juveniles lack the requisite mental capacity to understand the consequences of the waiver, the intelligence component cannot be automatically inferred. The end result is that under the totality-of-the-circumstances test, courts must still engage in subjective inquiries over the effect of the *Miranda* warnings on a juvenile's decision. The potential for arbitrariness therefore still exists.[29]

The Standards' recommendation requiring the presence of the parent during the administration of the warnings adds the element of certainty now lacking. The goal of the parental presence requirement is to compensate the juvenile for his vulnerability by giving him exactly what he lacks — an adult's emotional maturity and mental capacity. Thus, when a parent is present, the extra considerations associated with youth disappear, and a juvenile waiver can be treated as an adult waiver. By implementing the Standards' recommendation, the *Miranda* warnings will give rise to the same automatic inferences for juveniles as the Court intended for adults.[30]

The ultimate conclusion to be drawn from the above analysis is that the parental presence rule is constitutionally compelled.[31] At present, juveniles are entitled to the same fifth amendment protection afforded adults, but the courts have greater difficulty in ensuring that they receive it. Because of differences in sophistication, juveniles need greater procedural safeguards than adults in order to receive the same degree of protection. The Standards' recommendation furnishes these additional safeguards. By providing added advice and support, the parental presence test compensates juveniles for their weaknesses and thus places them on the same constitutional footing as adults.

An additional constitutional compulsion derives from the *Gault* requirement that both parent and child be advised of the right to counsel at trial.[32] The Court considered this added precaution necessary in *Gault* to assure the fairness of the proceeding[33] — a goal that was of equal concern to the Court in *Miranda* with respect to the trustworthiness of preadjudicatory confessions.[34] Thus, it is arguable that both parent and child should receive the *Miranda* warnings during custodial interrogation in order to protect the youth adequately during all stages of the proceedings and to preserve the integrity of the fact-finding process.[35]

C. Safeguards in Addition to Parental Presence

Even when courts require parental presence in order to implement a per se rule for juvenile waivers, a subsequent case-by-case analysis may sometimes be necessary to protect the juvenile. The parental presence recommendation assumes that parents — like adult defendants under *Miranda* — are fully competent to validly waive constitutional rights. Administration of the *Miranda* warnings to both parent and child therefore creates an inference that any waiver is voluntary, knowing and intelligent. However, evidence that the parent is not competent to understand the *Miranda* warnings[36] or is himself intimidated by police[37] would successfully rebut the inference.[38] Thus, these waivers would be invalid unless the state meets its heavy burden of proving that the waiver was indeed voluntary, knowing and intelligent. This could be accomplished by demonstrating either that the juvenile's unusual sophistication enabled him to validly waive his rights on his own, or that the juvenile received the assistance of counsel or other competent adult.[39]

In addition to assuming the competence of the parent, the Standards' recommendation also assumes that the parent and child will share common interests. This second assumption is rebuttable by the juvenile defendant. For example, if the parent, in the presence of police, actually coerces the child into confessing, the confession would not be admissible on due process grounds.[40] In this situation, it is unlikely that the police could produce countervailing evidence of voluntariness. The more subtle problem arises when the parent is either apathetic or antagonistic toward the child.[41] Because such parents do not provide the requisite advice and support, evidence of divergent interests would also rebut the inference of a valid waiver. Police could counter this rebuttal only by showing that the juvenile was unusually sophisticated. Therefore, once a conflict of interest situation appears, police would be better advised to immediately stop the interrogation and petition the court to appoint either a guardian *ad litem* or an attorney.[42] Although the procedure will admittedly require postponement of the interrogation, any delay will be no longer than if the juvenile himself had requested counsel.

The Standards recognize these shortcomings inherent in the parental presence test.[43] They therefore provide for mandatory consultation with counsel before actual questioning begins.[44] Although an attorney certainly provides additional protection, this recommendation cannot be viewed as constitutionally compelled. Mandatory attorney presence prior to interrogation would insulate the juvenile from errors in judgment in waiving his constitutional rights. Adults, however, remain subject to these errors. Thus, rather than placing juveniles on an equal footing with adults, the attorney presence recommendation confers superior constitutional benefits.

The attorney presence recommendation also poses certain inconsistencies with the *Gault* opinion. *Gault* extended to juveniles the same right to counsel at trial enjoyed by adults. As with adults, the defendant can waive this right without first consulting an attorney.[45] Thus, the Standards' proposal that counsel must be consulted prior to questioning essentially gives juveniles greater right at the preadjudicatory stage than at trial. Such a requirement is inconsistent with the Court's traditional approach of granting the most complete protection at trial and extending to earlier stages only those safeguards necessary for preserving the trial's integrity.[46]

In conclusion, although requiring parental presence does not in itself guarantee that every juvenile waiver of the privilege against self-incrimination will be valid, additional safeguards are available. The juvenile defendant can show either that his parent was incapable of properly advising and supporting him, or that his parent's interests conflicted with his own. Because such evidence is difficult for the state to rebut, police may attempt to avoid these problems by requesting the court to appoint a guardian *ad litem* in appropriate marginal cases. Finally, although attorney presence is not constitutionally mandated, the benefit of counsel is always available upon request.

CONSTITUTIONAL ANALYSIS OF THE STANDARDS' FOURTH AMENDMENT RECOMMENDATION

A. The Recommendation

The fourth amendment protects individuals against unreasonable searches and seizures.[47] Normally, in order to conduct a reasonable search, police must first obtain a warrant from a neutral magistrate on the basis of probable cause.[48] There are several exceptions to the warrant requirement, however. When an individual voluntarily consents to a police search, for example, neither a warrant nor probable cause is necessary.[49] Such consent searches are the next concern of this Note.

The constitutional standards governing consent searches are less rigorous than those governing confessions. Under *Schneckloth v. Bustamonte*,[50] courts inquire only whether the totality of the circumstances indicates that the defendant voluntarily consented to the search. No *Miranda*-type warnings are necessary prior to consent, and whether the defendant knew of the right to refuse consent is but one of the factors considered.[51] Although *Schneckloth* was restricted to noncustodial searches, the Court extended this rule to defendants in custody in *United States v. Watson*.[52]

Most courts that have considered the question in a juvenile context follow the *Schneckloth-Watson* rule;[53] the Standards, however, propose a different procedure. They provide that juveniles must be advised of the right to refuse consent prior to a search. This compensates juveniles for their lack of sophistication and greater susceptibility to coercion.[54] The Standards also diverge from the *Watson* rule by providing that in custodial searches the juvenile must also be advised of the right to counsel.[55] Both of these proposals are urged on constitutional and public policy grounds.

B. Advising Juveniles of the Right to Refuse Consent

As in the fifth amendment context, the greater vulnerability of juveniles must be given special consideration in determining whether a consent to search has been given voluntarily. For example, in *In re Williams*,[56] a fifteen-year-old had been arrested on a charge of burglary. After several hours of police pressure in the early morning hours, the youth consented to a search of his home. Although the police found incriminating evidence, the trial judge suppressed it on the ground that the consent was involuntary.[57] The court concluded that "because of the child's tender years . . . even more rigorous standards than those applied to adults should prevail."[58]

Although *Williams* involved a custodial search, *Schneckloth* recognized that police may exert subtly coercive pressures regardless of when or where the confrontation takes place.[59] A certain element of intimidation inheres in the very presence of an authority figure dressed in uniform, badge and weaponry. Because of their greater susceptibility to such intimidation, juveniles require extra protection before they can consent voluntarily to a search.

The Supreme Court has explicitly rejected the suggestion that adults must be informed of the right to refuse consent prior to a search.[60] As a result, it is not readily apparent that the Standards' recommendation to this effect for juveniles is constitutionally mandated. Nevertheless, a constitutional basis does appear to exist. As with the parental presence recommendation, the purpose of this proposal is to place juveniles on the same constitutional footing as an adult. However, the analogous solution of providing adult support is here simply impractical. Because juveniles not in custody may only be detained for brief periods, there will not always be sufficient time to locate parents.[61] Thus, to impose a parental presence requirement in this situation would effectively eliminate noncustodial consent searches involving juveniles.[62]

The Standards recognize this problem and thus attempt to compensate juveniles in a different manner.. Rather than providing juveniles with the additional support necessary to combat police pressures, the Standards' recommendation seeks to make police encounters less intimidating. When juveniles are informed of the right to refuse consent, they become aware that no compulsion to cooperate exists. This was partly the reasoning that applied in *Miranda*. The Court stated there that the warning of the right to remain silent ''is an absolute prerequisite in overcoming the inherent pressures of the interrogation atmosphere.''[63] The Standards' proposed warning serves a similar function in connection with consent searches.

The Standards' recommendation also serves to eliminate the same type of arbitrariness that was troublesome in the fifth amendment context. Determining voluntariness from the totality of the circumstances again results in subjective inquiries. By advising juveniles of the right to refuse consent, an objective determination of voluntariness is more easily made. Thus, as with the Standards' fifth amendment recommendation, this proposal results in clearer guidelines for police and less arbitrary decision making.

C. The Right to Counsel During a Custodial Search

The Standards' recommendation that juveniles in custody be granted a right to counsel prior to the consent decision is without firm constitutional support. *Watson* itself is ambiguous and may be construed either narrowly so as to prohibit this right or broadly so as to allow for its adoption. Moreover, putting *Watson* aside, the majority of juveniles receive this protection anyway as part of the standard safeguards surrounding interrogation.

The *Watson* decision requires a uniform standard of voluntariness in noncustodial and custodial searches. Thus, if advising juveniles of the right to refuse consent serves to place them on an equal footing with adults in the former situation, the same must be true in the latter. As a result, providing an additional right to counsel to juveniles in custody goes beyond the constitutional mandate.

Although *Watson* appears to establish a comprehensive rule governing all custodial searches, a narrower view of this case is possible. In *Watson*, the accused was taken into custody on the public street where he immediately consented to be searched.[64] This factual pattern suggests that *Watson* may be the appropriate rule only for consents obtained outside of a police station. Frequently, the atmosphere of a stationhouse is more intimidating than that of a public street,[65] and thus extra safeguards may be necessary at a police station. For juveniles, one such safeguard is providing for the assistance of counsel in making the consent decision.

Although theoretically sound, prartical considerations render this limited reading of *Watson* unnecessary. Once juveniles are taken into custody, they often receive adequate protection through fifth amendment safeguards. In most situations, consents result from extensive interrogations.[66] When this occurs, juveniles receive notice of the right to counsel as part of the *Miranda* warnings.[67] In addition, under the Standards' fifth amendment recommendation, juveniles receive the added benefit of parental presence. Thus, the apparent harshness of the *Watson* rule is largely mitigated by the extra safeguards available during custodial interrogation.

PUBLIC POLICY SUPPORT

This Note has concluded that two of the Standards' recommendations are compelled by analogy to Supreme Court implementation of constitutional protections afforded adults in the criminal context. These "compelled recommendations" are (1) parental presence during custodial interrogation and (2) advisement of the right to refuse consent prior to a warrantless search. Moreover, in view of important public policy considerations, the Note favors the immediate adoption of those recommendations by state legislatures rather than reliance on the necessarily cautious and hesitating process of judicial acceptance of these specific rules. Although different considerations obtain with regard to the two recommendations that do not appear to be so required, this Note suggests that state legislatures would be well advised to adopt them solely on public policy grounds. These "noncompelled recommendations" are (1) consultation with counsel prior to police questioning and (2) the right to counsel at the police station solely for making the consent decision.

A. The Compelled Recommendations

The parental presence requirement during interrogation is consistent with the instrumental role parents currently play in the juvenile court framework.[68] For example, many juvenile court statutes provide that parents should be notified as soon as a child is taken into custody[69] and that, whenever possible, the parents should retain custody of the child pending a hearing.[70] Further, under *Gault,* a parent is entitled to both formal notice of the charges[71] and notification of the right to counsel at trial.[72] Parents are also commonly required by statute to attend the adjudicatory hearing itself.[73] These provisions reflect a policy that parents should be involved at all critical stages of the juvenile court process. Thus, because a juvenile's preadjudicatory confession may determine his fate at trial, parental involvement at later stages may prove meaningless unless the parent is also present during custodial interrogation.[74]

Moreover, both of the compelled recommendations are consistent with the Supreme Court's philosophy for dealing with youthful offenders. The main thrust of *McKeiver* was to preserve those unique qualities of the juvenile justice system that do not jeopardize the fairness of the defendant's trial. Perhaps most important of these is the system's conception of juvenile offenders: "Reprehensible acts by juveniles are not deemed the consequence of mature and malevolent choice but of environmental pressures . . . beyond their control. Hence . . . his conduct is not deemed so blameworthy that punishment is required to deter him or others."[75] The major consequence of this philosophy is that juveniles are not to be punished but rather rehabilitated through the use of special procedures.[76]

In *Gault,* the Court indicated that a juvenile's prospects for rehabilitation are greatest when he perceives his treatment as fair. The Standards' compelled recommendations promote such perceptions.[77] By taking the time to locate a juvenile's parent, a policeman would impress upon the youth the integrity of the court process. Further, in receiving notification of the right to refuse consent, a juvenile would learn that compulsion has no role in the juvenile justice system.[78] Thus, both these recommendations would implement the juvenile court philosophy that rehabilitation begins with a perception of fair judicial procedures.

Although the primary goal of the compelled recommendations is to protect fully the juvenile defendant's constitutional rights, these procedures also benefit law enforcement officials in three ways.[79] First, the standardized guidelines would greatly reduce the policeman's need to second-guess courts on the constitutional validity of juvenile confessions and consents.[80] With this increased certainty, police will be able to perform more confidently. Second, although fewer consents and confessions may be obtained, those that are will stand a greater likelihood of holding up in court. Thus, policemen's time will be more productively spent. Finally, according to the *Gault* hypothesis that procedural fairness increases the prospects of rehabilitation, adoption of these proposals should help decrease the number of repeating offenders. All three of these advantages should, therefore, combine to increase police effectiveness in combatting juvenile crime.[81]

B. The Noncompelled Recommendations

The noncompelled recommendations both provide juveniles with greater access to counsel than presently afforded adults. To reiterate briefly, the Standards provide for mandatory consultation with counsel prior to police interrogation and for the right to consult with counsel solely for obtaining advice on whether to consent to a custodial search. In seeming opposition to exactly these kinds of rules, the Supreme Court has indicated that it would not condone procedures that necessitate a "station house lawyer."[82] However, from a policy standpoint, this potentially negative impact on the state's resources must be weighed against the degree of protection necessary to adequately protect juveniles.

The constitutional analysis in this Note concerning juvenile waivers of the fifth amendment privilege is predicated on the assumption that, in the great majority of cases, the juvenile's parent will provide satisfactory protection. Nevertheless, this Note has also indicated that, in a minority of instances, a guardian *ad litem* must be appointed because the parent either is incapable of advising the child or holds divergent interests.[83] In the latter cases, policy considerations suggest that an attorney would be the most suitable appointment. First, the problem of determining the capability of the guardian *ad litem* would be eliminated. In addition, appointment of counsel in these situations would minimize the delay involved. Although delay occurs while the court names a guardian, possible additional delay, caused by the guardian requesting the aid of counsel, would be avoided. Thus, although parents ensure the necessary degree of protection in the majority of cases, policy considerations suggest that providing counsel is the most expeditious alternative for the small but significant number of youngsters whose parents offer inadequate assistance.

Similarly, the noncompelled recommendation concerning custodial searches seems appropriate in a minority of instances. As noted earlier, the time when police normally request consent to conduct a custodial search is during interrogation — prior to which the juvenile has already been advised of the right to counsel as part of the *Miranda* warnings. Moreover, in these interrogations the juvenile also has the benefit of his parent's presence. On the other hand, when the only question the police ask of the juvenile is to consent to a warrantless search, the *Miranda* warnings need not be administered. In these instances, the child is left to make the decision completely by himself. Even though he is advised of the right to refuse consent under the compelled recommendation, he is still an easy target for subtle intimidation and may later feel resentful. Certainly, the juvenile court philosophy of creating a perception of fairness, discussed above, applies equally here.[84] If the juvenile is advised that he may consult with a lawyer, that juvenile will be more likely to view the judicial process as fair. As a result, his prospects for rehabilitation will be enhanced should he be adjudicated delinquent. Thus, the juvenile court philosophy strongly supports adoption of this noncompelled recommendation when the consent request is not part of interrogation.

The Standards, however, do not provide for adoption of its recommendations in some instances but not in others. The ultimate question, therefore, is whether policy considerations justify overprotecting the majority of arrested juveniles in order sufficiently to protect the minority. This Note concludes that they do. The whole system of juvenile justice is grounded on the principle of rehabilitation. But what is rehabilitation, if not a shorthand term for the hope that through individualized treatment a child's life may be changed for the better? The key word is "individualized," for the system aims at helping each individual it encounters rather than simply providing the greatest good for the greatest number. This philosophy necessitates the conclusion that full protection must be provided for all. And, even if these additional procedures compel increased expenditures on the part of the state, it will be an investment well made.

NOTES

1. The term "juvenile" in this Note refers only to those individuals who fall under a juvenile court's "delinquency" jurisdiction, as defined by state statute. This jurisdiction is limited according to age and offense. Normally, any person under eighteen years of age is included. *E.g.,* Uniform Juvenile Court Act § 2(1)(i) (1968). Some statutes, however, set a lower ceiling and/or a minimum age. *E.g.,* N.Y. Family Ct. Act § 712 (a) (McKinney 1977) (under sixteen and over seven). Most states define a delinquent act as one that would constitute a crime if committed by an adult, excluding traffic offenses. *E.g.,* Uniform Juvenile Court Act § 2(2) (1968).

2. *See In re* Winship, 397 U.S. 358 (1970); *In re* Gault, 387 U.S. 1 (1967).

3. *See* notes 17–24 and accompanying text [in the original, complete Note].

4. Institute of Judicial Administration & American Bar Association, Joint Commission on Juvenile Justice Standards, Standards Relating to Police Handling of Juvenile Problems (tent. ed. 1977) (Dr. Egon Bittner, Brandeis University, and Professor Sheldon Krantz, Boston University School of Law, Reporters) [hereinafter cited as IJA/ABA Standards].

5. Standard 3.2 reads as follows:
   Police investigation into criminal matters should be similar whether the suspect is an adult or a juvenile. Juveniles, therefore, should receive, at the least, the same safeguards available to adults in the criminal justice system. This should apply to:

    (a) Preliminary investigations (e.g., stop and frisk);
    (b) The arrest process;
    (c) *Search and seizure;*
    (d) *Questioning;*
    (e) Pretrial identification; and
    (f) Prehearing detention and release.

For some investigative procedures, greater constitutional safeguards are needed because of the vulnerability of juveniles. Juveniles should not be permitted to waive constitutional rights on their own. In certain investigative areas not governed by constitutional guidelines, guidance to police officers should be provided either legislatively or administratively by court rules or through police agency policies.

Id. at 54 (emphasis added). For a more detailed description of the fifth and fourth amendment standards, see text accompanying notes 11-15 and 53-55, respectively, *infra.*

6. 384 U.S. at 444. The *Miranda* Court adopted the traditional definition of waiver from Johnson v. Zerbst, 304 U.S. 458, 464 (1938): "an intentional relinquishment or abandonment of a known right or privilege." The Court then placed a "heavy burden" on the state to prove the validity of any waiver under the voluntary, knowing and intelligent test. When the state fails to meet its burden, the defendant's statements must be excluded from evidence. 384 U.S. at 475–76.

7. *E.g.,* West v. United States, 399 F.2d 467, 468 (5th Cir. 1968), *cert. denied,* 393 U.S. 1102 (1969).

8. Haley v. Ohio, 332 U.S. 596, 600 (1948) (opinion of Douglas, J.).

9. *E.g.,* People v. Hester, 39 Ill. 2d 489, 499–500, 237 N.E.2d 466, 474 (1968), *cert. granted,* 394 U.S. 957 (1969), *cert. dismissed as improvidently granted,* 397 U.S. 660 (1970); State v. Gullings, 244 Ore. 173, 182, 416 P.2d 311, 315 (1966).

10. *E.g.,* State v. Evans, 533 P.2d 1392, 1394 (Ore. App. 1975) (talked with attorney on telephone); Bradley v. State, 36 Wis. 2d 345, 356, 153 N.W.2d 38, 42 (1967) (consulted with husband and minister).

11. *E.g.,* West v. United States, 399 F.2d 467, 469 (5th Cir. 1968), *cert. denied,* 393 U.S. 1102 (1969); State v. Hardy, 107 Ariz. 583, 584, 491 P.2d 17, 18 (1971), *overruling* State v. Maloney, 102 Ariz. 495, 498–99, 433 P.2d 625, 628–29 (1967); People v. Lara, 67 Cal. 2d 365, 383–84, 432 P.2d 202, 215, 62 Cal. Rptr. 586, 599 (1967), *cert. denied,* 392 U.S. 945 (1968); T.B. v. State, 306 So. 2d 183, 185 (Fla. App. 1975); State v. Dillon, 93 Idaho 698, 707–08, 471 P.2d 553, 562–63 (1970), *cert. denied,* 401 U.S. 942 (1971); People v. Pierre, 114 Ill. App. 2d 283, 291, 252 N.E.2d 706, 710 (1969), *cert. denied,* 400 U.S. 854 (1970); State v. Melanson, 259 So. 2d 609, 612 (La. App. 1972); Commonwealth v. Cain, 361 Mass. 224, 228–29, 279 N.E.2d 706, 709–10 (1972); State v. Hogan, 297 Minn. 430, 440, 212 N.W.2d 664, 671 (1973); People v. Stephen J.B., 23 N.Y.2d 611, 616–17, 246 N.E.2d 344, 348–49, 298 N.Y.S.2d 489, 495–96 (1969); State v. Dawson, 278 N.C. 351, 362, 180 S.E.2d 140, 147–48 (1971); State v. Carder, 9 Ohio St. 2d 1, 9, 222 N.E.2d 620, 626–27 (1966); State v. Raiford, 7 Ore. App. 202, 204, 490 P.2d 206, 208 (1971); Commonwealth v. Moses, 446 Pa. 350, 354, 287 A.2d 131, 133 (1971); Vaughn v. State, 3 Tenn. Crim. App. 54, 456 S.W.2d 879, 882–83 (1970); Theriault v. State, 66 Wis. 2d 33, 41, 223 N.W.2d 850, 853 (1974); Mullin v. State, 505 P.2d 305, 309 (Wyo.), *cert. denied,* 414 U.S. 940 (1973). In addition, Texas has a statutorily created variation whereby the magistrate must administer the *Miranda* warnings and approve the waiver. Tex. Fam. Code Ann. tit. 3, § 51.09(b)(1) (Vernon Supp. 1975).

12. IJA/ABA Standards 69. The Standards acknowledge certain defects in its proposal but maintain that their effect is minimal. For example, although police efforts will be thwarted until parents can be located, most parents are available within a reasonable time. In addition, despite the existence of some juveniles sufficiently sophisticated to act on their own, the fifth amendment privilege is so fundamental as to warrant overprotection in a few isolated instances.

13. Lewis v. State, 259 Ind. 431, 439, 288 N.E.2d 138, 142 (1972); *In re* K.W.B., 500 S.W.2d 275, 283 (Mo. App. 1973). In addition, several lower New York courts have employed this test. *E.g., In re* Aaron D., 30 App. Div. 2d 183, 185, 290 N.Y.S.2d 935, 937 (1968). However, the Court of Appeals of New York still follows the totality of the circumstances test. People v. Stephen J.B., 23 N.Y.2d 611, 616–17, 246 N.E.2d 344, 349, 298 N.Y.S.2d 489, 495 (1969). Finally, one California judge has also spoken out in favor of the parental presence test. People v. Lara, 67 Cal. 2d 365, 396–97, 432 P.2d 202, 223, 62 Cal. Rptr. 586, 607 (1967) (Peters, J., dissenting), *cert. denied,* 392 U.S. 945 (1968). The parental presence test has also been adopted statutorily by four states. Colo. Rev. Stat. Ann. § 19 –2–102(3)(c)(I) (1973); Conn. Gen. Stat. Ann. § 17–66d(a) (West Supp. 1976); N.M. Stat. Ann. § 13–14–25(A) (1954); Okla. Stat. Ann. tit. 10, § 1109(a) (West Supp. 1976).

14. IJA/ABA Standards 71–72.

15. *Id.* at 71. The Standards also recommend that counsel should not be waivable without first conferring with counsel. *Id.* at 72. No state has yet required mandatory consultation with counsel. In Texas, however, although no attorney need be present if the magistrate administers the warnings and validates the waiver, Tex. Fam. Code Ann. tit. 3, § 51.09(b)(1) (Vernon Sup. 1975), an attorney must concur in the juvenile's waiver if the warnings are administered by a police officer, *id.* § 51.09(a). . . .

16. 332 U.S. 596 (1948).

17. *Id.* at 601 (opinion of Douglas, J.).

18. *Id.* at 599–600.

19. 370 U.S. 49 (1962).

20. *Id.* at 54.

21. 387 U.S. at 55.

22. *See* note 11 and accompanying text *supra.*

23. *See* Annot., 87 A.L.R.2d 624, 631–33 (1963).

24. *See* Malloy v. Hogan, 378 U.S. 1, 7 (1964).

25. Miranda v. Arizona, 384 U.S. 436 (1966).

26. 384 U.S. at 468–69. The Court there stated:
    Assessments of the knowledge the defendant possessed, based on information as to his age, education, intelligence, or prior contact with authorities, can never be more than speculation; a warning is a clearcut fact.

27. *Id.* at 469. This assumption may be successfully rebutted by showing that the defendant has unusually low intelligence. Dover v. State, 227 So. 2d 296, 300 (Miss. 1969).

28. 384 U.S. at 467. This inference may also be successfully rebutted by showing that the police used promises, tricks, or threats of coercion to elicit the confession. *Id.* at 476.

29. *In re* K.W.B., 500 S.W.2d 275, 282 (Mo. App. 1973); *see* Lewis v. State, 259 Ind. 431, 436, 288 N.E.2d 138, 141 (1972); State v. R.W., 115 N.J. Super. 286, 293–94, 279 A.2d 709, 713 (App. Div. 1971).

30. Lewis v. State, 259 Ind. 431, 439–40, 288 N.E.2d 138, 142 (1972); *see In re* K.W.B., 500 S.W.2d 275, 282 (Mo. App. 1973).

31. The term "constitutionally compelled," as used in this Note, requires clarification. Professor Monaghan has distinguished between two kinds of judicial review. The first he labels "constitutional interpretation," which, under the authority of *Marbury v. Madison,* 5 U.S. (1 Cranch) 137 (1803), cannot be altered by Congress. Constitutional interpretation is exemplified by the holding that electronic eavesdropping without a warrant constitutes an unreasonable search and seizure within the confines of the fourth amendment. Such judicial review is " an interpretive filling-out of the underlying constitutional guarantee. It is authoritative because the rule is 'part and parcel' of the underlying constitutional guarantee." Monaghan, Supreme Court Foreword: Constitutional Common Law, 89 Harv. L. Rev. 1, 23 (1975); *see* Cox, The Role of Congress in Constitutional Determinations, 40 U. Cin. L. Rev. 199, 251 (1970). In contrast, Professor Monaghan categorizes the second form of judicial review as "constitutional common law." Although escaping exact definition, constitutional common law includes judicially imposed prophylactic rules designed to safeguard underlying constitutional guarantees. The classic example is the *Miranda* warnings, for they represent only a method of protecting the privilege against self-incrimination. One significant result of segregating this second category is that constitutional common law can be overruled by federal statute. Indeed, *Miranda* itself clearly states that Congress is free to develop alternative rules that sufficiently protect the fifth amendment privilege. Monaghan, *supra* at 20–23.

    Even more significant for purposes of this Note, however, is the theoretical difficulty of imposing subconstitutional common law upon the states in areas primarily of state, rather than national, competence. *See id.* at 34–38. Without question, the procedures advocated by the Standards and critiqued in this Note fall into the latter category of constitutional common law rather than constitutional interpretation. Nevertheless, they constitute "prophylactic rule[s] [which] might be *constitutionally compelled* when it is necessary to overprotect a constitutional right because a narrow, theoretically more discriminating rule may not work in practice." *Id.* at 21 (emphasis added). Thus, when this Note asserts a certain procedure to be "constitutionally compelled," it does so with reference to constitutional common law rather than constitutional interpretation.

32. 387 U.S. at 42.

33. *Id.* at 36.

34. 384 U.S. at 466; *accord,* Schneckloth v. Bustamonte, 412 U.S. 218, 240 (1973).

35. Parental presence is also supported by language in two of the Court's earlier opinions. In *Haley,* Justice Douglas stated in a plurality opinion that the juvenile "needs someone on whom to lean," 332 U.S. at 600, and in *Gallegos,* the Court suggested that "[a]dult advice would have put him on a less unequal footing with his interrogators." 370 U.S. at 54; *accord, In re* K.W.B., 500 S.W.2d 275, 282 (Mo. App. 1973). *But see* Riley v. State, 237 Ga. 124, 226 S.E.2d 922, 926 (1976), *overruling* Freeman v. Wilcox, 119 Ga. App. 325, 327-29, 167 S.E.2d 163, 165-67 (1969).

36. Daniels v. State, 226 Ga. 269, 273, 174 S.E.2d 422, 424 (1970) (mother intoxicated); *see* Ezell v. State, 489 P.2d 781, 784 (Okla. Crim. App. 1971) no evidence showing that the mother or legal guardian could properly advise defendant).

37. *See In re* L.B., 33 Colo. App. 1, 4, 513 P.2d 1069, 1070 (1973) (Father himself incarcerated).

38. The same case-by-case analysis is necessary in the context of adult waivers when the adult defendant either has such low intelligence that he cannot understand the *Miranda* warnings or is intimidated by police. *See* notes 27-28 *supra.*

39. This problem of the incompetent parent must be distinguished from that of the perfectly capable parent who incorrectly concludes that an attorney is unnecessary. Although the juvenile clearly suffers in this situation, his plight is no worse than the adult defendant who unwisely waives his right to counsel. The Constitution provides no protection against the bad judgment of either an adult or a juvenile and his parent.

40. *See* Commonwealth v. Mahnke, 335 N.E.2d 660 (Mass. 1975), *cert. denied,* 425 U.S. 958 (1976), in which the Supreme Judicial Court of Massachusetts discussed the fundamental recognition that a statement obtained through coercion and introduced at trial is every bit as offensive to civilized standards of adjudication when the coercion flows from private hands as when official depredations elicit a confession. *Id.* at 672; *cf.* McBride v. Jacobs, 247 F.2d 595, 596 (D.C. Cir. 1957) (conflict of interest between parent and child would invalidate parental waiver of counsel) (dictum).

41. *See* Anglin v. State, 259 So. 2d 752 (Fla. Dist. Ct. App. 1972) (mother told son to tell "the truth" or she "would clobber him").

42. Appointment of an attorney is preferable to a guardian *ad litem* at this stage of the proceedings. *See* text accompanying note 83 *infra.*

43. IJA/ABA Standards 85.

44. *Id.* at 84.

45. 387 U.S. at 41.

46. For example, adults are afforded the right to counsel at trial, Gideon v. Wainwright, 372 U.S. 335, 342 (1963), and at some pretrial stages, Coleman v. Alabama, 399 U.S. 1, 9-10 (1970) (opinion of Brennan, J.) (preliminary hearing), while the right is denied at other stages, Kirby v. Illinois, 406 U.S. 682, 690 (1970) (opinion of Stewart, J.) (preindictment line-up).

47. U.S. Const. amend. IV provides, in part:
The right of the people to be secure in their persons, houses, papers, and effects, against unreasonable searches and seizures, shall not be violated, and no Warrants shall issue, but upon probable cause.

48. Coolidge v. New Hampshire, 403 U.S. 443, 449 (1971).

49. Davis v. United States, 328 U.S. 582, 593 (1946). Other cases finding exceptions to the warrant requirement include: Chambers v. Maroney, 399 U.S. 42, 50–52 (1970) (no warrant needed for car search based on probable cause, with exigent circumstances); Chimel v. California, 395 U.S. 752, 763 (1969) (no warrant needed for search incident to arrest); Terry v. Ohio, 392 U.S. 1, 20 (1968) (no warrant needed for stop and frisk); Camara v. Municipal Court, 387 U.S. 523, 538 (1967) (probable cause for warrant for administrative inspection of premises need only relate to area rather than specific building); Warden v. Hayden, 387 U.S. 294, 298-99 (1967) (no warrant needed when in hot pursuit); Henderson v. United States, 390 F.2d 805, 808 (9th Cir. 1967) (neither warrant nor probable cause needed to search persons, baggage, or vehicles crossing international border).

50. 412 U.S. 218 (1973).

51. *Id.* at 227. The Court distinguished *Miranda* in two ways. First, although interrogations are normally conducted in the inherently coercive atmosphere of the police station, most consents are obtained on

more neutral ground, such as a public street or even the defendant's home. *Id.* at 247. Second, although the *Miranda* procedures protect the fairness of the trial by eliminating unreliable, coerced confessions, *id.* at 240, hard evidence obtained from consent searches is reliable regardless of whether the consent was voluntary and knowing. *Id.* at 242.

52. 423 U.S. 411, 424–25 (1976).

53. *E.g., In re* Ronny, 40 Misc. 2d 194, 209, 242 N.Y.S.2d 844, 859 (Queens County Fam. Ct. 1963); State v. Evans, 533 P.2d 1392, 1394 (Ore. App. 1975). *But see* People v. Reyes, 174 Colo. 377, 381–82, 483 P.2d 1342, 1344 (1971) (statute interpreted to require parental presence when juvenile is in custody).

54. IJA/ABA Standards 67.

55. *Id.* The Standards also recommend that those jurisdictions that fail to adopt the proposals should give special consideration to such factors as the juvenile's age, intelligence, education, level of sophistication, and whether he was allowed to confer with a parent. Further, in those situations in which a very young or inexperienced juvenile cannot pass muster under this test, the Standards suggest that a valid consent still can be obtained if the juvenile's parent is present and consulted by the juvenile. *Id.* at 66–67.

56. 49 Misc. 2d 154, 267 N.Y.S.2d 91 (Ulster County Fam. Ct. 1966).

57. *Id.* at 169–70, 267 N.Y.S.2d at 110.

58. *Id.* at 169, 267 N.Y.S.2d at 109.

59. 412 U.S. at 229.

60. United States v. Watson, 423 U.S. at 425; Schneckloth v. Bustamonte, 412 U.S. at 231.

61. In discussing the constitutional bounds of a "stop and frisk," Justice White has stated that "given the proper circumstances, . . . the person may be *briefly* detained against his will while pertinent questions are directed to him." Terry v. Ohio, 392 U.S. 1, 34 (1968) (concurring opinion) (emphasis added).

62. Prohibiting consent searches in the case of juveniles would contradict the Supreme Court's stated conclusion that consent searches are a necessary police practice. Schneckloth v. Bustamonte, 412 U.S. at 227–28, 231–32.

63. 384 U.S. at 468.

64. 423 U.S. at 425.

65. Schneckloth v. Bustamonte, 412 U.S. at 247.

66. *See, e.g., In re* Williams, 49 Misc. 2d 154, 157, 267 N.Y.S.2d 91, 98 (Ulster County Fam. Ct. 1966).

67. In fact, the defendant in *Watson* received *Miranda* warnings prior to giving consent. 423 U.S. at 425.

68. *In re* K.W.B., 500 S.W.2d 275, 281 (Mo. App. 1973).

69. *E.g.,* Mo. Ann. Stat. § 211.131(2) (Vernon 1962).

70. *E.g., id.* § 211.141(1).

71. 387 U.S. at 33.

72. *Id.* at 42.

73. *E.g.,* Mo. Ann. Stat. § 211.101 (Vernon 1962).

74. *In re* K.W.B., 500 S.W.2d 275, 282 (Mo. App. 1973).

75. 403 U.S. at 551–52 (White, J., concurring).

76. *In re* Gault, 387 U.S. at 15–16.

77. *Id.* at 26.

78. *See In re* Carlo, 48 N.J. 224, 244–45, 225 A.2d 110, 121–22 (1966) (Weintraub, C.J., concurring). *See also* State v. Shaw, 93 Ariz. 40, 47, 378 P.2d 487, 491 (1963), where the Arizona court stated: "The need for special treatment begins at the instant the juvenile is contacted by peace officers. . . ."

79. *But see* Tex. Fam. Code Ann. tit. 3, § 51.09(a) (Vernon Supp. 1975), which, when enacted in 1973, required attorney concurrence for all juvenile waivers of the fifth amendment privilege. This statute, however, caused outrage within some law enforcement circles in Texas due to its severe limitations. Thus, it was amended in 1975 to include less restrictive options, *id.* § 51.09(b). *See* letter to author from Robert O. Dawson, Wright C. Morrow Professor in Criminal Law, University of Texas School of Law, Nov. 9, 1976 (on file at Boston University Law Review).

80. Lewis v. State, 259 Ind. 431, 436, 440, 288 N.E.2d 138, 141, 143 (1972).
81. *See* IJA/ABA Standards 1–2.
82. Miranda v. Arizona, 384 U.S. at 474.
83. *See* text accompanying note 42 *supra*.
84. *See* text accompanying note 77 *supra*.

The Front End of the Juvenile Justice System

B. Pretrial Detention and Its Alternatives

Introduction

The early advocacy for separate juvenile courts was motivated, in part, by the concern that youngsters were locked up with adults pending judicial hearings (as well as following sentence). The Illinois Juvenile Court Act of 1899 stated that pending final disposition, the child may be retained in the possession of a parent or custodian or in "some suitable place provided by the city or county authorities." Eighty years later, all too many communities and subregions of states lack suitable places providing constructive predispositional care for delinquent and status offense youths. Initially, the completion of the conversion of a private dwelling into a detention facility or obtaining the funds to construct such a facility seemed like the end of the task. In reality it represented only the beginning. Employing competent staff, securing teachers, arranging medical care for the youngsters, and insuring the safety of the children became additional objectives.

Serious deficiencies in the administration of detention facilities have become more evident during the past several decades; examples are the locking up of youngsters needlessly or for longer periods than necessary, physical attacks on youngsters by staff members and by other juveniles, as well as assaults on the staff by juveniles, suicides, and frequent inattention to the constitutional rights of accused youths. Though social science research and legal writings have emphasized the shortcomings in these programs, nonetheless many children must have received nourishment from caring staff and a renewal of their determination to resolve certain problems.

The initial article presents commentaries and observations by citizen volunteers who studied a number of detention programs around the nation. The report, by the National Council of Jewish Women [NCJW], depicts the detention experience, human and inhuman. What emerges is a call to minimize the use of detention and to substitute a variety of community-based alternatives aimed at reducing the trauma of separation from one's family and surroundings.

The professional research approach to detention services, by Rosemary Sarri, supports many of the observations and conclusions of the NCJW citizen volunteers. Additional approaches to curbing unnecessary detention, through legislative, programmatic, and judicial means, are urged.

An earlier work by Sarri, *Under Lock and Key,* also prepared as part of the University of Michigan's National Assessment of Juvenile Corrections, examined a range of detention data and issues. It reported the shocking fact that at least one-half million juveniles entered local adult jails annually; a similar number were admitted to juvenile detention facilities each year. If detention facilities provide difficult experiences for many youngsters, surely the jail experience produces far greater despair. An investigation into children in adult jails, published in 1976 by the Children's Defense Fund, revealed that numerous children were in local jails which were not included in the national jail census. Since Sarri's estimate was based in part upon the census, this finding indicates that substantially more than one-half million youngsters are jailed annually.

Four types of alternatives to secure detention are described and evaluated in Young and Pappenfort's concluding work in this section: home detention, also known as home supervision or in-house detention; attention homes; nonsecure residential programs for runaways; and private foster home programs. Of these, home detention appears to have proliferated across the nation more than the other models, probably because it is nonresidential in nature and easier to organize and operate. The California legislature mandated in 1976 that each county probation department provide a home supervision component with a probation officer or probation aide maintaining a caseload of no more than ten youngsters who otherwise would have required detention. Elsewhere, the caseload maximum guideline for this program is five youngsters.

Home detention fits well with the developing use of detention screening, an adaptation of the traditional juvenile intake function to screen juveniles away from the detention facility and return them to their families, place them under home supervision, or lodge them in nonsecure detention alternatives. The Wisconsin legislature in 1978 mandated twenty-four hour detention intake availability across that state. Further checks on unnecessary detention have been achieved through detention hearings, which most juvenile codes now require within forty-eight hours or so of admission, and which involve judicial officer review of the necessity for continued detention. Also, a growing number of statutes prohibit or severely constrain any locking up of status offense youths. The Young and Pappenfort review provides largely positive information as to the utility of these nonsecure alternatives.

14 *Detention as Punishment*
Edward Wakin

Generally speaking, when detention is properly used, the children in detention will be among the community's most disturbed and aggressively acting-out adolescents . . . Their detention experience cannot be a neutral one. It will either be a destructive experience confirming them in a pattern of delinquent behavior, or a constructive one that will help redirect them into becoming socially useful citizens. The mission of detention is to provide a constructive experience.[1]

These principles provide a point of departure for NCJW [National Council of Jewish Women] Sections visiting detention centers in their own communities to ob-

From *Children Without Justice: A Report by the National Council of Jewish Women* (New York: National Council of Jewish Women, Inc., 1975), pp. 43-58. Reprinted by permission.

serve them firsthand. Detention facilities, operating as way stations between the police and the courts, are designed to provide temporary care for children who require "secure custody." The care was of varying kinds, the custody was a matter of lock and key, the "constructive experience" was more the exception than the rule. Repeatedly detention emerged as a form of punishment without conviction — and often, without crime.

The resulting reports ranged from descriptions of "a very frightening and demoralizing place" to a detention center where "the children seemed happy (under the circumstances)." What became clear is that each community must look to its own detention centers to see what description fits and to learn what is being done for or to children in trouble. The descriptions from individual Sections of their own communities speak for themselves in introducing the subject of detention:

> Once in the detention center, the children lose their identity. They wear institutional clothing, eat institutional food, think and do in the way of the institution. There is no therapy; they may see a caseworker for a few minutes. . . . We did not see any children shackled to the beds or being beaten. But we also did not see any evidence of constructive work being done with the children. It is a very frightening and demoralizing place. It has been said that if a child is not a murderer or drug addict when he enters, he may well be after repeated times at the home. . . . The one improvement that I can see over the past ten years is that now infants, toddlers, and young children are not sent there.

> It was a very impersonal building, but in all fairness, I must say that the few staff members were extremely kind, dedicated, cooperative, and receptive. . . . The facility contains an open circular room where boys and girls eat and play (ping pong, pool, etc.), a classroom where one teacher attempts to teach approximately eleven students, all of whom have fallen behind in their studies and all of whom are at a different level of study. At night, boys and girls are locked in special small cells (some have sinks, others just a bed). The time lock then releases them in the morning. There is an intercommunication system if one of the children needs help, consultation, or becomes ill. At night, there is a part-time employed couple on duty available if a child needs help with a problem. . . . All belongings are locked and must be asked for. . . . The center was clean and the children seemed happy (under the circumstances). I tried to talk to a couple of the kids and they seemed polite, aloof, and uninterested.

> The center is overcrowded, staff turnover is great, many untrained, salaries are low. . . . Juveniles are assigned to rooms by age and sex. Nature of crime is not a factor. There is little or no privacy or freedom. All girls on admittance must undergo pelvic examination to determine if they are pregnant as no institution will take pregnant girls. Also, all children must go through the Cuprex Delouse test — yellow, burning substance sprayed on bodies. This is done in a group. . . . Our interviewer found the atmosphere to be that of a jail, monotonous, and very regimented. Physical conditions were barely adequate, due mainly to overcrowding. Children have to sleep on floors if rooms are filled. Some of the staff seemed aware of shortcomings but not all agreed that change and improvements are needed. This facility has been rated in the top five percent of all detention centers in the U.S. based on physical structure, quality of staff, and percent of recidivism (48 percent).

> We were deeply depressed by the general appearance and condition of the entire building. It was dreary, unattractive and actually many of the bedrooms were not fit for a reasonable

level of human comfort. In one room there were wall-to-wall cots and windows were covered with blankets to try to keep out the cold. All "social" rooms were barren with little, if any, comforts. There was an inadequate area for physical activity. Most children who were there at the time of our visit seemed lethargic and disinterested; not actively involved in anything constructive. The only two pleasant rooms in the building were closed because of lack of staff.

This detention center for girls is housed in a building that should have been condemned fifty years ago. There are huge cracks in the walls and ceilings. Water seeps through many of them because of the condition of the plumbing. We had to sidestep puddles in the hallways. The so-called gymnasium is a basement room with so many structural pillars that no real physical activity is possible. In their dormitories, the girls each have a "cubby" in which clothing and personal possessions are kept, explaining the generally disheveled look of their clothes. Many of the girls seemed to be slightly sedated, an impression confirmed by a member of the staff who cited heavy reliance on tranquilizers. Questioned about homosexuality among the girls, he said it was a misunderstood phenomenon: "They're just looking for families." (This detention center has since been closed.)

One step toward improving conditions may lie in the adoption of a National Advisory Commission recommendation that "Every detention facility for adults or juveniles should have provisions for an outside, objective evaluation at least once a year." This need for monitoring is emphasized by the fact that fourteen states have no laws requiring regular inspection of juvenile detention centers, and many states which do have such laws make no provision for compliance with recommendations arising from such inspection.[2]

As pointed out in Connecticut's 1971 Juvenile Court Manual, *"loss of liberty in any form is a serious matter."* The loss is compounded when children are unnecessarily detained while waiting for adjudication, further compounded when the conditions are punishing, compounded intolerably when the children are only accused of such status offenses as playing hooky and running away, or when children are themselves victims of parental anger, neglect, or crimes and the community is unable to find a place for them.

In community after community, detention centers were found to be places where the seriousness of losing liberty was not treated with the same gravity for children as for adults. The decision to detain was found to be a police as well as court power, particularly when no court or probation official was available. This was usually the case when juveniles were picked up late at night or on weekends — those periods which are also most likely to produce juvenile mischief. Police discretion on arresting or not arresting a child is thereby extended to release or detention as well, with detention less likely where children have backup from parents. Detention is liable to be used as a tactic in combatting delinquency as illustrated in two West Coast suburbs. When delinquency increased, orders went out to the police to detain almost every child on his second offense.

Yet, when proper criteria are applied, no more than 10 percent of all children arrested by police require detention according to the National Council on Crime and Delinquency. Secure custody, they maintain, is necessary only: (1) If the child is almost certain to run away while the court is handling the case; (2) If the child is almost certain to commit an offense dangerous to himself or the community before court disposition of his case; (3) If the child must be held for another jurisdiction.

In practice, as government studies have reported and as the NCJW study documented, detention is misused, abused, and overused. This was reflected in the proportion of juveniles detained on charges for which only children can be arrested — status offenses. Of 42 reports containing information on this point, 10 said "all" or "most" of the children in the detention centers visited were status offenders; in another 14, the proportion of status offenders varied from over 40 percent to 90 percent. At one center, when the director was asked how many of the 30 children there really needed to be detained, he reviewed each case separately, then answered, "Two." In another city, a 1968–1970 study of youths held in the detention center revealed that only three percent were charged with major offenses against persons. . . .

The most positive description of a detention center visited comes from a Midwest Section. As described by NCJW observers, the center tries to avoid confining children, following the philosophy of juvenile court that "no child should have his liberty curtailed if there is an alternative open to the court." The center operates a twenty-four-hour screening unit manned by staffers with degrees in social work or related fields, and considerable experience in working with troubled juveniles. After a policeman brings a youngster to the center and all pertinent information is taken down, the admissions staff tries to locate the parents, if the police have been unsuccessful in their attempts to do so. Most youngsters are released to their parents. Those who have committed no offenses and will not or cannot return home are sent to foster homes. Some can be placed in a Volunteers of America shelter. . . .

In deciding whether to detain a child, the staff considers attitude, seriousness of offense, and whether the child will appear in court if summoned. If juveniles are detained, their records are sent immediately to court intake so their case can be expedited. No child can be detained more than six court hours (excluding weekends and holidays) without a detention hearing and no more than twelve court hours unless a petition has been filed and a judge or referee decides that the child should remain in custody. To make certain no child is forgotten, a new detention hearing must be held every ten days.

Under this system, most children stay only a few days; the average stay is 4.8 days. Those in detention live in a thirty-bed center built in 1957 and remodeled in 1970 to add 29 beds, a gymnasium and new classrooms. It is composed of three levels: the lower level contains a large, cheerful cafeteria, gymnasium and classrooms, a second level consists of a large recreation room, counselors' offices and girls' living quarters; the third level houses the boys' sleeping quarters.

An effort is made to avoid depersonalization. Once a child is examined and takes a shower, he is allowed to wear his own clothes. A chaplain assigned to the center, working with a group of pastors learning clinical counseling, talks to the youngsters and holds voluntary interdenominational services on Sunday. Volunteers tutor youngsters and provide contact with an outsider who will listen to them. The classrooms are small and intimate; bulletin boards and windows are covered with children's work. Art projects done in the art classes are displayed throughout the building and even adorn the waiting room at juvenile court.

The atmosphere of the center and the attitudes of the staff were described by NCJW observers.

> There are many bulletin boards on the walls and the children are encouraged to write down their thoughts and post them. Music (the kind children like) can be heard in many places throughout the building. All of the staff in the center have been trained to work with troubled youth and are encouraged to provide as much warmth and support as possible. . . . The counselors are young people, college-educated in child care, psychology or sociology. They talk with the children, supervise their activities, and keep a log on each child's actions, attitudes, and problems as he spends his time awaiting a court hearing. Disruptive children receive extra help from the counselors, who have written guidelines to assist them in handling behavior problems.

Nonetheless, in this facility, as in the typical detention center, security means locked doors. From 10:30 p.m. until 7 a.m., each child is in his own room and the door is locked. An intercom system enables him to ask for the aid of a counselor if necessary. Corridor doors are locked night and day, and permission is required to go from one part of the building to the other. Even substantial professional services delivered in a compassionate manner cannot erase for the child the essential fact that he is locked up.

Security is a recurrent theme in reports on detention centers. One report from a southern city stated: "All detention is 'secure' in that doors are kept locked, and even when going to the bathroom there is always a guard in attendance. No toilet facilities have doors, so that there is no privacy." In upstate New York, a new director of a new facility noted that security is considered first and all else comes after, adding, "We are concerned with protecting the child and the community."

Surveillance extends to visitation and usually to mail. In one Midwest center, children are given a handbook which tells them about regulations and even more about the detention-center approach. On the one hand, the children read: "We think all people are important. This makes you important. . . . We really feel YOU *are important.*" This appears opposite a page which advises juveniles that all letters must be placed in an unsealed envelope which then goes to the probation officer handling his case: "If something in the letter is not clear, the probation officer may talk to you about it. Your assigned probation officer will read all of the mail that comes to you before giving it to you."

To encourage cooperative behavior, some detention centers use incentive programs. One center places youngsters in one of three groups — A, B, or C — depending on behavior. The A group gets the most privileges, including later hours and Saturday night pizza with the staff. A more usual approach involves "rewards" such as trips to town and movies or the earning of "merit" points that can be turned into treats at the canteen. (Such rewards raise questions about average length of stay.) No significant evidence was found of corporal punishment; isolation is used for recalcitrant youngsters. Its official use varied from one center where isolation lasted from five or ten minutes to three or four hours, depending upon change of attitude and behavior, to another center with a twenty-four-hour maximum in isolation. In the latter instance, the staff checks the child every fifteen minutes. In more than one instance, however, staff revealed broad discretion in the use of "solitary." One attorney described staff's placing a child in isolation, removing him before the lapse of the official twenty-four-hour limit, only to return him after a brief respite.

What emerges from inspection of detention centers and their many variations is an uncertain, uneasy, and uneven interplay between the need for security and the needs of children. It is complicated by the constant turnover of youngsters and the differences in reasons for detaining them. A Midwest Section report stated:

> The constantly changing population of the center with resulting psychological and physical problems of trying to work with many situations on a short-term basis must greatly frustrate the staff. The children usually resent being detained. They range from the frightened child who is a runaway or a drug user to the more sophisticated youths who have committed felonies and have appeared in court many times. Most of the girls who stay in the center are there because of family problems and are not segregated from more sophisticated offenders. There is a certain contagion factor involved, which the counselors try to minimize through program planning.

Shortages of money and of qualified personnel are cited as recurring problems. The money problem tends to squeeze out aspects that involve recreation and extra services and to reduce the centers to their custodial function. Depending on the community, the qualifications for personnel range from degrees in social work or the social sciences to high school diplomas. A more significant factor is harder to pinpoint and that is the staff attitude, which reflects the policies of the director who hired the personnel.

Because attitude is an intangible, there is no substitute for first-hand observation. In various instances, the reports cited the warm, positive attitude of directors and staff. Observers were also able to sense the gap between what was said and what was the actual atmosphere. One director stressed that he wanted to give the children the feeling that the detention center was "a home away from home" and that he and his wife were "just like parents — and in some cases better." NCJW observers questioned his description: "We felt that all was not well. The children that we saw seemed to be sitting around aimlessly watching TV or doing nothing. When asked about this, the director didn't seem to be too concerned or interested. In fact, he was very curt to one child who asked a question. The general feeling was one of fear of the director."

Volunteers perform a variety of roles in detention centers, with a number of centers reporting a greater need for them. Of sixty-six detention centers in which the question of volunteers was explored, about three-fourths draw on volunteers. Volunteers provide tutoring, recreation, and supportive services. Typical reports on their role: "Volunteers are an important part of the program and provide tutors for children having trouble with their school work." . . . "Volunteers come occasionally and give holiday parties and bring books, magazines, and treats. This is important because last year, only three of nineteen children detained at Christmas had a visit from family or friends of their own." . . . "The greatest need volunteer-wise is for volunteers to work on a one-to-one basis with the juveniles." . . . "The probation counselors indicated an interest in having volunteers act as consistent and close contacts for juvenile and family." . . . "This program consists of big brother and sister volunteers and foster grandparents." . . .

Minimizing the use of detention requires community alternatives such as group homes, temporary foster homes, detention boarding homes, and neighborhood supervision. Besides the all-important human factor, the cost factor argues for such alternatives. Detention centers have been estimated at costing between $20,000 and $35,000 per bed to build (an estimate that must be revised upward in the face of soaring building costs). Cost per child per day runs between $20 and $35. To cite one comparison: a program for detention boarding homes in upstate New York costs $6 per child per day.

From various parts of the country, NCJW Sections have reported on the success of these alternatives to detention centers:

Temporary Foster Homes — At about one-half the cost of institutional care, children are placed with families who take care of them until long-term arrangements are made. In one New England community, volunteers take into their homes children who are considered "low risks," often runaways. Children can be sheltered in these homes without parental consent with appropriate orders from the juvenile court.

Detention Boarding Homes — As a form of nonsecure detention, boarding homes are licensed and are under the supervision of juvenile authorities. Space is kept available on a standby basis and boarding home parents are paid according to a schedule that is increased when a child is placed there. In an upstate New York community, where six detention boarding homes operate, the parents vary widely in age from a couple in their late twenties to a grandmother. They maintain the same standards as foster homes, with boarding home mothers not permitted to work outside their homes. The children continue to attend their regular school, if possible; otherwise a school near the boarding home. The program, operating since 1967, has kept children for as long as six months in such homes; recently a state ruling limited the stay to forty-five days. Observers found this indication of the program's success: "Sometimes the children have to leave the boarding home when they much prefer to remain there."

Neighborhood Supervision —A program for supervising alleged delinquents enables them to live at home or in foster homes while the court disposes of their case. College students, housewives, and senior citizens have been used in such programs in different parts of the country. A St. Louis pilot project was found to be particularly successful. Community Youth Leaders were recruited from the neighborhoods in which the children were living and they supervised youngsters facing court action. The dropout rate was nil, the cost was considerably less than in an institution, and the rate of new delinquencies was far below that of children held in detention centers.

In Massachusetts, where statewide action was taken to close down all detention centers, a visit to one of the last remaining centers brought this reaction: "This facility, especially in contrast with the newer group homes and halfway houses, serves as a reminder of the deplorable conditions juveniles were exposed to under the archaic system of juvenile justice." After meeting with the director and his assistant following a tour of the facility, "it was easy to see why they both were primarily aiming for an eventual shutdown of the center as it now functions."

New Jersey has moved in the same direction with a new juvenile justice code that went into effect on March 1, 1974. Counties were barred from sending status offenders to detention facilities for juvenile delinquents. New facilities were ordered with an open-door rather than a locked-door policy. The shelters could not be physically restricting, allowing free access to the community. The head of the State Department of Institutions and Agencies described the ideal shelter as housing six to eight youths for periods of about two weeks or less, with the youngsters encouraged to attend local schools. Or a better solution: temporary foster homes.

Thus, in the interplay between the need of security and the needs of children, signs of revision can be identified. Current reassessment of secure detention has created a demand to put security in its very limited place and not to impose it unnecessarily on the majority of children in trouble. Communities are being challenged to emphasize the needs and rights of those children who await their day in court.

NOTES

1. *State Responsibility for Juvenile Detention Care,* Youth Development and Delinquency Prevention Administration, HEW, 1970.
2. *Statewide Jail Standards and Inspection Systems Project,* American Bar Association, Commission on Correctional Facilities and Services.

15 *Service Technologies: Detention*
Rosemary Sarri

. . . One of the most problematic aspects of juvenile justice is the detention of youth in juvenile detention facilities and in adult jails. Analysis of population distribution in juvenile justice indicates that on a given day, nine out of ten youth in residential facilities in the juvenile justice system will be found in detention units or adult jails (Sarri, 1974). It is conservatively estimated that nearly one million youth spend one or more days in jail or detention in the United States each year. Comprehensive information about detention practices is lacking because most of these programs are operated under local control and very few systematic studies have been completed. This section will not consider the general problem of jailing and detention, since NAJC [National Assessment of Juvenile Corrections] has already reported on state detention rates and practices in *Under Lock and Key* (Sarri, 1974). Instead, attention will be focused on the responses of detention unit directors to the questionnaire in the national sample survey. In that survey, responses were received from 147 juvenile detention units, 16 adult jails, and 8 shelter care facilities. Questionnaires were sent directly to the local juvenile court judge except in states with regional detention

From Rosemary Sarri and Yeheskel Hasenfeld, eds., *Brought to Justice? Juveniles, the Courts, and the Law* (Ann Arbor, Mich.: National Assessment of Juvenile Corrections, The University of Michigan, 1976), pp. 166-75. Reprinted by permission.

facilities, where the contact was made through the state director of juvenile corrections. Eleven states reported having state-administered facilities — a total of 18 such
units responded in this survey.

Detention is defined as the "temporary care of children who require secure custody for their own or the community's protection in physically restricting facilities
pending court disposition" (Sheridan, 1966:23). The object of pretrial detention in
the adult court is to assure the alleged offender's presence at trial; but in the case of
juveniles, the purpose is much broader because of the court's power to act in the
"best interest of the child" and to provide services that the judge or staff deems
necessary or desirable. [Some commentators believe] that probable cause evidence of
an alleged act or fear that the juvenile will abscond are less important to judges than
protection of the community or the needs of the youth.

The National Council on Crime and Delinquency has recommended that the percentage of youth detained should not exceed 10 percent of the cases referred to the
court. Seldom, however, is that standard achieved on a local or state level. For
example, in a study of juvenile courts in a large urban eastern state, detention rates
varied between 0.2 percent and 76 percent of the cases referred (Pawlak, 1972).
Further, McNeece (1976) noted that police who were located close to detention units
brought in many more youth than did police further away in the same county. Last, it
was reported that 83 percent of youth charged with incorrigibility in Hennepin
County, Minnesota, were detained, compared with 77 percent for armed robbery, 60
percent with assault, and 51 percent with burglary (Children and Youth in Crisis
Project, 1976). In that same court, status offenders constituted 46 percent of all
referrals to the court but 56 percent of all admitted to detention. Thus, as Lerman
(1970) and Ferster and Courtless (1971) point out, seriousness of offense is not a
useful basis for differentiating between detainees and nondetainees. Obviously, youth
who have no home or whose parents refuse to accept them run the highest risk of
detention regardless of what they have or have not done. Police are reluctant to
release youth on the street once there has been an apprehension.

WHO ARE THE YOUTH IN DETENTION?

Responses to the national sample indicate that systematic data about youth held in
detention are not kept in many courts. Thus our analysis is necessarily limited, especially with respect to age, offense, and other characteristics of these youth. . . .The
largest detention unit in the sample reported detention of 380 males and 170 females,
a total of 550. The vast majority (more than 90 percent) of youth detained in the
United States are held in large units, exceeding seventy-five beds. These are almost
exclusively in large urban communities.

Data on offense characteristics were often incomplete in this survey, but it is
clear that there are pronounced male and female differences. Status offenses were
predominant for females, while property, status, and person offenses were most frequent for males. When total population size and density were correlated with offense
characteristics, it was clear that the larger the size, the greater the likelihood of status

offenders (.51), property offenders (.66), and person offenders (.58). In addition, the larger units were more likely to have proportionally more nonwhite youth. Previous court referral was also an important variable: approximately 35 percent of the males and 34 percent of the females had a prior history in the court.

The median age was 14 years. This is similar to the 14.7 years reported by Pappenfort, Kilpatrick, and Kuby (1970). Only 3 percent of the youth were under 9 years old. . . .

WHAT IS DETENTION LIKE?

Health Services

Although 6 percent of the respondents stated that at least a quarter of the youth had severe emotional disturbances, screening examinations were not routinely provided except in the cases of medical and social-work examinations, where two-thirds of the youth were reported to have been examined. Social-work examinations are not surprising, since the professional staff most likely employed in detention are social workers. Concerning other personnel, only nurses were employed full or part time to any appreciable extent. Less than one nurse per unit, however, was the average. Only 9 units of the 171 sampled had full-time physicians; 2 units had dentists; 7 units had full-time psychiatrists. For the vast majority of the units, health care was provided on a special or emergency basis only. Thus, one should not overestimate the extent of screening that takes place given this great lack of resources. Only 13 percent of the units indicated that youth could see health care personnel on request. For many youth, detention is traumatic; thus, suicide and other evidences of trauma must be expected. But detention facilities have few or no resources to handle such problems. In the case of youth held in adult jails, few reported any type of servicing at all, not even medical examinations. These results are very similar to those presented in the earlier NAJC report (Sarri, 1974:55), indicating that almost no progress has taken place between 1966 and 1975. Shelter care facilities reported that they relied on the health care facilities of the local community.

TABLE 15-1 Screening Examinations in Detention*

	NONE	ALL OR MOST	SOME
Medical	6	62	32
Dental	24	17	59
Psychological	2	20	78
Psychiatric	4	10	86
Social work	3	64	33

*In percentages of units reporting services; N = 147.

In view of the frequent reports of suicide attempts, it was particularly interesting that 83 percent of the detention directors stated that between 1 percent and 10 percent of the youth in detention make one or more suicide attempts. These findings are in accord with those from the NAJC study of juvenile correctional programs (Vinter, 1976), which reported up to 17 percent of the youth attempting to seriously hurt themselves while in jail or detention. Obviously this proportion is alarmingly high, and it highlights the need for examination of conditions of incarceration and detention of youth who are no risk to the community's safety.

Education Services

Seventy-seven percent of the juvenile detention units reported that school facilities were available in the unit. In the remaining units, education was provided only on an irregular or special basis for certain youth. Of the facilities with education programs, 45 percent said all youth attended school but the majority attended part time. The mean number of teachers was between 1 and 2, and they were provided by the local public school system in 63 percent of the cases (where information was available). Obviously, any systematic education is limited under these circumstances.

Attendance at community schools was not permitted in 66 percent of the units; where permitted, 22 percent stated that only a few youth in each unit were allowed to attend. By way of contrast, jails reported no formal educational programs for juveniles, as would be expected, but the shelter care facilities all reported that more than 75 percent of their youth were enrolled in community schools. This finding would clearly support the use wherever possible of shelter care to prevent serious disruption of a youth's education.

Supplementary education programs were reported in the majority of the facilities — individual tutoring, remedial classes, religious education, and creative arts. Seldom did units report that more than 25 percent of the youth received such supplementary services.

Treatment Services

Specialized interpersonal treatment technologies are seldom employed in detention units. Small proportions of units provided these services:

- Counseling (4%)
- Reality therapy (2%)
- Guided group interaction (3%)
- Positive peer culture (1%)
- Behavior modification (1%)
- Family therapy (1%)
- Religious counseling (5%)

No pattern emerged about the providers. In some cases the service was provided by detention staff; in others it was contracted from external agencies; in others, both. Services often were provided by probation staff of the court, who also had control over these aspects of the detention program. Thus, distinctions between youth in a preadjudicatory status and those in a postadjudicatory status might well be obfuscated.

Community Interaction of Youth in Detention

Community contacts for youth in detention were sharply restricted. In a minority of instances, a few youth were permitted to work in the community or to attend religious services. On the other hand, 90 percent or more of the units reported that nearly all youth had opportunities to attend movies or other organized recreation in the community. Apparently youth could be securely handled in these situations but were not trusted in more individualized activity.

Although the parents are said to play important roles in juvenile justice, family contact is often not encouraged. Parents were permitted contact with the youth by 16 percent of the units at admission; by 38 percent on a weekly basis; by 13 percent on a biweekly basis; and less frequent contacts were arranged by the remaining 33 percent. The average time for a parent visit was thirty minutes. Youth contacts with parents by letter or telephone were also restricted, often censored: 40 percent of the units reported that all mail — incoming and outgoing — was censored. Denial of family visitation as a means of discipline was reported by 15 percent of the units.

Control and Custody

Detention units typically have extensive services to maintain physical control over youth and to prevent escape. Control and custody are asserted to be essential functions of all correctional programs, but nowhere is control more prominent than in detention. Staff reports of organizational goals . . . make it clear that control is an important goal priority for all staff.

Correctional programs have a vast array of technological devices and techniques for controlling disorder. Among the prominent security devices in most detention units were locked rooms, areas, and buildings, seclusion rooms, gates and fences, electronically controlled doors, and listening devices.

Surveillance and control of youth in detention is made more difficult because adolescent youth often strongly resent incarceration. Thus, actual control may be more difficult than in some adult facilities. Staff reported use of a variety of techniques to control behavior: continuous room monitoring, control of possessions, body checks, and so forth. Youth were monitored most often by having staff members accompany them, but passes and telephone surveillance were also used. Table 15-2 reports the types and frequencies of inspections in detention units. Random or daily checks are made in 75 percent or more of the cases. Random checks are particularly problematic because youth may readily perceive them as harrassment.

Contraband was reported as a problem by 61 percent of the directors, and it was often stated as a reason for the frequent searches. All types of contraband were reported found in detention units.

Phone and mail restrictions were reported by most units, especially on phone use. Mail censorship, as mentioned above, was reported by 40 percent of the units; the distribution of responses was bimodal, with another 40 percent reporting no censorship, and the remaining had variable patterns.

Youth were restricted to their rooms many hours each day. It is clear that not much is provided other than solitary activities. In 85 percent of the units, individual juveniles' rooms were used for discipline and seclusion, but they were also places for solitary studying and recreation, for listening to the radio, and for resting. There appeared to be little concern about negative effects of sensory deprivation through isolation. Moreover, the extensive use of television contributed to reduced interpersonal interaction. Few units restricted radio or television, so it was not surprising that youth watched television an average of 3-4 hours a day. Differences are noteworthy between viewing time and time spent in regularly scheduled, organized recreation. A mean of just less than 20 hours a week was reported — primarily in indoor and outdoor gymnastic and other sports activities.

Disruptive behavior is apparently frequent in correctional facilities: 68 percent of the units reported one or more incidents in the previous six months. Some units reported that disruptions occurred at least weekly. Only half of the units, however, reported standard operating procedures for handling such incidents; of those that did, only 10 percent had written rules and policies. It is probable that inconsistent handling is followed by more, not less, disruption.

The planned use of seclusion as a discipline measure was reported in all of the detention units except shelter care facilities (which did not have physical arrangements for secure holding). Thirty-four percent reported having special seclusion rooms; 20 percent had holding rooms; 8 percent had maximum-security wings or areas. The minimum time for youth to be held in these units averaged 30 minutes, while the maximum averaged 24-36 hours. The average length of time youth remained in them was reported as 6-12 hours. These are the reasons given by units for placing youth in seclusion:

- Hitting a staff member (84% of the units)
- Fighting with youth (67%)
- Escape (54%)
- Refusing to obey orders (49%)
- Use of drugs or alcohol (39%)
- Homosexual behavior (37%)
- Stealing (31%)
- Heterosexual behavior (26%)
- Hurting oneself (26%)

Youth whose disruptive behavior becomes problematic are sent to the adult jail by 69 percent of the units. In fact, 21 percent reported that more than one case a month is placed in the local adult jail because of disruptive behavior.

While youth are held in seclusion, their activities are further restricted, in most cases, to reading and listening to the radio. However, 15 percent of the units reported that youth in these situations were given no materials of any kind.

Staff in 97 percent of the detention units were not armed, but staff were permitted in 44 percent to use physical controls or restraints for youth who broke the rules.

TABLE 15-2   Detention Unit Inspections of Detainees*

	DAILY	RANDOM	WEEKLY	NEVER	NO INFORMATION
Youth's personal property	36	38	8	7	11
Living quarters	80	11	8	0	1
Person	52	37	4	1	6
Work area or school	63	20	4	3	10
Visitors	31	18	10	32	9

*In percentages; N = 171.

SYNOPSIS

The findings from this study suggest that detention should be used with great discretion since it is primarily a custodial program. The majority of detention facilities in the United States are operated in conjunction with the juvenile court; therefore the following recommendations are pertinent if the most negative consequences of detention are to be avoided.

• Intake screening should be available 24 hours a day and should be handled by professionaly trained court staff — not by law enforcement officials. The right to counsel and the availability of counsel in detention hearings must become a significant reality, not merely a formal gesture of little purpose and unrecognized value by juveniles and parents. Since several studies of adult court processing have observed that the mere fact of detention increases the probability of subsequent conviction and institutional commitment, such intervention should be most carefully controlled and avoided whenever possible. The Pawlak study (1972) substantially corroborated this finding among the more than sixty courts studied in one state.

• The court must take initiative in stimulating the development of alternatives to detention and, when necessary, must enjoin community child welfare and other agencies to provide services to youth in need. Too often detention facilities are misused for administrative convenience when another form of care would be more appropriate. As long as the court continues to accept youth inappropriately, those who apprehend and process youth will continue to overuse the court to aid police investigation, serve the diagnostic aspects of probation, hold for treatment, and so forth. Because so few of all detained youth are institutionalized following adjudication, court staff would be well advised to use preadjudicative detention more parsimoniously.

• Although detention is not supposed to be used as punishment, the reports from Sumner (1971) and the Montana survey (Logan, 1972) point to frequent use of preventive detention and of weekend holding. Nearly all of these detained youth were released without petitions being filed. Once criterion of effective detention practice could be the level of subsequent adjudication and institutional commitment: detainees subsequently institutionalized are more likely to have required detention. However, it would also be necessary to make sure that commitment rates did not become affected by having to prove the necessity of detention after the fact. After studying detention practices in the Denver Juvenile Court, Cohen (1975a) stated that youth who were held in detention were more likely to receive severe dispositions than those not detained. He also reported that the rate of detention for status offenses, auto thefts, and other property crimes was equal (22 percent of those referred). Moreover, the rate for youth charged with violent crimes was only 27 percent, which is 2 percent below that of those charged with alcohol violations (Cohen, 1975b:22). If one goal of detention is protection of the community, then such organizational behavior is clearly questionable.

• Accountability in detention decision making is urgently needed; and if it is to become a reality, more adequate information must be gathered and made available. Twenty-two states do not even bother to keep any detention statistics. And in states that maintain statistics our survey of courts indicates that their information is incomplete and seldom prepared for use by court administrators. If court staff can agree on the goal of facilitating the well-being of juveniles, regardless of their offenses, they can help reduce delinquency by judiciously and parsimoniously processing youth into and through the juvenile justice system. This idea of reducing penetration into the system is being attempted in several states. Research has indicated that apprehension and incarceration of youth at early ages increases rather than decreases the likelihood of subsequent delinquency and crime.

• The architecture and physical conditions of most detention facilities tend to increase the trauma associated with detention for many youth. We agree with most other observers that some youth must be held, but they need not be locked up in stark, frightening, jail-like units. Physically, each facility should permit privacy, adequate and healthful food, shelter, and personal care; recreation and education; use of the telephone; the right to have visitors and counsel daily; and a physical plant that permits visual and auditory supervision.

• Detention facilities need more professionally trained staff responsible to the court. They also need higher levels of child-care staff coverage with appropriate assignments of male and female staff. A total of 4.7 persons are required to cover one position for twenty-four hours a day, seven days a week. Staff should be able to relate to youth on a warm yet firm basis. They must have or be trained to use varied program skills so that youth can be constructively occupied during incarceration.

• Each presiding judge of a juvenile court should personally monitor the physical conditions and service delivery of his court's detention facility. This will require ongoing study of routine information about its operation as well as periodic visitations. Where private facilities are used for shelter care and holdover, they too should be subjected to the same monitoring and standards for adequate performance. Meeting such performance standards would probably require higher per diem allowances for shelter care than are currently provided.

• Education programs must be provided through the local community school and, whenever possible, youth should attend the local school and have some exposure to external community activities. The enforced idleness that characterizes many detention facilities can only lead to negative results and has no place in a system aimed at help and rehabilitation.

Detention in secure facilities is necessary for pretrial holding of youth, but the variation between states and between courts within states indicates that it is often used far more extensively than necessary and for youth who present no serious threat to community safety. Many youth report that their most frightening experiences in the justice system occurred when they were held in detention units, police lockups, or adult jails. Nevertheless, incarceration of youth in these types of facilities appears to be increasing throughout the country faster than incarceration in any other type of residential correctional facility (Wisconsin, 1976; Lerman, 1975). If another generation of youth is not to be harmed irrevocably, greater parsimony in the use of detention is essential.

REFERENCES

Children and Youth in Crisis Project   1976, HENNEPIN COUNTY'S STATUS OFFENDERS. Minneapolis: Community Health and Welfare Council.
Cohen, Lawrence E.   1975a, JUVENILE DISPOSITIONS: SOCIAL AND LEGAL FACTORS RELATED TO THE PROCESSING OF DENVER DELINQUENCY CASES. NCJISS Analytic Report 4, SD-AR-4. Washington: Law Enforcement Assistance Administration
1975b, WHO GETS DETAINED? AN EMPIRICAL ANALYSIS OF THE PREADJUDICATORY DETENTION OF JUVENILES IN DENVER, NCJISS Analytic Report 3, SD-AR-3. Washington: Law Enforcement Assistance Administration.
Ferster, Elyce Zenoff, and Thomas F. Courtless   1971, "The Intake Process in the Affluent County Juvenile Court." 22 HASTINGS L.J. 1127.
Lerman, Paul   1970, "Beyond *Gault:* Injustice and the Child." In Lerman (ed.), DELINQUENCY AND SOCIAL POLICY 236. New York: Praeger.
1975, COMMUNITY TREATMENT AND SOCIAL CONTROL. Chicago: University of Chicago Press.
Logan, Robert   1972, STATE OF MONTANA JAIL SURVEY. Helena: Governor's Crime Control Commission.
McNeece, Carl Aaron   1976, "Juvenile Courts in the Community Environment." Ph.D. dissertation, University of Michigan.
Pappenfort, Donnell N., Dee Morgan Kilpatrick, and Alma M. Kuby, comps.   1970, A CENSUS OF CHILDREN'S RESIDENTIAL INSTITUTIONS IN THE UNITED STATES, PUERTO RICO, AND THE VIRGIN ISLANDS: 1966. 7 vols. Chicago: University of Chicago, School of Social Service Administration.
Pawlak, Edward J.   1972, "The Administration of Juvenile Justice." Ph.D. dissertation, University of Michigan.
Sarri, Rosemary C.   1974, UNDER LOCK AND KEY: JUVENILES IN JAILS AND DETENTION. Ann Arbor: University of Michigan, National Assessment of Juvenile Corrections.
Sheridan, William   1966, STANDARDS FOR JUVENILE AND FAMILY COURTS. Children's Bureau Pub. No. 437. Washington: Government Printing Office.
Sumner, Helen   1971, LOCKING THEM UP: A STUDY OF JUVENILE DETENTION DECISIONS IN SELECTED CALIFORNIA COUNTIES. New York: National Council on Crime and Delinquency.
Vinter, Robert D.   1976, TIME OUT: A NATIONAL STUDY OF JUVENILE CORRECTIONAL PROGRAMS (ed.). Ann Arbor: University of Michigan, National Assessment of Juvenile Corrections.
Wisconsin Department of Health and Social Services   1976, JUVENILE DETENTION IN WISCONSIN: FINAL REPORT. Madison.

16 *Secure Detention of Juveniles and Alternatives to Its Use*

Thomas M. Young and Donnell M. Pappenfort

SITE SELECTION AND VISIT METHODOLOGY

. . . The selection of sites was purposeful and not random. We wanted to visit programs from which we could learn something. We tried to include programs in large, middlesize and small cities; programs designated for status offenders or alleged delinquents or both; residential and nonresidential programs. We also tried to achieve some geographic spread across the country.

The fourteen programs visited in January and February, 1976, and reported on here are listed below alphabetically by city.

- Discovery House, Inc., Anaconda, Montana.
- Community Detention, Baltimore, Maryland.
- Holmes-Hargadine Attention Home, Boulder, Colorado.
- Attention Home, Helena, Montana.
- Transient Youth Center, Jacksonville, Florida.
- Proctor Program, New Bedford, Massachusetts.
- Outreach Detention Program, Newport News, Virginia.
- Non-Secure Detention Program, Panama City, Florida.
- Amicus House, Pittsburgh, Pennsylvania.
- Home Detention, St. Joseph/Benton Harbor, Michigan.
- Home Detention Program, St. Louis, Missouri
- Community Release Program, San Jose, California.
- Center for the Study of Institutional Alternatives, Springfield, Massachusetts.
- Home Detention Program, Washington, D.C.

Readers should note that there is no basis for considering these fourteen programs as representative of all alternative programs now operating in the United States. The list does include seven programs based upon the Home Detention model which has been adopted by jurisdictions in several areas of the country. It also includes three Attention Homes which have been adopted by jurisdictions in a few western and mountain states. But the programs listed were selected more for anticipated learning value than for representativeness. While they may not be representa-

From *Secure Detention of Juveniles and Alternatives to Its Use*, National Evaluation Program, Phase I Summary Report. National Institute of Law Enforcement and Criminal Justice, Law Enforcement Assistance Administration, U.S. Department of Justice (Washington, D.C.: Government Printing Office, 1977), pp. 12-25 and 31-33. Reprinted by permission.

tive of all such programs, we found visiting them an informative experience and we think almost any juvenile court jurisdiction will find the descriptions here useful in planning an alternative to secure detention.

Site visits were conducted over a two- or three-day period during which court and other officials were interviewed and statistical data were assembled. After our reports were written informants in each jurisdiction were given an opportunity to read them and comment on the accuracy of our assertions of fact. They were indeed helpful. The conclusions and judgments given here, of course, are our own.

Eight of the alternative programs are administered by public agencies and six by private organizations. Seven of them were nonresidential in the sense that the juveniles remained in their own houses (in some a few were placed in surrogate homes). Five of the residential programs used group homes; the other two placed the youths in foster homes.

The programs are described in the following order. An initial section considers seven public, nonresidential programs based on the Home Detention model as originally conceived for and carried out in St. Louis, Missouri. They are sufficiently similar to discuss as a group. The second section takes up, one at a time, three Attention Homes, including the original one in Boulder, Colorado, and two others modeled after it. Each of the three had its own features, so they are described separately. The third section presents information on two programs for runaways. One of them is in an area where runaways are mainly local. The fourth section contains descriptions of two foster home programs under private auspices. The first is for girls only. The second receives almost all cases awaiting adjudication in the region it serves.

HOME DETENTION PROGRAMS

The seven Home Detention Programs are similar in format and can be thought of as a family of programs. All of them are administered by juvenile court probation departments. For the most part their staffs were made up of paraprofessional personnel variously referred to as outreach workers, community youth leaders or community release counselors. Usually a youth worker supervised five youths at any one time. In all programs youth workers were expected to keep the juveniles assigned to them trouble free and available to court. They achieved the essential surveillance through a *minimum* of one in-person contact with each youth per day and through daily telephone or personal contacts with the youths' school teachers, employers and parents. Youth workers worked out of their automobiles and homes rather than offices. Paperwork was kept to the minimum of travel vouchers and daily handwritten logs. In some programs the youth workers collaborated so that one could take over responsibility for the other when necessary. All programs authorized the workers to send a youth directly to secure detention when he or she did not fulfill program requirements — for example, daily contact with worker or school or job attendance. Typically, youths selected for the programs would have the rules of program participation explained to them in their parents' presence. These rules generally included attending school; observance of a specified curfew; notification of parents or worker as to whereabouts at all times when not at home, school or job; no use of drugs and avoidance of companions or places that might lead to trouble. Most of the programs allowed for the setting of additional rules arising out of discussions between the youth, the parents and the worker. Frequently, all of the rules would be written into a contract which all three parties would sign.

One key operating assumption of all of these programs is that the kind of supervision just described will generally keep juveniles trouble free and available to the court. Six of the seven programs rest on a second operating assumption as well. This assumption is that youths and their families need counseling or concrete services or both and that the worker can increase the probability that a juvenile will be successful in the program by making available the services of the court. The degree of emphasis on counseling and services varied. In some programs workers always try to achieve a type of "big brother" counseling relationship, sometimes combined with advocacy for the youths at school and counseling or referral of the youths' parents. In three programs workers organize weekly recreational or cultural activities for all juveniles on their caseloads.

Four of the programs in this category were said to have been started to relieve the overcrowding of a secure detention facility. Two began with explicit concern about the possibly harmful effects of secure detention. One began as an experiment to test the value of the program as an alternative to secure detention for status offenders; however, intake was not restricted to status offenders.

Youths Served

Only two of the seven programs had been designed for alleged delinquents only. The others accepted both alleged delinquents and status offenders. No program was used exclusively for the status offender. All but two were relatively small in absolute number of juveniles served — between 200 and 300 per year. The other two had accepted just over 1,000 youths each during the last fiscal year.

Of the nonstatus offenses, burglary is the delinquency alleged most often in each of the programs for which information was available. In general, the alleged delinquencies of program participants do not differ markedly from those encountered on the rosters of secure detention, with the exceptions of homicide, aggravated assault and rape which are few in number and rarely released. The delinquency charges that predominate in numbers are in the middle range of seriousness.

Rates of Success or Failure

All of the programs in this group themselves classify youths as program failures when they either run away and so do not appear for adjudication or when they are arrested for a new offense while participating in the programs. We have obtained data on youths by type of termination for six of the seven programs visited. It is presented along with other pertinent information about each program in Table 16-1. The tabular presentation risks implying a comparison between programs that is not truly possible. The data presented have not been gathered as part of a comparative evaluation research design. Other variables of importance, such as selectivity in referral to court, social characteristics of juveniles and their families, type of offense and length of prior record have not been controlled. The tabular presentation, however, does have the advantage of facilitating a discussion of success and failure for the programs in this category and it is for this purpose that we present it here.

If one combines what each of the programs views as program failures, it may be seen in Table 16-1, column 3, that the range of such failures is from 2.4 percent to 12.8 percent of all terminated juveniles. The combined failure rate for four programs falls between 2.4 percent and 7.5 percent, while the rate for one other is 10.1, a percentage that may not include runaways.

Reciprocally, column 6 presents the percentages of juveniles who had been kept trouble free and available to the courts — that is, had not been accused of committing a new offense and had not fled jurisdiction. The smallest percentage was 87.2 for program B. The largest was 97.5, at program C.

In the remaining programs, the percentages were 95.7, 94.8, 89.8 and 92.5 It is tempting to declare these "percentages of success." But are they?

Another view of the data at hand may be seen in a comparison of columns 1 and 2, where for five programs statistics are given separately for new offenses and running away. The data are not very enlightening, except to note that alleged new offenses exceeded running away in every instance except one (program B). We have no information that explains why no youths ran away from programs C and D.

A complication is the use of secure detention for certain program participants. We have already reported that all of these programs authorized their youth workers, for cause, to return juveniles to secure detention. In all programs they did so, as may be seen in column 4 of Table 16-1. Further, the percentages so returned in every instance exceeded the percentage of juveniles in the same program who had committed a new offense or who had run away while being supervised.

Is use of secure detention to be considered a program failure in this context? The youths for whom it was used did appear in court. If they are to be considered something less than successful in the programs then the statistics in column 5 — percentages of youths completing the programs without incident — should be considered. The smallest was 70.8 percent; the largest was 89.4 percent. Still, it seems a bit unfair to consider use of a preventative procedure planned from the start as a program weakness: the youths did get to court. . . .

ATTENTION HOMES

The Attention Home concept originated in Boulder, Colorado.

> The term attention as distinct from detention, signifies an environment which accentuates the positive aspects of community interaction with young offenders. The homes are structured enough for necessary control of juveniles, but far less restrictive and less punishing than jail. In fact, the atmosphere is made as homelike as possible — to give youngsters exactly what the term describes —attention. (Kaersvang, 1972:3.)

This quotation reflects the philosophy guiding the operation not only of the home we visited in Boulder but of the Attention Homes visited in Helena and Anaconda, Montana, as well. We had expected to treat the three homes as a family or programs.

TABLE 16-1. Percentages of Youths, by Type of Termination from Six Home Detention Programs

PROGRAM	PERCENT						
	1 New Offenses	2 Running Away	3 Runaways Plus New Offenses	4 Returned to Secure Detention	5 Completed Without Incident	6 Trouble-Free and Available to Court	7 Total 3 and 6
A: N=200. Delinquents Only.	4.5	3.0	7.5	12.0	80.5	92.5	100.0
B: N=274. Delinquents and Status Offenders.	4.4	8.4	12.8	16.4	70.8	87.2	100.0
C: N=246. Delinquents and Status Offenders.	2.4	0.0	2.4	8.1	89.4	94.5	99.9
D: N=252. Delinquents and Status Offenders.	5.2	0.0	5.2	21.0	73.8	94.8	100.0
E: N=206. Delinquents and Status Offenders.	2.4	1.9	4.3	24.8	70.9	95.7	100.0
F: N=276. Delinquents Only.	...b	...b	10.1b	13.3	76.4	89.8	99.9

[a]Totals may not add to 100.0 because of rounding.
[b]Information obtained from interview and may not include runaways.

However, each had adapted itself to unique circumstances in such a way that generalizations tended to obscure important differences. The Attention Home in Boulder is closely attached to court process and functions almost exclusively as an alternative to secure detention. Other Attention Homes have been developed in that jurisdiction to assist with probation and other postdispositional problems.

The Attention Home in Helena is multifunction. It serves a mixture of court cases and other kinds of agency referrals as well. It in fact functions as a resource for other agencies as well as a resource for juveniles in preadjudicatory status.

The Attention Home in Anaconda, as in Boulder, is tied closely to court process. However, it places a great emphasis on treatment through purchase of services and has taken on an important diversionary function. For these and other reasons the programs have been described separately. We will return to their similarities and differences later in a brief summary.

Boulder, Colorado

The Holmes-Hargadine Attention Home, the first of its kind, opened in Boulder in 1966 as an alternative to jail. In 1975, approximately 150 youths were admitted, two-thirds of them boys. About three-fourths were alleged delinquents; the rest were referred for status offenses. Most youths charged with more serious offenses are not referred to the home but, rather, are transferred to a regional detention center opened since the Attention Home was established.

The intake unit of the Boulder Juvenile Court refers youths to the home. The houseparents make the admission decisions, but they seldom reject referrals. They try to create as homelike an atmosphere as they can, spending time and talking with each of the youths. Some youths continue to attend their schools, but most work in a county sponsored program which pays two dollars an hour. In the afternoons, evenings and weekends volunteers (students from a nearby university) organize activities both in the home and elsewhere.

Systematic statistics were not available, but we estimate, based on what we were told, that the rate of those who ran away and those returned to secure detention was 2.6 percent each (there were no new offenses), producing a success rate of 94.8 or up to 97.4 percent depending upon how one believes returns to secure detention should be interpreted. There is no unusual aspect to the operation of the Attention Home with which rates of success can be linked, unless it is a felt "quality" that is difficult to define. It is not a fancy program, but it is a program to which the judge, the probation department and the houseparents are deeply committed.

Helena, Montana

The residential program of the Helena Attention Home is much like the one in Boulder. It differs, however, in the type of youths for whom it is used and in the kinds of agencies using it.

The home was a response to the needs of four youth-serving agencies in the city: the Probation Department of the Juvenile Court; the State Department of Institutions,

Aftercare Division (responsible for youths discharged from mental hospitals and for youths released on parole from juvenile correctional institutions); the State Department of Social and Rehabilitation Services (welfare) and the Casey Family Foundation (a private social work agency providing specialized foster care homes and an independent living program for youths who either were running away from or were unwelcome in their own homes or foster homes. Frequently they ended up in Helena's county jail, as did many other youths.

Thus, juveniles awaiting adjudicatory hearings at the home are a minority of the residents, but it is the only nonsecure program for them in the jurisdiction.

It is difficult to say what measures of success or failure should be applied to this program. Only rarely do youths run away from it, we were told. Even when they do, they usually return on their own within twenty-four hours. And only twice in 1975 did a youth have to be transferred from the home to jail.

Anaconda, Montana

The Attention Home in Anaconda is also an alternative to jail. Most referrals to Discovery House, as it is called, are from the court probation department. Youths excluded from referral are those charged with serious offenses against persons or those who have failed previously at the home due to aggressive behavior. Two-thirds of the admissions (47 in all) in 1975 were alleged status offenders.

Discovery House receives juveniles who differ greatly in the problems they present. At one extreme are youths who stay for short periods, an average of 3.3 days and no more than two weeks. At the other are a small number of youths with complicated personal problems for which it is difficult to find solutions. These adolescents may remain in residence for long periods — two to five months.

Because of the seriousness of the problems of certain youths and because of the commitment of the director of Discovery House to provide treatment, when needed, the program invests heavily in professional services. They are purchased with contractual monies; there are no professional personnel on the program's staff.

The court, in view of the treatment services provided by Discovery House, quashes the petitions on about three-quarters of the youths while they are in the program. Thus, many of the juveniles referred to the program as an alternative to jail end by being diverted from court jurisdiction.

Only rarely are youths asked to leave Discovery House or returned to jail. Those who run away from the program generally return on their own. The home's policy is to take them back. . . .

PROGRAMS FOR RUNAWAYS

We selected for visits two programs designed for runaways, a category of status offenders considered very troublesome to deal with. One program mainly handled juveniles running away locally. The other had been started to return out-of-state runaways to their homes.

Pittsburgh, Pennsylvania

Amicus House had been in operation since 1970. Only recently has it begun to accept referrals from the Allegheny County Juvenile Court. From the beginning the program provided a residence for runaway youths, using individual counseling, group treatment and family casework in an attempt to reconcile youths with their parents. The target population has always been runaways from the local area, and it is this group of youths that is now sent to Amicus House following detention hearings.

The program's operating assumptions are that the runaway youths referred to them are experiencing fairly serious emotional or family problems. Intensive treatment interventions of a problem-solving nature are required for the youth and the parents if the family situation is to be stabilized. The agency does not try to provide long-term treatment. Its goal is to make a successful referral if such help is needed. Its staff includes the program's director, an administrative assistant, ten counselors, a cook and two program coordinators who also supervise the counselors. Counselors are responsible for maintaining the house in addition to working with the juveniles and their parents.

A youth is restricted to the house without telephone privileges for forty-eight hours after arrival. He is told that he is there to think: to identify and begin working on whatever problems led to his running away. The juvenile's personal participation in the process is what is emphasized, the counselors being available to help him. If after forty-eight hours he is working to define his problem, a counselor may contact his parents and set an evening appointment for a family session. These may last two and one-half hours and are repeated regularly while the youth is in the program. Daily group meetings of all youths in residence are held after dinner in the evenings with guided group interaction techniques used to encourage and support problem-solving efforts. Programming that might distract juveniles from their problems is avoided.

If, as sometimes happens, a youth's parents refuse to cooperate, Amicus House petitions the court for custody of the youth and authorization to provide counseling. The petitions almost always are granted. Most parents then decide to cooperate, but if they do not Amicus House approaches the court to petition that the youth be declared "deprived" and thus eligible for foster placement. The practice of bringing petitions to court on behalf of youths whose parents are reluctant or unwilling to participate in the program is an important one to note. Too often juvenile courts have allowed themselves to become disciplinary agents for angry parents rather than using court authority to change the behavior of the parents.

For youths referred from court, the average length of stay is two to three weeks, varying with how rapidly the court docket is moving. Most of the youths terminate from the program by returning home; program officials reported that 8 percent of the youths admitted since July, 1975, ran away from the program, but the statistics were not specific to court referrals only. On occasion disruptive youths are asked to leave — but this is rare. The staff's principal response to disruptive behavior is to encourage ventilation of feelings.

Jacksonville, Florida

The Transient Youth Center was designed for out-of-state runaway youths. The Child Services Division of Jacksonville's Human Resources Department operates the Center which has residential capacity for twelve youths (both boys and girls) and accepted 560 youths in its first ten months of operation.

Local law enforcement agencies and court intake officials agreed to bring runaways directly from the police station or court intake to the center, thus avoiding secure detention altogether.

The principal objective for out-of-state juveniles is to return them to their families. The operating assumption is that provision of food, shelter and positive human contact of a crisis intervention kind will help youths decide to contact their parents and return home. To carry out this program, counselors are available twenty-four hours a day. A youth arriving at the center is fed, assigned a bed and given an opportunity to talk with a counselor. Daily staffings assess the youth's willingness to work out the details of contacting his parents and returning home. For most out-of-state youths this process takes one to three days. The center's close working relationship with Traveler's Aid appears to be a major factor in expediting return.

Although the Transient Youth Center was designed for juveniles running away to Florida, 40 percent of its clientele is now from Jacksonville and other parts of Florida. The local youths have presented needs and problems different from youths from other states. They need concrete services and an opportunity to talk, but often they present serious personal and family problems as well. The staff attempts to engage such youths and their families with the local social agencies for longer-term service. On the average, Florida youths stay at the Transient Youth Center a few days longer than do those from out-of-state. . . .

PRIVATE RESIDENTIAL FOSTER HOME PROGRAMS

The two private, residential foster home programs have little in common except that both are located geographically in the state of Massachusetts. This may not be a coincidence.

In Massachusetts, the Department of Youth Services (DYS) is the state agency responsible for juvenile corrections. In that state this responsibility includes the operation and provision of pretrial detention facilities and services for juveniles. During the early 1970s both the structure and organization of DYS was altered dramatically under the administration of its Commissioner, Dr. Jerome G. Miller. He closed most of the state's juvenile training schools and encouraged community-based programs to take their places. He organizationally divided DYS into seven semiautonomous administrative regions and encouraged each region to develop nonsecure community-based alternatives to incarceration for youths in their care. This, of course, included alternatives to detention for juveniles awaiting court.

New Bedford, Massachusetts

The New Bedford Child and Family Service, a private social work agency, operates the Proctor Program under contract with DYS Region 7. Region 7 has no secure detention for girls. Girls remanded by courts by DYS Region 7 for detention are placed in either the Proctor Program or in shelters, group homes or other foster homes.

The New Bedford Child and Family Service (NBCFS) Proctor Program assigns girls received from DYS to a "proctor" who provides twenty-four-hour care and supervision for the girl and works with the NBCFS professional staff to develop a treatment plan for rehabilitation. Twelve proctors are paid about $9,600 each per year for thirty-two child-care weeks. Each makes her own home or apartment available to one girl at a time. The proctors are single women between the ages of twenty and thirty who live alone and are will to devote all their time to the girls assigned to them.

The idea for this program grew out of NBCFS's previous experience with female juvenile offenders and their families. The agency had observed that foster home care and other substitute care arrangements often seemed to make troublesome girls' behaviors worse but that a positive one-to-one relationship with a female caseworker seemed to cause improvement. The Proctor Program began with the operating assumption that many adolescent girls referred to court lacked a positive relationship while growing up and that the one-to-one proctor format would provide such a relationship. This, in turn, would lead to short-term behavioral stability assuring appearance in court and the beginning of the rehabilitative work viewed as necessary for growth and development in the longer run. The immediate objective is to see that the girl appears in court at the appointed time. The long-term goal is to help the girl begin a course of rehabilitation by providing a type of care that will eventually improve her relationship with her parents. To accomplish these goals, the counseling and other resources of NBCFS are brought to bear in addition to the personal help of the proctor.

One hundred and sixteen girls were placed with proctors during 1975. About three-fourths were status offenders, petitioned for incorrigibility or running away. About 10 percent ran away while in the program.

The Proctor Program cannot be compared with any of the other programs visited. It is a specialized program for a particular (and particularly difficult) population of youths who often are referred to juvenile court when all other resources have failed. In many other jurisdictions they are admitted to secure detention even though intake and court officials know that the court's resources are not adequate to deal with the range of complex problems they present. The Proctor Program maintains close working relationships with both the Bristol County Juvenile Court in New Bedford and the regional office of DYS. It may be that the Proctor Program is one of the kinds of alternative programs needed to provide effective care for youths who are most inappropriately placed in secure detention.

Springfield, Massachusetts

The Center for the Study of Institutional Alternatives (CSIA) is located in Springfield, Massachusetts, and serves the four western counties that make up Region 1 of the State Department of Youth Services (DYS). It is a private, nonprofit corporation that operates two alternative programs under contract with Region 1. Each program accepts both boys and girls and together they provide 95 percent of all detention services in the region. DYS operates a nine-bed regional secure detention facility in Westfield, Massachusetts.

The Intensive Detention Program (IDP) was designed for juveniles charged with more serious offenses or who, regardless of charge, are more difficult to manage behaviorally. It consists of a Receiving Unit Home (four beds), two Group Home units (five beds each) and two foster homes (two beds each). Thus, space is available for a maximum of eighteen juveniles at any one time. The doors and windows of the Receiving Home Unit can be locked with keys, but that is the maximum degree of mechanical security possible in this network.

The Detained Youths Advocate Program (DYAP) consists of seventeen two-bed foster homes and was designed for youths charged with less serious offenses or who, regardless of charge, are behaviorally less difficult to manage. The combined capacity of these programs at any one time is fifty-two youths, although it could expand by recruiting additional DYAP foster homes.

The operating assumptions of the CSIA programs are that decent, humane care provided by people who can develop relationships with youths awaiting court action will keep most such youths free of trouble and assure their appearances in court at the appointed times. The IDP is staffed with a director, a receiving home unit supervisor and an assistant, two full-time and two part-time counselors and three office personnel who often double as resource personnel. Group and foster home parents are carefully screened and selected. As the main program thrust is relationship building, program staff and houseparents work closely together in attempting to match each youth with an adult (staff or houseparent) that the youth can relate to and trust. This person, who tries to help the youth understand the legal process ahead of him, is prepared to be an advocate on the youth's behalf when he or she appears in court. Counselors frequently involve the youths' families, schools and other concerned persons in planning for the future.

The DYAP is less labor intensive and relies for the most part on the program director and the foster parents, who are frequently young couples, some with children of their own. The operating assumptions and program activities are the same as those of the IDP.

The two CSIA programs combined accepted 650 youths during fiscal year 1975. Two-thirds were males and all were petitioned either as alleged delinquents or Children in Need of Services (CHINS). During the first six months of that year, 475 youths were placed in the CSIA programs, of whom six (1.2 percent) committed new offenses while in the program and 32 (6.8 percent) ran away, for a combined failure rate of 8 percent. The rest appeared in court as scheduled. Our own randomly selected sample of all youths terminating from a CSIA program between July 1 and December 31, 1975, showed that the average length of stay for youths in both programs was 20 days. . . .

CONCLUSIONS ABOUT ALTERNATIVE PROGRAMS

In concluding this document we set forth certain generalizations about programs currently in use as alternatives to secure detention for youths awaiting adjudication in juvenile courts. The reader should remember that we visited only fourteen such programs and that selection of programs in different jurisdictions might have resulted in other generalizations. Still, we will summarize conclusions that we believe to be of immediate importance to individuals and organizations that may be considering the development of alternatives in their jurisdictions.

1. The various program formats — residential and nonresidential — appear to be about equal in their ability to keep those youths for whom the programs were designed trouble free and available to court. That is not to say that any group of juveniles may be placed successfully in any type of program. It refers, instead, to the fact that in most programs only a small proportion of juveniles had committed new offenses or run away while awaiting adjudication.

2. Similar program formats can produce different rates of failure — measured in terms of youths running away or committing new offenses. The higher rates of failure appear to be due to factors outside the control of the programs' employees — e.g., excessive lengths of stay due to slow processing of court dockets or judicial misuse of the programs for preadjudicatory testing of youths' behavior under supervision.

3. Any program format can be adapted to some degree to program goals in addition to those of keeping youths trouble free and available to the court — for example, the goals of providing treatment or concrete services. Residential programs seem the most adaptable in that they are able to serve youths whose parents will not receive them or those who will not return home — often the same juveniles.

4. Residential programs — group homes and foster homes — are being used successfully both for alleged delinquents and status offenders.

5. Home Detention Programs are successful with delinquents and with some status offenders. However, a residential component is required for certain juveniles whose problems or conflicts are with their own families. Substitute care in foster homes and group homes and supervision within a Home Detention format have been combined successfully.

6. The Attention Home format seems very adaptable to the needs of less populated jurisdictions, where separate programs for several special groups may not be feasible. The Attention Home format has been used for youth populations made up of (a) alleged delinquents only, (b) alleged delinquents and status offenders and (c) alleged delinquents, status offenders and juveniles with other kinds of problems as well.

7. Thoughtfully conceived nonsecure residential programs can retain, temporarily, youths who have run away from their homes. Longer term help is believed to be essential for some runaways, so programs used as alternatives to detention for these youths require the cooperation of other social agencies to which such juveniles can be referred.

8. Certain courts are unnecessarily timid in defining the kinds of youths (i.e., severity of alleged offense, past record) they are willing to refer to alternative programs. Even when alternative programs are available, many youths are being held in secure detention (or jail) who could be kept trouble free and available to court in alternative programs, judging by the experiences of jurisdictions that have tried.

9. Secure holding arrangements are essential for a small proportion of alleged delinquents who constitute a danger to others.

10. The costs per day per youth of alternative programs can be very misleading. A larger cost can result from more services and resources being made available to program participants. It also can result from geographical variation in costs of personnel and services, differences in what administrative and office or residence expenses are included and underutilization of the program.

11. A range of types of alternative programs should probably be made available in jurisdictions other than the smallest ones. No one format is suited to every youth, and a variety of options among which to choose probably will increase rates of success in each.

12. Appropriate use of both secure detention and of alternative programs can be jeopardized by poor administrative practices. Intake decisions should be guided by clear, written criteria. Judges and court personnel should monitor the intake decisions frequently to be certain they conform to criteria.

13. Since overuse of secure detention continues in many parts of the country, the main alternative to secure detention should not be another program. A large proportion of youths should simply be released to their parents or other responsible adults to await court action. . . .

The Front End of the Juvenile Justice System

C. Intake and Diversion

Introduction

The juvenile court intake process has its analogs in other fields: the applicant for a bank loan whose employment, assets, and liabilities are evaluated by a loan officer before a decision is made; the personnel department of a company that assesses a job applicant's prior employment record and apparent job performance capabilities before reaching a hiring decision; the duty officer at a mental health clinic who evaluates an applicant for services and measures this person's problems and motivations against the kinds of persons the clinic can help and the space it has in its present workload. In the human services field, the decisions made at the intake stage govern workloads at subsequent stages. At the same time, the nature of the workload at the later stages affects whether the intake worker screens in, screens out, or develops a waiting list.

Juvenile justice intake has several special characteristics. The prosecutor has not participated in this procedure until quite recently. The intake probation officer, following his preliminary investigation, has wide latitude in his decision to dismiss, divert, adjust, utilize informal supervision, or file a formal petition. In contrast to the criminal justice system, juvenile intake decisions place great emphasis on the "social facts" such as the child's attitude toward his offense, parental cooperativeness, parental control over the child, child and parent interest in utilizing external community agency services, the child's school achievements and adjustment, his peer group and neighborhood, his psychiatric history and psychological makeup.

Until recently, the social facts were considered more important than the legal facts in reaching the intake decision to file a petition, counsel and release the child, or effect some strategy in between. The legal facts include the child's age, seriousness of the present offense, prior offense record, prior court dispositions, the time space between this offense and prior offenses, prior detentions, a legal status of probation or parole, the county where the offense occurred, and the prosecutive merit of the case.

A spin-off from the intake function was "informal probation" or "informal supervision," a trial run on probation without actual probation status, sometimes with and sometimes without the counseling services of a probation officer. By cooperating with the probation officer, his parents, and the law, the youth could have his case dismissed. There would be no appearance before a judge; the judge's time could be spent on more difficult cases, and the child would be spared a formal record. The informal record, however, would be considered by the intake officer if the youth committed another offense.

Diversion to services provided by other community agencies has developed rapidly, but not without criticism and problems.

The public probably views the juvenile court judge as the most influential figure in dealing with juvenile problems. The Cressey and McDermott article states that the intake officer is the most important official. Their position gains credence from juvenile processing statistics which show, typically, that 50 percent of referrals never pass the intake stage, and that this figure reaches 80 percent or more in many courts. The judge sees only what comes to him. Even with judicial dispositional hearings concerning formal cases, other authorities such as the probation officer who conducted the social study, the prosecutor, and defense counsel assert substantial influence on the ultimate judicial decrees. However, in a growing number of states, the probation department's dominance of the intake function is yielding to the prosecutor, much as in an earlier era police dominance of what came before a juvenile court judge yielded to the emerging intake authority of the probation department. It may now be suggested that the prosecutor is becoming the most powerful functionary in the juvenile court process.

The descriptive and analytic Cressey and McDermott work equates the intake role with discretionary decision making. Both probation departments and individual intake officers utilize decisional norms, often unwritten, or broadly based if recorded, which guide the decisions they make. Both intake norms and intake procedures have come under increasing attack as being subjective, irregularly and unequally administered, and as subversive of legal protections.

The research report which follows examines the characteristics of youngsters referred to juvenile court intake in Upstate County, New York. It assesses the characteristics which were significant in the intake decision to file or not to file a formal petition. This intake unit of three probation officers and a supervisor was part of a county level executive branch probation agency which served the family court in that mid-sized county. In New York, eligibility for family court jurisdiction terminates upon a juvenile's sixteenth birthday. This fact may have influenced the finding that only a small number of the offenders had been referred for offenses against persons. In Upstate County, and perhaps in all juvenile or family courts, the primary delinquent offense referral involves property. Status offenses were also prominent. Further, New York State intake officers operated with substantially less authority than is true in most states. The complainant who insisted upon formal court action had the right to obtain court review by obviating the intake process.

The study discovered that poor home quality and poor school performance are more powerful predictors of formal processing than the severity of the present offense or the existence of a prior record. One can describe this court as more concerned with social than legal facts, and as interested in asserting court authority in the pursuit of rehabilitation. The editor observed the Upstate County family court in operation in late 1978 and found youngsters nominally represented by defense counsel, but with counsel cooperating with the court's latter day *parens patriae* approach which continually emphasized the need for the child to conform to parental controls and school regulations as well as legal norms.

The final article describes the Sacramento, California diversion project, an early demonstration (beginning in late 1970) which has been widely replicated. It utilized family oriented crisis intervention within its objective to minimize detention and formal petitioning and to reduce recidivism. Initiated with section 601 youngsters (status offenders), it was expanded to include the less serious of the section 602 offenders (juvenile delinquents). The research findings were largely positive, supporting the concept of "front end" rather than "back end" service provision. That so few status offenders required formal petitions furnished further support for the postition that those youngsters should no longer fall within juvenile court jurisdiction, or, alternatively, that community resources should be exhausted before court review should be authorized.

17   *Diversion from the Juvenile Justice System*
Donald R. Cressey and Robert A. McDermott

INTAKE PROCEDURES

The design of the buildings and rooms used for giving justice to juveniles hides the fact that the intake officer is the most important person in the juvenile justice system. This man's workroom is smaller and barer than the "chambers" of juvenile court judges, the suites used by Chief Probation Officers, and the offices of the probation department section chiefs called supervisors. In his little cubicle there are no flags, no polished wood furniture, no panelled walls, no carpet, and no statue of the blindfolded lady. The cubicle is equipped with a cheap metal desk and a couple of straight-backed chairs. A few unframed prints and a diploma or two are temporarily taped on the walls. The intake officer doesn't wear a robe or a wig. He sits at his bare desk, often wearing an open-collared shirt, and does justice.

Policemen screen out, and dismiss with no further action, a good proportion of the suspected juvenile offenders they encounter on the street. Another proportion are referred to some unofficial or official police diversion program. The remainder are either escorted to the intake officer's cubicle or ordered to appear there in the company of their parents or guardians. The intake officer, in turn, filters out most of these cases and orchestrates action on the rest.

In the adult criminal justice system a "complaint officer" deals with pieces of paper rather than with people. Policemen bring criminal complaint forms to his desk, and he must decide which ones to "file," meaning that they are sent along the criminal justice path, not that they are put away in a drawer. But in the juvenile justice system, the intake officer deals with people. Children and parents are there, in his cubicle, and he must tell them where to go next.

He tells most children to go home with their parents, dismissing them with only an official warning. He places others on "informal probation," meaning that they

---

From *Diversion from the Juvenile Justice System* (Ann Arbor, Mich.: National Assessment of Juvenile Corrections, The University of Michigan, 1973), pp. 11-20 and 30. Reprinted by permission.

will be on probationary status for an offense for which they have only been accused, not convicted. He tells other children to go to a special diversion unit that his probation department runs, and he diverts a few more to private or public social welfare agencies. Those remaining are told to appear before a juvenile court referee or judge for a formal hearing.

The intake process is one of dramatic discretionary decision making. The decision to send a child home with a warning or to put him on one of the juvenile justice system paths is affected by what the intake officer decides are the facts of the case, the technicalities of the arrest, the probabilities of proof. The decision is affected even more by the intake officer's sense of what is right, just, fair, and proper. He sends children home because he thinks the offense is not serious enough to justify what in the criminal justice system would be called prosecution. He sends other children home or diverts them, or puts them on informal probation, because he believes the circumstances of the offense and the background of the child call for less serious consequences than those likely to follow if the child is sent on for a formal hearing. The juvenile's attitude plays a paramount role here. In all these actions, the intake officer clearly acts as a judge, just as a policeman acts as judge when he informally settles juvenile delinquency cases without arrest or citation.

Even in probation departments with official diversion policies, diversion is likely to occur only if the intake officers want it to occur. Although these men surely are influenced by the policies, programs, and philosophies favored by thier superiors — especially their immediate supervisors — they still have great latitude to decide who shall be diverted and who shall not. The degree and direction in which juvenile offenders are diverted is influenced by the individual intake officer's conception of justice and his philosophy and theory of correction, as well as by his knowledge of community resources, by his relationships with other professional welfare workers both within and without his department, by his personal assumptions, attitudes, biases, and prejudices, by the size of his case load and the work load of his department, and by many other subtle conditions. He cannot easily be ordered to make his decisions in a specified way. Ultimately, then, decisions to divert or not divert are his to make. Pressuring him to make his decisions in a certain way, overruling his decisions, and even hesitant questioning of his decisions are usually viewed as unwarranted interference by both intake officers and their superiors.

Initial Contact

Children come to intake officers' cubicles along three major paths. Terminology and administrative procedures differ from place to place, but the routes are essentially the same:

Detained juveniles are brought over from the juvenile detention center. These are the juveniles whom law enforcement officers arrested and officially booked into the detention center yesterday afternoon or last night. Some were detained because their alleged offense was serious, but most were held because the arresting officer could think of nothing better to do with them. A hitchhiker or runaway, for example, can hardly be released to his parents. Detained juveniles are by law entitled to an intake hearing withing forty-eight hours of their booking. Further detention is allowable only with the consent of a juvenile court referee or judge.

Juveniles who have promised to appear arrive at a designated time, usually accompanied by their parents. Law enforcement officers have recently released these youths to their parents or guardians, issuing a citation (much like a traffic ticket) that specified the complaint. A parent or other responsible adult has signed the citation/ticket, thus agreeing to appear with the juvenile before an intake officer on a specified day. Intake officers themselves sometimes write up such agreements. For example, in some jurisdictions the police release the juvenile but submit a contact report to the intake officer, who then notifies the family and makes arrangements for a hearing.

Informal contacts seek out the intake officer. These teenagers (and their parents) are usually called "walk-ins" or "phone contacts." Note that there is a significant difference here between the criminal justice system and the juvenile justice system. No burglar walks into the courthouse and applies for criminal justice. It is the welfare aspects of the juvenile system that make the difference. Some walk-in cases are handled officially and others are not, depending principally upon the seriousness of the problem as viewed either by the intake officer or the clients.

Intake officers often work for the probation department which, in Mountain State, is part of the *judicial* branch of county government. This contrasts with the policemen and assistant district attorneys serving as complaint officers in the *criminal* justice system, and it makes a difference. As part of the executive branch of government, a policeman or prosecutor either dismisses a case, handles it informally, or turns it over to the judicial branch for further processing. But intake officers, as members of the judicial branch, have cases turned over to them. Accordingly, their decisions are judicial, no matter how administrative they appear. A policeman can divert children *from* admission to the juvenile justice system, but an intake officer can only divert them *out* of the system they have entered, or minimize their penetration after they have entered.

Intake units ordinarily have only two levels of rank — a supervisor and the intake officers. The unit supervisor's essential contribution to the diversion process seemingly lies in the general "tone" or "atmosphere" he establishes with reference to punishment or treatment, and the degree to which he becomes involved in the allocation of cases. For example, if he takes the percentage of petitions filed for formal hearings as his yardstick for unit success or failure, he *might* strongly discourage or encourage diversion. In dividing the work load among the intake officers, he *might* allocate cases to officers according to type of offense, sex, age, race, and his estimate of the individual officer's ability to handle them. If he doesn't favor diversion of a specific case, he can hand it to an intake officer who doesn't favor diversion for any case. Some supervisors deny such specialized allocation of cases, invariably on the grounds that "all my officers are equally qualified or they wouldn't be here." It is true, of course, that large numbers of cases are both allocated and disposed of without the direction of any supervisor. At night and especially on weekends, all cases may be handled by the intake officer who happens to be on duty.

There is wide variation among intake units in the age, experience, and civil service rank of the intake officers. If the chief probation officer recognizes the critical importance of intake officers' decisions, all the officers are likely to be Senior Probation Officers. On the other hand, if the intake process is viewed as mere routine screening, intake officers might be Deputy Probation Officers or even Probationary Probation Officers.

No matter what their rank or experience, all intake officers are likely to engage in four different roles or sets of activities. Variation in units is principally variation in the mix of these activities — in one unit the focus may be on screening, in another on conducting hearings, and so on.

As a *screening officer,* the intake officer separates out minor cases either for informal handling or specialized handling: for example, all "predelinquents" are sent to a special unit. He may also work out screening routines that amount to perfunctory handling of the caseload: all first offenders get released, second offenders get informal probation, all third offenders get petitioned. Sometimes intake officers are specifically assigned as screening officers, but more commonly, there is a know attitude about intake work. No matter what the practice of an intake unit, routine processing according to formula is quite common and is frankly admitted to "off the record," but is is officially denied on the basis of the ideal of "individualization" of cases. One man seems to have viewed his work as similar to police and district attorneys who serve as criminal complaint officers but who rarely see a criminal: "You know what you are going to do or recommend after reading the report and records," he said. "You don't have to see the kid."

As a *hearing officer,* the intake officer disposes of a case only after a detailed reading of all records on file; taking a sample of the opinions or recommendations of school officials, the arresting officer, and others; interviews with the parents and the juvenile; and the professional evaluation of the "attitude" and "needs" of the juvenile as evidenced during a hearing. This is the most commonly accepted "official" function of the intake officer. The intake officer thus views his job as one of diagnosing a problem and referring it to public or private agencies capable of resolving the issue. But is should be pointed out that all this work is done in hearings that rarely last more than an hour; in the vast majority of cases, only a few minutes are used to review, hear, and dispose of a case. Bear in mind that only this one individual at this particular point in time determines "penetration into the system" or the manner of diversion. His knowledge of public and private resources thus is crucial, but it is often minimal. As a result, typical disposition is either dismissal or entrance into some sector of the system — "true" diversion is the exception.

As *counselor*, the intake officer tries to give advice, help, and even tnerapy. All intake officers "counsel" most of their cases in some manner, but such counseling is usually limited either to lecturing the juvenile about his responsibilities or trying to scare the hell out of him. This kind of counseling is ordinarily referred to in the most common disposition of cases by intake officers as "CWR" — "counseled, warned, and released." Some specialized intake officers, however, do engage in a different kind of counseling and identify themselves as counselors rather than as intake officers. For example, in separate diversion units with intake power it is typical for participating officers to view counseling as an important part of their job. Such specialized individuals are often, in fact, torn between diverting children out of the unit and keeping them in it for intensive counseling. Only in such settings with such officers do the delinquent and his family receive professional and in-depth counseling at the intake level.

As *intake investigator,* the intake officer goes to the field and personally conducts a probation investigation, which is then presented, with his recommendations to the referee or judge when the petition for a hearing is filed. It was commonly believed in the past — and even today many persons believe — that probation departments at intake merely gather "facts" and leave decision-making to the judge. The variation is the intake officer who may "screen," "hear," or "counsel" (as above), but who also personally investigates those cases in which he decides to file a petition. This practice is found in areas as diverse as metropolitan Londondale County and small rural counties with few probation officers.

Once an official petition has been filed, the juvenile's case passes from the intake officer to the discretion of a probation investigating officer. It is the latter's task to verify the facts of the case and to submit a report of his findings to the juvenile court. In addition to looking at the evidence behind the complaint and petition, the officer looks at the background of the juvenile and the circumstances of his offense. His report to the court will contain a "probation plan" if probation rather than incarceration or detention for further diagnosis (or punishment) is recommended. As part of a proposed probation plan the officer may recommend a specific program — such as drug abuse education — conducted either by the probation department or by some other agency, public or private. His report may, alternatively, ask for dismissal of the petition so that the juvenile can be placed on informal probation. Another alternative, rarely used, is to ask for dismissal with no further action. In one jurisdiction, the juvenile court judge grants such dismissals by signing a supply of blank request forms. Dismissal, then, may occur with a minimum of "official" action.

Most investigating officers feel confident that officers of the intake unit would not file a petition without due cause. Consequently, they, like assistant district attorneys, view their primary responsibility as that of developing cases that can be "won" in a courtroom. In some cases, however, the presumption of probable cause is overcome by the investigation. Perhaps the investigator becomes convinced that the juvenile has had a change of heart since the intake interview, or that sending him into the courtroom would be too hard on him. In the first instance the officer simply asks that the petition be dismissed. In the second instance, he will recommend that the petition be dismissed if the juvenile agrees to participate in some special program, one that is community based or one conducted by the probation department.

Such "arrangements" are wholly informal. The process resembles that which occurs when a prosecuting attorney lets an accused armed robber plead guilty to disturbing the peace or some other lesser offense. Although in the juvenile justice system the *name* of the offense does not determine or even limit dispositional alternatives, as it does in the criminal justice system, the juvenile nevertheless in effect pleads guilty in exchange for a mild disposition. Like an accused felon, he somehow comes to understand that compromise is better than forcing court action.

Since the most common reason for dismissal of a petition is lack of evidence, it is quite possible that the investigating officer's willingness to "compromise" often stems from his judgment that the case is not likely to stand up in court.

The great majority of cases are either reported on or dismissed, although dismissal with referral back to intake for placement on informal probation is common. Few cases are referred directly to community agencies because investigating officers, like other probation workers, either are unfamiliar with available services or are dubious of their value. If a case is referred to an agency other than the probation department, it is most likely to end up in the hands of the welfare department or the mental health department. Whenever an investigating officer becomes too involved in diversion, he is apt to be reminded that his job is one of case preparation rather than case disposition. The segmented responsibilities of trained professionals serve to place subtle controls upon their discretionary power.

Little difference was found between the operations of the investigation units in Westlane, Van Dyke, and Scottville. In Londondale, however, there is a partial combination of the role of intake officer and investigator. "Intake investigating officers" do preliminary investigations on juveniles who are being considered for informal probation. Intake officers delay formal petitioning until an investigating officer has completed his study and made a recommendation. If a petition is filed, the case goes to a regular probation investigation unit, as in Metropolitan Mountain View.

The Londondale procedure seems meant to relieve the pressure on intake officers, and at the same time give greater attention to the due process rights of juveniles. The broad discretionary power available to investigating officers could be — and perhaps is — a major diversion device. But using their power for diversion purposes is surely offset by high case loads that frustrate adequate analysis of the juveniles' needs; by lack of awareness and understanding of alternative community programs; and by professional needs to support the decision of a professional colleague and coworker — the intake officer.

Intake Options

No matter what the organzational structure of an intake unit, and regardless of the orientation of supervisors and individual officers, six different dispositional options are available to intake officers. We shall list them in the decreasing frequency with which we believe they are used, but it should be understood that there are variations from unit to unit.

Counsel, Warn, and Release is the most commonly utilized option. This disposition is an almost automatic response to cases brought in via citations. The child is usually discharged after a warning, a lecture, or a short conference with him and his parents. The case is not carried in the official records as "dismissed," even though CWR is sometimes called "dismissed" rather than a disposition.

Informal probation is the option whereby, under Mountain State law, a juvenile might be placed on a maximum of six months informal probation if he and his parents agree to it. In practice, the term of probation is rarely less than six months.

Probation diversion units may be used for the particular types of cases they have been established to receive. The intake officer may be required to refer certain cases (usually predelinquents or minor lawbreakers) to such a unit. In addition, or in some locations, he may opt to send other cases there. When a child is sent to a diversion unit, his case is officially logged as "dismissed." However, the child is strongly urged to participate in the special unit's program. Diversion units will be discussed later in some detail.

Referral to another agency (or to a person) is a common disposition of walk-in and phone contact cases. Such referral is an attempt to handle the case "unofficially" by sending the juvenile to someone that "is better able (qualified) to handle his case." This disposition is sometimes used for other than "walk-ins" by intake officers on night duty. These officers tend to be viewed by detention center staff members and the police as "trouble shooters." Intake officers receive cases from them that have not "officially" come to the attention of the juvenile justice system, and they dispose of them unofficially. It is questionable, then, whether such referrals are "dispositions," "diversions," "dismissals," or something else.

Petition for an official hearing before a juvenile court referee or judge is the "classic" disposition used in "serious" and "last resort" cases. It is something like the filing of charges in criminal cases. The papers on the case are simultaneously filed with the court and with a regular probation officer (as indicated above) who makes an investigation and reports back to the court, which then conducts a hearing.

Dismissal is the least used option. It occurs most frequently when the intake officer decides there is not enough evidence to justify further action, or when he believes the technicalities of the arrest were improper. . . .

Conclusions

The probation department's intake officers are the first officials of the juvenile court with whom a youth in trouble must negotiate his fate. A "fair," "just," and "reasonable" disposition flows from pitting various techniques of "impression management" (on the part of both the juvenile and his parents) against the specific intake officer's theories of delinquency and correction; his awareness of the existence of alternative public and private social agencies; and his judgment of the worth of these agencies. Only rarely are the dispositions satisfactory to all the parties in the case, and often they are satisfactory to none of them, principally because they are merely stopgap actions. When "true" diversion of individual cases occurs, or even when effective diversion/minimization of penetration occurs, the quality of the alternative program is likely to reflect the capacity of an intake officer and his immediate superior to transcend the bureaucratic roadblocks (and the community apathy) that so often divert diversion programs from their objectives.

18   Characteristics of Youngsters Referred to Family Court Intake and Factors Related to Their Processing

Henry Paquin with: Philip Harris, Janet Rothacker,
Marguerite Q. Warren

. . . This study has examined over 300 record and interview variables in the attempt to better understand who the youngsters referred to family court intake are, and how they are processed in the juvenile justice system. In this section, the major findings are reviewed in the form of answers to fundamental questions about juvenile delinquency and the manner in which it is handled at the county level.

Who were the youngsters referred to family court intake ?   Most of the referrals were white boys, with an average age of slightly over fourteen years old; almost half came from low status neighborhoods, and very few from high status neighborhoods. Most youngsters referred to family court intake were living with their parents/parent figures at their home prior to the referral, and not residing in institutions or other placements.

What were their families like ?   The great majority of the youngsters were in the legal custody of at least one natural parent prior to their referral and almost half lived with both natural or adoptive parents. Most of the youngsters had three siblings, and typically, none of the siblings had ever had contact with the family court. By age, the youngsters were equally likely to be from the lower, middle, and upper age group in their families.

Almost half of the youngsters had mother/mother figures and father/father figures judged by probation staff to be rejecting, and more than half were described as having had difficulty getting along with their parents for some time. In most of the cases, probation staff estimates of the appropriate of the home indicated that is was suitable as a placement for the youngster. Only in a small percentage of the cases had neglect petitions ever been filed against the parent(s), and in only very few cases had the parent(s) actually been adjudicated neglectful.

In general, the youngsters who came from broken homes were the most likely to have their homes characterized negatively by probation staff, and they were the youngsters most likely to have trouble getting along at home, and most likely to live in low status neighborhoods. In short, the youngsters with intact homes were the most likely to have "healthy" environments as measured across a number of other variables.

From Henry Paquin, with Philip Harris, Janet Rothacker, and Marguerite Q. Warren, *Characteristics of Youngsters Referred to Family Court Intake and Factors Related to Their Processing* (Albany, N.Y.: School of Criminal Justice, State University of New York, 1976), pp. 162-75. Reprinted by permission.

What were their school situations like ? Most of the youngsters had completed at least their seventh grade of schooling, and most attended public, city schools. Almost half of the sample were in the eighth or ninth grade at the time of their referral, and slightly more than half had a record of poor academic performance. In addition, one-third of the youngsters had difficulty getting along with their teachers, and a similar number had problems getting along with their school peers. The majority of the youngsters had a record of at least some level of truancy.

In general, the youngsters attending public, city schools had more school problems than did the suburban school youngsters. Moreover, school problems (with teacher, peers, academically, and truancy) tended to go together, so that most youngsters how had one or two were likely to be experiencing them all. Finally, poor school situations and poor home situations were also very likely to go together, so that the youngsters having difficulty at home were the most likely youngsters to also have difficulty at school.

What were their records of past delinquency like ? Most youngsters had never been to family court intake or family court before, and most had never been placed outside of their homes. Most had never been on probation, even informal, and those who had been on probation had generally experienced it only once, and for a short time.

More than half of the youngsters had no prior offenses at all, and most of those who did have prior offenses had one prior property offense. The males and females differed greatly with regard to past delinquency, the males much more likely than the females to have past offenses, adjudications, probation, and placements. In addition, the youngsters with poor home situations were much more likely than youngsters with stable homes to have past delinquency in their records, as were the youngsters who currently had poor school performance and behavior records.

What were their current offenses ? The youngsters were referred to family court intake by different kinds of referring agents or agencies ranging from parents, school and private parties and business establishments to various city and town police departments. Most of the referring agents (official complainants) were male, largely because of the male dominated police departments in the city and surrounding towns and slightly more than half of the referring agents had little familiarity with the youngster they were referring. Most of the youngsters referred were informal referrals, i.e., complaint rather than petition cases, and most alleged crimes rather than status offenses.

By type, slightly more than half of the offenses alleged in the referrals were property offenses, almost one-third were status offenses, a small number were person offenses, and a few were other violations (neither status offenses nor crimes). Most of the property offenses were burglaries or petit larceny, while the status offenses were cases of truancy, ungovernable behavior, and running away. Almost all of the person offenses were cases of assault.

Most of the youngsters had committed one current offense, and the largest proportion of youngsters had been charged with offenses which were Class A Misdemeanors, followed by a slightly smaller proportion of youngsters charged with noncriminal status offenses. The great majority of the youngsters had no mention of violent behavior in their current or past records. With regard to the time lag between the act of the present offense and processing at intake, more than two-thirds of the youngsters reached intake within fourteen days of their offense.

While the property offenders were typically referred by male complainants, the person and status offenders were typically referred by females. Generally, youngsters with more severe and a greater number of offenses were more often than youngsters with less severe and fewer offenses to be referred by petition — demanding formal court action. As with past delinquency findings, females were less likely than males to have current property or person offenses, and much more likely to be PINS referrals.

Typically, youngsters with records of past delinquency were more likely to commit more severe present offenses, and were more likely to be referred by petition than were youngsters with no past involvements with the juvenile justice system. In fact, youngsters with poor home situations, poor school performance, and residence in low status neighborhoods were generally more likely than other youngsters to be referred by petition.

How were the youngsters processed ?   Slightly more than half of the youngsters referred to family court intake were handled at intake and went no further; the remainder at least reached formal processing at family court, of which almost two-thirds were eventually adjudicated PINS or JDs. Of the youngsters who reached family court, one-third were held in detention during their proceedings. All but a very small percentage of the youngsters were represented by court-appointed law guardians, and most of the youngsters processed at family court admitted to the allegations made against them. Most youngsters experienced three to five . . . hearings.

Typically, at least one parent/parent figure was present during the proceedings, and a police official was present in half of the cases. In a small number of cases, a complainant who was neither a parent, school or police official was present. The adjudication and disposition hearings typically spanned an eight to ten week period from first hearing to final court appearance.

Half of the youngsters who were adjudicated were placed in the legal custody of their parents; one-third were placed in the legal custody of the Department of Social Services, and a small percentage were placed with the Division for Youth. Generally, with regard to custody, placement, and program, the family court followed the recommendations of the probation staff.

In summary, slightly more than half of the youngsters in the sample were processed at intake on one occasion during the study and proceeded no further; almost one-third went directly to family court on one occasion without processing at intake; a small percentage went to court after having been to intake; and a very small percentage went to court more than one time, without ever having been to intake.

How were the youngsters characterized by probation staff ?   Most of the youngsters were viewed by probation staff as essentially prosocial in their general social attitude, and most were estimated to have a good or very good chance of avoiding future delinquency. In most cases, the youngster was characterized by probation staff as sorry for what he/she had done, and the most common recommendation of probation staff was that of returning the youngster to his/her own home.

Were different groups of youngsters handled differently ?   Females and blacks were less likely than white males to be represented by private attorneys at their proceedings, and blacks were typically more often adjudicated as juvenile delinquents, and more often given poor prognosis with regard to future delinquency. In general, youngsters residing in low status neighborhoods were handled more severely for their current interaction, and had more substantial delinquency histories than did other youngsters.

Typically, the youngsters with poor home and poor school performance characteristics were much more often processed severely than were other youngsters; i.e., they were more often sent to court instead of handled at intake, detained during proceedings, adjudicated PINS or JDs, and placed away from home, in the custody of someone other than their parents. The same pattern was observed for youngsters with past delinquency records: they were much more often handled severely for their present interaction than were first offenders.

Property and person offenders (current offenses) were more often adjudicated JDs than were status offenders, though they were not more likely to be sent to court than were status offenders, nor more likely to be placed away from home. While what youngsters had done was related to what they would be classified as if they went to court (PINS or JDs), it was not related to more severe handling. In fact, even the technical severity of the present offenses (under New York law) was not related to going to court, being placed, or being put in the custody of someone other than the parents. The offense factor found to matter most with regard   ıdling is that of repeating; repeat past and/or present offenders were more often   .ed severely than youngsters with only one offense, regardless of the type of severity of the offenses.

In summary, the most meaningful way of examining different groups of youngsters (according to record data) was by categorizing them according to their home and school situations, since these factors seemed to matter most to the decision makers who processed the youngsters in the system.

What were the youngsters' attitude toward police and probation personnel ?   Almost half of the youngsters were very negative or negative about their experiences with the police, though most felt that they had been handled fairly. More than one-third of the youngsters were frightened, nervous, "shook up" during the experience, and few were unaffected. Equal proportions of youngsters knew little about what was going on, knew some, and knew a great deal about what was happening at the police, with regard to the way in which the process worked.

Typically, the youngsters were much more positive about the probation officer they were in contact with at intake than they were about police, and they were even more likely to feel that they had been handled fairly at intake than at police. A considerable proportion were frightened during the intake contact, and a similar number were relieved; smaller proportions were angry and resentful. One-fifth felt that the intake contact had no meaning and no effect.

Most youngsters felt thay they played little or no part in the intake process, and most felt that the decision regarding their handling was made by the probation officer. A smaller proportion felt that the decision had been made by the complainant who had referred them to family court intake.

How did the youngsters feel about their offenses ?   Most youngsters were judged to be uncomfortable with a delinquent identity, and most blamed others for their trouble, suggesting that they had been led into the offense behavior. Similar proportions of youngsters felt that they had gotten into trouble because of family problems, or because there just wasn't enough to do around their neighborhoods. Slightly more than half of the youngsters were familiar with the complainant who referred them into the system, and almost half were negative or very negative in their attitutes toward that complainant.

How did the youngsters feel about their families ?   Only one-third of the youngsters felt positive or very positive about their mother/mother figures, and a far smaller proportion felt positive or very positive about their father/father figures. The youngsters generally described their parents/parent figures in terms which focused on concern or power, though the younger age groups were likely to give stereotype descriptions ("nice"; "gives us things").

Slightly more than half of the youngsters felt that they received little or no supervision at home, and that they could pretty much do as they pleased; a similar proportion felt that their families weren't very close. Typically, youngsters were more likely to feel that their mother/mother figures understood them than they were to feel that their father/father figures understood them. More than half of the youngsters said that there was physical violence in their homes on a regular basis.

Generally, the youngsters felt that their parent/parent figures were "mad" as a result of their involvement in the juvenile justice system, though a substantial proportion of youngsters felt that their father/father figures didn't really care about their involvement.

The youngsters' feelings about various dimensions of their families were quite consistent, so that negative attitudes toward parents, poor home supervision, lack of family closeness, and physical violence tended to appear together in the youngsters' families.

What did the youngsters say about past delinquency ?   Almost half of the youngsters indicated that they had no past offenses whatsoever, and most of the remainder said that they had committed one to three past offenses for which they were not processed in the system; i.e., which did not cause apprehension by police or referral to family court intake. Most of the youngsters who admitted to past delinquency indicated that their offenses had been property offenses.

Most of the youngsters used alcohol and marijuana at least occasionally; a small proportion were frequent consumers. A very small proportion of the youngsters used narcotics occasionally. Alcohol and marijuana use were related so that youngsters who participated in one typically participated in the other at least occasionally.

How did they feel about school ?   Slightly less than half of the youngsters felt that school was "o.k."; one-third said that they had difficulty in getting along with their teachers, and a smaller proportion said that they had trouble getting along with their school peers. More than half of the youngsters were negative or very negative in their general attitude toward school, though only a small percentage expressed a desire to quit as soon as possible. In fact, more than one-third said that they wanted to graduate from high school, and one-third indicated that they wanted to try going to college.

One-third of the youngsters were negative or very negative in their attitudes toward teachers in general, though most said that they had one favorite teacher whom they really liked.

The youngsters most likely to say that they wanted to quit school as soon as possible were the youngsters most negative about school, and those having most trouble getting along with their teachers and school peers.

What did they say about their friends ?   Most youngsters said that they had many friends, though most described relationships which were judged to be superficial or reciprocal rather than really close. Almost half of the youngsters felt that their friends had little or no past delinquency, and a similar proportion felt that their friends infrequently used alcohol or marijuana, or narcotics.

How did they describe themselves ?   Almost one-third of the youngsters used stereotype terms in describing themselves; almost half chose terms which were comparative, of which equal proportions suggested comparative, inferior descriptions, and comparative, superior and antisocial descriptions. Half of the youngsters said that they had problems, and of these youngsters, most said that their problems were external, i.e., behavior problems. Slightly more than half of the youngsters felt little or no control over their own lives, and half felt that they would like to make external changes. One-third indicated that they would like to make internal changes — in their personalities.

What did they say about the future ?   Most youngsters were optimistic or very optimistic about the future, and almost half expressed and described fairly long-term plans. With regard to typical time orientation, however, most youngsters were judged to be oriented to the "now"; i.e., they did not make decisions by looking backward or forward in their lives. Slightly more than half of the youngsters felt that they would be involved in no further delinquency, one-third were unsure, and the remainder anticipated future contact. . . .

COMPARISON OF FINDINGS WITH THOSE OF PAST STUDIES

The literature search conducted as part of the present study uncovered only four past research efforts which addressed the area of family court and family court intake processing of youngsters and which were also designed for empirical analysis. All four studies shared certain design factors which make direct comparison of findings between past studies and the present study difficult. The past studies were based on inactive (i.e., past) populations of male youngsters only, and generally included only delinquent and not status offenders. As a result, the referred youngsters making up those study populations were overwhelmingly police referrals, and not referrals from parents, schools, and private agents. Further, past studies have relied on record data alone, and on very few variables; youngsters were not interviewed, and no classification system was utilized as a means of organizing the data.

There are additional factors which make direct comparison of findings problematical. No past studies examined the court-level decision point, and none examined both the severity of handling and severity of placement decisions across several decision points. Instead, past studies concentrated on precourt handling, and ranked the fact of referral to court as the most severe among handling alternatives.

Despite these limitations, certain comparisons are possible. Past studies have found sex, race, and socioeconomic status to be relatively unimportant predictors of handling, and the present study findings are in agreement. Two of the four studies. . . found family variables to be fairly important predictors; in both studies, the youngsters' past delinquency record was found to be the most important predictor. The regression analyses conducted in the present study have shown family and school data to be far more powerful predictors of severity of handling and placement than any past or present delinquency information. The number of decision points examined in the present study was expanded however, and the entire population was defined as youngsters handled *at least* at intake. It may well be the case that family and school data are of less importance (or perhaps less known) to decision makers determining whether to refer youngsters to intake or handle without that contact.

CONCLUSION

This study set out to discover the characteristics of youngsters referred to Upstate County family court intake and to determine the factors related to their processing; this report represents the extent to which these goals have been met. Research efforts of this kind are most useful in the hands of the criminal justice theoretician/researcher and the practictioner, especially when they serve to narrow the gap between the two. It seems clear, at any rate, that before it is possible to meaningfully discuss where we want to go in the operations of family court intake and family court, we need to accurately grasp where we have been and where we are currently.

Feedback of these findings to Upstate County court and intake personnel, as well as resulting dialogue between these individuals and the researchers, will lead to a discussion of implications and possible recommendations for changes in processing procedures. Two major topics which should be included in the dialogue are: (1) the implications of decision making based on family and school status for services to be delivered to the family by family court and probation; and (2) the discrepancy between the decision-making criteria and the current legal focus on determinate sentences bases only on the offense behavior. It is hoped that some of the answers provided in this study serve ultimately to raise new, more sophisticated research questions.

19 *Preventing Delinquency Through Diversion*
The Sacramento County Probation Department 601
Diversion Project — A Second Year Report
Roger Baron and Floyd Feeney

This is the second major report about the results of the Sacramento County Probation Department 601 Diversion Project. This project is concerned with youths beyond the control of their parents, runaways, truants and other youths falling within Section 601 of the California Welfare and Institutions Code. This kind of case constitutes over one-third of all juvenile court cases in Sacramento County and high percentages elsewhere in California and the nation. Many judges and probation officers have long felt these to be among their toughest cases and the least appropriate for handling through the juvenile court.

The Sacramento 601 Diversion Project is an experiment designed to test whether juveniles charged with this kind of offense — the 601 or "predelinquent" offense — can be handled better through short term family crisis therapy at the time of referral than through the traditional procedures of the juvenile court. Its objective is to demonstrate the validity of the diversion concept of delinquency prevention by showing that:

- runaway, beyond control and other types of 601 cases can be diverted from the present system of juvenile justice and court adjudication
- detention can be avoided in most 601-type situations through counseling and alternative placements that are both temporary and voluntary
- those diverted have fewer subsequent brushes with the law and a better general adjustment to life than those not diverted
- this diversion can be accomplished within existing resources available for handling this kind of case.

The intent of the project is to keep the child out of the juvenile hall, keep the family problem out of the court and still offer counseling and help to the family.

This approach relies on the following features:

- immediate, intensive handling of cases rather than piecemeal adjudication
- avoidance of compartmentalized service by the creation of a prevention and diversion unit handling cases from beginning to end
- spending the majority of staff time in the initial stages of the case — when it is in crisis — rather than weeks or months later
- the provision of special training to probation staff involved

From *Preventing Delinquency Through Diversion*, The Sacramento County Probation Department 601 Diversion Project, A Second Year Report (Davis, Calif.: Center on Administration of Criminal Justice, University of California, 1973). Reprinted by permission.

- the provision of on-going consultative services on a periodic basis to enable staff to continue to improve their crisis handling skills
- avoidance entirely of formal court proceedings
- avoidance of juvenile hall through counseling and the use of alternate placements that are both temporary and voluntary
- maintenance of a twenty-four-hour, seven days a week telephone crisis service
- closer ties with outside referral services.

The project began handling cases on October 26, 1970. For purposes of the experiment the project handles cases on four days of the week with the regular intake unit handling the other three days as a control group. Days are rotated monthly, so that each day of the week will be included approximately the same number of times for both the project group and the control group.

On project days when a referral on a 601 matter is received — whether from the police, the schools, the parents or whatever — the project arranges a family session to discuss the problem. Every effort is made to insure that this session is held as soon as possible and most are held within the first hour or two after referral. Through the use of family counseling techniques the project counselor seeks to develop the idea that the problem is one that should be addressed by the family as a whole. Locking up the youth as a method of solving problems is discouraged and a return home with a commitment by all to try to work through the problem is encouraged. If the underlying emotions are too strong to permit the youth's return home immediately, an attempt is made to locate an alternative place for the youth to stay temporarily. This is a voluntary procedure which requires the consent of both the parents and the youth.

Families are encouraged to return for a second discussion with the counselor and depending upon the nature of the problem for a third, fourth or fifth session. Normally, the maximum number of sessions is five. Sessions rarely last less than one hour and often go as long as two or two and a half hours. First sessions take place when the problem arises. Since the project operates until 2 a.m., some begin after midnight.

All sessions after the first session are essentially voluntary, and whether the family returns is up to the family itself. In many cases counselors are in contact with the family by phone whether there is a follow-up visit or not. All members of the family are encouraged to contact the counselor in the event of a continuing problem or some new additional problem.

The data available for the First Year Report indicated that 601 cases could be diverted from court using project techniques. The number of court petitions, the number of informal probations, the number of days spent in detention, and the cost of handling were all less for project than for control cases. In addition, after seven months project cases had fewer repeat acts of delinquency than did those in the control group.

These results indicated that the project was a highly promising one, but a number of important questions still remained. Perhaps the most important was whether the results concerning recidivism would hold up over a longer period of time and a larger number of cases. Were the differences reported the results of initial project staff enthusiasm or of the project technique itself? Was the improvement in recidivism a permanent improvement in the situation or simply the delaying of trouble that would ultimately occur?

RESULTS — REPEAT OFFENSES

Because these questions are so central to the project, this second report was designed to provide answers to the extent possible. In order to provide both a larger number of cases and a larger follow-up, all cases — project and control — handled during the first year of the project were followed for a period of twelve months from the date of initial handling.

The rate for both groups of repeat behavior involving conflict with the law was high. Project cases, however, did noticeably better than did control cases. Thus, while at the end of the one-year period 54.2 percent of the control group youths had been rebooked for either a 601 offense or for a violation of the penal code (section 602 of the California Welfare and Institutions Code) the comparable figure for the project group was 46.3 percent. Out of any 100 youths handled, 7.9 fewer will repeat under project handling than will repeat under control handling. In percentage terms this represents an improvement of over 14 percent.[1]

Looking at offenses committed after initial handling which involved only criminal conduct (section 602), the improvement was even greater. For these cases the repeat rate for control was 29.8 percent and 22.4 percent for the project group. This is a drop in the rate of repeated offenses of 24.8 percent. Because of greater consistencies in classification among all agencies involved, the repeat rate for 602 offenses is perhaps the single best measure for the project.

If consideration is limited to felony and drug 602 cases, generally regarded as the more serious cases, the improvement is greater still. The percentage of project youths having rebookings for these offenses was 13.1 percent as compared with 22.1 percent for the controls, a difference of over 40 percent.

There are also substantially fewer project youths who are rebooked twice — 24.6 percent as compared with 31.6 percent for two or more rebookings of any kind; 7.4 percent as compared with 12.2 percent for two or more 602 rebookings and 3.6 percent project versus 5.9 percent controls for two or more rebookings for felony or drug offenses.

TABLE 19-1   Percent of Juveniles Rebooked within Twelve Months*

	PROJECT (674 YOUTHS)	CONTROL (526 YOUTHS)	DIFFERENCE
Any Recidivism	46.3	54.2	+14.6
602 Recidivism	22.4	29.8	+24.8
Serious 602 (Drug or Felony)	13.1	22.1	+40.7
Double	24.6	31.6	+22.2
Double 602	7.4	12.2	+39.4
Double 602 Serious	3.6	5.9	+39.0

*Youths initially referred October 26, 1970 through October 25, 1971.

The figures above reflect the differences in the number of youths rebooked for an offense within the twelve-month period. Since each youth who is rebooked for a new offense may be rebooked more than one time, the previous figures do not, however, show any differences in the total number of new offenses committed. This aspect of the problem was consequently examined separately, and the results indicated below. In this table one repeat offense is counted as one and four repeat offenses by the same youth as four. In the previous table each of these two situations was counted as one.

TABLE 19-2   Number of Bookings for a New Offense within Twelve Months per 100 Youths Initially Handled*

	601 REPEAT BOOKINGS (PER 100 YOUTHS HANDLED)	602 REPEAT BOOKINGS (PER 100 YOUTHS HANDLED)	601 OR 602 REPEAT BOOKINGS (PER 100 YOUTHS HANDLED)
Control (526 youths)	71	49	120
Project (674 youths)	64	35	99

*Youths initially referred October 26, 1970 through October 25, 1971.

What this table shows is that for each 100 youths initially handled, the control group had 71 subsequent bookings for 601 offenses, 49 subsequent bookings for 602 offenses, and a total of 120 subsequent bookings. This compared with totals of 64, 35 and 99 for the project. These figures in effect indicate that for each 100 project youths there were 17.5 percent fewer new bookings than there were for the same number of control youths, 9.9 percent fewer 601 new bookings and 28.6 percent fewer 602 bookings.

Basically these figures indicate that the difference in recidivism indicated in the first year report on the basis of a seven-month follow-up are being maintained. Repeat bookings increased between the seventh and the twelfth months by about the same amount for each group. (Statistically this maintains the absolute difference but decreases the percentage difference).

These figures suggest that most of the project impact comes early in the process. Given the project emphasis on providing immediate help to youth and families this is not too surprising, and is what could be expected. Moreover, the fact that the difference in the number of repeat bookings persists over a period as long as a year suggests strongly that the improvement involved for the youths concerned is of relatively long duration and not simply temporary.

RESULTS — DIVERSION FROM COURT

Another important objective of the project is to test the idea that 601 cases can be diverted from the juvenile court. Data for the first twelve months of the project continue to indicate rather clearly that this objective has been accomplished. During this period the project handled 977 referrals to the probation department involving opportunities for diversion, but filed only thirty-six petitions. Court processing was consequently necessary in only 3.7 percent of these referrals as opposed to 19.8 percent of the referrals handled in the control group. Because a youth may be referred to the probation department two, three, or more times before a petition is filed or without a petition being filed, the number of referrals handled exceeds the number of individuals handled.

TABLE 19-3   Referrals and Petitions*

	NUMBER OF REFERRALS	NUMBER OF PETITIONS	PERCENT
Control	612	121	19.8
Project	977	36	3.7

*First twelve project months.

This table is concerned with petitions filed while there is an opportunity for diversion from court rather than petitions filed as a result of the recidivism. Consequently, if a petition is filed on a youth handled by either the project or the control group and that person subsequently returns on another 601 matter and an additional petition is filed, the additional petition is not included in these totals. Similarly, if a youth handled on a 601 matter by either the project or the control group subsequently returns for some kind of 602 behavior and a 602 petition is filed, that petition is also not included.

If these kinds of petitions were included as well as those resulting from referrals involving opportunities for diversion, project data indicate that during a twelve-month follow-up period 41 percent of all control group youths and 20 percent of all project group youths ultimately went to court. The total number of petitions filed for 526 youths handled in the control group was 401, while the total for 674 project group youths handled in the same period was 219.

In California a second entry point from intake into the juvenile justice system is through informal probation. Informal probation is provided for by Welfare and Institutions Code Section 654 and is a voluntary procedure entered into when the probation intake officer believes the matter can be handled without going to court but requires some probation supervision. During the first twelve months of the project a total of 117 control cases were placed under informal supervision as a result of initial handling as opposed to 22 project cases.

TABLE 19-4   Informal Probation

	NUMBER OF REFERRALS	INFORMAL PROBATIONS	PERCENT
Control	612	117	19.1
Project	977	22	2.3

*First twelve project months.

Taking both petitions and informal supervision together, the number of cases going forward in the system from intake were 38.9 percent of the control cases, but only 6.0 percent of the project cases.

TABLE 19-5   Petitions Filed and Informal Probations*

	NUMBER OF CASES	PETITIONS & INFORMALS	PERCENT
Control	612	238	38.9
Project	977	58	6.0

*First twelve project months.

While these figures show some increases in the number of project cases with a petition filed or an informal probation — from 3 percent in the first year report to 6 percent in this report — the percentage remains quite low.

RESULTS — DETENTION

A third major project concern is that of detention. A great deal of evidence suggests that detention is itself a harmful factor which serves on the one hand as a school for crime and on the other as an embittering factor which makes family reconciliations necessary to the resolution of 601 cases more difficult. The table below compares the extent of overnight detention in juvenile hall as a result of initial arrests.

Under California law all cases involving detention longer than forty-eight hours (not including weekends and other nonjudicial days) must be brought before the juvenile court judge or referee for approval.

TABLE 19-6   Overnight Detention in Juvenile Hall as a Result of Initial Referral*

	CONTROL (PERCENT)	PROJECT (PERCENT)
No Overnight Detention	44.5	86.1
1 Night	20.7	9.9
2-4 Nights	19.2	3.0
5-39 Nights	14.4	0.7
40-100 Nights	1.1	0.3
Over 100 Nights	0.0	0.0

*Youths referred October 25, 1970 through October 25, 1971.

These figures indicate that more than 55 percent of all control group youths spent at least one night in juvenile hall as compared with 14 percent for youths handled by the project. These initial differences in the amount of detention are also reflected in the average number of nights each youth spent in detention. Thus, while project group youths had an average of 0.5 nights in detention as a result of initial handling, control group youths spent an average of 4.6 nights in detention.

In addition to spending more nights in detention as a result of initial referral, control group youths also spent more nights in detention over a twelve-month follow-up period.

TABLE 19-7   Overnight Detention in Juvenile Hall Either as a Result of Initial Arrest or as a Result of Subsequent Arrest During Twelve-Month Follow-Up*

	CONTROL (PERCENT)	PROJECT (PERCENT)
No Overnight	30.6	57.7
1 Night	14.8	12.9
2-4 Nights	17.1	12.5
5-39 Nights	24.5	10.4
40-100 Nights	11.2	6.1
Over 100 Nights	1.7	.7

*Youths referred October 26, 1970 through October 25, 1971.

These figures indicate that considering both initial arrest and subsequent case history more than 69 percent of the youths handled by control spent at least one night in juvenile hall as compared with 42.3 percent of the project youths. The average number of nights spent for project youths was 6.7 per case as compared with 14.5 for control youths.

These figures indicate some improvement in the number of control youths spending at least one night in juvenile hall (73 percent in the first year report as compared with 69 percent in this report) and at the same time an increase in the number of project youths spending the night (from 34.4 to 42.4 percent). The differential remains a very substantial one, however, and it seems clear that diversion handling results in a much lower amount of detention.

WORKLOAD AND DIVERSION

From the beginning one important objective of the diversion project has been to demonstrate not only that the diversion idea was sound from a treatment point of view, but also that this kind of service was no more costly and perhaps less costly than the kind of service more regularly provided.

Figures developed in the first year report based on the handling for a seven-month period of cases referred in February 1971 indicated that diversion-type service was considerably cheaper than regular service. Average handling time for this group of cases was 9.9 hours for project cases as compared with 17.0 hours for control cases. These figures indicated a substantial difference in average handling costs for the two kinds of cases. There were also substantial differences in the average costs for detention and placement.

Recomputation of these figures based on the larger sample of cases and the longer period of time covered by this report indicates that these cost differences continue to hold true.

TABLE 19-8. Average Cost for Case Handling, Detention, and Placement for Seven-month Period

	PROJECT	CONTROL
Handling	$ 79.20	$136.00
Detention	65.60	196.27
Placement	25.28	73.50
Total	$170.08	$405.27

Using all cases referred during the first year of the project and following these for a one-year period, the average total handling time for each of the 674 project youths was 14.2 hours. The comparable average time for the 526 control youths was 23.7 hours.

The average costs for the two groups were as follows:

TABLE 19-9. Average Costs for Case Handling, Detention, and Placement for One-Year Period

	PROJECT	CONTROL
Handling	$113.60	$189.60
Detention	98.98	214.27
Placement	61.43	157.76
Total	$274.01	$561.63

Thus, the cost to the probation department of regular intake care for this kind of case continues to be more than twice as expensive as the cost of diversion.

A second method of evaluating the cost impact of the project used in the first year report was an analysis of the manpower savings engendered by the program. This analysis focuses on the direct manpower savings in case handling and does not consider other savings such as those involved in detention and placement. This method of analysis is based on comparing the manpower required to handle the diversion caseload with that required to handle cases in the normal way.

The average work required for handling cases in the first seven months as reported in the first year report was as follows:

TABLE 19-10. Average Work Required for Handling in First Seven Months (Based on February 1971 Referrals)

	PROJECT	CONTROL
Average Number of Petitions per Youth	.19	.61
Average Months of Supervision per Youth	.55	2.40
Average Months of Placement Supervision per Youth	.12	.61

The comparable figures for handling for one year all the cases referred during the first year are:

TABLE 19-11.   Average Work Required for Handling in First Year (Based on First Year Referrals)

	PROJECT	CONTROL
Average Number of Petitions per Youth	.32	.76
Average Months of Supervision per Youth	1.06	3.67
Average Months of Placement Supervision per Youth	.34	.88

In each category youths handled by the project continued to require less work. If both project and control figures are multiplied by the number of youths handled by the diversion unit per month, the difference will be the work displaced by diversion at points past intake. The figures for this during the first four months of the project and reported in the first year report were as follows:

TABLE 19-12.   Work Displacement for Four-Month Period

NUMBER OF WORK UNITS DISPLACED	NUMBER OF OFFICERS DISPLACED
31 court cases per month	2.1 court officers
139 supervision hours per month	2.0 supervision officers
37 placement supervision hours per month	1.1 placement officers
90 intake cases per month	1.5 intake officers
Total	6.7 positions

The comparable figures for the whole year are:

TABLE 19-13   Work Displacement for One-Year Period

NUMBER OF WORK UNITS DISPLACED	NUMBER OF OFFICERS DISPLACED
25 court cases per month	1.7 court officers
147 supervision hours per month	2.1 supervision officers
30 placement supervision hours per month	.9 placement officers
90 intake cases per month	1.5 intake officers
Total	6.2 positions

Thus, while the displacement figure dropped slightly somewhat from the first report, it remained above the number of officers in the diversion unit — resulting in a net displacement, of two-tenths of a position within the probation department, not including such other savings as detention, court and placement costs. . . .

NOTES

1. The difference in recidivism between project and controls is 7.9 percent (54.2 percent less 46.3 percent). Using the project rate of recidivism as a base, the rate of improvement is 14.0 percent.

$$\frac{\text{difference between rates}}{\text{lowest rate of recidivism}} = \text{rate of improvement}$$

$$\frac{7.9}{46.3} = 14.0 \text{ percent}$$

The Juvenile Court Treatment Rationale: Restriction and Expansion

INTRODUCTION

To help children, or to use the more contemporary language, to obtain treatment services needed by youngsters, has been the emotional wellspring of the juvenile court movement. The juvenile court's treatment rationale was bound to run into trouble, in time. Judges and probation officials often blended treatment offers with punitive sanctions. Treatment resources were neither sufficient nor effective. Many citizens preferred the lockup and the rod to more conciliatory approaches. Lawyers, for some time, did not question the treatment purposes, but instead expressed concern with the court's absence of legal regimen prior to and during the treatment effort. Accelerated legal challenge since the mid-1960s reflected defense attorney skepticism over the court's assertion of authority on the basis of a need for treatment and the subsequent failure to obtain quality services. Feeding fuel to the lawyers' fire was the array of social science research and evaluation revealing, in the main, that there was no clear correlation between individual treatment approaches and an acquisition of law conforming behavior. Increasingly repressive legislation in the 1970s expressed the public's concern for safety and a growing preference for a punishment rationale. Child advocates expressed concern that individualized justice based on an individual's "needs" caused discriminatory and disparate sanctions. The more conservative and the more liberal viewpoints coalesced in proposals recommending the legitimation of a punishment rationale. The duration and nature of restrictions would be correlated with the severity of the offense, prior criminal history, and age, rather than offender needs or family strengths. A further objective was the more equal handling of equals. Punishments would be relatively modest; the great bulk of juvenile offenders would be handled in the community. The treatment interest would not be eliminated, but it would not be primary. This perspective, adopted by an influential national commission and several legislatures to date, represents an important new approach.

A further development during the 1970s was the expanded testing of the doctrine of the right to treatment, possibly an inappropriate term for an important concept. The doctrine arose in the field of mental illness law to challenge the involuntary hospitalization of patients in the absence of mental health treatment, and expanded to the fields of mental retardation and juvenile justice. The theory was suited to a juvenile court with an avowed purpose of treatment, but less suited to a penal model of juvenile justice. The limited but growing juvenile court enactments which have set forth punishment as an objective have not repealed other statutory purposes such as rehabilitation. Overseeing juvenile justice practices is the due process clause of the Fourteenth Amendment, from which the right to treatment has derived certain constitutional support.

The first article in this section is a case from a family court in Syracuse, New York which reflects the careful efforts of a trial judge to weigh punitive legislation enacted by that state in 1976 against constitutional precepts and the statutory ban on jury trials for juveniles. Earlier, in 1971, the United States Supreme Court had held that the Sixth Amendment's right to a jury trial in a criminal proceeding did not mandate state juvenile court provision of a jury trial. The rationale for that decision was based upon the differences between juvenile and criminal courts and their respective emphasis on rehabilitation versus punishment. The judge's task, in this instance, required a conscientious examination of the strictures of the new legislation in contrast to the juvenile court's rhetoric of treatment.

The concept paper by Professor Fred Cohen sets forth the basic assumptions of a proportionality or just deserts principle for juvenile court decisions and argues that there are greater values inherent in this doctrine than in an individualized treatment rationale. Although failures in treatment achievements are cited to support the proportionality model, the theory can stand by itself without an underpinning of treatment failures; its philosophy of equal justice and humanistic punishment is a self-contained rationale. Cohen's paper served as a foundation for principles adopted by the Institute of Judicial Administration-American Bar Association Juvenile Justice Standards Project, and its basic outline was adopted in 1977 Washington state legislation. The administration of a proportionality model can be expected to present numerous problems, such as increased plea and sentence bargaining and a shifting of discretion from judge to police and prosecutor. However, its widespread adoption would significantly transform the juvenile justice system.

The final article in this section, by Adrienne Volenik, traces the evolution of the right to treatment doctrine through case law. Application of the doctrine, limited to date to detained and incarcerated youngsters, has received support from a number of United States district courts but conflicting opinions from two United States circuit courts of appeal. Whether the right to treatment is a consititutional right is currently unsettled. Many of the juvenile cases have been accompanied by court findings of other constitutional violations such as cruel and unusual punishment and unequal protection of the laws. Right to treatment rulings have improved institutional care conditions for juveniles in a number of states and have triggered marked expansion in community-based service alternatives to institutionalization.

20 *Matter of Felder*

Family Court, Onondaga County. Feb. 8, 1978.
402 N.Y.S.2d 528

DECISION — EDWARD J. McLAUGHLIN, JUDGE.

This juvenile delinquency proceeding involves a designated felony pursuant to the *Juvenile Justice Reform Act of 1976*, N.Y. Family Court Act §§ 711–767, 29 A

From *Matter of Felder* 402 N.Y.S.2d 528, Family Court, Onondaga County, New York, February 8, 1978.

McKinney's Consolidated Laws 1977. It presents a case of first impression for this court. Respondent, a boy of fifteen, allegedly committed a robbery in the first degree, Penal Law § 160.15, a designated felony. F C A § 712(h). When the case came before the Court, the Respondent moved for a jury trial, asserting that under *Baldwin v. New York,* 399 U.S. 66, 90 S.Ct. 1886, 26 L.Ed.2d 437 (1970), an individual charged with a crime where the penalty could exceed six months imprisonment is entitled to a jury trial. The respondent alleged that since he can be confined in a secure facility for a period of time up to twelve months, pursuant to section 753–a(4)(a)(ii) of the Family Court Act, the *Baldwin* doctrine applied, and he is entitled to a trial by jury.

On the other hand, the petitioner alleged that the United States Supreme Court decision in *McKeiver v. Pennsylvania,* 403 U.S. 528, 91 S.Ct. 1976, 29 L.Ed.2d 647 (1971), is controlling. *McKeiver* holds that a juvenile charged with a delinquency, which precludes, by definition, criminal consequences and tried in a civil court, does not have a due process right to a jury trial. Petitioner further alleged that while New York is not constitutionally precluded from granting a jury trial under *McKeiver,* it has determined not to do so, citing *In re Daniel G.,* 27 N.Y.2d 90, 313 N.Y.S.2d 704, 261 N.E.2d 627 (1970) and *Matter of George S.,* 44 A.D.2d 352, 355 N.Y.S.2d 143 (1st Dept., 1974).

The issue before the court, then, is whether the instant proceeding is controlled by *McKeiver* or by *Baldwin.* Specifically, the question turns on whether this is a juvenile proceeding within the meaning of *McKeiver,* or, whether so many of the attributes of a juvenile proceeding have been discarded that the proceeding is in effect "criminal" in nature and thus within the ambit of *Baldwin.*[1]

A. IS A DESIGNATED FELONY PROCEEDING A JUVENILE PROCEEDING?

The concept of designated felony was created as a part of the *Juvenile Justice Reform Act of 1976* (Chapt. 878, Laws of 1976).

The Legislature has chosen to label this new "designated felony concept" as a "juvenile" proceeding. It is axiomatic that this court is not bound by that designation if, in fact, the new proceeding is indeed a criminal proceeding.[2] The Supreme Court recognized this principle in *Trop v. Dulles,* 356 U.S. 86, at 94, 78 S.Ct. 590, at 594, 2 L.Ed.2d 630 (1958), when the Court taught us:

> But the Government contends that this statute does not impose a penalty. . . . We are told that this is so because a committee. . . said it "technically is not a penal law." How simple would be the task of constitutional adjudication and of law generally if specific problems could be solved by inspection of labels pasted on them . . .

Further, "[N]either the label which a state places on its own conduct, nor even the legitimacy of its own motivation, can avoid applicability of the Federal Constitution." *Vann v. Scott,* 467 F.2d 1235, at 1240 (7th Cir. 1972) (decision per Judge Stevens, now Mr. Justice Stevens, on an Eighth Amendment challenge to a training school commitment).

B. BACKGROUND OF THE JUVENILE JUSTICE SYSTEM

The fundamental substantive distinction between a juvenile proceeding and a criminal proceeding is that a juvenile disposition is limited to treatment, while a criminal proceeding may impose punishment regardless of whether the punishment results in retribution and, or, deterrence. The view that the difference between criminal and juvenile proceedings is the difference between retribution and deterrence, on the one hand, and treatment, on the other, is confirmed by an examination of the history of the juvenile court system. This examination will also show that a denial of a juvenile's full exercise of his constitutional rights can only be predicated upon the presence of the treatment principle of the juvenile justice system.

At common law there were no juvenile courts or juvenile proceedings. If a child, over the age of seven, committed a criminal act, he was tried in a criminal court, and afforded all of the privileges of an adult charged with the same conduct. Thus, he was arrested, indicted by a grand jury, tried by a petit jury, and, if convicted, sent to prison. Mack, *The Juvenile Court,* 23 Harv. L.R. 104, at 106 (1909).

The reformers of the nineteenth century were appalled by the fact that juveniles could be given long prison sentences to be served with hardened criminals. They recognized that criminal jurisprudence was founded not on "Reformation of the Criminal, but punishment; punishment as expiation for wrong, punishment as a warning to other possible wrongdoers." Mack, *supra,* at 106. To alleviate this situation, special juvenile centers were established which were authorized to admit children convicted of petty criminal offenses. The premise of these juvenile centers was that children were not criminal offenders, and, if properly treated, could be saved from a life of crime. The juvenile reform movement later became concerned not only with the disposition received by the juveniles but with the adjudication of juveniles as well. Thus, separate court proceedings were established.

The juvenile statutes were early challenged on the basis that the statutes were criminal in nature and the procedures employed were, therefore, violative of the constitutional protection applicable to criminal proceedings. In most cases the challenges were rejected on the ground that the disposition was rehabilitative and not grounded on motivations of punishment and deterrence. E.g. *Commonwealth v. Fisher,* 213 Pa. 48, 62 A. 198 (1905). Where the challenge succeeded was in those situations where the proceeding was, in effect, criminal in nature. E.g. *Robinson v. Wayne Circuit Judges,* 151 Mich. 315, 115 N.W. 682 (1908).

This historical examination of the origins of the juvenile justice system shows that the informality, flexibility, and, concomitantly, the absence of constitutional safeguards at juvenile proceedings was justified on the ground that the juvenile was to be treated and rehabilitated. Conversely, when the juvenile proceeding was primarily for retributive and deterrent purposes, it was considered criminal in nature, and hence subject to all of the limitations of a regular criminal proceeding. Sometimes referred to as the "exchange principle of juvenile law",[3] the trading of the constitutional protections of a criminal proceeding for rehabilitation still remains today the *sine qua non* of juvenile proceedings. Typical is the comment of the court in *Inmates of Boys' Training School v. Affleck,* 346 F.Supp. 1354, at 1364 (D.R.I.1972). The court said:

(T)he constitutional validity of present procedural safeguards in juvenile adjudications, which do not embrace àll of the rigorous safeguards of criminal court adjudications, appears to rest on the adherence of the juvenile justice system to rehabilitative rather than penal goals. . . . Rehabilitation, then, is the interest which the state has defined as being the purpose of confinement of juveniles. Due process in the adjudicative stages of the juvenile justice system has been defined differently from due process in the criminal justice system because the goal of the juvenile system, rehabilitation, differs from the goals of the criminal system, which include punishment, deterrence and retribution.

It is against this background that *McKeiver v. Pennsylvania, supra,* must be viewed. It is true that *McKeiver* stated that in a juvenile proceeding trial by jury is not a constitutional requirement. The Court specifically refused to abandon the salutary goals of the juvenile system and rejected the jury trial because it could "tend to place the juvenile squarely in the routine of the criminal process." 403 U.S., at 547, 91 S.Ct. at 1987. Indeed, the Court acknowledged that when a child is adjudicated as a juvenile, but treated as a criminal, an inconsistency results, for the Court stated: "Of course there have been abuses. . . . We refrain from saying at this point that these abuses are of a constitutional dimension." *Id.,* at 547–48, 91 S.Ct. at 1987. In effect, the Court deferred until a more appropriate occasion the determination of when a juvenile disposition fails to meet the rehabilitative premise of the juvenile system. The determination in *McKeiver* that in a juvenile proceeding a jury trial is not required, is, therefore, necessarily limited to those proceedings that are juvenile in nature. Thus, there is no requirement of a jury trial in family court where the disposition is rehabilitative and nonpenal. When, however, the protections provided to the juvenile criminal offender have so eroded away that what is actually a punishment is characterized as a treatment, an abuse of constitutional dimension has occurred, and, a jury trial is required before punishment, although appropriate, may be inflicted.

C. BACKGROUND OF THE 1976 ACT

In response to the reported increase in the frequency and severity of crimes committed by juveniles, the Legislature in the 1976 session enacted the *Juvenile Justice Reform Act*. This bill significantly amended Article 7 of the Family Court Act. The express purpose of Article 7 was redefined to include, for the first time, consideration of the needs of the community: "In any juvenile procedure under this article, the court shall consider the needs and best interests of the respondent as well as the need for protection of the community." F C A § 711. To this end, the Legislature created restrictive placement. Rejecting proposals to transfer seriously violent juveniles to the adult criminal system, the Legislature adopted restrictive placement as a method of dealing with the juveniles within the juvenile system. Gottfried, R. and Barsky, S. *Practice Commentaries,* F C A § 753–a, *29A McKinney's Consolidated Laws of New York, 1977.*

The amendments to Article 7 define four new terms — designated felony act,[4] designated Class A felony act,[5] secure facility,[6] and restrictive placement.[7] F C A § 712. Further, the amendments allow the County Attorney to be assisted by members of the District Attorney's staff, F C A § 254(c); provides that the probation service may not attempt to adjust some cases without the prior written approval of a judge, F C A § 734(a)(ii); requires that, with a few exceptions, the judge presiding at the fact finding hearing shall preside at the dispositional hearing, F C A § 742; and, eliminates in designated felony cases the judge's discretionary right to prevent disclosure of portions of the juvenile's reports and histories to either the respondent or the petitioner. F C A § 570.

D. AN ANALYSIS OF THE 1976 ACT

A significant change made by the *Juvenile Justice Reform Act* is the requirement that restrictive placement may be ordered for a juvenile found to have committed a designated felony, when the court determines that a juvenile requires such restrictive placement. F C A § 753−a. Once restrictive placement is ordered by the court, the delinquent must remain in the placement for twelve months, if the placement results from an adjudication on a Class A designated felony, or for six months, if the placement results from the adjudication of any designated felony. F C A § 753−a(3)(a)(ii); (4)(a)(ii). Further, during the period of restrictive placement, the right to petition the court to stay the execution, to set aside, modify, or vacate the disposition is suspended. It is this suspension of the provisions of part six, Article 7, of the Family Court Act which distinguishes a restrictive placement disposition from all other dispositions under Article 7. Thus, the Legislature has created a definite sentence of placement nearly indistinguishable from definite sentences imposed upon adults under section 70.20(2) of the Penal Law.

Further, in mandating the minimum period of restrictive placement, when restrictive placement has been found to be needed at all, the Legislature has introduced two other concepts of the criminal justice process previously unknown in the juvenile system. First, the length of the commitment is determined by the act committed rather than by the needs of the child, and second, the sentence is mandatory. In effect, the Legislature has determined that a child who at the time of his dispositional hearing requires restrictive placement will continue to require restrictive placement for the entire period of the minimum sentence. Prior to the enactment of this statute, the court was only required to determine that at the time of the dispositional hearing the needs of the child were for placement in an institution and that at any time during that initial period, if the child was successfully rehabilitated, he was entitled to release. Consistent with this philosophy of treatment was the provision that if at the end of the initial placement the child was not successfully rehabilitated, then, the period of placement could be extended. In effect, once the court makes a finding that restrictive placement is needed at the time of the disposition, the act then mandates a minimum sentence, a result which is more harsh on the juvenile than is the criminal procedure for the adult who is entitled to an indeterminate sentence in nearly all cases. P L § 70.00.

The distinction between indeterminate and determinate sentencing is not semantic, but indicates fundamentally different public policies. Indeterminate sentencing is based upon notions of rehabilitation, while determinate sentencing is based upon a desire for retribution or punishment.

In his vigorous dissent *In re Gault,* 387 U.S. 1, 87 S.Ct. 1428, 18 L.Ed.2d 527 (1967), Mr. Justice Stewart succinctly distinguished the purpose and mission of the juvenile system of justice from the purpose and mission of the criminal system. "The object of the one[juvenile] is correcting a condition. The object of the other [criminal] is conviction and punishment for a criminal act." 387 U.S., at 79, 87 S.Ct., at 1470. By mandating restrictive placement in a secure facility for a minimum of six months, the Legislature has created a disposition that more nearly resembles a punishment than a treatment and, thereby, has blurred the clearly distinct objectives of the juvenile justice system with those of the criminal justice system.

The thinly disguised intent of the Legislature to punish an adjudicated designated felon, based upon the criminal act and upon the characteristics of the victim of the criminal act, as opposed to rehabilitating and treating a juvenile offender is revealed by the 1977 amendment to section 753–a of the Family Court Act which states:

> . . . the court shall order a restrictive placement in any case where the respondent is found to have committed a designated felony act in which the respondent inflicted serious physical injury . . . upon another person who is sixty-two years of age or more. F C A § 753–a(2–a).

This court does not deny that punishment may be appropriate for certain designated felons. This court does insist, however, that deprivation of liberty for purposes of punishment based on the nature of criminal acts committed must be surrounded by constitutional protections not now available in family court proceedings.

The very heart of the rehabilitative nature of the juvenile justice system in New York is the array of remedies provided in part six of Article 7 of the Family Court Act, for it is these remedies that have protected the right of a juvenile to an indeterminate sentence. Cf. *In the Matter of Ilone I.,* 64 Misc.2d 878, 316 N.Y.S.2d 356 (Family Court, Queens County, 1970). It is the indeterminate quality of a juvenile disposition that makes the disposition rehabilitative. To refuse to allow a part six motion to modify or to terminate a placement gives the disposition clearly criminal characteristics.

E. TREATMENT

The *Juvenile Justice Reform Act* requires that treatment be available at restrictive placement facilities. The availability and quality of treatment available to the respondent is not at issue here. What is at issue is the mandatory time period required for treatment. F C A § 753–a.

Analogies may be made between the treatment of persons confined because of mental illness and juveniles confined because of delinquency. Serious consideration has been given recently to the constitutional rights of persons involuntarily committed to mental hospitals following noncriminal dispositions. In identifying treatment as a right for the mentally ill, for instance, a court concluded that at the least an institution must make a *bona fide* effort to cure, since the purpose of the involuntary hospitalization is treatment, not punishment. *Rouse v. Cameron,* 125 U.S.App.D.C. 366, 373 F.2d 451 (1966). Similarly, another federal district court found that non-criminal procedures for commitment which lacked constitutional safeguards were valid only for treatment and not for punishment. *Wyatt v. Stickney,* 325 F.Supp. 781 (M.D.Ala.1971). Cf. *O'Connor v. Donaldson,* 422 U.S. 563, 95 S.Ct. 2486, 45 L.Ed.2d 396 (1975); *Jackson v. Indiana,* 406 U.S. 715, 92 S.Ct. 1845, 32 L.Ed.2d 435 (1972).

Juveniles also have a right to treatment. *Martarella v. Kelley,* 349 F.Supp. 575 (S.D. N.Y.1972); *Inmates of Boys' Training School v. Affleck, supra; M. v. M.,* 71 Misc.2d 396, 336 N.Y.S.2d 304 (Family Court, Bronx County, 1972). Moreover, one court has found that "the right to treatment" includes "the right to *individualized* care and treatment." *Nelson v. Heyne,* 491 F.2d 352, at 360 (7th Cir.), *cert. den.* of 417 U.S. 976, 94 S.Ct. 3183, 41 L.Ed.2d 1146 (1974) (emphasis in the original). The reasoning of the court in *Nelson* is helpful in analyzing time limited restrictive placement:

> Because children differ in their need for rehabilitation, individual need for treatment will differ. . . . Without a program of individual treatment the result may be that the juveniles will not be rehabilitated, but warehoused, and that at the termination of detention they will likely be incapable of taking their proper places in free society; their interests and those of the state thereby'being defeated. *Id.*

Clearly, treatment may result in a cure in six days, or in six weeks, or in six months, or in one year, or never! By setting a mandatory minimum time period for restrictive placement, treatment becomes indistinguishable from punishment.

F. INTAKE — A CRITICAL STAGE IN DESIGNATED FELONY ACT PROCEEDINGS

Intake proceedings are a unique feature of the juvenile justice system in this state. The intake conference provides for a screening out of cases not suited to court intervention. *In the Matter of Charles C.,* 83 Misc.2d 388, 371 N.Y.S.2d 582 (Family Court, New York County, 1975). It is designed to return the juvenile to the community prior to the formulation of a petition. *In the Matter of Frank H.,* 71 Misc.2d 1042, 337 N.Y.S.2d 118 (Family Court, Richmond County, 1972). The intake'procedure of the family court, as it applies to juvenile delinquency, confers authority on the probation service to offer informal, voluntary conferences to settle the differences between the petitioner and the respondent. In fact, in his concurring opinion in *McKeiver, supra,* Mr. Justice White said that "the distinctive intake policies and procedures of the juvenile court system to a great extend obviate [the] important function of the jury." 403 U.S., at 552, 91 S.Ct., at 1990.

. Under the 1976 amendments to the Family Court Act, a juvenile accused of a designated felony must obtain the "prior written approval of a judge of the court" before an adjustment may take place. F C A § 734(a)(ii). It had been the rule in New York that "no statement made during a preliminary conference may be admitted into evidence at a fact finding hearing." F C A § 735; 22 NYCRR 2507.4(a)(6), 1977, (previously NYCRR 2506.3(d), 1976). This rule had been interpreted as a protection for the respondent against self incrimination, and, thus, the intake conference had not been considered a "critical" stage of adjudication and, therefore, the child was not entitled to counsel at the conference. *In re Frank H., supra; In the Matter of Anthony S.,* 73 Misc.2d 187, 341 N.Y.S.2d 11 (Family Court, Richmond County, 1973).

It now appears that the kind of information previously protected during intake proceedings and not admitted as evidence in fact finding hearings must be made available to the court before the court can determine whether the case is, or is not, suitable for adjustment. Thus, the informality, responsiveness, and flexibility of the intake proceeding, a unique tool of the juvenile justice process, is vitiated, and intake becomes a critical stage of the proceedings and the protection of the constitutional rights of the respondent becomes essential. Whether a respondent is entitled to counsel at a designated felony intake conference is now certainly a consideration.[8] See, *Argersinger v. Hamlin,* 407 U.S. 25, S.Ct. 2006, 32 L.Ed.2d 530 (1972).

G. OTHER FEATURES OF THE ACT

Other features of the *Juvenile Justice Reform Act* are traditionally more associated with criminal proceedings than with civil proceedings. While these procedures are legally less significant than those discussed above, the new procedures do serve to flavor the act with criminal spice.

For instance, in a juvenile proceeding the petitioner's case is presented by the county attorney. F C A § 254–a, but in a designated felony case the district attorney may present the case. F C A § 254–c. This provision, at the least, demonstrates a recognition by the Legislature of the criminal nature of a designated felony proceeding. Further, the court must authorize the fingerprinting and photographing of juveniles adjudicated as designated felons. F C A § 753–b. Then, the assignment of the same judge to both fact finding and dispositional hearings represents a major shift in juvenile justice processes. The *New York Juvenile Justice Act of 1976,* 45 Fordham L.R. 408, at 420. The Legislature's intent was "to insure that the judge who makes . . . the disposition . . . will have a familiarity with all the circumstances surrounding the case." Gottfried, R. *Practice Commentary,* F C A § 742, 29 A *McKinney's Consolidated Laws of N.Y.* 1977. The presentencing hearing has its parallel in criminal proceedings. Compare CPL § 380.30, 390.20, 390.50, 400 and F C A § 753–a(2). The requirement of psychological tests, reports, and histories fails to distinguish the designated felony proceeding from a criminal proceeding. Compare CPL § 390.20 and F C A § 750(3).

In a criminal proceeding the court may in its discretion except from disclosure to counsel portions of the presentencing investigation reports "which might seriously disrupt a program of rehabilitation." CPL § 390.50(2). The same discretion is not afforded the court in a juvenile designated felony case. F C A § 750(4). Ironically, the juvenile court judge is faced with restrictions that fly in the face of rehabilitation the very purpose for which there is a system of juvenile justice distinct from the criminal justice system.

H. THE NEED FOR A JURY TRIAL

The revision of the Family Court Act by the *Juvenile Justice Reform Act of 1976* transformed a purely rehabilitative juvenile statute into a statute that mirrors a retributive criminal statute, but fails to reflect the constitutional protections presumed to apply to such statutes. This transformation is most particularly evidenced by the requirement of restrictive placement in a secure facility for a definite period of time for a person found to have committed a designated felony and to be in need of restrictive placement with no provision for changing the placement if rehabilitation of the juvenile offender is found to have occurred. Other aspects of the revision also indicate that the designated felony proceeding is in its very essence a criminal proceeding, although labeled a juvenile proceeding. Since it is essentially a criminal proceeding, it is required that all the safeguards mandated by the United States Constitution be afforded the accused.

The particular constitutional safeguard now before the court is the Sixth Amendment right to a trial by jury. Since it is the conclusion of this court that the designated felony portions of the *Juvenile Justice Reform Act of 1976* are fundamentally criminal in nature, the respondent is entitled to a trial by jury for a criminal prosecution.

Were it possible to extend this right to the respondent, no serious problem would arise. Unfortunately, it is not possible for this court to have the facts determined by a jury, since the law in this state is clear that no court may conduct a trial by jury unless such proceeding is authorized by statute. *People v. Carroll*, 7 Misc.2d 581, 161 N.Y.S.2d 339 (Kings County, County Court, 1957), *In re Daniel G., supra.*

The quandry thus created for the court is, may it proceed in this case given its inability to extend a right to a trial by jury? And further, if it may so proceed, how does it protect the rights of the respondent and the rights of society?

It is the determination of this court that it is entitled to proceed to the fact finding hearing on this alleged act of delinquency without a jury, provided that prior to the taking of any testimony the court advises the respondent that regardless of the outcome, this court will not order restrictive placement, and this it now does. *Baldwin v. New York, supra.*

If the alleged facts are proven, thereby giving this court jurisdiction to make a disposition, and if at that dispositional hearing it is determined that placement is necessary, such disposition will be ordered and the respondent may be placed for an initial period of eighteen months. If the treatment is not completed at the end of such time, placement will be extended within the provisions of the law and, accordingly, the right of society to be protected from further depredations will be as effectively insured as if a restrictive placement were ordered, and at the same time the right of the respondent to modification of that disposition as soon as he responds to treatment will be preserved.

Accordingly, motion for trial by jury is denied.

NOTES

1. Without reaching the conclusion that a proceeding in a designated felony case was a *juvenile* proceeding, the Family Court of King's County recently concluded that the U.S. Constitution Sixth Amendment right to a trial by jury in a *criminal* prosecution did not apply. *William M. v. Harold B.,* 90 Misc.2d 173, 393 N.Y.S.2d 535 (1977). While *McKeiver* left to the discretion of the states the use of jury trials in *juvenile* proceedings, the right to a jury trial in a *criminal* proceeding applies to the states through the Fourteenth Amendment. *Duncan v. Louisiana,* 391 U.S. 145, 88 S.Ct. 1444, 20 L.Ed.2d 491 (1968).

2. In holding that the Fifth Amendment protection from double jeopardy applied to juvenile proceedings, a constitutional guarantee traditionally associated with criminal prosecutions, the U.S. Supreme Court in *Breed v. Jones,* 421 U.S. 519, 95 S.Ct. 1779, 44 L.Ed.2d 346 (1974), noted:

   We believe it is simply too late in the day to conclude . . . that a juvenile is not put in jeopardy at a proceeding whose object is to determine whether he had committed acts that violate a criminal law and whose potential consequences include both the stigma inherent in such determination and deprivation of liberty for many years. For it is clear under our cases that determining the relevance of constitutional policies, like determining the applicability of constitutional rights, in juvenile proceedings, requires that courts eschew ''the civil labels-of-convenience which have been attached to juvenile proceedings,'' *In re Gault,* 387 U.S. 1, 87 S.Ct. 1428, 18 L.Ed.2d 527, and that ''the juvenile process . . . be candidly appraised.'' 387 U.S., at 21, 87 S.Ct., at 1428. 421 U.S., at 529, 95 S.Ct. at 1785.

   Doubtless even a clear legislative classification of a statute as ''nonpenal'' would not alter the fundamental nature of a plainly penal statute.

3. For an extensive analysis of the exchange principle in juvenile law see Katz, *Juveniles Committed to Penal Institutions – Do They Have a Right to a Jury Trial?,* 13 J.Fam.Law 675 (1973).

4. F C A § 712(h) ''Designated felony act.'' An act committed by a person fourteen or fifteen years of age which, if done by an adult, would be a crime (i) defined in sections 125.27 (murder in the first degree); 125.25 (murder in the second degree); 135.25 (kidnapping in the first degree); or 150.20 (arson in the first degree) of the penal law; (ii) defined in sections 120.10 (assault in the first degree); 125.20 (manslaughter in the first degree); 130.35 (rape in the first degree); 130.50 (sodomy in the first degree); 135.20 (kidnapping in the second degree), but only where the abduction involved the use or threat of use of deadly force; 150.15 (arson in the second degree); or 160.15 (robbery in the first degree) of the penal law; or (iii) defined in the penal law as an attempt to commit murder in the first or second degree or kidnapping in the first degree.

5. F C A § 712(i) ''Designated class A felony act.'' A designated felony act defined in clause (i) paragraph (h) of this section.

6. F C A § 712(j) ''Secure facility.'' A residential facility in which the juvenile delinquent may be placed under this article, which is characterized by physically restricting construction, hardware and procedures, and is designated a secure facility by the division for youth.

7. F C A § 712(k) ''Restrictive placement.'' A placement pursuant to section seven hundred fifty-three-a.

8. The quasi-criminal nature of juvenile proceedings has long been recognized. *In the Matter of Gregory W.,* 19 N.Y.2d 55, 277 N.Y.S.2d 675, 224 N.E.2d 102 (1966). The current recognition of the critical and criminal nature of the early stages of these proceedings is evidenced by the strict application of the Criminal Procedure Law to these juvenile proceedings. For instance, a court held that the more stringent pretrial discovery procedures of the CPL should apply to such proceedings rather than the more generous disclosure provisions of the CPLR. *Matter of Tony T.,* 178 N.Y.L.J. 1, July 26, 1977 (Family Court, New York County, 1977). Another court denied a respondent's motion for an identification hearing, a suppression order and a bill of particulars because the motion was not timely under CPL § 255.20. *In the Matter of Archer,* 89 Misc.2d 526, 392 N.Y.S.2d 362 (Family Court, Queens County, 1977). On the other hand, a court found that in the case of a six-month delay between initial detention and initial appearance that Article 30 of the CPL did not apply and no speedy trial problems resulted. *Matter of Walters,* Misc., 398 N.Y.S.2d 806, 1977 (Family Court, Suffolk County, 1977). It would appear that juveniles have *quasi-rights* in *quasi-criminal* proceedings.

21   *Juvenile Offenders: Proportionality vs. Treatment*

Fred Cohen

CURRENT LEGAL STRUCTURE

Although there are some variations, it is generally accurate to state that at the formal level juvenile court philosophy seeks to focus on the personal condition and social situation of the child and architecturally invites this through standardless and procedurally barren dispositional law. In so doing, juvenile law more closely resembles therapeutic civil commitment law than criminal law.

There are, however, differences of some magnitude. Civil commitments can be, and frequently are, wholly indefinite in duration. Inherent in the pure civil commitment model is the notion that the duration of an intervention cannot be subject to prior time constraints and therefore release from coercive treatment must be governed by "improvement" or "cure." Indicative of the mixed-model prevalent in juvenile justice is the fact that "cure" can be attained merely by the passage of a determinate time — the attainment of majority.

Putting aside the problems of status offenses, a juvenile must first be proved to have engaged in proscribed conduct before the State can coercively offer its help. In civil commitment law, conduct is secondary to the diagnosis of a particular condition and relevant to the extent that it contributes to the diagnosis.

Thus, juvenile delinquency law is something of a hybrid and conceptually falls in the cracks between criminal and civil commitment law. Conduct is primary for the adjudication; the adjudication leads not to a determination of guilt but to a finding of a nonclinical status, delinquency; this in turn is followed by a dispositional process which supposedly seeks to flesh out the broad status of delinquency by determining the precise condition and needs of the child. The particular disposition is then to be related to this comprehensive assessment of the child and a treatment program adopted consistent with this determination.

Probation is the most frequently used disposition and available in every state. The most common pattern is to allow for probatory supervision until the juvenile is 21, or any lower age of majority. The judge may discharge sooner whenever he sees fit. Seven states now require periodic review and seven others put a time limit on the duration of probation. Institutionalization is the most drastic disposition available and in 1971 there were 35,931 juveniles in state Training Schools and another 6,611 in ranches, camps, farms and halfway or group homes. Indeterminate commitment, usually limited to the attainment of majority, is the rule although some eight states now have a maximum time limit. The indeterminate term is not formally related to any judgment concerning the seriousness of the offense, the prior record of the

From *Children's Rights Report,* American Civil Liberties Union Foundation, II (May 1978): 2-7. Reprinted by permission.

juvenile or his age. In practice, of course, these factors may well influence the judge in the choice of a disposition and then influence the duration of intervention.

Statutory guides for the selection of dispositions and for the conduct of dispositional proceedings are virtually nonexistent. The "best interests of the child" and "the protection of the community" represent the most frequently used statutory language and are so obviously broad and inherently contradictory as to call for little comment. It is curious that many judges will not acknowledge the inherent conflict and wish to perpetuate the existing system. My guess is that they wish to continue making whatever decision seems correct at the moment without having to openly elect one objective rather than the other, and to continue to make punitive decisions in the guise of benevolence without the attendant consequences of appearing to have made a choice. For my purposes this composite is completed by repetition of the fact that neither the nature nor the duration of a disposition is limited by the nature of the underlying conduct; conduct which can vary from a minor misdemeanor to an atrocious felony.

BASIC ASSUMPTIONS

First, I raise no question about the right and authority of society through its officially designated representatives to impose some forms of coercion on youths and adults following a legally proven offense. I assume that one of our efforts in fashioning standards for juveniles justice will be to define with precision and select with rationality and fairness those forms of conduct that are so harmful that coercion is deserved.

I assume further that we shall promote, and hopefully set some standards, for an organized system of delivery of services for children in general, and children in trouble in particular.

A critical assumption is that we shall rid the coercive court system of status offenses and at the same time identify those former status "offenders" who are in fact victims in order to provide help within a dependency-neglect-abuse framework.

The most widely accepted theory of cause for criminal and delinquent behavior is that there is no single theory which will explain such diverse behavior. Left then with a multi-varied theoretical approach which goes from the highest level of abstraction — e.g., a racist, economically unbalanced, materialistic society — to more concrete levels of abstraction — e.g., a broken home — we must begin to question the extent to which a justice system can function if cause is a primary dispositional concern. To put the same thought in a more declarative style, what actually causes certain conduct more often than not either is unknown or unknowable; and when known, the identified cause usually is beyond the inherent power of a justice system to redress.

Since the curent fad in information gathering is to maximize information and to collect both social and psychological data one must ask whether the data is obtained in order to redress the causal factor or to understand the juvenile in order to design an individual program for treatment. It is perfectly obvious that courts cannot cure problems of the magnitude of those encompassed at the highest level of abstraction and to design a coercive treatment program around such factors as a broken home is *unfair* (by not being conduct related); and *unequal* (by providing a relative benefit to those juveniles with intact homes who engage in the same conduct).

THE COMPETING MODELS:
I — INTRODUCTION AND POSITION

The treatment-rehabilitation ideal is under legitimate attack and for good reasons. Before providing what I believe are the good reasons let me first summarize my position.

Neither the individual characteristics nor the social situation of the juvenile provide a supportable rationale for determining either the nature or the duration of a coercive intervention.

In selecting among competing rationales, only a principle of proportionality (or "deserts") provides a logical, fair, and humane hinge between conduct and an official, coercive response.

While the nature and duration of a coercive response should be conduct related, it does not necessarily follow that within the particular sanction, and for the allowable time, the state may not make every reasonable effort to *facilitate* individual change.

Efforts to facilitate individual change cannot be based on the assumption that an act of delinquency is pathological in origin and whatever efforts are made must, on the one hand, be limited by principles of law, and, on the other hand, guided by the principle of voluntariness.

A separate juvenile justice system can and should be supported by the Juvenile Justice Standards Project. Juveniles may be viewed as incomplete adults, lacking in full moral and experiential development, extended unique jural status in other contexts, and deserving of the social moratorium extended by this and all other societies of which I am aware. Thus, removal of the treatment rationale does not destroy the rationale for a separate system or for the utilization of an ameliorative approach; it does, however, require a different rationale.

Among the principal objectives of this approach are:

a. to reduce discretion and disparity;

b. to achieve a modicum of impartiality and equity;

c. to remove "the noble lie" from the system, face candidly what we do, and limit the opportunity for even greater incursions upon the individual in the future;

d. to bring to focus objective factors in disposition as opposed to the wholly subjective factors associated with treatment;

e. to assure that the most severe deprivations of liberty (which at the outside should be minimal) reflect the seriousness of the culpable conduct and the harm caused or threatened;

f. to provide a rationale for the specific definition of offenses; and for the utilization of justification and excuse as defenses, and for factors relating to mitigation and aggravation as appropriate for the limited discretion available at disposition; and finally

g. to eliminate from the prospect of any coercion those juveniles whose conduct is lacking in culpability and to insist on independent resources for those juveniles whose mental condition is such as to call for some form of help.

THE COMPETING MODELS:
II — DISCUSSION

Accurate diagnosis, whether through predisposition reports, clinical findings or classification programs, is the foundation for any treatment program. A survey of the literature reveals that there is no classification-diagnostic system capable of reliable application and that is generally acceptable to professionals working in the field.

Diagnosis is not only a framework in which to design and provide relief, it is also a prediction. Parenthetically, the treatment intervention can only be to interrupt the inevitability of the outcome predicted by the diagnosis. Representative of the state of the art of diagnostic prediction are two California studies reported by Norval Morris in his Cooley lectures at the University of Michigan Law School, 1974. Morris reports on the efforts by Dr. Wenk and his associates to develop a "violence prediction scale" for use by parole boards. The result was that 86 percent of those identified as potentially violent failed to commit a violent act while on parole. A parallel effort to predict Youth Authority wards as likely to be violent on parole produced a 95 percent overprediction of violence.

Thus, I mean to assert that diagnostic capability is extremely poor and hardly a sound foundation upon which to build a system that imposes coercive treatment based on that construct. Suppose, however, that the problem is not inadequate theory but, as is so often asserted, a lack of resources. If we only had the money, so the argument goes, we would hire the best people and do accurate diagnoses as well as effective treatment.

There are several flaws in that argument. First, to argue lack of resources is not even responsive to the assertion that the capability to make accurate diagnoses — or make them with sufficient regularity and accuracy to support deprivations of liberty — does not exist. Second, there is no evidence of any willingness to commit the amount of resources necessary for the time consuming and intensely individualistic task of differential diagnosis. Indeed, we have three-quarters of a century experience upon which to draw to conclude that there is no such willingness.

The elimination of the rehabilitative ideal as a basis for dispositions and retention decisions has the virtue of honesty. Rena K. Uviller, Director of the A.C.L.U. Juvenile Rights Project, expressed my thoughts at a recent conference:

> The factor affecting disposition, however, which is most avoided and vociferously denied by the more disingenuous of us, is that of retribution or punishment. It matters little to me whether social reformers instruct us that retribution ought *not* be cognizable in a system of

juvenile justice. It *is* an operative factor because society does and will insist we sanction those who hurt others. And it ought to be recognized as a factor in juvenile dispositions so that it is kept in its proper perspective. In a humane system, punishment and retribution hopefully are tempered by the individual facts of a given case. But I would rather acknowledge and confront its proper presence in any system which purports to deal with law violators of whatever age, than to feel the palpable presence of retribution under the clock of the euphemisms for which the family court is famous — whether the euphemism be treatment, rehabilitation, or a righteous bemoaning of the absence of community resources.

Honesty in terms of what we actually do is not the only advantage of cleansing the system of the traditional rehabilitative ideal. Treatment, rehabilitation and benevolence are terms which carry with them the seeds for natural expansion. I know of no instance either in civil commitment law, or juvenile justice where the rhetoric of treatment has not pushed out to encompass more people, often for more time, and regrettably, to no avail. Punishment, or the more antiseptic word coercion, should give us pause and evoke concern for restraint and care in its imposition.

I know that it will be argued that while it is true that coerced rehabilitation does not work, the "noble lie" does serve to restrain the atavistic impulses of judges, legislators and others and thus ultimately reduces the harshness of the system. Set the judges and legislators free with punishment in their arsenal and they will know no limits, the argument goes.

Is that possible? Yes, I think it is possible. I also think that it is possible, given the desire, to raise the ante in the current rehabilitative system. What is to prevent raising the age for treatment retention beyond majority? (In California, e.g., this already is possible.) What's to prevent an increase in waivable offenses? (In my scheme, there would be *no* waiver!)

I submit that the argument for sanctioning culpable conduct on a principle of proportionality, severely limiting the amounts and types of deprivations that are available, and honestly recognizing that the deprivation is a "hurt" has less chance for perversion than the perpetuation of the system we now have. I grant that this is speculative and suggest that a similar stipulation is in order for the proponents of the position that treatment acts as a restraint. The choice is, at bottom, one between legislatively imposed limitations and untrammeled judicial discretion; and as a legislatively-oriented project we ought not to hesitate placing our "risk money" on the legislature as that organ of government better suited to the determination of basic policy.

I should add here, that in my scheme principles of humanization and limits on intervention are co-equal and must enter into any revision simultaneously. By this assertion I mean that proportionality limits the initial intervention and humanization is then a limitation which accompanies the specific deprivation. Thus, where secure confinement is an available sanction, any further deprivation either is unavailable or limited to the maintenance of the particular setting and even then further limited by such specific prohibitions as no corporal punishment, no alteration of diet as a disciplinary measure, and so on.

Thus, to the extent that any set of words in the form of standards-turned-law can control a situation, we must act to limit the possible abuse of the system being proposed here.

The perpetuation of the rhetoric of rehabilitation, and surely its expansion, does not augur well for imposing the rule of law on the system. On this proposition we have the hard evidence of the past and the resistance of the present on which to rely. What is at issue here then are such items as maximal discretion in all system functionaries; claims to secrecy concerning decisions and information; total confusion in the various roles of such persons as the judge, defense attorney, and probation officer; lax procedures; broad and ambiguous statutes on substance and procedure; training and professional educational efforts that are uncertain and confused; information about young people and their families which know no boundaries — and more. By adopting a system which responds to harm-producing conduct and which frankly recognizes that deprivations of liberty are painful sanctions, we can legally recognize the adversary stance of the parties, emphasize the importance of factfinding and diminish the scientific jargon which parades as expertise; we can bring some visibility to decision making, further tighten procedures, and give some focus to the requisite training of system functionaries.

I would not argue that this is impossible under a therapeutic regime. But I would argue that it is more difficult and that it perpetuates conceptual and logical absurdities (e.g. How can you argue for close attention to fact finding for the collection of clinical data? Do you bring a lawyer to your doctor's office? Do you appeal your psychiatrist's opinions? These are the sorts of claims one encounters from "treatment people," as foolish as they look when committed to writing).

Let us look at the end of the coerced therapeutic process. There is little reason to believe we have found a sure way to reduce recidivism through rehabilitation. The few instances of full or partial success are isolated and produce no clear pattern to indicate the efficacy of any particular method of treatment. Evaluative measures are primitive and often self-serving. The one hopeful item is that the reduction of coercion — the use of probation, for example, instead of incarceration — is less expensive and produces at least as good results, probably better, than confinement. The suggestion is that success even with community supervision is not related to the casework dynamic but rather to the avoidance of the more destructive potential of incarceration.

I have mixed evaluation potential with program failure in the above discussion, so let me now simply assert the following:

a. We are at a loss to construct acceptable measures of success or failure. Recidivism rates, after all, tend to be controlled by those with a vested interest in the particular program. Thus, those few programs claiming success in treatment based on the reduction of recidivism are highly dubious. Also, they are more than offset by programs showing higher rates of recidivism for those in the test group.

b. The level of legitimate success in treatment for any particular modality is either so low or so uncertain that to continue to use treatment for initial sanctions or retention decisions is to perpetuate a pious myth.

To complete the point, a sanction whose nature and duration is linked with conduct can be meted out fairly and evaluated with some certainty. That is, we would ask only for similar treatment for similar offenses committed under similar circumstances. Under the "similar circumstances" condition there is room for factors relating to aggravating and mitigating circumstances surrounding the offense. These factors can, and should be, part of the dispositional process and allow the judge to revise the legislatively fixed disposition upward or downward but within legislatively fixed time periods.

[This may corrupt the relentless logic of "just deserts" but since the factors are objectifiable and discretion limited I see no reason not to have some play in the joints. A compelling reason for my position is that factors on aggravation and mitigation relate to the way most of us judge behavior and there is no reason for law to constantly be at war with experience.]

With aggravating and mitigating factors as the discretionary dispositional base, as opposed to the effort to diagnose the youngster, we give the courts a task they are accustomed to doing and, also, put a crimp in later (correctional) decision making based on treatment-rehabilitative factors. I do not believe we should endorse an adult parole model for juvenile justice with its trinity of discretionary release-supervision-reincarceration components. Treatment factors at disposition feed right into that sort of correctional mechanism. I do think we can devise some means for release short of full term based on compassionate factors, but this is not the occasion to spell that out. I note only the potential for incremental releases to test the reaction under increasing freedom, clemency-type releases, good time releases necessary for program-institutional maintenance, and so on.

Dr. Gerald Wheeler, in his work for the Ohio Youth Commission, studied some thirty states to determine the influence of the indeterminate sentence on the lives of the nation's incarcerated youth. Among his findings are that states with a high commitment to treatment (as measured by use of I-level or Quay classification systems) retained juveniles whose conduct was minimal in terms of harm longer than others; and that youth are in fact subjected to a "fixed" sentence (that is standardized retention terms) but the length of stay is *not* related to offense and *not* even related to individual needs; and, finally, one outcome of this is the disproportionate application of correctional resources to youths who pose no danger to the community. He recommends, in part:

1. Adoption of a modified fixed sentence for youthful offenders who commit felonies or serious crimes against the person or property;
2. Abolishment of status offenses and the prohibition of such cases being committed to the juvenile correctional system;

3. Unequivocal rejection of the indeterminate sentence as it applies to involuntary incarceration for the purpose of rehabilitation; this implies rejecting the current "right to treatment" movement. This, in effect, is more "treater" than "treatee" oriented. That is, states may be enjoined to provide more "professional" staff in existing institutions to assure some notion of "treatment." If the national trend holds, a "right to treatment" may result in nothing less than a right to confine people longer against their will in remote, rural-based institutions, or a right to practice psychosurgery indiscriminately; . . .

One final thought; given the relatively low average length of stay in state institutions — either 8.6 or 8.8 months depending on whose data is used — would a flat sentence based on seriousness of conduct tend to raise or lower that figure? Also, would more or less young people be subjected to confinement?

The National Assessment of Juvenile Corrections Study, in its preliminary and incomplete findings, reports that about 50 percent of those in closed institutions are confined for Level 1 offenses (status, vagrancy, drunkenness) with only 12 percent of those confined for the most serious felonies. Indeed, 75 percent of the females confined were committed for status offenses.

If we remove status offenders from coercive juvenile justice we obviously cause a substantial reduction in the number of persons confined. That, of course, still does not fully answer the specific questions posed. The removal of status offenders from the prospect of confinement can be accomplished without the use of a conduct-proportionality approach. Eliminating the prospect of any custodial disposition from the least serious offenses also can be accomplished in the same manner, although the rationale for doing so under a treatment approach becomes increasingly strained. That is, the natural tendency is to ask not what the juvenile has done, but what we can do for the juvenile.

On the other hand, it seems likely that more juveniles who commit the more serious offenses — certainly those offenses which involve the threat or imposition of substantial harm to other persons — will receive custodial dispositions whether or not such pieties as "amenable to treatment" are employed. Thus, we face the prospect of a tradeoff; a tradeoff I would strongly support — we eliminate the prospect of coercion for perhaps 50 percent of those now in confinement and under supervision; we eliminate the prospect of custodial disposition for another substantial percentage; and we assert the right to impose coercion, including confinement, for those juveniles who engage in voluntary conduct which causes or directly threatens substantial harm.

So far as raw numbers in confinement go, I would assert that the elimination of most of our confining institutions is more important than procedural or substantive law revision. As Kai Erikson, and many others of the societal reaction to deviance school, points out — the units (beds, cells, jails etc.) assigned to any particular form of deviance tend to remain filled although turnover rates within the units may fluctuate. Thus, I would urge that the Commission speak early and forcefully to the objective of closing nearly all of the nation's Training/Industrial Schools, substituting a minimal number of small, residential facilities with varying levels of security, and reserved only for the chronic offender whose offense is great, *not* whose problems seem severe.

22 Right to Treatment: Case Developments in Juvenile Law

Adrienne Volenik

Momentous changes have occurred in the juvenile justice system in the last decade. In particular, there has been a change in the basic outlook toward juvenile rights. The *parens patriae* philosophy that gave rise to the system has steadily given way to demands for due process. Nearly all due process rights that adult criminal defendants enjoy are now also accorded to juveniles. Further, demands to eliminate many of the remaining differences between the adult and juvenile system continue.

While the cry for increased due process continues, other aspects of the system have experienced less structured scrutiny. One of the most interesting of these is the concept of a right to treatment for juveniles found to have committed delinquent acts. It is interesting for two reasons: (1) it has no parallel in the adult criminal system, but arises instead from the area of mental health; (2) it has had its genesis in the same climate that gave rise to the increase in due process rights for juveniles, yet has had an erratic history that does not parallel that systematic, steady development of due process rights.

This article seeks to trace the development of the right to treatment in the juvenile justice system from its origins to the present. This exposition does not represent an in-depth analysis of the concept. Instead it seeks to acquaint the reader with how the right has been interpreted as being applicable to various phases of the juvenile system. This is accomplished through a summary of individual cases.

The author does not intend to posit her views on the future role the right to treatment will play in the juvenile justice system or the influence that it will have on decision makers. Whether the right will be part of the vocabulary of the system in ten years is uncertain. Indeed, we are, perhaps, now at the turning point where the idea will be either totally rejected or accepted as an integral part of the juvenile justice system.

THE ORIGINS OF THE RIGHT TO TREATMENT

The concept of a right to treatment is one that arose in conjunction with adults deprived of their liberty because of mental impairments.

According to the concept originally conceived in 1960 by Morton Birnbaum,[1] a person who is deprived of liberty because of a mental illness so serious as to result in involuntary commitment to a mental institution is entitled to treatment. If that treatment is not provided, that person is, or should be entitled to release. Birnbaum postulated that a right to treatment derived from the constitution. Recognition of the concept would mean that "substantive due process of law (would not) allow a men-

From *The Justice System Journal: A Management Review 3* (Spring 1978): 292-307. Reprinted by permission.

tally ill person who has committed no crime to be deprived of his liberty by indefinitely institutionalizing him in a mental prison.''[2] Thus, due process would not be
limited to procedural safeguards aimed at guaranteeing a fair commitment procedure
but would also assure that continued confinement conform to fundamental fairness.

In the years between Dr. Birnbaum's articulation of the concept and the present,
his theories have become reality as courts have recognized that a right to treatment
does exist. Just as the concept first arose in conjunction with the adult mentally ill,
the first court decisions recognizing it were the result of litigation in that field.

In *Rouse v. Cameron,*[3] a defendant in Washington, D.C., charged with possession of a gun and ammunition, was found not guilty by reason of insanity. Although
the charge, a misdemeanor, could have resulted in only a one-year sentence, Rouse
was involuntarily committed to a mental institution for a period that ultimately lasted
much longer. *Rouse* is an important right to treatment decision for many reasons, not
the least of which is that it identifies the sources of the right. Although the decision
was based upon a right to treatment stemming from a statute, the 1964 Hospitalization of the Mentally Ill Act, the court implied that it could have reached the same
conclusion on constitutional grounds. As Chief Judge Bazelon stated:

> Had appellant been found criminally responsible, he could have been confined a year, at
> most, however dangerous he might have been. He has been confined four years and the
> end is not in sight. Since this difference rests only on need for treatment, a failure to
> supply treatment may raise a question of due process of law. It has also been suggested
> that a failure to supply treatment may violate the equal protection clause . . . Indefinite
> confinement without treatment of one who has been found not criminally responsible may
> be so inhumane as to be "cruel and unusual punishment."[4]

Since the decision in *Rouse,* a number of other courts have recognized the right
of the civilly committed to receive treatment.[5] The Supreme Court, however, has
consistently rejected any opportunity to rule on the issue as it pertains to the mentally
ill. In *O'Connor v. Donaldson,*[6] the court specifically concluded:

> [T]he difficult issues of constitutional law dealt with by the Court of Appeals are not
> presented by this case in its present posture. Specifically there is no reason now to decide
> whether mentally ill persons dangerous to themselves or to others have a right to treatment
> upon compulsory confinement by the State or whether the State may compulsorily confine
> a nondangerous, mentally ill individual for the purpose of treatment.[7]

Although the Court also stated that its decision vacating the judgment of the Fifth
Circuit "deprives that Court's opinion of precedential effect . . . ''[8] it subsequently
declined to review *Burnham v. Georgia,*[9] another Fifth Circuit opinion that explicitly
reaffirmed its initial analysis of right to treatment as expressed in *Donaldson v.
O'Connor.*[10]

DEVELOPMENT OF THE CONCEPT OF A JUVENILE'S RIGHT TO TREATMENT

The juvenile system has always had as its philosophical base the idea that children,
instead of being punished by the state for antisocial behavior, should receive the care,
attention and treatment needed to rehabilitate them. With this end in mind nearly

every state has enacted, as part of its juvenile code, a purposes clause that normally includes language similar to that of the *Uniform Juvenile Court Act* drafted by the National Conference of Commissioners on Uniform State Laws (1968) which states in part:

> This Act shall be construed to effectuate the following public purposes:
>   (1) to provide for the care, protection, and wholesome moral, mental and physical development of children coming within its provisions;
>   (2) consistent with the protection of the public interest, to remove from children committing delinquent acts the taint of criminality and the consequences of criminal behavior and to substitute therefore a program of treatment, training and rehabilitation;
>   (3) to achieve the foregoing purposes in a family environment whenever possible, separating the child from his parents only when necessary for his welfare or in the interest of public safety.[11]

With rehabilitation and care the stated goals of the juvenile system, it was logical that juveniles would eventually begin to assert that they, like the mentally ill, had a right to treatment once their liberty was curtailed. Because of the similarities in civil commitment and delinquency proceedings, it was equally logical that the courts would find that juveniles too have a right to treatment.

Courts have justified the denial of certain rights to juveniles on the grounds that there are certain advantages to being processed as a juvenile that would be lost with the extension of these rights. For example, the Supreme Court concluded that the extension to juveniles of the right to a jury trial would add both the formality and the clamor of the adversary system to a hearing and thus be inimical to the ideal of an intimate and informal juvenile hearing.[12]

Longer periods of confinement for a juvenile who has committed an offense than for an adult convicted of the same offense have been justified because the purpose of a juvenile proceeding is not punishment but rather "rehabilitation and restoration" of the minor to useful citizenship.[13] The similarities to an involuntary commitment which provides for institutionalization of a mental patient until a cure can be effected are unmistakable.

The justification for a right to treatment for juveniles, like the justification for the right for the civilly committed, is found both in state codes and in state and federal constitutions.

This has been recognized by those courts that have acknowledged a right to treatment for juveniles. In articulating the justification for a right to treatment, courts normally begin with a discussion of the history of the juvenile court, stressing the *parens patriae* philosophy that gave rise to the concept that rehabilitative treatment should be substituted for punishment when children are brought before the bar. This acts as a preamble to discussion of the individual state statute, which will often contain language similar to the purposes clause of the *Uniform Juvenile Court Act*.[14] From this analysis the court may conclude that there is either a common law or a statutory basis for the right.

The constitutional bases for the right vary slightly. It may be found to be grounded in the Eighth and Fourteenth Amendments[15] or in the Equal Protection and Due Process Clauses of the Fifth and Fourteenth Amendments.

RAISING A JUVENILE'S RIGHT TO TREATMENT: INTRODUCTORY OVERVIEW

The idea that a child has a right to treatment has important repercussions for many phases of the juvenile process. As outlined in some detail below, courts have considered the applicability of the concept to: (1) detention prior to adjudication, (2) cases involving transfers of jurisdiction to criminal courts, (3) instances where specific treatment has been ordered at the dispositional stage of trial court proceedings, and (4) post dispositional reviews of the adequacy of treatment once commitment has occurred. Acceptance of the right, however, is far from complete and, as noted above, the future integration of the vocabulary and substance of the right to treatment concept in the formal law affecting juveniles is uncertain.

DETENTION PRIOR TO ADJUDICATION

That a juvenile has a right to treatment that he is not receiving may be alleged when a child is confined prior to an adjudication of his guilt or innocence. *Creek v. Stone*,[16] one of the earliest juvenile right to treatment cases illustrates this situation.

On May 31, 1966, a juvenile was arrested on a charge of robbery and detained at the District of Columbia Receiving Home for Children for several months before being brought to trial.[17] During that period of confinement, he filed a petition for a writ of habeas corpus in the District Court for the District of Columbia alleging that his detention at the home was unlawful because the home had no facilities to provide him with needed psychiatric assistance. As a corollary to this, he objected to the Juvenile Court's refusal to hold a hearing on whether or not the home was a suitable place of detention because it could not provide the care he needed. The District Court refused to hear evidence on this issue concluding that suitability of the home, based upon failure to provide allegedly necessary psychiatric assistance, was not relevant to the issue of the lawfulness of the actual detention.

In a *per curiam* opinion by Chief Judge Bazelon and Circuit Judges McGowan and Leventhal, the appeal to the Court of Appeals for the District of Columbia was dismissed as moot. In dismissing the appeal, however, the Court of Appeals recognized that the District of Columbia Juvenile Code was premised on the assumption that the juvenile court, acting in its *parens patriae* capacity, had an affirmative duty to provide a child with an environment as similar as possible to the one he should have been receiving at home. It, therefore, stated that the juvenile court, when faced with a claim that a need for treatment exists that is not being met, should make an inquiry to discover whether the child is being treated in accordance with the statute. *Creek* illustrates the major problem with raising the issue of a juvenile's right to treatment when he is detained prior to adjudication: before the Circuit Court could rule on the case, the juvenile had been adjudicated delinquent and committed to the National Training School, rendering the appeal moot.

TRANSFER OF JURISDICTION TO CRIMINAL COURTS

All but two states, New York and Vermont,[18] provide a statutory mechanism whereby a juvenile may be transferred, when certain circumstances have been met, to the criminal court system for prosecution. Generally a hearing is required before transfer can be effected. At that hearing a crucial issue, and one frequently established by statute, is whether the juvenile is amenable to treatment. For example § 31 of the *Model Act for Family Courts and State-Local Children's Programs,* Department of Health, Education, and Welfare (1975) states in part that:

> The court shall conduct a hearing . . . for the purpose of determining whether there are reasonable prospects of rehabilitating the child prior to his 19th birthday. If the court finds that there are not reasonable prospects for rehabilitating the child prior to his 19th birthday . . ., it shall order the case transferred for criminal prosecution.

Likewise the *Uniform Juvenile Court Act,* § 34,[19] provides in part that transfer of jurisdiction may be authorized if the court finds that "the child is not amenable to treatment or rehabilitation as a juvenile through available facilities." These statutory provisions clearly imply that if a juvenile is amenable to treatment he should not be transferred. The logical corollary to that is that treatment will be provided if he is retained within the system.

This raises two right to treatment issues in connection with transfer of jurisdiction: (1) can a child be transferred if he is considered amenable to treatment but no suitable programs exist within the state to provide the treatment necessary for his rehabilitation, and (2) if a juvenile has a statutory or constitutional right to treatment, can he be transferred from the juvenile system and hence denied that right?

The first question was recently considered by the Minnesota Supreme Court in *In re Welfare of J.E.C.*[20] The court was asked to decide whether the juvenile court had acted properly in authorizing the transfer of a juvenile for criminal prosecution when evidence indicated that the juvenile was amenable to treatment, but not amenable to treatment in any of the programs currently in operation in the state. Essentially, the juvenile argued that he had a right to treatment that could rehabilitate him.

Although the court recognized that Minnesota law is grounded on the theory that a juvenile has a right to treatment, it was unwilling, without a more complete record before it, to exercise any of the options available to it: retention of the juvenile within the system for placement in a program unlikely to have any beneficial effects, or transfer of jurisdiction over the juvenile to the criminal system with its services that would, at best, have doubtful rehabilitative value.

Instead the court remanded the case with specific instructions that the [juvenile] court inquire into:

> (1) whether there is presently any program available for treatment for this and other similar juveniles; (2) if no program is available, whether it is feasible and possible to put together an effective program which could treat this and other similar juveniles; (3) if so, why has the Department of Corrections failed to make such a program available?[21]

Availability of rehabilitative programs for persons prosecuted and convicted as adults was also to be investigated.

On remand the juvenile court was presented with evidence indicating that the treatment of this juvenile and others like him within the juvenile system would be neither practical nor effective. Accepting this conclusion, the appellate court upheld the transfer decision . . . without attempting to resolve the important question of whether it or the juvenile court could direct the Department of Corrections to establish a particular program designed to provide rehabilitative treatment for a juvenile with special problems.[22]

The second question, whether, if a juvenile has a statutory or constitutional right to treatment, he can be transferred from the juvenile system and so deprived of that right, has never been addressed squarely. While it is possible that a court might conclude that transfer denies a juvenile the right to treatment and so is unconstitutional, it is more likely that a court would conclude that a juvenile's right to treatment does not vest until the court affirmatively indicates that it is exercising jurisdiction over the child by prosecuting him as a juvenile.[23]

THE RIGHT TO TREATMENT AT DISPOSITION

An issue arising with considerable frequency recently is whether the juvenile court may order state agencies to provide specific treatment for a child, particularly if that treatment is unavailable within the state. Note this situation differs from that presented in *J.E.C., supra,* in that the decision has already been made to treat the child within the juvenile system. Therefore, if his right to treatment is recognized, delivery of treatment becomes the raison d'etre for placement in a juvenile program.

In Mississippi the courts have recognized that, according to state law, children committed to training schools or other facilities operated by the Mississippi Department of Youth Services are entitled to treatment reasonably calculated to rehabilitate them back into society. Because this is true, no child can then be committed to an institution unless the child will there receive treatment reasonably calculated to rehabilitate him.

Even beyond the statutory right, one court concluded that the Due Process Clause of the Fourteenth Amendment also required that confinement be reasonably related to treatment and rehabilitation.[24] Faced with the problem of how to deal with a child adjudged delinquent who was suffering from both organic brain damage and a behavior disorder, the court found no reasonable solution. The consensus of the psychiatric testimony before the court was that the child needed a structured residential treatment center with individual and group psychotherapy available. Unfortunately no such facility existed within the state and the court did not believe that it had the inherent power to direct the Department of Youth Services by dictating the kinds of facilities that should be provided. While out of state placement via purchases of services was authorized, no placement had been effected. However, the court did order that the State either provide the juvenile with treatment "reasonably calculated to rehabilitate" him or release him.

In reaching this conclusion the court utilized an interesting analysis. It first found that the juvenile was amenable to treatment that could rehabilitate him. It then identified the kind of treatment that the child needed and concluded that no facilities capable of providing the treatment were available to the court. To do this, it specifically examined and eliminated as acceptable alternatives certain facilities within the state. Once the child's right to treatment was established and his specific needs identified, the court's conclusion became the only logical one, short of ordering the development of a new facility (an alternative specifically discarded), that was available to the court.

The Oregon Court of Appeals, clearly recognizing a statutory right to treatment but raising a question as to the existence of a constitutional right, dealt with a similar question recently.[25] In *Matter of L.* a Children's Service Division (CSD) worker recommended a child be given care and treatment in an out of state institution that would provide a relatively secure setting. CSD ultimately declined to place the child in this institution because it had exhausted its budget allocations for out of state placements. The Juvenile Court, reviewing CSD's actions, found that funds were available and that failure to use them for treatment of the juvenile was an abuse of discretion. It then ordered the implementation of the recommended treatment plan.

The state appealed this decision alleging that the juvenile court exceeded its authority in ordering treatment. While the court of appeals concluded that ordering CSD to provide treatment, irrespective of budgetary limitations, was an act in excess of its authority, it found that the court could order CSD to secure treatment or certify to the court that it was unable to do so. If such certification were forthcoming, the court would then have the option of terminating CSD's custody over the child

since the statutory basis for CSD's custody no longer exists when it becomes evident that CSD will not provide a child with responsive treatment.[26]

The Appellate Division of the Superior Court of New Jersey overturned a similar decision by a Camden County juvenile court.[27] A fifteen-year-old, adjudicated delinquent on seventeen different charges of breaking, entering, and larceny was before the court for disposition. The juvenile court, like the court in Mississippi, made certain findings of fact: the juvenile was suffering from a severe emotional disorder requiring immediate treatment in a structured facility; the juvenile was not an appropriate candidate for placement in a state training school; failure to provide the juvenile with prompt and adequate treatment could result in his becoming irreversibly psychotic; the juvenile needed intensive psychotherapy unavailable at private facilities within the state; and a residential placement at a psychiatric institute would provide the treatment needed by the juvenile.

The court recognized that two questions needed to be decided: whether the Juvenile Court could order the State Division of Youth and Family Services to place a child in a specific private residential facility for treatment of his mental illness; and whether a juvenile has a right to treatment. Addressing the second question first, the court recognized that the juvenile code purposes clause constituted a mandate to the court to exercise its *parens patriae* power to assure, "that a juvenile adjudicated delinquent will get effective rehabilitative treatment, and to choose a dispositional alternative most likely to achieve that result.''[28] Beyond that, the court recognized that the constitution required, on due process and equal protection grounds, that an adjudicated child obtain effective rehabilitative treatment.

The answer to the first question was also answered in the affirmative. The court declared that its power to place a child in a specific residential facility was rooted in common law, state law, and the state and federal constitutions, and was essential in order to implement the statutory mandate of the purposes clause to ''secure for [a child] custody, care and discipline as nearly as possible equivalent to that which should have been given by his parents.''[29]

On appeal, the Superior Court concluded that the juvenile court exceeded its authority in its order committing the youth to the state agency, the Division of Youth and Family Services (DYFS). The commitment order, which invoked agency responsibility for the youth's care, foreclosed the exercise of any discretion by the agency in the ultimate selection of a placement. Instead the court selected a placement for the youth without regard to agency budget limitations and without concern for the treatment needs of other youths committed to the agency.

The Superior Court, commenting on the Juvenile Court's discussion of a right to treatment, declined to affirm whether or not such a constitutional right existed and further indicated that ''it was inappropriate in the context of this case.''[30] The court took the position that the youth had not been confined for purposes of treatment that was then denied him and that the right, if it existed, was ''triggered by confinement, not by the adjudication of delinquency.''[31]

Had the New Jersey juvenile court gone only so far as to order DYFS to provide treatment that would meet the juvenile's already ascertained needs, without ordering placement in a specific institution, the judgment might have survived appeal. Both the Oregon and Mississippi decisions tend to support this position since in each of those cases, the courts were ultimately taking a position of ''treat or release,'' without mandating all details of treatment.

Delivery of treatment to a child entitled to it took a somewhat different turn in a recent Pennsylvania case.[32] In 1973, a juvenile court ordered that Janet D., a sixteen-year-old deprived child, be placed in shelter care. In the order, the court noted that the girl had run away from the McIntyre Shelter, operated by the Allegheny County Child Welfare Services (CWS), on previous occasions and therefore CWS was directed ''to make suitable arrangements that said child does not run away subsequent to her placement in the shelter facility to be provided by CWS.''[33]

The girl was then again placed at McIntyre. Shortly thereafter, her appointed counsel wrote to Thomas Carros, the Director of CWS, to complain that suitable arrangements had not yet been made and to ask for compliance with the court order. The same evening Janet D. ran away.[34] The following day her attorney petitioned the lower court for a rule to show cause why Carros should not be held in contempt. After hearing, the court did find him in contempt.

Reviewing the propriety of the contempt order, the Superior Court of Pennsylvania first addressed the issue of whether Janet D. had a right to treatment. Because the right was so clearly mandated by the Pennsylvania Juvenile Act, 11 P.S. §50–101 *et seq.,* the court did not decide whether the constitution similarly established a right.

However, the Juvenile Act and the Department of Public Welfare Regulations were interpreted to require a right to treatment for Janet D. conforming to the following minimum requirements:

1. An analysis of her personal history, to determine her physical, psychological, and educational needs;
2. The development of an individualized treatment program based upon those needs;
3. The provision of the counseling, psychiatric, educational, recreational, and social work services required by the individualized treatment program, and the incorporation of her caseworker into the program;
4. The formulation of a longer-term placement plan, based on analysis of her needs;
5. Adequate communication and consultation about her and the plans for her future among all levels of the staff;
6. Periodic reevaluation of the treatment program developed for her in terms of her behavior in response to the treatment, and revision of the program as necessary;
7. Application of disciplinary measures consistent with her dignity.[35]

Without ordering a specific plan, the court recognized that individualized planning for Janet or any child was needed in order to assure that more than mere custodial care would be delivered.[36] The court also concluded that while contempt would be a proper method of enforcing a child's right to treatment, the court had improperly exercised the power in that case.

THE RIGHT TO TREATMENT AFTER COMMITMENT

A number of cases have discussed the issue of right to treatment in terms of whether institutions to which children have been committed are providing required treatment. As suggested by the court in *Pena v. New York State Division for Youth*,[37] this can require that a court evaluate the punitive and the therapeutic aspects of practices at these institutions, a task for which the judicial branch may not be ideally suited, but one which must be assumed if constitutional rights have been violated.[38]

In *Pena,* the court was specifically asked to rule on whether the use of isolation, hand restraints, and thorazine and other tranquilizing drugs at Goshen Annex Center was violative of the inmates' rights to treatment under the Fourteenth Amendment and whether these acts amounted to cruel and unusual punishment prohibited by the Eighth Amendment. Their conclusion was that, indeed, these practices were used in punitive and antitherapeutic ways and were, therefore, unconstitutional. The court did not, however, conclude that these practices wer *per se* unconstitutional, merely that they had been used that way at Goshen and for that reason issued an injunction to end the practices.

Different practices have been the target of litigation in other cases. In *Inmates of Boys' Training School v. Affleck,*[39] a class of Rhode Island juveniles challenged the conditions of their confinement alleging that certain practices constituted cruel and unusual punishment while others were antirehabilitative and so violative of both equal protection and due process. The court held that conditions in the former women's reformatory, then being used to house children, were such as to be antirehabilitative and enjoined them as in violation of equal protection and due process.[40] Juveniles transferred to the Youth Correctional Center of the Adult Correctional Institute had to be provided with at least three hours of outdoor exercise daily.[41] Further, education equivalent to that provided in the Boys' Training School was ordered for all youth confined in this facility.[42]

For juveniles confined in any facility, the following minimum conditions were ordered:

a. a room equipped with lighting sufficient for an inmate to read by until 10:00 p.m.;

b. sufficient clothing to meet seasonal needs;

c. bedding, including blankets, sheets, pillows, pillow cases and mattresses; such bedding must be changed once a week;

d. personal hygiene supplies, including soap, toothpaste, towels, toilet paper and a toothbrush;

e. a change of undergarments and socks every day;

f. minimum writing materials: pen, pencil, paper and envelopes;

g. prescription eyeglasses, if needed;

h. equal access to all books, periodicals and other reading materials located in the Training School;

i. daily showers;

j. daily access to medical facilities, including the provision of a twenty-four-hour nursing service;

k. general correspondence privileges.

The court refused to order other specific relief requested by the plaintiffs largely because it was unwilling to interfere with the management of the Training School in those areas where the record failed to clearly show the deprivation of a constitutional right. It also recognized that while the defendants were handicapped by lack of facilities and trained personnel, this was no excuse for failing to protect the constitutional rights of the youth interred.[43]

The detention of "Persons in Need of Supervision" (PINS) in secure facilities was challenged in *Martarella v. Kelley.*[44] The district court was asked to determine whether the conditions were punitive, hazardous and unhealthy and, if so, whether confinement of nondelinquents in these conditions, absent rehabilitative treatment, constituted cruel and unusual punishment and a violation of due process. The Court recognized that decisions "clearly pronounce the constitutional requirement of 'treatment' as a quid pro quo for the exercise of the state's rights as *parens patriae,*" but that, even so, they provide little guidance as to what is adequate treatment.[45]

Agreeing with Judge Bazelon's observations in *Rouse v. Cameron*,[46] the court viewed the following guidelines as valuable for measuring a facility's programs to determine whether or not it furnishes effective treatment:

> (1) The institution need not demonstrate that its treatment program will cure or improve, but only that there is "a bona fide effort to do so," (2) the effort must be to provide treatment adequate in light of present knowledge, (3) the fact that science has not reached finality of judgment as to the most effective therapy cannot relieve the court of its duty to render an informed decision, and (4) continued failure to provide suitable adequate treatment cannot be justified by lack of staff or facilities. . .[47]

The court also found useful the following considerations suggested in the American Psychiatric Association's "Position Statement on the Question of Adequacy of Treatment":

> (1) the purpose of institutionalization, and reference to the length of custody, (2) the importance of interrupting the "disease process" as in separating the addict from his drugs or the psychotic from his family stress situation, (3) efforts to change the emotional climate around the "patient" and (4) the availability of conventional psychological therapies.[48]

In depth scrutiny led to the conclusion that "the program at the centers does not furnish adequate treatment for children who are not true temporary detainees, and thereby violated their right to due process."[49]

In the order issued subsequent to the decision, the court held that detention of a child for thirty days or longer without treatment constituted a deprivation of constitutional proportions.[50] The court then specifically outlined what it considered to be a constitutionally adequate standard of treatment. This included specific educational and training requirements for caseworkers, recreational workers and counselors. It defined treatment and outlined the process by which the decisions for living assignments for a child would be made. It specified the amount of recreational time to be provided daily, called for reasonable access to a psychiatrist and the formulation and review of individualized treatment programs, and established minimally acceptable ratios of children to workers. The court order also required that a complete file be compiled and maintained on each child, and that the information be considered privileged and confidential. Lastly the court ordered the appointment of an independent ombudsman to hear and act on all grievances of the inmates.[51]

Not so specific in its dictates was the Seventh Circuit's decision in *Nelson v. Heyne*,[52] upholding a district court's action in enjoining the unconstitutional practices and policies of the Indiana Boys School.[53] In doing so it agreed with the district court that juveniles have a right to rehabilitative treatment pursuant to state law and the federal Constitution.

The specific practices with which the court was concerned were the infliction of corporal punishment and the administration of tranquilizing drugs. Without holding all corporal punishment in juvenile institutions per se cruel and unusual, it did find the beatings administered at the Boys School unnecessary and therefore excessive, hence, cruel and unusual. Likewise, the use of tranquilizing drugs in the circumstances evidenced in the record constituted cruel and unusual punishment.

The court did not, however, decide that minimum treatment would be required to provide constitutional due process. Instead it remanded the case to the district court for further proceedings on the question but noted that the right to treatment includes:

the right to minimum acceptable standards of care and treatment for juveniles and the right to *individualized* care and treatment. Because children differ in their need for rehabilitation, individual need for treatment will differ. When a state assumes the place of a juvenile's parents, it assumes as well the parental duties, and its treatment of its juveniles should, so far as can be reasonably required, be what proper parental care would provide. Without a program of individual treatment the result may be that the juveniles will not be rehabilitated, but warehoused, and that at the termination of detention they will likely be incapable of taking their proper places in free society; their interests and those of the state and the school thereby being defeated.[54]

In 1973, the United States District Court for the Eastern District of Texas ruled that confined juveniles have a right to treatment.[55] In conjunction with that decision, it held that numerous criteria would have to be followed by the state of Texas in order to assure that proper treatment would be afforded incarcerated juveniles.[56] Included in these criteria were extensive requirements for establishing minimum standards for assessing and testing children committed to the state before a placement decision could be made. Similar standards were set for assessing educational skills and handicaps and for providing programs aimed at advancing a child's education. Criteria were also established for the delivery of vocational education, medical and psychiatric care, and treatment programs designed to return the child to the community. Finally minimal standards for conditions at the institution were established in order to assure that a child's daily environment would not be so deprived as to confound all effort at rehabilitation.

That order, no doubt the most extensive ever justified by a child's right to treatment, has been harshy assailed. The order was vacated on procedural grounds by the Fifth Circuit on the theory that a three-judge court should have been convened to hear the case.[57] On certiorari to the Supreme Court, that Court reversed the Court of Appeals and remanded the case.[58]

When once again faced with the extensive order entered by the District Court, the Court of Appeals stated that while it was not deciding the legal issues presented because of its decision to remand for further evidentiary hearings, it had reservations concerning the constitutional right to treatment theory relied on by the district court judge.[59] These reservations were based on questions concerning the lack of universal acceptance of a constitutionally based right to treatment for the adult mentally ill especially since the argument espousing the right for juvenile offenders is less forceful. While the Fifth Circuit did not totally reject the concept, it did state that the minimum requirements established by the District Court were excessively detailed[60] and implied that such requirements might result in a rigidity that would make it difficult for the Texas Youth Council to adjust to new treatments and testing techniques.

At present it is unlikely that the 1974 order of the District Court can withstand the assaults against it. Whether the constitutional right to treatment concept, still in infancy in the juvenile system, will be served a mortal wound along with the order is an open question and one of major importance to those who chart developments in the field of juvenile justice.

CONCLUSION

Despite the uncertain status of the right to treatment insofar as it relates to juveniles, the right has served as the basis for many substantive changes within the last fifteen years. Just as the Supreme Court, during that same period, improved the lot of children by extending to them the procedural due process protections afforded adults, lower courts have implemented meaningful and beneficial changes in the substantive law governing children on the grounds that these changes are mandated by the right to treatment.

The most dramatic and noticeable change has been the improvement of the physical conditions within many juvenile institutions. Perhaps the most important, however, is recognition by the judiciary that they can and must become more involved in the juvenile justice system. Many judges are evidencing an awareness that their role in the juvenile process does not end when they dispose of a child. They can and must become involved in monitoring the agencies that treat children if for no other reason than that these agencies are generally protected from public scrutiny. While the authority of the court may not go so far as to order the creation of new programs nor so far as to diagnose the specific treatment needed by a child, it does encompass the right to make a decision that minimum standards of treatment have not or are not being met. It further allows the court, after eliciting expert testimony, to make findings that existing programs either are or are not capable of treating individual children.

This means that a judge can, if he or she is so inclined, change the nature of the disposition hearing. When examination reveals problems that may lie at the root of a child's difficulties, representatives of the state social agency often recommend to the court specific courses of treatment that may be of benefit to the youth. Often these recommendations are made without any thought to the alternatives that, realistically, are available to the court. The court will note the recommendations and then order placement of the youth in whichever available facility appears most likely to suit the youth, based, often, upon a set of criteria totally unrelated to the child's needs: age, size, and seriousness of the offense. While not unimportant considerations, these factors may bear no relationship to the child's problems.

Relying on the theory that the child has a right to treatment, the judge may wish to request that the social agency representative recommend specific programs or facilities designed to deal with the individual problems of the youth. If no such facilities exist, the judge may then direct the agency representative to prepare an assessment of existing programs with an eye toward evaluating their capabilities for providing services to the youth. Where the capability exists, the judge may seek to enter an order directing that facility to make those adjustments necessary to implement a needed program of care, realizing that any program beyond the financial capabilities of the program or agency will never be implemented, despite court order. As indicated by the cases discussed *supra,* the final sanction that the court apparently has in ordering specific treatment plans is the option that it retains of releasing the child if no suitable program can be found for him or her.

Requiring that social agencies provide detailed and specific treatment plans for youths adjudicated delinquent can serve a very useful collateral function. These recommendations should be screened for the purpose of accumulating information on the number of times during the course of a set interval, a particular kind of recommendation is made. It may become obvious that a certain jurisdiction has a great need for a facility capable of providing certain services, and that a campaign to erect such a facility is appropriate. It may also become obvious that certain available treatment facilities are obsolete and should be either altered or abolished. Additionally, the juvenile court judge has a continuing duty to ascertain that programs and facilities that promise treatment actually provide it. Just as it would appear to be within the realm of the juvenile court judge to determine that a youth has obtained the maximum benefit from a program or facility and so should be released, so too should it be within his authority to determine that the program or facility is not delivering the treatment promised. This failure ultimately could also be the basis for the release of the child.

This kind of involvement by the court is not only not in excess of its authority, it is imperative if the juvenile court is to fulfill the promise that gave birth to it at the turn of the twentieth century. It is imperative to assure that a child does not receive the worst of both worlds — receiving neither "the solicitous care and regenerative treatment postulated for children" nor "the protections accorded to adults."[61]

NOTES

1. *Birnbaum,* The Right to Treatment, *46 A.B.A.J. 499 (1960).*
2. Id. *at 503.*
3. *125 U.S. App. D.C. 266, 373 F. 2d 451 (D.C. Cir. 1966).*
4. *125 U.S. App. D.C. at 368, 373 F. 2d at 453.*
5. See, e.g., Wyatt v. Aderholt, *503 F. 2d 1305 (5th Cir. 1974) aff'g* Wyatt v. Stickney, *325 F. Supp. 781 (M.D. Ala. 1971); 334 F. Supp. 1341 (1971); 334 F. Supp. 373 (1972); 344 F. Supp. 387 (1972), in which the court held that civilly committed mental patients had a right to treatment stemming from the Due Process Clause of the Constitution;* Stachulak v. Coughlin, *364 F. Supp. 686 (N.D. Ill. 1973), in which the court noted its agreement with* Wyatt v. Stickney, *insofar as it recognized a constitutional right to treatment for civilly committed mental patients. In accord,* Welsch v. Likens, *373 F. Supp. 487 (D. Minn. 1974);* Burnham v. Dept. of Pub. Health of State of Ga., *503 F. 2d 1319 (5th Cir. 1974),* cert. denied *422 U.S. 1057, 95 S. Ct. 2680 (1975); contra* N.Y. St. Ass'n For Retarded Children, Inc. v. Rockefeller *357 F. Supp. 752 (E.D. N.Y. 1973);* Renelli v. Dept. of Mental Hygiene, *340 N.Y.S. 2d 498 (1975).*
6. *422 U.S. 563, 95 S.Ct. 2486, 45 L.Ed.2d 396 (1975).*
7. Id. *at 573.*
8. Id. *at 578, n. 12.*
9. *503 F. 2d 1319 (1974),* cert. denied, *422 U.S. 1057 (1975).*
10. *493 F. 2d 507 (5th Cir. 1974).*
11. Uniform Juvenile Court Act, *§1, page 5.*
12. McKeiver v. Pennsylvania, *403 U.S. 528 (1971).*
13. See, e.g., In re Juvenile, *274 A.2d 506 (Vt. 1970).*
14. *See pp. 5–6 for text.*
15. See, e.g., Martarella v. Kelley, *349 F. Supp. 575 (S.D. N.Y. 1972).*

16. *379 F. 2d 106 (D.C. Cir. 1967).*

17. *Five days after the juvenile was apprehended the Juvenile Court entered an order authorizing his continued confinement. Before a petition was actually filed nearly three months later, the Court considered but rejected after a hearing the possibility of waiving jurisdiction over him.*

18. *Levin and Sarri,* Juvenile Delinquency: A Comparative Analysis of Legal Codes in the United States, *National Assessment of Juvenile Corrections (1974) p. 19.*

19. Uniform Juvenile Court Act *drafted by the National Conference of Commissioners on Uniform State Laws (1968).*

20. *225 N.W.2d 245 (Minn. 1975).*

21. Id. *at 253.*

22. In re Welfare of I.Q.S., *224 N.W.2d 30 (Minn. 1976).*

23. Cf. United States v. Bland, *472 F. 2d. 1329 (D.C. Cir. 1972).*

24. In the Interest of R.R., *#10,513 Youth Court First Judicial District of Hinds County (3/10/76)* [*unreported*].

25. Matter of L., *546 P. 2d 153, 158 n.3 (Ore. App. 1976).*

26. Id. *at 160.*

27. State of New Jersey in the Interest of D.F., *367 A. 2d 1198 (Sup. Ct. N.J. 1976).*

28. State in the interest of D.F., *351 A. 2d 43, 47 (Juv. & Dom. Rel. Ct. 1975).*

29. Id. *at 57.*

30. *367 A. 2d at 1203.*

31. *Id.*

32. Janet D. v. Carros, *362 A. 2d 1060 (Pa. Super. 1976).*

33. Id. *at 1062.*

34. During the forty-two days Janet D. was held at McIntyre, she ran away five times.

35. Id. *at 1074.*

36. Id. at 1076.

37. *419 F. Supp. 203 (S.D. N.Y. 1976).*

38. Id. *at 207.*

39. *346 F. Supp. 1354 (D.R.I. 1972).*

40. Id. *at 1367.*

41. Id. *at 1370.*

42. Id. *at 1373.*

43. Id. *at 1374.*

44. *349 F. Supp. 575 (S.D. N.Y. 1972).*

45. Id. *at 585.*

46. Supra *at note 3.*

47. *349 F. Supp. at 601.*

48. Id.

49. Id. *at 603.*

50. Martarella v. Kelley, *359 F. Supp. 478 (S.D. N.Y. 1973).*

51. Id. *at 485–486.*

52. *491 F. 2d 352 (7th Cir. 1974),* cert. denied *417 U.S. 976, 94 S.Ct. 3183, 41 L.Ed.2d 1146 (1974).*

53. *355 F. Supp. 451 (N.D. Ind. 1973).*

54. Id. *at 360.*

55. Morales v. Turman, *364 F. Supp. 166 (E.D. Tex. 1973).*

56. Morales v. Turman, *383 F. Supp. 53 (E.D. Tex. 1974).*

57. Morales v. Turman, *535 F.2d 864 (5th Cir. 1976).*

58. Morales v. Turman, *430 U.S. 322, 97 S.Ct. 1189, 51 L.Ed.2d 368 (1977).*

59. Morales v. Turman, *562 F. 2d 993 (5th Cir. 1977).*

60. Id. *at 999.*

61. Kent v. United States, *383 U.S. 541, 556 (1966).*

Community Intervention with Juvenile Court Youths

INTRODUCTION

This final section reviews certain policy and programmatic issues concerning community-based intervention with court youths. The discussion omits the more or less universal probation services, traditional or innovative, important as they may be; probation offerings have served well but not well enough to minimize the need for institutionalization. Nor do the articles dwell on the range of counseling services, mental health treatment, alternative educational projects, or citizen volunteer programs. Rather, the emphasis is on group homes and certain more intensive local programs, largely private agencies reimbursed through public funds, which are classified as alternatives to institutionalization. National commissions repeatedly have urged an expansion of these programs in order to fill the space between basic probation capabilities and the availability of institutional beds. Retaining more youngsters in the community comports with the purpose of juvenile legislation favoring community-based juvenile corrections, and squares with the rehabilitation theory that a child's improved adjustment is better accomplished without full removal from the community. Admittedly, an enriched network of community-based services has intrinsic value without being posed as a strategy to reduce institutionalization.

Private residential facilities are not new inventions. Under sectarian and nonsectarian auspices, they have received juvenile court youngsters for decades. The numbers of youngsters they have housed and the quality of their services have spanned a wide range. There has been a new focus in the past ten or fifteen years on small group homes, neighborhood residences leased for this purpose using child care employees and housing from six to ten or even fifteen youngsters. Here too, the variation as to size, location, type of administration, and type and quality of program have varied widely.

These facilities have been promoted as being substantially cheaper than state institutional care. While the latter's annual cost per bed has escalated sharply and now, in some states, exceeds $25,000 per year, the costs of the smaller private group home programs are running $10,000 to $15,000 and more per year in many communities. For other reasons as well, these facilities are not unmixed blessings, but in general, they can be more innovative, more flexibly programmed, and more easily related to a broader community experience. They can also be more readily closed down following poor performance or inadequate administration than can state institutions.

The first article, by Rutherford and Bengur, examines fifteen community-based programs, most of them residential, from policy and program perspectives. The authors note the individuality of programs, observe that some facilities develop characteristics which parallel state institutional life, and express concern with the blurring of treatment objectives and social control purposes. Because they find only limited correlation between an increase in community-based resources and decarceration of juvenile offenders, with the basic exception of Massachusetts which is described but not named in their recent account, they contend that the web of state intervention is widening and that more youngsters are being cared for in costly community facilities without diminishing state institutional populations. Most of the programs they observed were for "shallow end" juveniles, the less serious and less repetitive offenders, than for "deep end" youths. In other research, Rutherford describes similar findings with youngsters served by juvenile diversion agencies.

Coates and Miller analyze the panoply of factors which relate to community acceptance (tolerance) or rejection of the establishment of a group home residence for juveniles who are in the custody of a state youth agency. The evaluation begins from the recognition that most people believe community halfway houses are useful correctional strategies, but they should be placed in someone else's neighborhood. The analysis of attempts to establish group homes in six communities, three of which were successfully opened and three of which failed to open, points to the need for thoughtful planning in locating a group home, ways to more constructively interpret the program, and methods for dealing with the resistance which invariably arises. Since private agencies sponsored all six efforts, an initial conclusion is that private agency sponsorship is not a guarantor of successful establishment. The issues are more complex and contextually related to a host of local contingencies. The group home enterprise is more than the development of a soundly conceived and well executed in-house rehabilitative program. Citizen concerns over the perceived threat to their property values and their physical and emotional well-being are among the reasons for resistance which require neutralization.

The Albrecht work is an original article, written for this book to provide an examination of the use and implications of subcontracting for juvenile services. Albrecht's definition of subcontracting is a broad one, extending beyond the direct purchase of services to include the myriad of ways juvenile courts and public children's agencies obtain outside services for youths. Subcontracting is perceived as a vehicle for aggregating judicial control over other organizations while delegating operational accountability away from the judiciary. While the literature is scant on this subject, subcontracting has proliferated and is likely to extend still more vigorously in the juvenile justice arena as well as in other human services fields.

The final article is a return to the Massachusetts decarceration initiative. While many observers contended that the departure of Dr. Jerome Miller, the architect of deinstitutionalization policy, from his position as Commissioner of the Massachusetts Department of Youth Services would result in extensive reinstitutionalization of juveniles, such a result has not yet occurred. The report of the Task Force on Secure Facilities, appointed by the Massachusetts Attorney General, must be interpreted as a vindication of a community-based system of juvenile corrections as launched by Miller and as refined by his successors, Joseph Leavey and John A. Calhoun. The report's fundamental findings provide a powerful message: for a state of some six million people whose age for initial juvenile court processing ends at seventeen years, a maximum of only 129 to 168 secure placement beds are required, of which 100 to 130 should be provided by the Department of Youth Services and the remainder by the state mental health agency. Further, the Task Force holds, 114 secure pretrial detention placements are clearly adequate for that state. It is doubtful that Massachusetts youths are any less delinquent than those of other states which have urban centers, industrialized cities, and suburban and rural areas. Rather, viable networks of nonsecure program alternatives, regionally organized, have enabled that state to prevent its dollars and youngsters from being swallowed up by costly and unnecessary state institutionalization.

23 *Community-Based Alternatives to Juvenile Incarceration*

Andrew Rutherford and Osman Bengur

. . . A major task of the project was to select twelve site visit locations for the field research. To this end, information was collected concerning programs through: (1) telephone interviews and correspondence with state planning agencies, juvenile justice personnel and programs; (2) program descriptions provided by LEAA's Grant Management Information System (GMIS) and by the National Council on Crime and Delinquency; (3) a search of the available literature. From a universe of 400 programs the list was reduced to twelve site locations representative of the universe. In all, fifteen programs were examined during twelve site visits. . . .

PLACEMENT CRITERIA

Though program placement criteria reflected the view that youths should be placed in programs according to their specific needs, the field investigations found that referral agencies (probation, DYS, etc.) depended on other factors when making their placement decisions. These included organizational considerations such as the availability of placements or the types of intervention efforts at various phases of the juvenile justice process.

Placement criteria are also defined relative to the types of youth that should be sent to incarcerative facilities and the types of youth considered appropriate for community-based programs. In the twelve sites visited, most juvenile justice officials expressed the view that incarcerative facilities are appropriate and necessary for serious offenders. However, there are widely varying opinions as to what constitutes a serious offense. This is clearly illustrated by the fact that one-third of all incarcerated youth in the United States (and in the case of girls alone, more than half) are status offenders.

The field research did reveal two broad strategies which determine the type of youth for whom community-based programs are being used: a) shallow end; and b) deep end.

Shallow End

The most common criteria that was found (in eight of twelve site visits) insured the placement of relatively minor first and nonserious offenders into the community-based programs. Many of these community-based programs for shallow end offenders exist in a correctional milieu in which more youths are place in incarcerative

From *Community-Based Alternatives to Juvenile Incarceration,* National Evaluation Program, Phase I Report. National Institute of Law Enforcement and Criminal Justice, Law Enforcement Assistance Administration, U.S. Department of Justice (Washington, D.C.: Government Printing Office, 1976), pp. 10-35. Reprinted by permission.

facilities than in community-based programs. It appears that many youths are being placed in community-based programs for whom the chances of incarceration would have been slight. It may well be that such placement criteria are *widening the net* to include youth who do not require any type of program.

Deep End

Two of the community-based programs visited exist in a state where the minimal use of incarceration necessitates community-based programs for the vast majority of juvenile offenders.[1] Within this context, referral criteria to community-based programs are considerably broader. In another state, MSA, an experimental program, has strict criteria in order to insure that only those youths in imminent danger of being incarcerated are referred. The program director commented that the youths in the program were "hard core," and implied that the program was pursuing a deep end strategy. The field research found that:

> because of the . . . criteria, 55.6 percent of all the clients of MSA were arrested for major felonies, 23.6 percent for minor felonies, 5.3 percent for major misdemeanors, 2.8 percent for minor misdemeanors, and 2.8 percent for miscellaneous delinquency.

CLIENT CHOICE

A final important placement criterion involves the question of choice. Many program staff and juvenile justice personnel feel that expressed desire to enter a program is a necessary prerequisite for successful completion of the program. The nature of this choice, however, in many instances is affected by the consequences, especially when incarceration is held as the option to not choosing the program. Despite the attempt to give the youth some say in the placement process, the placement decision is commonly made by juvenile justice personnel for the youth. Even where the explicit threat of incarceration is not used the authority of the court or correctional agency generally appears sufficient to ensure that the recommendations are followed.

PROGRAM ISSUES

Community-Basedness

The extent, frequency and quality of linkages among program staff, clients, and the local community provide a basis for determining the degree to which programs are community-based relative to incarceration.

Extent and Frequency of Linkages with the Community One aspect of incarceration is its social separation from the community. In this respect, the extent of linkages with the community is extremely limited, if not in many cases nonexistent. One community-based program encountered during the field research was similar to incarceration in that it did not allow any community contact during the initial thirty days of residence.

The majority of programs visited placed varying limits on the extent and frequency of community linkages. This was particularly the case with residential programs, many of which use an achievement system to regulate the extent of community contacts. One program example illustrates how this works: "Girls on the third level and above can take forty-five-minute walks in the neighborhood after dinner." Attainment of a higher level brings increased contact in the form of weekend outings.

There is a great difference between programs which do and programs which do not limit the extent to which youths and staff interact with the community. The extent and frequency of linkages with a community are *not* necessarily determined by whether a program which is residential or nonresidential. One nonresidential program that serves as an alternative school, for example, has limited linkages with the community during the enrollment period as most of the program's focus is upon classroom related activities. In contrast, two residential programs insisted on youth being present only for meals and housemeetings, and that they must return to the house by a certain time at night.

Quality of Community Linkages   The *quality* of linkages that a program has with a community is a critical measure of community-basedness. Though the extent and frequency of community linkages might be high within a particular program, quality of linkages may be lacking. For example, in one residential program examined in the field research, the youths attended the local public schools on a daily basis. Apparently the youths felt stigmatized by their identification with the group home; other students referred to them as the "San Quentin girls" and this had a profound effect on the quality of their relationships at school.

Within this particular program, quality also depended upon whether the youth was from the community in which the program was located, or from another part of the state. Girls from other parts of the state had to adjust to a new school situation and were not able to see their families often. Similarly, in another program, 60 percent of the youths were from communities other than the one in which the program was situated. Though the program emphasizes community linkages, experiences take place outside of the community to which the youth will eventually return. "The youth's own community is not involved in, nor aware of the progress the youth is making and consequently, his reintegration into his community (may) not be any easier because of his community contacts while in the program."

Other programs felt that it is sometimes necessary to remove the youth from his/her own community in order to enable the youth to experience new relationships, or to alleviate some of the pressures that may have developed as a consequence of the offense that the youth committed. One interviewed youth, who is presently incarcerated in a state prison, felt that the nature of his offense made placement within his own community detrimental to his chances for rehabilitation. He stated that he was never able to overcome the stigma the community had attached to him by virtue of the offense he had committed.

Some programs which deal with older youths place a great deal of emphasis upon the youth maintaining a job within the community. Finding quality employment for youths is difficult. As far as could be determined in interviews with youth and staff in one program, the jobs the youth could get were menial, low paying and unexciting; even these were rarely available. For those youth in job training programs, there is no guarantee that their training will lead to meaningful employment.

Sexist attitudes affect the quality of linkages; a discrepancy was noticed within one group home for girls, compared with group homes for boys. Girls' needs for meaningful activity were not considered a priority. For example, while the boys in a similar program in one state were encouraged to find jobs, the girls did volunteer work. Despite the likely possibility of holding menial jobs the girls in this particular program preferred to earn some money.

Though this study cannot draw firm conclusions on the relative quality of community linkages between residential and nonresidential programs, the nonresidential programs studied during this project placed a strong emphasis on the quality of linkages with the community. This was not equally true for all residential programs.

In summary, community-based programs exhibit varying degrees of community-basedness along the dimensions of extent, frequency and quality of linkages that the program has with a community. In this respect, the programs can be placed on a continuum according to their "community-basedness."

Control

Control in correctional programs can be examined from the perspectives of: type; degree; duration; and the use of discretion.

Types of Control. Incarceration, or physical confinement is one of the more extreme types of control found in correctional programs.[2] In many training schools visited, this type of control is manifested by confinement in a locked cell or locked facility. In those training schools where the majority of the population is not held behind locked doors or high fences, surveillance and geographical distance can be equally effective as controlling mechanisms.

In the field examination, only one alternative program (investigated during a site visit to a community-based program) used physical confinement for control purposes. Though it only had fifteen clients at a time, it had twenty-five full-time staff and was located on the fourth floor of a thousand-bed public hospital. In addition to the high degree of surveillance by staff, the youths were physically confined.

All of the project-selected community-based programs used five types of control to varying degrees: achievement systems; the threat of incarceration; peer pressure; program regimentation; and surveillance.

Degree of Control. In most of the state training schools studied during the site visits, a high degree of control was maintained through constant surveillance; the staff closely watched youths and controlled their activities. In extreme cases some of these incarcerative settings used four-hour lock-ups or confinement in a 6' by 4' steel cage for 38 days.

None of the community-based programs maintained either the intensity or degree of control found in most of the state training schools. Five major degrees of control were evidenced in these programs and are as follows:

• *Achievement Systems*. The achievement system was used in over half of the community-based programs visited. The staff feel that the use of a point system compels the youth to be responsible for his/her behavior. With the accumulation of points comes privileges, the final privilege being successful discharge from the program. The point system on one program monitors the youth's behavior while the youth attends public school during the day or when the youth goes home for a weekend, by sending along activity report cards which must be filled out by teacher or parent respectively.

• *Threat of Incarceration*. In the majority of programs that were examined, the threat of incarceration was used as a control mechanism.[3] However, it was difficult to determine the extent to which the "hammer" is used within individual programs. One program did have extensive use of a detention facility on a weekend basis until this activity was prohibited by a local judge. More often, there was an implicit awareness among youths that improper behavior on their part could lead to incarceration.

• *Peer Pressure*. In programs which use peer pressure, the responsibility for control rests with the youth. The daily group meeting pressures individuals to conform to the dominant values of the group. Groups can, as an aspect of controlling each other's behavior, impose sanctions upon individual youths. The degree of control maintained in such programs can be quite intense. While the daily group meetings focus on establishing behavioral guidelines, constant mutual vigilance throughout all program-related activities insures a high degree of behavior control.

• *Program Regimentation*. Rigid scheduling in two programs is the basis for a high degree of control. One of these programs is a modified therapeutic community. Intensive counseling and highly controlled activities over an extended period of time are considered necessary for rehabilitating clients who have usually been heavy drug users for years.

• *Surveillance*. The fifth type of control evidenced in community-based programs is surveillance. A nonresidential program employs what it calls a client tracking system to supervise youth "all the time." Counselors use detailed forms to log their efforts with youth on a daily, weekly, and monthly basis. Such a high degree of control over youths makes it a valued placement by the state Department of Youth Services.

Finally, two programs were noteworthy in functioning without any overt control techniques. In these programs, a close relationship between staff members and the youths appeared to be a more subtle control device.

To some extent, the above types of control were manifested in all the correctional programs visited, incarcerative and community-based. Where the programs differ is their emphasis on one type of control and the degree to which it is used.

Duration of Control.   The existence of alternative community-based programs may be in some instances increasing the duration of control that programs have over youth. In one program, for example, all youth spent more time under the direct control of the alternative program than they would have in the state training school.

Furthermore, the time the youths spent in the alternative program was often not counted toward their commitment period. Thus a youth could end up spending up to four months in a community-based program and still run the risk of being incarcerated without having committed any further offenses. In more than half the community-based programs visited, the possibility existed that a youth might be incarcerated following completion or termination from a community-based program, in some cases because there was no other available placement. One youth who had completed a community-based program and was then sent to the state training school commented bitterly on the difference between time "done" in an alternative program and time "done" in a training school: "Four months in the program [community-based] may or may not get you out. [You] may just get sent up after all with another four months to do. At least [at the training school] you can do your time without being afraid of another commitment."

Discretion. Discretionary decision making by program staff was evidenced in two major areas: in the administration of controls and sanctions, and in establishing criteria for program success and failure and length of stay. Discretionary judgments can have both positive and negative consequences. Particular sanctions can be applied by staff based upon arbitrary definitions of unacceptable behavior. In some programs, the accumulation of a record of poor behavior can result in increased length of stay or termination. Termination in two programs resulted in automatic incarceration for the youths involved. In the other programs efforts were made to insure that the administration of sanctions for specific behaviors were not capricious. However, in some cases program staff have the authority to define certain types of behavior as delinquent, and then impose sanctions which can increase the degree and duration of control over a youth.

It is of major concern that in many instances the imposition of sanctions is justified as a form of treatment. Thus, for example, in many programs increased length of stay in a program or restricting community linkages is justified for reasons of treatment.

Staff

Program staff are largely responsible for maintaining a balance between a positive environment and the necessary degree of control within a program. Staff background, in all programs, is considered important for relating to the youths. The apparent trend in many programs is toward a staff comprised of ex-offenders, former program graduates, and persons who have grown up in, or experienced, an environment similar to that of the youths with whom they work. The majority of the programs examined use a paraprofessional staff instead of professionally trained social workers. In at least one site visit, however, the use of paraprofessional staff caused considerable controversy in the juvenile justice system which emphasized the use of probation staff and other workers with proper professional training. Two other programs placed great emphasis on a professional staff with masters degrees and formal job training with classroom instruction and workshops. These programs tended to be very structured in their approach towards youth.

An element common to all programs encountered was the high level of staff commitment to the program and the youth. Staff work extraordinary hours in the programs, feeling that their ability to provide quality services depends upon "our being there when (the youth) need us. . . ." It was anticipated that the problem of the staff "burning out" would be regularly encountered; this did not turn out to be the case. Only once was it cited as a problem with respect to staff commitment.

Finally, in a majority of programs, a favorable impression was gained of staff-youth relationships. The best indication of the kind of relationships that staff were able to maintain came from the youth within a program. The intangible balance between caring and control maintained by staff appears to have an important effect upon the youth's view of the program. In many instances this determines whether a youth feels s/he is being helped by the program, or whether the youth primarily views the program as a controlling experience.

FACTORS EXTRINSIC TO COMMUNITY-BASED ALTERNATIVES TO INCARCERATION

Single Programs versus Program Network Strategies

In nine of the twelve site visits individual community-based programs operated in isolation from other programs. While individual programs may use different treatment strategies, the program itself is expected to provide the primary rehabilitation services.

The single program method of intervention can best be understood when contrasted with the program network strategy of intervention. In a network strategy a number of individual programs may be used to provide several services for the individual youth either sequentially or simultaneously.

An example is provided by one program which operates as a network in itself. This program serves as a brokerage agency and uses the network strategy to offer widely varying alternative settings from minimal supervision by a voluntary advocate while the youth lives at home, to extended psychiatric treatment in a private hospital or six weeks of wilderness training. The network strategy can link programs in sequence so that a youth may undergo short-term treatment in a psychiatric hospital, followed by residence in a group home, and then return to his own home under the supervision of a community advocacy program.

Funding

Issues arise out of the differences between programs operated by public agencies, and programs whose services are purchased by the state and operated by private agencies. Privately operated programs appear to provide a certain flexibility lacking in publicly operated programs. This flexibility is particularly apparent in their ability to maintain staff on rigorous and unorthodox schedules.

Another area in which a privately operated program is seen as advantageous is when it is associated with a well respected local organization. As illustrated in a number of site visits, such relationships enable a program to become established and maintain considerable community support.[4]

Juvenile justice officials in one state cited other positive aspects of privately operated programs: (a) they allow more innovation as they do not have to contend with a state bureaucracy; (b) they can hire and fire personnel on the basis of ability obviating state civil service requirements; (c) programs which do not work can be more easily closed or changed. This is more difficult with public programs which often continue, regardless of their effectiveness, for years.

A disadvantage of the public-private liaison is that well established private programs can wield considerable power over youth placement and program development, while becoming as fossilized and resistant to change as many state agencies. In addition, some privately operated programs become tied to the funding requirements of state agencies. In one program youths had to be labeled "mentally disabled" in order to qualify for funding from the state Department of Vocational Rehabilitation. In addition, many private agencies are dependent upon funding from sources other than the state Department of Youth Services. As such, they can be forced to make substantive changes in programmatic content and/or intake policies to conform to these other funding agencies' demands.

Finally, recent status offender legislation in some states is having a profound effect on traditional funding arrangements. Some state youth corrections agencies have been mandated to handle only delinquent youths; status offenders are being picked up by child welfare agencies. One of the consequences is that many programs are no longer taking status offenders because child welfare agencies have not been able to provide adequate funding. The seriousness of this situation is illustrated by one state which has status offenders (CHINS) spending up to forty-five days in detention while awaiting placement.

Program Costs

The wide variety of funding arrangements and the bewildering array of cost accounting formulas and procedures makes it very difficult to obtain reliable information on the cost of running community-based programs. As a result, it was difficult to substantiate cost claims made by programs and thus make a comparative analysis regarding different types of community-based programs and training schools. Three somewhat limited conclusions can be drawn: (a) with one exception, the costs quoted by programs were comparatively less than the cost of incarceration quoted by state agencies; (b) cost information was more easily obtainable from state run programs than from privately operated programs; (c) some programs did not have cost figures readily available, and were unable to explain precisely how they arrived at their figures.

Monitoring

The monitoring of private agency programs appears to be limited or nonexistent. Only one state agency, which operates its own community-based programs, monitored the programs closely. In this case, operating procedures appeared to aid in the maintenance of relatively consistent levels of services.

The Political Context of
Community-Based Alternatives to
Incarceration

During the field visits, the overall political context of each of the programs was not always apparent. However, there were three significant exceptions to this. In one site visit the development of an experimental network, or strategy type program was influenced when key figures in the field of juvenile justice formed a policy board.[5] The policy board was viewed as a major breakthrough in uniting critical juvenile offenders. In effect, the policy board provided the mandate for the program's attempts to provide a range of alternative programs for relatively serious offenders who otherwise would have been incarcerated.

Another example comes from a state which has all but abandoned traditional forms of incarceration in favor of over two hundred community-based programs. This policy has focused attention on the state Department of Youth Services' plans for those youth who are in need of secure custody. The limited availability of secure settings (a quota system limits the number of youth who may be placed in such facilities to a total of one hundred statewide)[6] is a constant source of friction with juvenile court personnel who feel more secure facilities are needed. This controversy illustrates a central question for the development and use of community-based alternatives to incarceration: what types of offenders can be placed in community-based programs, and what types of offenders should be placed in secure settings?

A third state more clearly illustrates the politics that surround the fundamental question of how juvenile offenders should be handled. This state has pursued a deliberate strategy of reducing the number of youth within their state training school system through the development of community-based programs. The reforms initially did not generate much controversy. However, eventually a battle ensued between those supporting the reforms, and those with a more punitive orientation who felt the new emphasis on community-based programs was coddling youthful criminals. Eventually a reactionary response to the department's policies resulted in a dramatic increase in the numbers of youths being incarcerated throughout the state.

In short, the policy of this state was to slowly decrease the population of its training schools while shifting to a community-based approach. However, the training schools remained in use during the attempted reforms even while community-based programs were being used for an increasing number of offenders. It is the view of some correctional observers that if training schools themselves are not closed concurrent with the creation of alternatives, then such incarcerative facilities will continue to be used at or near their full capacity despite the availability of community-based programs. This appears to have happened in this state as a consequence of its gradualist policy of decarceration.

CONCLUSIONS

Despite the criticism that has been leveled at juvenile institutions and the training schools, and the demands for alternatives to them, they have demonstrated great resilience. David Rothman offers an insight as to why they continue to be the major strategy for dealing with juvenile offenders.

> The history of the discovery of the asylum is not without relevance that may be more liberating than stifling for us. We still live with many of these institutions, accepting their presence as inevitable. Despite a personal revulsion, we think of them as always having been with us, and therefore always to be with us. We tend to forget that they were the invention of one generation to serve very special needs and not the only possible reaction to social problems.[7]

This study has assessed the contemporary state of community-based alternatives to incarceration. An attempt has been made to focus upon issues which have relevance for research and policy considerations. In particular, this has included immediate issues concerning the day-to-day operation of community-based programs, and extrinsic factors which place community-based programs within the context of the juvenile justice process. Qualitative data has been obtained using two techniques: (1) a review of the available literature; and (2) field research to cover a range of programs in which interviews were conducted with program participants, and juvenile justice personnel from judges to state administrators.

The program issues examined in the field research have also been raised in the research and other literature concerning the use of community-based programs. Several important findings relative to program operation have been highlighted in this report. These findings require considerably more attention from researchers and administrators alike.

Community-Basedness

The field research was aided by the conceptual exploration of community-based corrections undertaken by Robert Coates.[8] The findings of this study indicate that programs differ in important respects depending upon the linkages that are developed with the community. The dimensions of extent, quality and frequency of community linkages still require translation into measures which determine the degree to which programs are community-based.

Control

In examining community-based programs, an attempt was made to distinguish between purposes of control and services. The importance of making such a distinction has been made by several researchers and most forcefully in a recently published study by Paul Lerman.[9] The strong impression gained from the field research in this study is that community-based programs are viewed by juvenile justice personnel primarily in terms of treatment services rather than control. In support of Lerman's findings, it appears that distinctions are rarely made by program personnel or other juvenile justice staff between activities related to the provision of treatment services for youths and those that serve a control purpose. A number of instances were observed during the field research of increased control over youth being justified by a treatment rationale. As Lerman notes:

> The issue is not whether, on reasonable grounds, wards should ever be locked up. The issue is whether a correctional agency . . . can accept the responsibility for depriving youth of rights and privileges — and can then forthrightly address the issues associated with the administration of sanctions. If the conceptual distinction between social control and treatment is not made, then the responsibility of organizing a nonarbitrary administration of sanctions is not likely to occur.[10]

Discretion

Again the findings of this study tend to support Lerman's conclusion that the wide use of discretion by program personnel results in ad hoc policymaking which has direct consequences for youths in programs.[11] Some of the consequences of discretionary decision making observed during the field research included increased duration and degree of control over youths in programs for arbitrary purposes. Specific examples were found of youths being incarcerated because of program failure, not because they had committed another delinquent offense.

Another study which has examined the effects of discretionary decision making found that the development of special juvenile delinquency police units was associated with higher rates of juvenile delinquency.[12] The fact that juvenile justice personnel exercise enormous discretion in making diversion decisions was highlighted in a study by Cressey and McDermott.[13] Yet policies and litigation attempting to reduce the use of arbitrary and capricious discretion have not been common in the juvenile justice field, especially compared to efforts being made in this regard in adult corrections. The few efforts in this area of juvenile justice have been almost entirely concerned with institutional and not community settings. This study's field research strongly supports the importance of developing more precise conceptions of fairness and justice; policies which place parameters around the use of discretion in programs; and the monitoring and evaluation of programs in these terms.

Costs

This research effort experienced considerable difficulty in obtaining reliable cost information on programs. Fiscal data is generally not recorded in a manner which allows for a careful analysis of program costs. The cost issue is receiving attention from National Assessment of Juvenile Corrections; hopefully the methodology developed during the course of that study will aid in the development of more sophisticated cost accounting measures. The NAJC researchers have reported that states spend considerably less on community-based programs than on the operation of institutions, and that average per-offender costs were less than half the average institutionalized cost.[14]

Careful accounting of fiscal costs is important at both the individual program level and with respect to their impact on policy decisions. Paul Lerman's reanalysis of the fiscal impact of probation subsidy in California provides an important warning that there may be unanticipated and unmeasured fiscal costs resulting from policy decisions.[15]

Recidivism

Most research efforts in both juvenile and adult corrections have centered upon attempts to measure programs in terms of their impact upon recidivism. The accumulated research has underlined that there is little empirical evidence to support the view that community-based programs are more successful in this regard than incarceration. Comprehensive surveys of the research literature, most recently by Martinson, show that such alternative programs are no less successful than incarcerative programs.[16] Even if it is not possible to demonstrate that alternative programs are *more* effective in reducing crime, it is necessary to show that the public is not being exposed to greater danger as a consequence of their operation. Measures of recidivism are clearly important, but they should not be used as the sole determinants of correctional policy.

The Central Policy Issue

This study has been concerned both with issues that arise in viewing an individual program and in the broader context of which programs are a part. Reference has been made to the important work being undertaken at the Harvard Law School's Center for Criminal Justice in this regard. The Center's researchers have made a distinction between *programs* and the *strategies* that they might be said to represent. This model allows for the state of flux which characterizes individual programs, and for the possibility that youths may be associated with more than one program, either simultaneously or sequentially. The Harvard study is unique in addressing both linkages between programs, and the relationship of a range of programs to wider strategies for change.[17]

The role that community-based programs are playing as a strategy to provide alternatives to incarceration has been a central issue addressed by this report. The main question is whether community-based programs are in fact serving to replace or to supplement juvenile incarceration. In the majority of cases, the findings of the field research strongly indicate that community-based programs appear to be serving a supplementive rather than an alternative role. This is in concert with recently published findings of the National Assessment of Juvenile Corrections which has addressed the same issue. The University of Michigan researchers state:

> The development of community corrections is not associated with reduced rates of institutional incarceration. States that place more offenders in community-based programs do not place fewer in training schools although there are several exceptions. In general as the number of offenders in community-based facilities increases, the total number of youth incarcerated increases.[18]

In eight of the twelve site visits conducted by this project, community-based programs were found to be dealing with shallow end offenders who in all likelihood would not have been incarcerated had a community-based program not been available. It appears that the use of community-based programs for shallow end offenders neither limits the penetration of youth into incarcerative programs, nor reduces the level of incarceration. In this regard, an important research question to be asked is: *to what extent does the development of community-based programs lead to a widening of the juvenile justice net?* Although this study did encounter instances of community-based programs being used for deep end offenders as part of a strategy to reduce the number of incarcerated youth, such programs were the exception.

Given the policy directions set by the Juvenile Justice and Delinquency Prevention Act of 1974, and by a series of national commissions in favor of reducing the level of incarceration and the overall extent of control in the juvenile justice process, there remains a critical policy decision that must be made with respect to the funding and use of community-based alternatives to incarceration. This policy decision revolves around a fundamental question: *should community-based programs be tied to a policy of decarceration?* This study has underlined the importance of making an explicit policy decision, rather than allowing policies to develop through default, which often results in a series of unanticipated or undesired consequences. The present community-based programs might well become significant in providing alternatives to incarceration but this is generally not the case at present. If such programs are to serve that purpose, explicit policy decisions are required and the implementation of these decisions must be closely monitored.

NOTES

1. Of approximately 2000 youths being handled by the state correctional agency, less than 150 are being held in incarcerative facilities.

2. Physical abuse was reported by youths in some incarcerative facilities but its extent could not be determined.

3. Incarceration might involve temporary placement in a local facility, or transfer to a longer-term setting, such as a training school.

4. One of the apparent disadvantages of state operated programs is the difficulty they have in eliciting community involvement. Such programs are sometimes seen as being the responsibility of the state and not the community.

5. Members of the Policy Board include representatives of the juvenile court, police department, state child welfare agency, department of youth services, and the state attorney general's office.

6. This state is one of the largest in the nation.

7. David J. Rothman, *The Discovery of the Asylum* (Boston: Little Brown, 1969), p. 295.

8. Robert B. Coates, "A Working Paper on Community-Based Corrections: Concept, Historical Development, Impact and Potential Dangers" (Harvard Law School: Center for Criminal Justice, undated). Unpublished paper.

9. Paul Lerman, *Community Treatment and Social Control* (Chicago: University of Chicago Press, 1975).

10. Ibid., pp. 83–84.

11. Ibid., pp. 79–90.

12. James Q. Wilson, "The Police and the Delinquent in Two Cities," ed. Stanton Wheeler, *Controlling Delinquents* (New York: John Wiley and Sons, Inc., 1974).

13. Donald R. Cressey and Robert A. McDermott, *Diversion from the Juvenile Justice System,* National Assessment of Juvenile Corrections (Ann Arbor, Michigan: University of Michigan, 1973).

14. Rosemary Sarri and Elaine Selo, "Some Selected Findings From the National Assessment of Juvenile Corrections." Paper presented at the American Correctional Association, Nashville, Tennessee, August, 1975.

15. Lerman, *Community Treatment and Social Control,* pp. 157–187.

16. Douglas Lipton, Robert Martinson and Judith Wilks, *The Effectiveness of Correctional Treatment: A Survey of Treatment Studies* (New York: Praeger Publications, 1975), p. 247.

17. Robert B. Coates and Alden D. Miller, "Evaluating Large Scale Social Service Systems in Changing Environments: The Case of Correctional Agencies" (Harvard Law School: Center for Criminal Justice, undated). Unpublished paper.

18. Sarri and Selo, "National Assessment of Juvenile Corrections."

24 Neutralizing Community Resistance to Group Homes

Robert B. Coates and Alden D. Miller

Part of the effort to reform the treatment of juvenile offenders in recent years has focused on changing the treatment setting. Attempts have been made to handle more youth within community residential centers or group homes in order to reduce the numbers of youth served by traditional reform schools and exposed to the degrading effects that are so often part of such institutional experiences. While the group home concept for troubled youth is often philosophically accepted in both professional and nonprofessional circles, the actual establishment of group homes in local communities is often vehemently resisted by residents.[1] Thus a very pragmatic issue confronting both state and privately operated agencies is how to handle community resistance to group homes. How can community resistance be avoided or ameliorated when it arises?

This chapter describes the first results of a continuing investigation into the dynamics of locating a group home in a community setting. We are concerned here with the political aspects of coping with community resistance to the initial establishment of the group home. We will not, in this report, deal with community reaction to the program of the group home once it is in operation, nor with the effect of the program on the youth residing in the group home. We will deal with the program only as it is represented as a proposal in the process of gaining entry into the community. Our analysis of resistance and strategies for neutralizing resistance will focus on the community level. Analysis at the statewide and governmental levels is not included here.

From *Juvenile Correctional Reform in Massachusetts,* National Institute for Juvenile Justice and Delinquency Prevention, Office of Juvenile Justice and Delinquency Prevention, Law Enforcement Assistance Administration, U.S. Department of Justice (Washington, D.C.: Government Printing Office, 1977), pp. 81-91. Reprinted by permission. This chapter was first published in slightly different form under the title "Neutralization of Community Resistance to Group Homes," in Yitzhak Bakal, *Closing Correctional Institutions* (Lexington, Massachusetts: Lexington Books, © 1973 by D.C. Heath and Company), pp. 67-84. Reprinted by permission.

The data supporting this study were gathered within the Massachusetts Department of Youth Services. Massachusetts ranks in the forefront of states seeking to discover viable community-based alternatives to the institutionalization of juvenile delinquents. As part of the deinstitutionalization process during the spring and summer of 1972, the DYS sought to establish several group homes throughout the state under a purchase of service arrangement. That is, the DYS proposed to buy group home services from private agencies. This arrangement was adopted for several reasons: (1) it was believed that the closer the ''treatment'' program to the community and the more involvement of private agencies and private citizens, the greater the likelihood of successful reintegration of program clients; (2) it was also believed that private agencies, particularly the more experienced agencies, were better prepared to handle group residential homes than most DYS line staff who had only worked with youth in an institutional context; and (3) it was considered to be an easier task for existing or even newly created private agencies to work with communities in establishing group homes than it would be for DYS with its controversial image. The DYS had been strongly opposed by some interest groups in the state because they felt that the DYS deinstitutionalization effort was moving too quickly, and that the department's treatment approach was too permissive.

METHOD

In order to isolate those issues that are most sensitive to community resistance and to identify the various strategies for handling resistance, we looked at several planned group homes that failed primarily because of community resistance, and at several other homes that were able to neutralize resistance and establish on-going residences. Three homes were selected within each of the two categories. Two of the agencies that failed had previously operated similar homes and had therefore been confronted with some of the same problems before, while one agency that failed had never before operated such a program. Two of the successful agencies had previously operated similar programs; the third agency had a parent structure with some prior experience, but the specific people involved in setting up the group home had had no prior experience.

The homes were located in six of the seven DYS regions. The seventh region was not studied because there was at the time considerable political turmoil within the region over other issues related to corrections. Although the selected group homes do not necessarily represent the full range of all probable conflict situations, they do present a range sufficient to identify at least some of the key issues of strategy.

The data collection strategy focused on extensive interviewing of key actors. To learn most about the plans for each home, the first person contacted was either the executive director of the sponsoring agency or the director of the proposed home. During this initial discussion the interviewer identified other significant actors or interest groups to be interviewed at a later time. This snowball technique was followed until it became apparent that little additional, useful information could be gained by further interviewing. Typically the interviewing included agency representatives, police, clergy, neighbors, and city officials. In two cases the snowball technique was modified to accommodate the wishes of the group being studied. One involved an agency that failed and the other an agency that succeeded. The research team respected the intricacies of the ongoing political processes and tried not to endanger an operating program or the chances of any proposed home.

The interviews, although structured, were also quite flexible. During the course of an interview with a representative of the social service agency, the interviewer obtained the following information: (1) the goals of the program and strategies for implementing the program; (2) the process of communication of goals to interest groups; (3) the kinds of people who agreed or disagreed with agency goals and strategies; (4) the communications from vested interest groups; (5) the strategies for handling opposition and support; and (6) the expected outcome. When interviewing representatives of interest groups outside the agency, the major blocks of information included: (1) perceptions of the private agency and DYS goals; (2) the source of information about the group home; (3) interest group goals for home; (4) the strategies for attaining those goals; (5) the communication of goals and strategies — to whom, how, and why; (6) the kinds of people or groups that agreed or disagreed with goals and strategies; (7) the strategies for handling opposition and support; and (8) expected outcome. Three interviewers were involved in the data collection process. Each covered one group home that failed and one that succeeded.

In addition to interviewing the key actors, researchers analyzed local newspaper accounts as well as letters of support or opposition and minutes of planning meetings and hearings where available. Together the data project a fairly good picture of the process and problems of placing a residential home in a community.

Throughout this paper we will refer to group homes and their communities by fictitious names. Many persons cooperated with us in our data collection efforts in order to contribute to the understanding of the process of establishing or resisting a group home, with the express understanding that we would respect certain confidentiality about the information and not identify our sources. Fortunately this need for confidentiality does not interfere with our purposes in this analysis, since the actual identity of the communities and group homes is not important for the kinds of inferences we are seeking to make and support.

RESULTS

The major variables and strategies involved in the process of establishing the group homes in this study are summarized in Table 24-1. Data from the individual case studies will be compared and contrasted in order to derive at least tentative responses to a number of policy and strategy issues. The nine critical variables include such items as selection of community, strategy for entering community, and resolution of conflict. These nine variables provide the backbone of our analysis. Before proceeding with a detailed comparative analysis of the six homes in the study, it will be helpful for the reader to have an understanding of the general flow of the processes involved in setting up group homes and the kinds of opposition encountered. We will

TABLE 24-1. Successful and Unsuccessful Group Homes.

CHARACTERISTICS of GROUP HOMES

| | Laurel | Failures | | | Successes | |
		Palmyra	Whitewater	Eagle Grove	Sullivan	Hebron
Who established it?	An "established" agency with experience in group homes for drug cases	A sectarian religious group new to this sort of work	An established agency treating children with physical disabilities	"Ex-con" group new to this sort of work	An established agency with experience in group homes for welfare youth	An established agency with experience in group homes for delinquents
Selection of community	Knew community but not with respect to reaction to delinquents	Did not know neighborhood community	Knew community but not with respect to reaction to delinquents	Knew community well	Knew community well	Learned community well *after* site selection
	Residential are a working and middle class	Residential middle to upper class	Residential middle to upper class	Transient community, disorganized	Mixed transient but neighborly and "liberal"	Residential working and middle or upper class
Strategy for entering community	Talk to "significant few" and then campaign	Talk to "significant few"	Talk to "significant few"	Low profile ("quiet")	Low profile ("quiet")	Talk to "significant few" and then campaign
Selection site	Across from school and no space for recreation	Fire trap, small yard	Busy road, small yard	Youth involved in improving house	Youth involved in improving house	Estate more than adequate, for expansion

CHARACTERISTICS of GROUP HOMES

	Failures			Successes		
	Laurel	Palmyra	Whitewater	Eagle Grove	Sullivan	Hebron
Selection of name for program	Name designed to challenge youth	Name or label emphasized community's responsibility	Name or label emphasized community's responsibility	Name was de-emphasized	Name was de-emphasized	Name designed to challenge youth
Presentation of program content	Presented as related to DYS-plan for a kind of problem-kid community did not have	No clear presentation or conception	Vague and too technical presentation	Presentation through youths' activity	Presentation through youths' and house parents' activity	Presentation in direct, informative style in meeting
Client and staff residence	Staff and supporters did not live in neighborhood	Staff and supporters did not live in neighborhood	Staff live in group home	Staff lived in group home	Staff lived in group home	Staff lived in group home
Serving the community	*Home* an unwanted service to community	*Home* an unwanted service to community	*Home* an unwanted service to community	*Youth* serve community	*Youth* serve community	*Youth* serve community
Resolution of conflict	Looking for middle ground	"Holy War"	"Righteousness" in getting community to meet problems	Avoidance of creating issues	Avoidance of creating issues	Straight-forward meeting of issues

therefore present two brief hypothetical case studies: one representing failure, Clarion, and one representing success, Kimberly. The nine critical variables will emerge in these hypothetical case studies, as they did in the six real case studies, as the major steps in the flow of action, resistance, and effort to neutralize resistance.

Clarion

A long-established social service agency, BURN (Boys United: Resources, Neighbors), attempted to set up a small group for juvenile delinquents in the middle-sized city of Clarion. BURN had been operating a program designed to address learning disabilities in the city for six years. Its reputation was thought to be quite good, and on the basis of that reputation little opposition to the program's expansion was anticipated. The actual program was to consist of a "free school" environment and provision of work experiences within the community. The group home would house eight to twelve boys ranging in age from thirteen to seventeen.

The initial strategy for setting up the home involved talking to a few key people in the community — people who were generally considered to be friendly toward the agency. These people included the mayor, two of the town's five selectmen, and other wealthy backers of the agency. Response from the mayor was noncommittal; the two selectmen and the financial backers were quite supportive. After these initial conversations a site was selected. The selected neighborhood was primarily residential in character, with one gasoline station and a small store. Although unknown to the agency administrators, the neighborhood had in the recent past taken two actions to maintain its residential atmosphere. The residents had organized to prevent a light industrial plant from moving into the area, and they had also closed a teenage drop-in center that had operated for a brief period of time. This lack of knowledge about the neighborhood's capacity for organizing was to be a major factor in the failure of BURN.

Before the purchase arrangements were completed, it was necessary for BURN to go before the town zoning committee to request modification of the zoning regulations in the case of the group home. Upon hearing of the group home for juveniles, abutters were incensed and alarmed. They were incensed because no one had told them about the plans previously, and they were alarmed because they believed that "gansters were moving in next door." Over the next two-week period the abutters held a number of informal meetings to determine how the group home could be stopped. Neighbors indicated that their primary motivation for keeping the halfway house out of their neighborhood was to protect their own children. In addition it was pointed out that the neighborhood did not have any delinquency problem and did not want to be an "experimental lab for other neighborhoods who could not solve their own problems."

By the time of the zoning hearing, BURN was aware that it would encounter a little opposition. But it believed that the support of various public officials would outweigh a few "strident antagonists." This did not prove to be the case. The hearing was underscored by a very well thought out confrontation on the part of the informal citizens' group. They listed three reasons why the group home should not be allowed: (1) the site selected was inadequate for ten to twelve teenagers because of its small size and tiny yard (the lack of space would also cause an undue nuisance burden for nearby neighbors); (2) children and elderly persons would be endangered by the "criminal types" who would be associated with the halfway house; and (3) the agency had no experience working with juvenile delinquents. One woman suggested that much of the fear expressed by residents was related to the acronym, "BURN." She said, "Why couldn't they simply call it AIDE or something like that."

Rather than attempting to deal with each of the specific reasons cited by the citizens' group, BURN administrators suggested that the citizens did not care about children, but only cared about property values. This righteous stance on the part of BURN only served to strengthen the bond among the citizens. Seeing the rift between the citizens and BURN the town selectmen had "no other choice" but to reject the home.

Kimberly

Several individuals who had previously worked with juvenile delinquents decided to set up a group home in the town of Kimberly. Eight to twelve boys would reside in the home; in addition another eight boys would participate in the program on a non-residential basis. The program would focus on informal counseling and getting the youth into activities occurring in the community. These would include work, schools, and recreation. According to the staff the program was to project the image of a "large but concerned family," concerned about its members and the community. Youth would typically stay in the residential program for three to four months. After their residential stay, program staff would maintain contact in order to support the youth as they returned to their own or foster homes.

The program staff selected an area of Kimberly they believed best fitted their needs. The locality had a junior high school and a senior high school nearby; a number of small businesses were also within walking distance.

The strategy for setting up the home operated on two levels. Program staff were talking with various influential town officials about their proposal, and concurrently they were talking with local residents and leaders of civic organizations functioning in the target area. Initially some of the neighbors expressed fear and concern for their own welfare. However, the program staff handled this situation well. They explained that dangerous youth would not be participating in the group home and that if youth did seriously act out in the community they would be transferred elsewhere. At the same time it was said that the community could expect some minor incidents but these inconveniences would be balanced by the service to the community that the home offered. First, the home obviously offered a service to area youth who may be beginning a delinquent career, and second, youth would repair the house used for the group home and would hire out their services to improve and maintain the neighborhood. This concern for property values handled some of the more subtle opposition to the proposed home. Moreover, many residents were concerned about the occurrence of delinquent acts in their neighborhood and saw the group home as one means for dealing with the problem.

Town officials were for the most part supportive of the proposed home. This was particularly the case once it became apparent that the bulk of opposition had already been mollified. The police chief had been contacted by the program staff. He did not anticipate problems, but was taking a "wait and see" attitude.

A zoning hearing was called to pass on the proposed home. Three or four residents living in the area voiced opposition. They indicated fear for their children's safety and did not believe the program staff to be particularly qualified to work with troubled youth. The program staff responded very straightforwardly. They acknowledged that there were minimal risks but argued that the value of the home for the community outweighed the risks. They also described the program in detail, thereby answering any question about their competency to work with youth. In addition to the defense put forth by the program staff, other community residents spoke on the group home's behalf. Preparation of the community and cooperation with the community had paid off; the group home passed the zoning hearing and was established.

Having these two brief vignettes in hand and a feeling for the general flow of the processes involved in setting up community-based group homes, we can now turn to a more detailed analysis of the data summarized in Table 24-1.

DISCUSSION

The usefulness of studying the community resistance process comes from comparing those proposed homes that failed and those that were successfully established. This analysis should yield results which directly relate to policy and strategy considerations.

One of the initial questions administrators within the DYS raised as they closed the institutions and became involved in setting up community residences was whether the state should set up the homes, or whether it should contract this task to private agencies. DYS opted for the latter strategy for three reasons: (1) the DYS image was burdened by past controversy, and the private agencies were seen as potentially the easier way of obtaining the group homes; (2) privately run group homes appeared to offer better prospects for real community involvement in the youth corrections process; and (3) private agencies with a number of years of experience were expected to have a greater level of expertise about moving into communities and operating community-based programs than DYS had at that time.

Because there are no state-operated group homes within this study we cannot speak directly to this issue, but we can say something about the use of private agencies. There is no guarantee that the well-established private agency has the capacity to set up a new residence without meeting the same opposition that a newly formed private agency, or for that matter the state itself, might face. The data within this study suggest that experience cannot be equated with finesse. Two of the proposed homes that failed (those in Laurel and Whitewater) were planned by agencies that had operated in those communities for a number of years. It may be that both agencies suffered from overconfidence, misreading of the community, and poor preparation for handling any resistance. In Hebron and Sullivan, we again have two agencies with years of experience, but each approached the communities very cautiously, with considerable preparation, and overall strategies for handling community resistance. As for the newly established private groups, one was a failure and one a success. The agency in Palmyra failed. And the agency in Eagle Grove, although it did have a nominal umbrella agency, was for all intents and purposes newly created and quite successful.

Therefore we must beg the question for the moment; it is apparent that the answer to successful entry is not simply a longstanding privately established group or a newly created group. The answer is probably more directly related to the way the agency plans strategy and approaches the community. Some of the issues discussed seem likely to arise from use of a sectarian religious organization in a pluralistic community if the organization stresses religion as an issue. It is certainly reasonable for a Catholic church or any other to function well as a sponsor in a community where no other church exists or where the religious inclinations of the community are predominately in that direction, and for that church to use religious arguments. But where there is much religious diversity, religious groups may be more successful as sponsors if they are ecumenical or nonsectarian in nature, and do not emphasize religious differences. Any strictly sectarian operation in a religiously diverse community has a good probability of becoming embroiled in a "holy war." The effect of such a conflict is to focus debate on false issues related to other interests and to personalities rather than toward the issue of community responsibility for handling troubled youth.

Selection and Survey of the Community

Comprehensive understanding of the community and the particular neighborhood in which the proposed home will reside is requisite for the sort of planning that is demanded. It seems reasonable to anticipate some community resistance to any group home; the question is where will that resistance come from and how can it be neutralized. The form the resistance will take can be anticipated if enough is known about how the community has reacted in similar situations. Has the community recently organized to defeat a drug program or an alcoholism center? What sort of people live in the area — are they professionals or day laborers? Is the community an integrated area? Do the people in the community recognize a crime or delinquency problem in their area? Who has power and how do they exercise it?

The lack of such knowledge was detrimental for agencies in Laurel and Palmyra. In Palmyra, particularly, the proposed home ran into a very well organized community that had already gotten together to make a "passive park" and to object to college dormitories. This information perhaps should have suggested that the agency look elsewhere for the site or at least suggested potential problems which would have to be handled if the community were to be approached successfully in setting up the home. The agency in Hebron took ample preparatory time to study the area, the needs of the region, and the interests of the community. Here the primary problem involved the matter of timing. The agency took so long to complete the first phase of the preparation plan (that is, gaining support of regional professionals) that the second phase (talking with community leaders and abutters) was then made more difficult by news leaks. Information gleaned by surveying the community, its makeup and concerns, can be used for devising the appropriate strategy for entering the community. As we will see, some strategies are appropriate for some communities but not for others.

Strategy for Entering the Community

Once one knows something about the context of the community, the focus of power, and the way it organizes itself to serve the interests of its residents, one is in a position to consider alternative strategies for entering the community to establish a group home.[2] Three general strategies seem to have been put into operation by the group homes represented within this study: (1) maintaining a low profile; (2) focusing communication on a significant few; and (3) focusing communication both on the significant few and on the local resident. Some of these strategies seem to be appropriate for certain kinds of communities and very inappropriate for other kinds.

In general, the low profile entry into the community appears quite adequate for communities which are characterized by mobile populations, which have diverse groups in terms of age and race, and which have little experience in organizing to present a collective response to an issue. The purest type of low profile approach was discovered in the Eagle Grove community which could be described by each of the above characteristics. The agency sought a community with great diversity so that little attention would be attracted by a group of youth or by a staff made up of ex-offenders. This low profile approach, which could be called the "quiet approach," has certain risks which are minimized in the transient community but which could be exacerbated in a residential community. That is, the danger of being discovered before the program has had a chance of proving itself is always a risk. It seems improbable that one could actually place a group home in a middle-class residential community without being discovered and then becoming involved in a bitter struggle to remain before having a chance to show what one's program can do.

The other community in which a low profile approach was used successfully was Sullivan. That community can also be characterized as having a diverse and mobile population, but it also had the capacity to organize itself to promote community interests. The approach of the group home was to win community support by means of a functional approach. That is, the nondelinquent youth and staff became involved in the community on a personal level. They projected themselves as worthwhile persons and therefore sold the program. Then DYS youth were introduced into the existing group home, and were also urged to sell themselves. This approach probably works best where there is a sympathetic and widespread concern about community problems. In Sullivan, the residents recognized that a crime and delinquency problem existed and had to be handled; furthermore, they believed that the program was one way to deal with delinquency. It is problematic, however, whether this approach would work in a relatively isolated suburb unwilling to acknowledge the existence of delinquency in the community or to accept responsibility for coping with it. As long as delinquency is seen as another community's problem, the sympathetic support and understanding requisite for this low-key functional approach would be missing.

The approach that emphasized communication with a significant few persons in the community — the mayor, the selectmen, and key professionals — has had mixed success in residential areas. Usually it has worked fairly well only where it has been expanded to include a fairly comprehensive communication flow with grass roots neighbors and abutters. In communities where there are upper-middle-class persons who recognize the value and use of collective power, elected town officials and professionals will be unable to force acceptance of a group home even if the officials are in favor. In most cases in a conflict, the officials, because of their desire to be reelected, will probably go with the majority or a very vocal minority of the residents. The proposed group homes for both Whitewater and Palmyra were very dependent on political and professional support. The agency in Whitewater had an international reputation among professionals but that reputation was not particularly useful when community residents resisted the idea of a group home in their neighborhood. In Palmyra, the power and influence of the Protestant Council with town officials was considerable, but it could not match the tenacity of the neighborhood residents. In both cases, the agencies were open to the rather serious charge that support came from the outside, or from suburban communities that would probably not themselves accept such a group residence in their own neighborhoods.

This approach has a rather glaring liability. The fears and emotions of a few are allowed to spread and to be voiced in group meetings where such feelings can easily be reinforced. One-to-one contact, with its greater likelihood of neutralizing the fear, was not employed sufficiently in these two cases.

The combined approach which incorporated both communication with significant leaders and with the neighbors and abutters is perhaps more time consuming than the above strategy. And it also has its risks. After all, the best managed communication scheme may still be unconvincing, or perhaps the community is simply unwilling to accept the kind of responsibility that goes along with a group residence. However, for the organized residential community, the combined approach seems the most workable. The strategy revolves around a desire for a community to assess its needs and to take an active cooperative role in meeting some of those needs. This strategy was backed into in Laurel, where it became a face-saving if not agency-saving strategy, and it was the planned approach in Hebron. The original approach in Laurel seemed to emphasize the professional, civic leader, and town official support. It depended a great deal on what was believed to be a good reputation in the community. This strategy blew up. Negative publicity was so rampant that one would wonder about the safety of the agency's existing programs. The program staff withdrew from direct confrontation with the residents of the community and began a massive education campaign directed at the press and at the local residents. This intensive communication with the grass roots seems to have stabilized the situation a great deal. Although the proposed site will be forgotten and the proposed home may be established in another community, the ongoing programs of the agency do not seem to be in immediate danger. In Hebron, the agency sponsoring the group home had developed a strategy which included emphasis on both the significant regional leaders and the community residents. There, however, the strategy was seen as sequential: first the significant leaders would be contacted and then the community residents. The time lag and the almost inevitable news leaks nearly proved to be the end of the proposed home. Again, a fairly concerted effort to communicate with concerned residents was instituted and the proposal was saved. Although initial groundwork may be necessary, requiring communication with the leadership of a community or a region, contact with the local residents cannot lag far behind or once again one will be open to the charge that the program does not care about the residents' concerns and that someone is trying to sneak a halfway house into the community.

This discussion suggests that specific approaches for entering a community with a group home can be tailored to the contextual makeup of the community. The "low profile" approach is most appropriate for the mobile, pluralistic community. The "significant few" approach may be adaptable in a residential community where the local residents are not particularly capable of organized opposition, but where the town and civic leaders are playing an active role in redirecting or shaping the image of the community. The combined approach, which stresses communication with both the significant leaders and the grassroots residents, seems to be one of the few strategies with potential for gaining access to a community that has the ability to organize itself in support of, or in opposition to, issues.

A survey of the selected community should provide the information necessary for choosing the best entry strategy. Well-laid strategies can be devastated, however, if conflict cannot be avoided over such technical problems as appropriateness of the site, presentation of the program content, and intake procedures. We will now describe some of the more technical issues that could produce conflict and impede entry into the community; such conflict might result in focusing debate on what the agency would view as nonessential issues, and away from the basic issue of what a community is going to do to help its youthful offenders. After this discussion we will describe the third major step for neutralizing community resistance — how to resolve conflicts.

The *selection of the site* is of great importance. Care should be taken to avoid giving grounds for legitimate complaints about the suitability of the site for a group residence that will house, let us say, eight to ten youths and two house-parents. If structural questions are legitimate, the whole proposal can be scuttled simply because the agency did not do its homework well. Certain problems can be anticipated, such as a small yard, heavy traffic, or an inadequate house. These are problems that any family buying a house must consider. The appeals board decisions in both Whitewater and Palmyra made specific reference to the shortcomings of the particular sites selected. One can debate such issues as maintaining the residential character of a community or the selection procedures to insure that only certain ages and certain offenders will be residing in the home, but it is most difficult to argue with these physical and structural issues which will inevitably be couched in terms of what is "good for kids."

Selection of a name for the program can also be strategically relevant. Program names are symbols that say something to the community as well as something to the clients. Some names may serve only to threaten and increase the anxiety of potential neighbors. In Hebron, one woman suggested that the name of the program caused as much concern within the community as any other factor. In many cases social service agencies try to put together acronyms that challenge the client but they may also raise red flags for community residents. Names such as BURN, SCARE, SMACK, BLOW-UP or JD may simply cause more problems with community relations than they are worth. Acronyms in the mental health field such as HELP and RECOVERY seem more neutral.

An issue related to selecting a name is deciding what generic label should be used to describe the program. Most of the agencies in this study did not refer to their proposals as halfway houses, even though many of the community's residents referred to them as such. Preferred labels were group homes, child-care centers, schools, or "family." Choice of a label has an effect not only on how the program will be perceived in the community, but also on whether a zoning variance will be required in residential areas. A residence with an educational program that will enable it to be called a school may find that in some areas the zoning question can be eased. In some communities the best strategy might be to set up a "family," which might avoid raising the issue of zoning regulations. This could be done by employing a couple, full time, to work with five to eight residents and who would bring into their home from time to time other persons with specialized skills to provide services for the youth. This could be seen as an expansion of the foster home model.[3]

Presenting program content carelessly can raise needless problems. It is ridiculous for a social service agency to lay itself open to the charge that it does not have a well-planned, well-articulated program for the residence. The proposed home in Palmyra was particularly susceptible to this charge, as was, initially the program in Laurel. In Laurel, an added complication arose because residents did not believe that a program which had been fairly successful with youthful drug abusers would necessarily be successful with juvenile delinquents. The program staff did not seem ready to handle this issue.

Issues involving selection criteria and procedures are included under program content. In Laurel and Whitewater residents were particularly upset over the possibility that tough older juveniles would be admitted to the program. The selection procedures must be worked out and articulated so that the community is assured the plan does not call for working with "dangerous youth" and that if such does manage to make his way through the screening process and become unmanageable in the program, he can be rejected. The residents may still not believe the argument, but at least a straightforward program has been presented.

The importance of this presentation of program content can best be illustrated by the experience in Hebron. Because of a news leak and because of the name of the program, many residents were ready to organize opposition to the proposed home. At the Taxpayers' Association meeting, convened to discuss the group home proposal, however, the program staff presented a very honest, straightforward appraisal of their program. While they could not guarantee the community's safety, they did present the safeguards built into the program. Most of the participants agreed that the presentation neutralized any further efforts to prevent the establishment of the group residence.

In Sullivan, the program was actively presented to neighbors by both staff and the boys. They did not seek to dramatically publicize the program, but they did quietly solicit the assistance of some neighbors, and the youth became involved in various work projects within the community. Again, the staff and youth knew what the program was about and could intelligently talk about it.

Client and staff residence can also materially affect acceptance of a group home. An issue that arose in the Laurel, Whitewater, Palmyra, and Hebron communities was the desire not to be a dumping ground for the problems of other communities. This was particularly the case in Laurel where councilmen from other communities were kidding the Laurel councilmen about Laurel's being the leader in social service and saying that other communities would like to send their "tough kids" to Laurel. In Palmyra there was the complaint that the support for the group home came from the suburbs. And in Hebron, there was concern that the home would serve youth from Boston and Brockton. Residents in Laurel seemed willing to serve the needs of their own youth. And most residents in Hebron were willing to serve youth as long as the youth resided in the resort area.

A similar issued has been raised about staff. In Laurel, it was said that the program staff worked in the program during the day but then drove home to rather plush suburbs at night. And in Palmyra, it was said that the Protestant Council should set up their group home in their own neighborhood. Although these issues were not raised in Sullivan or Eagle Grove, in both cases some program staff resided within the home or the community.

The issue of community control is related to this question. If a community recognizes the need for a residential program for its troubled youth, such as the need to generate more community contact while the youth are in a "treatment" program and being reintegrated into that community, it also is reasonable for the community to make certain demands on the program. This may include a request that at least a specific portion of the staff reside within the community, that youth from the community have priority for entry into the program, and that residents have some influence on decisions about the nature of the program. A problem with community control arises when a community decides it has no delinquency and can therefore simply reject the notion of a group residence; at that point it seems the state must assume an *in loco parentis* role and provide services for troubled youth. Where there is community interest, however, one probably should not resist real "community-based corrections" by denying *shared control* over the program.

Finally, emphasizing that the *program will serve the community* can greatly ease entry. Obviously the home should have some impact on handling the community's delinquency situation. Successful integration of clients will prevent at least some crime. But the clients can also be used as resources while participating in the program. One woman in Hebron recognized this when she suggested that some of the youth could help her with a local historical society. Youth in the Sullivan residence became a resource for filling part-time jobs. Youth in the Eagle Grove residence are becoming active in a delinquency prevention program.

Resolution of Conflict

We must reiterate that in most instances, with the possible exception of the very low profile approaches, any attempt to establish a group home in a community will incur some sort of resistance. Even if the issues discussed above have been well handled, some conflict will still probably arise over such issues as "we don't need a halfway house in this area," "this is not the kind of issue with which this organization should be involved," or "halfway houses are needed but in the next county." For successful entry into a community, it seems imperative for the social agency to develop strategies for resolving conflicts.[4] In general, an all-out fight will work against the interests of the social service agency and the youth whom the agency wants to serve. The administrators in Laurel recognized this when they said that it would be better for the youth to be located in a business-zoned area than to be in a residential community which simply did not want them. If all attempts to resolve conflict fail, this backing off may be one of the preferable alternative choices. Let us then turn our attention to ways of neutralizing conflict that may hold open the opportunity for establishing the proposed home. With this goal in mind, it is important to recognize that those conflict resolution strategies that make continued relationships of cooperation between the conflicting parties difficult or impossible are inappropriate in this case, although they may be helpful in other situations.

Any conflict will have at least two disagreeing parties. If each has a level of power sufficient to thwart the desires of the other, a situation where there can be no outright winner will probably result. Even if the social agency can "beat" the opposition on a particular issue, if its tactics are unjust, the opposition may simply regroup and become an even more intense enemy.[5] It is desirable therefore to have available face-saving devices. The opposition should be given the sense that it has had some impact on the outcome. In Laurel, when the agency sponsoring the group home realized that its whole program could be lost, it withdrew from direct confrontation to begin a massive education campaign. In a sense the education effort was a face-saving device; it provided a reason for avoiding direct confrontation and was a strategy which may reestablish the agency in the minds of the residents as a viable, worthwhile organization. Palmyra exhibited quite the opposite extreme. There, emotional invectives such as "unchristian" and "property-conscious" and "do-gooder" served to escalate the conflict and to make satisfactory resolution that much more difficult. In Hebron conflict was neutralized by confronting it, letting all the questions come, and dealing with them on the spot. There was no particular effort to "snow" the residents, but rather to be honest about the strengths and weaknesses of the program. The style that one uses to handle conflict can have considerable impact on its resolution.

A classic distinction in the study of conflict and conflict resolution is between realistic and nonrealistic conflict.[6] A basic principle that underlies this discussion is that of generating and rising to only realistic conflict.[7] Realistic conflict is over an actual difference of interest clearly and accurately defined. Nonrealistic conflict is over something other than an actual difference of interest, and is therefore not susceptible to resolution. Nonrealistic conflicts often tend to be impersonal, couched in terms of ideas rather than actual personal interest. Such abstractly defined conflicts can be pursued with greater fury than can personal conflicts. This truth is represented in the common recognition that holy wars are more bloody than others, in the fact that "lynch law" has frequently been activated by couching a personal economic interest in terms of some widely held ideal, such as the saving of Southern white womanhood, and in the fact that when the federal government has been actively and successfully involved in solving racial problems, it has done so by focusing conflict on genuine economic and social interests, not on symbols. The role of the mediator in labor-management relations is also to focus the conflict on realistic issues and to get rid of unrealistic ones.

The direct identification of the real issues and frank discussion of them by the group entering Hebron is a good example of focusing on realistic conflict with good results. So is the strategy of representing oneself to the neighbors in terms of what one is doing, and in terms of who the youth actually are, instead of as a halfway house, an abstract idea with nonrealistic connotations, or representing oneself by a highly symbolic name. The strategy of the Protestant Church Council in Palmyra is a good example of failure because of stubbornly generating and rising to nonrealistic conflict. Alinsky was fond of pointing out that when he approached church groups, he did it on pragmatic grounds of economics, power, and the like, not on the grounds of religious belief.[8] The conflict in Palmyra had clear realistic components, relating to property value, possible danger to residents, and the intrusion of an outside group. The Protestant Council, instead of meeting these problems and resolving them, chose to generate a nonrealistic conflict over the practice of religious values, a conflict it could never win. Realistic conflict, probably susceptible to solution by compromise, since many of the objections of the community were probably quite valid, was escalated by the Protestant Council into a "holy war," perhaps either out of naiveté or because of a need for martyrdom. It was perhaps fortunate for DYS as well as for the community that the Protestant group was decisively defeated, because their tendency to make a holy war would have had a generally alienating effect in the community.

To summarize, one must know the other side, its power and interests, be clear on the difference between one's own interests and the other side's, and do everything possible to focus the conflict on those realistic issues, avoiding nonrealistic conflict over loaded symbols. The voice of a group in determining the course of the community in which it lives should always be considered as one of the issues over which realistic conflict may arise. Thus one must consider the importance of face-saving. The possibility of escalating nonrealistic conflict by using a symbolic name, or by using a loaded shorthand description, such as halfway house, should also be considered, as should the danger of creating a holy war. Also much of the conflict about technical issues, such as the program name, selection procedures, and site selection can *simply be avoided* if one plans well and anticipates the consequences of decisions related to these technical issues. It is absurd as well as unfortunate to have a proposed home rejected because the sponsoring agency did not carefully do its own homework. Debates over technical problems and nonrealistic concerns allow for proponents and opponents to engage in cconflict over petty issues while altogether avoiding discussion of the real issues. On the other hand, once the technical issues are out of the way, the possible value of forthrightly dealing with the real, unavoidable issues involved in differences of interest should not be underestimated, and meetings and educational campaigns designed to focus and resolve realistic onflict should be seriously considered.

NOTES

1. For example, a study conducted by Louis Harris and Associates for the Joint Commission on Correctional Manpower found that 77 percent of a representative sample favored the idea of a halfway

house, 50 percent would personally favor a halfway house in their neighborhood, and only 22 per-
cent believed that most people in the neighborhood would favor a halfway house in the area. Joint
Commission on Correctional Manpower and Training, *The Public Looks at Crime and Corrections*
(Washington, D.C.: Government Printing Office, 1968), pp. 16–17.

2. The importance of understanding the power structure and process of a community to facilitate community action is underscored by Roland Warren, *The Community in America* (Chicago: Rand
   McNally, 1972), pp. 308–309; and Robert C. Wood, *Suburbia* (Boston: Houghton Mifflin, 1958).

3. The Massachusetts Department of Mental Health has undertaken research concerning the definition
   of "family" in zoning ordinances. The department contends that "there is growing legal precedent
   in zoning cases in Massachusetts and other states to support the emerging definition of family [as]
   that of a group of people sleeping, cooking, or eating on a premises as a single housekeeping unit
   rather than as a group of people related by blood or marriage."

4. This is not to say that a certain level of conflict does not futher efforts to establish group homes.
   Conflict does clarify boundaries of interest groups for example. The function of social conflict has
   been discussed in numerous works, for example Georg Simmel, *Conflict and the Web of Group
   Affiliations* (Glencoe, Ill.: The Free Press, 1955), pp. 17–20; Ralf Dahrendorf, *Class and Class
   Conflict in Industrial Society* (Stanford, Calif.: Stanford University Press, 1957), pp. 206–213;
   Lewis Coser, *The Functions of Social Conflict* (Glencoe, Ill.: The Free Press, 1956).

5. It has nearly become a sociological dictum that conflict often tends to strengthen the opposition into
   an even more formidable opponent. *See* Kurt Wolff, *The Sociology of Georg Simmel* (Glencoe, Ill.:
   The Free Press, 1950), p. 192; and Coser, *Functions of Social Conflict*, p. 38.

6. Dahrendorf, *Class and Class Conflict:* In order to regulate conflict "both parties to a conflict have to
   recognize the necessity and reality of the conflict situation, in this sense, the fundamental justice of
   the cause of the opponent," p. 225.

7. Coser, *Functions of Social Conflict*, pp. 48–55; and Simmel, *Conflict and the Web of Group Affiliations*, pp. 27–28.

8. Saul D. Alinsky, *Rules for Radicals: A Pragmatic Primer for Realistic Radicals* (New York: Vintage
   Books, 1972), p. 88.

25 *Subcontracting of Youth Services: An Organizational Strategy*

Gary L. Albrecht

Social critics and scholars devote much attention to the ideologies and programs of
the juvenile court but often neglect detailed analyses of how the court relates to other
legal institutions and human service agencies. In our complex society, the satisfactory
performance of the juvenile court is dependent upon the coordination of services
among many institutions. This paper analyzes the subcontracting of services by
juvenile courts as a strategy designed to elicit interorganizational cooperation in an
uncertain and demanding institutional environment. The paper uses a resource dependency perspective to examine the extent, rationale, process and consequences of
subcontracting in the juvenile justice system.

Government contracting for services began in colonial times and continues in the present. For example, the Community Action Program (CAP) provides the authority to delegate "portions or all of a component project to another public or private non-profit agency by means of a contract or agreement."[1] Furthermore, the Community Mental Health Act of 1963, the Economic Opportunity Act of 1964, amendments to the Social Security Act of 1967 and Title XX of that Act allow the use of federal monies to purchase services from other public agencies, nonprofit organizations and the private sector.[2] Governmental subcontracting of services has reached such proportions that Paul O'Neill, deputy director of the U.S. Office of Management and Budget from 1974 to 1977, argues that one of the primary functions of our government is the redistribution of income and wealth.[3] Since 1971, the government has spent more on transfer payments and grants in aid to state and local governments than on the purchase of goods and services to operate its own direct operations like defense, space, courts, and foreign service. In 1978 the government spent $102 billion more on contracts than on direct operations. This general trend toward increased government subcontracting is also being experienced in the juvenile courts.

Juvenile courts receive operating budgets and special project monies from state, local, and federal governments to perform their basic functions, but subcontract many services to outside agencies. In this context, juvenile court judges use their authority and capital resources to design and coordinate youth services. Through this role, judges formulate and enact social policy. In his discussion of the judicial role, Nathan Glazer points out the consequences of such activity:

> It seems reasonable to conclude that the overall effect of judicial intervention in social policy administration is to reduce the responsibility and range of discretion of administrators and service workers; to reduce their authority; to give greater weight to theoretical than to practical or clinical considerations; to give greater weight to the speculations, considerations, and research of social scientists in formulating policy; and to increase the power of the legal profession and the more theoretical professions in each branch of social service over that of professionals who deal directly with the clients of the service.[4]

Thus, judges not only oversee court operations but extend their influence through subcontracting to control the work of professionals in other human service organizations.

Silberman contends that the relatively unmitigated power of juvenile court judges has frequently resulted in inconsistent, arbitrary, and unconscionable behavior toward youth and their families.[5] The *Kent* and *Gault* Supreme Court delinquency cases illustrate that juveniles often did not receive the same legal protections as adults.[6] The juvenile courts which were originally established to prevent the mistreatment found in adult courts have unwittingly become parodies of the abusive institutions they replaced. Although there is evidence to support these accusations, it is simplistic to blame juvenile court judges for every problem in the court and treatment system. This paper argues that the effect of court intervention is a product of the judge and court system working in a specific social, economic, and political environment. Even though judges exercise awesome power in the court and human service system, their actions are constrained by organizational structures and environments.

ORGANIZATIONS AND THEIR ENVIRONMENTS

Recent literature in behavioral science focuses on the symbiotic relationship between organizations and their environments.[7] All organizations respond to or anticipate the threats and opportunities of an external environment given the limitations of their goals, structure and resources.[8] The pattern of responses to the environment, which usually is modified and sequenced over time, constitutes the organization's strategy. The success of the organization in maintaining its domain and resources is contingent on the appropriateness and implementation of its strategies. This paper is concerned with the juvenile court's use of subcontracting as an organizational strategy designed to respond to a specific environment.

The political environment of the juvenile court is uncertain. Public concern over crime, which remains a critical issue in public opinion polls, seems justified. Over 20 percent of the people questioned responded that they stay off the streets at night, do not speak to strangers, use cars and cabs at night, and would like to move to another neighborhood because of their fear of crime.[9] Victimization studies reveal that many more crimes are experienced than are reported.[10] Furthermore, the young, poor, urban citizens are more likely to be victimized than the older suburbanite.[11] In addition, victimizations appear to be on the increase.[12] Recent uniform crime reports and more sophisticated analyses of crime rates reveal that juvenile crimes also have been on the rise — especially crimes of violence and auto theft.[13] These sobering statistics and public perceptions are of critical importance because the police and the courts do not seem to be able to deal effectively with the problems. The highly touted LEAA Impact Program and juvenile prevention programs have been notable in their lack of effect. Juvenile courts are perceived to be operated by judges in a whimsical fashion where the severity of punishment often does not correspond to the seriousness of the offense.[14]

Problems with juvenile courts have prompted some observers to suggest that adolescent offenses ought to be heard in a family court that would combine juvenile jurisdiction with divorce and custody matters, criminal offenses against family members, and mental illness procedures.[15] Certainly there is a growing consensus to make juveniles more accountable for their behavior and courts more accountable for their programs.[16] The increased emphasis on responsibility is reflected in discussions of community involvement, retribution, determinate sentencing, and deterrence. The impact of tax reduction legislation such as Proposition 13 has made politicians and public programs more accountable for monies spent and services delivered.

Meanwhile, in the legal arena juvenile courts are becoming more due process oriented. Over the eighty-year history of the juvenile courts, the rights of children have suffered while attention was focused on their welfare. The *Kent, Gault, Winship* and *Breed v. Jones* Supreme Court cases reversed this trend by ruling that juveniles have rights to fair hearings, notice, counsel, the privilege against self-incrimination, a beyond-a-reasonable-doubt standard of proof, and protection of the individual from duplicate trials in juvenile and adult courts.[17] Concerns over the legal rights of the child likewise have led to rulings and new statutes that allow the judge less discretion in hearing and sentencing youth. A call for sentences that are proportionate to the offense is heard frequently.

The social and economic environment of the courts is influenced by concerns for labeling,[18] diversion,[19] deinstitutionalization,[20] protection of youth under custody from assault and homosexual rape,[21] community-based rehabilitation programs,[22] family involvement in the case,[23] and confidentiality of court records.[24] Because of well publicized court abuses and a recognition of the limited funds to operate government services, increasing pressures are being exerted by the public and government to make the court more socially and financially accountable for its actions. Groups of court watchers are observing court proceedings, rating judge performance, interesting the press in court policies and offering suggestions for improved performance. Governments are asking the courts to use zero-based budgeting, management by objectives, and more careful accounting procedures to document the cost efficiency of their programs. Program evaluations are more often required. The effect is a more regulated and potentially threatening environment than that which the juvenile courts previously enjoyed.

THE HUMAN SERVICES DELIVERY MODEL
IN THE JUVENILE JUSTICE SYSTEM

The function of the court is influenced by its internal organization and process as well as by its external environment. The child saving movement of the progressive era has grown from small juvenile courts supported by community reformers and philanthropists into massive bureaucracy that regulates the behavior of children who typically belong to the working classes.[25] Today's juvenile court is a human service organization with two goals that reflect its development: the processing of cases and the rehabilitation of youth.[26] There are three large staff groups in the juvenile justice system who work towards these goals: legal professionals such as judges, clerks, prosecutors and attorneys; probation officers and social workers; and bureaucrats who are typically under the control of the judges. Legal professionals generally are concerned with processing cases through the court in an expedient fashion by applying the law to the facts under due process guidelines. Probation officers and social workers are interested principally in rehabilitating or protecting troubled youth. The court management staff assumes the responsibility of assisting the legal and social service professionals to achieve court goals under serious budget restrictions and increasing public scrutiny. All three groups also talk of using the court system to protect society from dangerous juveniles and violent youth from themselves.[27]

The juvenile court is then a complex bureaucracy with multiple goals that are frequently in conflict.[28] The professional groups in the court have somewhat different vested interests in these goals. Furthermore, the roles of the professionals in achieving the goals of the court often become confused. For example, some activist judges actually get involved in setting social policy and administering rehabilitation programs. Attorneys forget their legal advocacy role and are co-opted by the judge or probation staff to cooperate in obtaining services for youngsters. Similarly, probation officers often become so wedded to their case investigations, disposition recommendations, and treatment plans that they apply strong pressures on the judge to make specific decisions. Finally, court administrators enter into the legal and social service arenas of the court by seeking monies for defense counsel, purchase of videotape equipment, computerized information systems or new treatment programs. The multiple goals and role confusion in the juvenile court make evaluations of this human service organization difficult.

The juvenile court bureaucracy is further complicated by the subcontracting of rehabilitation programs for court youth through court and state or county welfare departments to private agencies. There is no one dominant or uniquely successful interorganizational model of youth service delivery. In fact, the forms of these interorganizational relationships differ depending upon whether the services provided are mandated by law, based on a formal agreement, or voluntary.[29] Given the uncertainty of the environment, the strong lobby and public support for youth services, and the vast funding and subsidies to the juvenile justice system over the last ten years,[30] the juvenile courts have responded by decentralizing their delivery of services. This system response is predicted by the resource dependence model of the relationship between organizations and their environments.[31] This form of a political economic argument states that the survival and growth of an organization is contingent on its ability to maintain its domain and acquire ample resources. Although the juvenile court has a well established domain and has been able to generate an abundant supply of resources, it is also a complex, conflictful bureaucracy operating in a stressful and uncertain environment. Resource dependence theorists predict that when services do not come clearly under one authority and are not carefully coordinated, decentralization benefits the dominant organization, in this case, the juvenile court.

Decentralization results in a loose coupling of organizations that cooperate to achieve mutually beneficial goals. This "loose coupling" form of organizational relationships is an "important safety device for organizational survival."[32] Under the loosely coupled interorganizational arrangement, the convulsions or demise of one institution does not predetermine hard times for another because the impact of one organization on another is imperfect and buffered.[33] In this context, the dominant organization can control smaller groups because of its power and resources. The dominant organization frequently becomes a linking pin institution that has extensive and overlapping relationships to different parts of the interorganizational network through which it controls services and products. Aldrich points out three advantages of linking pin organizations: "(1) they serve as communication channels between organizations; (2) they provide general services that link third parties to one another by transferring resources, information and/or clients; and (3) if they are dominant or high status organizations, they serve as models to be imitated" or exercise their power to control the work of others.[34] The juvenile court is the dominant linking pin organization in the juvenile justice system that is loosely coupled to many other agencies and institutions that cooperate in delivering services to youth. The decentralized, loosely coupled structure of the juvenile court fits well with its goals, objectives, structure, resources and environment because it allows the court to control the juvenile justice system, to diffuse accountability, to enhance its autonomy, to utilize community and other institutional resources, and to attempt innovative programs.

THE STRATEGY OF SUBCONTRACTING

Subcontracting is a cooperative organizational strategy that allows the dominant organization to control its work and simultaneously maintain some distance through loosely coupled interorganizational relationships. Subcontracting involves the negotiation of an agreement between two or more organizations to exchange information, goods or services during a specific time period.[35] Under such an arrangement, money may actually be exchanged for services or a particular function or responsibility may be delegated from one agency to another without any transfer of funds. This form of cooperation is particularly effective when the tasks are complex and demanding and the environment is uncertain. The subcontracting strategy multiplies the options, increases flexibility, reduces risk and spreads the accountability for the dominant organization. Thus, for example, the Department of Defense used subcontracting to produce the main battle tank and the National Aeronautics and Space Administration used subcontracting to put a man on the moon.[36] Juvenile courts, given their own brand of complex problems and uncertain environment, employ the subcontracting strategies to process cases legally and to attempt to rehabilitate youth.

An extensive literature review and in-depth interviews with thirty-eight juvenile court administrators from across the United States reveals a broad range of juvenile court subcontracting. In the legal arena, arrangements often are made between the local bar association and the juvenile court to provide voluntary counsel for youth appearing in court. Such a contract saves the court considerable money, elicits support from the public and legal community, and provides representation to eligible juveniles. Elsewhere, judges appoint counsel to represent indigent youth, and the lawyers are compensated through public funds.

Many courts subcontract with the state department of family and children services or a department of youth services for transportation, custody, or incarceration services.[37] Once juveniles receive a disposition of incarceration in a state facility or are placed in the custody of a welfare department, the state agency picks up, transports, and cares for the child until release from the institution or program. Juvenile courts also subcontract with privately owned and operated group homes and private families for child care and rehabilitation services.[38] These homes run the gamut from foster homes for abused children to behavioral modification programs for violent offenders. During this time period, the child is usually a ward of the state under the direct supervision of a subcontracted family or institution.

In small or rural counties, detention and rehabilitation services frequently are shared or subcontracted to larger counties where facilities and staff are underutilized or resources are available. In some instances children are even ordered out of state to residential institutions. For example, until recently some Illinois youth were housed in Texas facilities. High risk or extremely violent offenders often are transferred over to adult jurisdictions and institutions where they are treated more as adults in secure correctional environments. While most laws require that they be separated from and treated differently than adults, these youth sometimes end up incarcerated with adults where they can be assaulted and abused.[39]

Diversion programs also can be planned and funded through the juvenile court but subcontracted to police departments, schools, private agencies or community groups. There is a movement in the juvenile justice system to take traffic cases and status offenders out of the juvenile court. In some locales status offenders are immediately referred to the welfare department and traffic offenders to the county traffic court; other jurisdictions handle all these cases internally in the juvenile court. Some courts even subcontract status offender cases to other institutions, agencies, or volunteer homes; thus, although nominally responsible, the court does not have to process the case directly.[40]

Volunteer probation is another area in which traditionally operated court services are subcontracted to a community group. A University of Michigan study shows that these programs have had differential effects; some have had deleterious consequences on recidivism and self-image, while others have been shown to be as effective as traditional probation programs.[41] A positive aspect of these programs is that they do involve the community and save the court considerable cost. Overnight shelter care is another service that frequently is subcontracted or occasionally operated through volunteer programs.

Juvenile courts have traditionally subcontracted psychological evaluations, psychiatric counseling, alcohol and drug treatment, health care, pregnancy counseling, and school programs. Sometimes these services are performed at the juvenile court by public or private professionals; in other instances the youth receive these services at separate facilities. Finally, juvenile courts are increasingly beginning to subcontract institutional functions such as accounting and information services, research and computer work, food and janitorial services.

REASONS FOR SUBCONTRACTING

Massachusetts was the first state to undertake a massive deinstitutionalization program designed to remove youth from dehumanizing institutions.[42] This program was praised by national leaders as being exemplary and innovative. The horrors and injustice of juvenile confinement were highlighted by Bartollas, Miller, and Dinitz's book on juvenile victimization,[43] and by the National Council on Crime and Delinquency which estimates that of the 100,000 youth held in correctional institutions by juvenile courts in 1975, 23 percent of the boys and 70 percent of the girls were status offenders.[44] Severity of punishment seemed inversely related to seriousness of offense. Jerome Miller, architect of the Massachusetts deinstitutionalization program, has been lauded for being one of the innovators in correcting these injustices. When he was asked about the advantages of deinstitutionalization and subcontracting of youth services to community based group homes, he responded that in addition to the justice done, the subcontracting strategy is useful because: "It is a lot easier to get rid of an unsatisfactory program which is on a service contract to the state than it is to phase out a budgeted state program."[45]

The subcontracting of services is a particularly useful strategy in a turbulent environment because it also allows full utilization of specialized work groups. As Terreberry has suggested, the organizations that are most apt to survive in an uncertain and changing environment are those that decentralize and make use of small, specialized, functional units.[46] Small focused programs permit the organization to be problem specific and adaptable. For example, through subcontracting the juvenile court is able to encourage delinquency prevention programs and place youth in specially designed group homes and schools.

An additional benefit of subcontracting by juvenile courts or departments of youth services is that youth services can be conducted in a cooperative, businesslike manner that closely approximates the free enterprise system.[47] The contracting parties are more visibly accountable for their services; if they do not fulfill their contracts, they are subject to economic sanction or loss of future contracts. On the other hand, this strategy benefits the court because it diffuses responsibility from one institution to many; the subcontractors are held tightly accountable, while the juvenile court is less directly responsible for services provided. The court is in the position of the controlling, linking pin organization purchasing services from a variety of competitive subcontractors. This can be called a behavioral distancing of accountability.

Because of the subcontracting strategy, the court is better able to utilize soft money funding. By generating grant monies from the federal and state governments, private foundations, and community groups, the court is able to hire specialized staff for short periods of time to undertake experimental, innovative programs. When the grant runs out, the court may choose to put the program on its hard-line budget, subcontract to a similar independent group, or allow the program to lapse. In any event, the court does not have the same personnel problems that it might if it hired the staff on its hard-line budget. Numerous court administrators have said that subcontracting services frequently is more cost efficient than directly providing services, since the strategy creates competition in the area of service delivery.

The subcontracting model permits judges to maintain control over the work of the court, and at the same time introduces cost efficiencies, treatment alternatives, management flexibility, innovation mechanisms, and decreased personal accountability.

ORGANIZATIONAL AND ENVIRONMENTAL EFFECTS OF SUBCONTRACTING

Although the subcontracting organizational strategy has many beneficial consequences, it also has some ominous implications. Horowitz, Empey, and Rubin demonstrate how juvenile courts increasingly are becoming courts of law concerned with due process and protection of the legal rights of the child.[48] While these efforts to forestall capricious treatment of youth in the juvenile justice system are laudable, less attention has been focused on the juvenile court judge, the critical decision maker whose authority shapes the direction and policy of the court. Extensive observation of American courts led Silberman to declare: "As we have seen, criminal courts do an effective job of separating the 'garbage' cases from the 'real crimes,' so that resources can be concentrated on the latter. The opposite is true of juvenile courts . . . For the most part, sentences bear little or no relation to the seriousness of the offense or to the offender's culpability. In 'juvie' court, unlike criminal court, sentences really *are* arbitrary . . . "[49] The present structure of the juvenile court system and the enactment of subcontracting strategies reinforce the judge's position of social control and extend his power beyond the courthouse to social service agencies and even to some for-profit businesses. Justice William O. Douglas was concerned with the juvenile court judge's self-perceived role and authority when he described his conversation with a well-known juvenile judge: "I, the judge, and the bailiff and the other court attendants are like those on a hospital staff, dressed in white. We are doctors, nurses, orderlies. We are not to administer a law in the normal meaning of criminal law. We are there to diagnose, investigate, counsel and advise. We are specialists in search of ways and means to correct conduct and help reorient wayward youngsters to a life cognizant of responsibilities to the community."[50] The juvenile court judge is a powerful agent of social control who uses his authority to set social policy both in the court and in service institutions.[51] Most juvenile court judges enjoy the full exercise of this influence.

From the perspective of the judge and the juvenile court, the organizational strategy of subcontracting services is highly desirable because it further establishes the court as a powerful, linking pin, coordinating agency in the community. The judge is the critical decision maker and source of power. Thus, the subcontracting strategy enhances the prestige and authority of the legal profession, consolidates power in the juvenile court, and provides both the judge and the court with adaptive techniques and programs to maintain the strong court position in a threatening and ambiguous environment. This particular strategy makes theoretical sense and seems quite functional in the everyday operational world.

However, the consequences of vesting relatively unchecked power in a single professional decision maker in a resource rich, authoritative institution may be significant. The judge, as a social control agent, can misuse his available power. For example, in several communities, a judge's support for youth placements in a particular costly private residential facility was at variance with professional staff criticism of this agency and their reluctance to use its services. Reaction to this practice has been expressed recently. Judicial orders that executive agencies place court youth in expensive, out of state placements have been vetoed on appeal.[52] "Therapeutic detention" is another practice that demonstrates potential judicial abuse of professional discretion. This practice allows the judge to incarcerate youth in 'his own jail' for punishment purposes without having to sentence them formally to a state correctional institution. As Van Maanen observes, "much of the control over individual behavior in organizations is a direct result of the manner in which people are processed."[53] Judges direct the socialization of those youths who contact the juvenile justice system by controlling the people processing functions of the court and the dispositional hearings. Critics contend that many judges actually manufacture delinquency by inappropriately processing cases. For example, Silberman points out how status offenders are often processed and incarcerated while serious delinquent offenders are not detained.[54] Contact with the police, court and correctional institutions has many deleterious effects. Youth who contact the court because of status offenses are locked up with delinquents who teach them how to behave as delinquents. Those who spend time in juvenile correctional facilities are likely to be labeled, victimized, sexually assaulted, and suffer loss of self-esteem, and often must join gangs for protection.[55]

Certainly, these results are not what the advocates of rehabilitation had in mind.

Highly touted diversion and deinstitutionalization programs similarly have their problems as implemented by many juvenile courts. After an extensive analysis, Platt asserts that "efforts to divert minor offenders from the stigmatizing influence of the juvenile court and into local service agencies have apparently served either to reinforce existing programs or expand state surveillance and control."[56] A national study of diversion shows that it is likely that contact with a "softer" diversion program has many of the same harmful effects as formal treatment by the court.[57] Cressey and McDermott even go so far as to question whether programs have been changed while consequences to youth remain the same: "The faddish nature of diversion has produced a proliferation of diversion units and programs without generating a close look at whether the juvenile subject to all this attention is receiving a better deal. It is quite possible that participating personnel have revamped terminology and procedures without seriously altering what happens to the juvenile."[58]

There have even been accusations that the juvenile court has been and remains offense-, race-, sex- and class-biased. Judges and court administrators tend to come from middle and upper middle classes. A common referral to the juvenile court is the black, male, urban working class youth who is overrepresented in the juvenile justice system.[59] Some maintain that the system is equitable because black male, inner city juveniles proportionately commit more crimes than other youth. However, the self-report and victimization evidence does not substantiate this charge.[60] Platt contends that: "It is impossible to conceive of the juvenile court system as an agency of 'rehabilitation' and social equality in a society where most working class and minority youths are tracked into deadend or low wage jobs, where institutional racism and sexism systematically segment people into antagonistic social relations, and where the criminal justice system is blatantly used to undermine and repress progressive political movements."[61]

Even if these conditions are somewhat overstated, the fact remains that the current organization of the juvenile court system maintains the status quo with the judge in strong control of a resourceful, linking pin institution. The judge and the court are able to exercise tremendous power and control over human service agencies through referral power.[62] The judge is able to determine through dispositions and court orders who must receive treatment, the type and duration of the treatment, and what agency will provide the care. This is another instance in which professionals exercise monopolistic control over human service delivery systems in a fashion that may not be beneficial either to the youth or the community.

JUDICIAL ACCOUNTABILITY AND PROGRAM EVALUATION UNDER SUBCONTRACTING

A major problem with the present organization of the juvenile justice system combining a powerful judge and subcontracting strategy is that it is difficult to assign accountability. After judges assign a case to a particular disposition, they frequently do not receive any feedback on the case status unless the individual is released and becomes a recidivist in the same jurisdiction. If a delinquent becomes hardened, recidivistic, and commits more serious offenses, it is difficult to know whom or what program to blame. However, each part of the system eagerly takes credit for successful cases, general declines in recidivism and decreases in offense statistics. As a consequence, the system is difficult to monitor or evaluate.

The juvenile justice system is not well coordinated. The judge issues orders and subcontracts services but does not have effective management mechanisms for holding others accountable for their work or program outcomes. Likewise, it is difficult to hold judges accountable for their decisions. This lack of accountability reinforces the status quo and preserves judicial power. The judge can always discount mistakes by the subcontractors, stop the contracts, and try new providers. Juvenile justice system contracts frequently are poorly managed; there is little feedback, and court executives are just beginning to receive formal management training. Zero-based budgeting, management by objectives [MBO], program evaluation review technique [PERT], and behavioral accounting systems are being introduced in some courts but are rarely employed with the subcontractors.

The Institute of Judicial Administration-American Bar Association Juvenile Justice Standards Project was aware of the need for coordination and case follow-up in the justice system to provide continuity and protect the individual from abuses. Standards for the prosecution read "while the safety and welfare of the community is their paramount concern, juvenile prosecutors should consider alternative modes of disposition which more closely satisfy the interests and needs of the youth without jeopardizing that concern."[63] Discontinuity and poor supervision in the system is evidenced by the admonition, "Juvenile prosecutors should undertake their own periodic evaluation of the success of particular dispositional programs that are used in their jurisdiction, from the standpoint of the interests of both the state and the juvenile."[64] Defense counsel receive similar advice to follow the client after disposition: "The lawyer's responsibility to the client does not necessarily end with dismissal of the charges or entry of a final dispositional order . . . If the client has been found to be within the juvenile court's jurisdiction the lawyer should maintain contact with both the client and the agency or institution involved in the disposition plan in order to insure that the client's rights are respected and, where necessary, to counsel the client and the client's family concerning the disposition plan."[65] While these are heartening standards, they are ideal guidelines and do not reflect the actual operation of the uncoordinated system. More formal checks and balances are required to control the power of judges and the court.

SUMMARY AND CONCLUSION

This paper has analyzed the subcontracting of services by juvenile courts as an organizational strategy designed to preserve the power and domain of the court in an uncertain and stressful environment. The judge as the key decision maker in the court is able to acquire resources for the court and control the delivery of most youth oriented human services by striking cooperative subcontracts with many other organizations and agencies. Subcontracting is a marvelously adaptive strategy for a powerful, complex organization functioning in an ambiguous, changing environment. Although the strategy consolidates the resources and control of the court, it has both positive and negative consequences. A useful strategy for the juvenile court and the judges, it requires operational checks and the infusion of accountability to protect the welfare of the juvenile.

Further research and analysis of subcontracting in the juvenile court could take numerous perspectives. The most popular approach to the study of juvenile court management is that of scientific management originating with the work of Frederick Taylor.[66] This model focuses on management techniques for improving organizational productivity. In this context, the task force of the National Conference on Social Welfare proposed the following principles, summarized by Sarri and Hasenfeld, for delivering more effective services to clients:

1. Clearly articulated and operational goals based on valid data, staff participation, and client needs.
2. Enforcement of worker accountability for achieving results, not merely performing activities.
3. Facilitation of staff behavior and implementation activities which involves discretion and flexibility in means to achieve results.
4. Implementation of objective methods of evaluation linked to goals, with rewards to staff and clients for successful output.
5. Securing of necessary resources for ongoing activities and also for innovations and experimentation.
6. Facilitation of personal and professional growth in staff, including career development for new managers.
7. Simplification of bureaucratic procedures and reduction of paper work.
8. Developing ongoing problem solving and change mechanisms.
9. Goal oriented case management as a basic strategy of programming for workers.
10. Creation of ongoing mechanisms for effecting sound interorganizational relationships.[67]

This model of scientific management is reflected in the court literature and in the educational and training programs for court administrators across the country.

While this is a good beginning, a major assumption of this paper has been that scientific management does not adequately address the theoretical issues in court organization nor can it alone, as a set of techniques, drastically improve service delivery. Juvenile courts are organizations with peculiar histories, resources, and domains that function in a larger social system. The goals and service delivery of the court are shaped by the internal and external environments of the institution. The interest groups that control the court's resources, goals and functions determine, or at least modify, the manner in which services are delivered. A fuller understanding of court organization and operation must take into account the specific social, economic, and political environments of the juvenile courts in order to make the strategies enacted by the court effective.

NOTES

1. Community Action Program Guide, Vol. 1, Instructions for Applicants (Washington, D.C.: Office of Economic Opportunity, February 1965).

2. Kenneth R. Wedel, "Government Contracting for Purchase of Service," *Social Work* (March 1976), pp. 101–105. Title XX is social security legislation to provide social services through welfare.

3. Paul H. O'Neill, "How Government Makes Its Living, *Commonsense* 1 (Fall 1978), pp. 27-36.

4. Nathan Glazer, "Should Judges Administer Social Services?", *The Public Interest* 50 (Winter 1978), pp. 64–80.

5. Charles E. Silberman, *Criminal Violence, Criminal Justice* (New York: Random House, 1978), pp. 309–370.

6. Donald L. Horowitz, *The Courts and Social Policy* (Washington, D.C.: Brookings Institution, 1977), pp. 177–219.

7. Howard E. Aldrich and Jeffrey Pfeffer, "Environments of Organizations," *Annual Review of Sociology* 2 (1976), pp. 79–105.

8. Donald T. Campbell, "Variation and Selective Retention in Socio-Cultural Evolution," in H.R. Barringer, G.I. Blansten and R.W. Mack (eds.) *Social Change in Developing Areas: A Reinterpretation of Evolutionary Theory* (Cambridge, Mass.: Schenkman, 1965), pp. 19–48. Michael T. Hannan and John H. Freeman, "The Population Ecology of Organizations," *American Journal of Sociology* 82 (March 1977), pp. 929–964.

9. President's Commission on Law Enforcement and Administration of Justice, *The Challenge of Crime in a Free Society* (Washington, D.C.: Government Printing Office, 1967).

10. Criminal Victimization in the United States, 1973, Advance Report May 1 (Washington, D.C.: Law Enforcement Assistance Administration, 1975).

11. Criminal Victimization in the United States: A Comparison of 1973 and 1974 Findings (Washington, D.C.: Law Enforcement Assistance Administration, 1976).

12. Criminal Victimization Surveys in the Nation's Five Largest Cities (Washington, D.C.: Government Printing Office, 1975).

13. Federal Bureau of Investigation Uniform Crime Reports for the United States, 1973 (Washington, D.C.: Government Printing Office, 1974).

14. Silberman, op. cit.

15. H. Ted Rubin, *The Courts: Fulcrum of the Justice System* (Pacific Palisades, Cal.: Goodyear Publishing Co., 1976), p. 99.

16. Raymond A. Bauer and Dan H. Fenn, Jr., *The Corporate Social Audit* (New York: Russell Sage, 1972).

17. LaMar Empey, *American Delinquency: Its Meaning and Construction,* (Homewood, Illinois: The Dorsey Press, 1978), pp. 462–465; Rubin, op. cit., pp. 82–84; Horowitz, op. cit.

18. Gary L. Albrecht and Maryann H. Albrecht, "A Critical Assessment of Labeling in the Juvenile Justice System," *The Justice System Journal* 4, (Fall 1978), pp. 114–129.

19. Edwin M. Lemert, *Instead of Court: Diversion in Juvenile Justice* (Rockville, Md.: National Institute of Mental Health, 1971).

20. Yitzhak Bakal (ed.), *Closing Correctional Institutions* (Lexington, Mass.: Lexington Books, 1973).

21. Clemens Bartollas, Stuart J. Miller and Simon Dinitz, *Juvenile Victimization: The Institutional Paradox* (New York: John Wiley and Sons, 1976).

22. Paul Lerman, *Community Treatment and Social Control: A Critical Analysis of Juvenile Correction Policy* (Chicago: University of Chicago Press, 1975).

23. Rubin, op. cit., p. 99.

24. Michael Altman, "Juvenile Information Systems: A Comparative Analysis" in Lawrence Boxerman (ed.), *Computer Applications in the Juvenile Justice System* (Reno: National Council of Juvenile Court Judges, 1974).

25. Allan Nevins and Henry Steele Commager, *A Pocket History of the United States,* 6th ed. (New York: Pocket Books, 1976), pp. 336–356. Anthony M. Platt, *The Childsavers: The Invention of Delinquency,* 2nd ed., (Chicago: University of Chicago Press, 1977), pp. 183–192.

26. Rosemary Sarri and Yeheskel Hasenfeld (eds.), *Brought to Justice? Juveniles, the Courts, and the Law.* (Ann Arbor, Mich.: National Assessment of Juvenile Corrections, 1976).

27. Walter I. Trattner, *From Poor Law to Welfare State: A History of Social Welfare in America,* 2nd ed., (New York: Free Press, 1979).

28. Gary L. Albrecht, "Defusing Technological Change in Juvenile Courts: The Probation Officer's Struggle for Professional Autonomy," *Sociology of Work and Occupations* 6 (1979), pp. 283–311. Yeheskel Hasenfeld, "People Processing Organizations: An Exchange Approach," *American Sociological Review* 37 (1972), pp. 256–263.

29. Richard H. Hall, John P. Clark, Peggy C. Giodano, Paul V. Johnson, and Martha Van Roekel, "Patterns of Interorganizational Relationships," *Administrative Science Quarterly* 22 (September 1977), pp. 457–474.

30. Anthony M. Platt, op. cit.

31. Jeffrey Pfeffer and Gerald R. Salancik, *The External Control of Organizations: A Resource Dependence Perspective·*(New York: Harper Row, 1978).

32. Ibid., p. 13.

33. Karl E. Weick, "Educational Organizations as Loosely Coupled Systems," *Administrative Science Quarterly* 21, pp. 1–19.

34. Howard Aldrich, "Centralization versus Decentralization in the Design of Human Service Delivery Systems: A Response to Gouldner's Lament," in Rosemary C. Sarri and Yeheskel Hasenfeld (eds.) *The Management of Human Services* (New York: Columbia University Press, 1978), pp. 51—79.

35. Jay R. Galbraith, *Organizational Design* (Reading, Mass.: Addison Wesley), pp. 211–214.

36. Raymond G. Hunt and Gregory W. Hunt, "Some Structural Features of Relations Between the Department of Defense, The National Aeronautics and Space Administration, and Their Principal Contractors," *Social Forces* 49 (March 1971), pp. 414–431.

37. For example, see Bakal, op. cit. and government documents from DHEW.

38. Bakal, op. cit.

39. Silberman, op. cit.

40. Jane C. Latina and Jeffrey L. Schembera, "Volunteer Homes for Status Offenders: An Alternative to Detention," *Federal Probation* (December 1976), pp. 45-49.

41. Robert J. Berger, Joan E. Crowley, Martin Gold and John Gray, *Experiment in a Juvenile Court: A Study of a Program of Volunteers Working with Juvenile Probationers* (Ann Arbor, Mich.: Institute for Social Research, University of Michigan, 1975).

42. Bakal, op. cit., and Robert B. Coates and Alden D. Miller, "Neutralizing Community Resistance to Group Homes," in Lloyd E. Ohlin, Alden D. Miller and Robert B. Coates (eds.) *Juvenile Correctional Reform in Massachusetts* (Washington, D.C.: Government Printing Office, 1977), pp. 81–91.

43. Bartollas, Miller and Dinitz, op. cit.

44. Latina and Schembera, op. cit.

45. U.S. Department of Justice, *The Serious Juvenile Offender* (Washington, D.C.: Government Printing Office, 1978), p. 58.

46. S. Terreberry, "The Evolution of Organizational Environments." *Administrative Science Quarterly* 1968, 12: 590–613.

47. Norman V. Lourie, "Public-voluntary Agency Relationships in the 70's," *Child Welfare* 49 (July 1970): 376–378.

48. Horowitz, op. cit.; Empey, op. cit.; Rubin, op. cit.

49. Silberman, op. cit., pp. 311–312.

50. William O. Douglas, Foreword in Edward Wakin, *Children Without Justice: A Report by the National Council of Jewish Women* (New York: National Council of Jewish Women, Inc.), 1975, p. V.

51. Glazer, op. cit.

52. See State in re D.F., 367 A. 2nd 1198 (N.J. Super. 1976); In re Doe, 390 A. 2nd 390 (R.I. 1978).

53. John Van Maanen, "People Processing: Strategies of Organizational Socialization," *Organizational Dynamics* (Summer 1978), p. 35.

54. Silberman, op. cit.

55. Bartollas, Miller and Dinitz, op. cit.

56. Platt, op. cit., p. 189.

57. Andrew Rutherford and Robert McDermott, *Juvenile Diversion* (Washington, D.C.: Government Printing Office, 1976).

58. Donald R. Cressey and Robert A. McDermott, *Diversion from the Juvenile Justice System* (Ann Arbor, Michigan: National Assessment of Juvenile Corrections, 1973), p. 59.

59. Empey, op. cit., pp. 440–483.

60. Empey, op. cit.; Albrecht and Albrecht, op. cit.

61. Platt, op. cit., p. 192.

62. Arlene Kaplan Daniels, "Advisory and Coercive Functions in Psychiatry," *Sociology of Work and Occupations* 2, pp. 55–78.

63. Institute of Judicial Administration-American Bar Association Juvenile Justice Standards Project, *Standards Relating to Prosecution,* (Cambridge, Mass.: Ballinger, 1977), p. 78.

64. Ibid., p. 80.

65. Institute of Judicial Administration-American Bar Association Juvenile Justice Standards Project, *Standards Relating to Counsel for Private Parties* (Cambridge, Mass.: Ballinger, 1977), pp. 187–188.

66. Frederick W. Taylor, "What is Scientific Management?" in Michael T. Matteson and John M. Ivancevich (eds.), *Management Classics* (Santa Monica, Cal.: Goodyear, 1977), pp. 5–8.

67. Rosemary C. Sarri and Yeheskel Hasenfeld (eds.), *The Management of Human Services* (New York: Columbia University Press, 1978), pp. 10–11.

26 *The Issue of Security in a Community-Based Juvenile Corrections System: the Final Report of the Task Force on Secure Facilities*

INTRODUCTION

For the past eight years, the Commonwealth has been engaged in a dramatic experimental approach to juvenile corrections which is unique in this country. The traditional state institutional system, dominated by large, centrally administered youth facilities, has been dismantled. In its place, the Department of Youth Services (DYS) administers a regional, community-based program network consisting of a broad and diverse range of placement and open setting options, the vast majority of which are privately run. This comprehensive reform effort is now being challenged by a renewed concern focused on, and symbolized by, the issue of security. Can the community-based system accommodate effectively the public's right to protection from demonstrably serious and dangerous juvenile offenders *and,* at the same time, provide humane care and treatment geared to the individualized needs of youth? This controversy and the administrative problems which attend any major systemic change threaten the form and substance of the community-based reform approach.

From *The Issue of Security in a Community-Based System of Juvenile Corrections,* The Final Report of the Task Force on Secure Facilities to Commissioner John A. Calhoun, Commonwealth of Massachusetts, Department of Youth Services, November, 1977, pp. 1-11. Reprinted by permission.

The Task Force on Secure Facilities was appointed in this context in April, 1976, by the then new Commissioner of DYS to serve as an independent advisor on the problems and issue of security. The Task Force was composed of individuals representing a broad spectrum of interests and perspectives. All members had substantial experience and recognized expertise in the field of juvenile justice. The Task Force process was designed to draw upon the backgrounds and observations of this group and to provide practical and meaningful assistance to the Commissioner.

This Report is the product of that process and the consensus which emerged in the course of a fourteen-month review. It represents the collective wisdom and best judgment of the Task Force on the problems and issues which must be addressed in connection with security. It is a measured, comprehensive response to this important but highly politicized subject.[1]

The Report has two dominant themes. First, the issue of security is not merely a matter of numbers. Like the underlying problem of juvenile violence, the issue of security is complex and multifaceted; neither can be addressed responsibly in a vacuum nor are there simple solutions or panaceas. Security must be addressed comprehensively in a context which recognizes the integral relationship of articulated principles and objectives, administrative reform, the nature, content and quality of secure programs, and a viable network of nonsecure program alternatives, to effective public protection. Second, the community-based system is a viable approach to juvenile corrections which can uniquely balance, accommodate and moderate the competing concerns about, and inherent tensions between, public protection and individualized care and treatment. The reforms that are needed can and should be effected within the existing structure. However, prompt action by all concerned is required to implement these reforms.

The Task Force recognizes clearly that the issue of security and the problems involved in addressing it are of long standing, are not unique to this jurisdiction, and are not solely the responsibility of DYS. In the past year, DYS has made real progress and should be allowed additional time to effect the remedies. The case should be continued for one more year. The best advice the Task Force can offer the Commissioner is that, thereafter, there can be "no more continuances." If substantial progress is not made, regardless of the reason, the justification for the approach advocated by the Task Force will inevitably be weakened and may give way to more drastic and less desirable alternatives. . . .

SUMMARY OF MAJOR RECOMMENDATIONS, THEMES AND CONCLUSIONS

This section summarizes many of the key aspects of the *Final Report* of the Task Force. It is primarily a guide to, not a comprehensive review of, the approximately one hundred pages. . .

General Overview

The Task Force recommendations are designed to implement the following general conclusions:

• The Commonwealth's commitment to the deinstitutionalized, community-based approach to juvenile corrections should be preserved and strengthened. A viable balance can be maintained in the existing system between the need for security for purposes of public protection and the needs of youth for individualized care and treatment.

• The vast majority of DYS youth can be effectively and appropriately placed in the broad and diverse range of nonsecure community-based settings and alternatives without detriment to public protection. However, while the number is clearly limited, a small percentage of DYS youth do need secure placements of some kind for some period of time for purposes of public protection. To meet this need, an increased emphasis on security by DYS is required.

• An increased emphasis on security which focuses primarily on the number of secure placements is inappropriate and may well be counterproductive. Therefore, the Task Force recommended a multipronged approach which conditioned an increase in the number of secure placements on administrative reform, the availability of a range of quality secure programs, and significant increases in the resources available for nonsecure program alternatives.

• Secure and nonsecure programs are integrally and inextricably linked in terms of success, effectiveness and quality. The need for a secure placement often results from the absence or inadequacy in the past of other alternatives which are less costly in human and fiscal terms and have greater potential for success. Increases in secure programs at the expense, or in the absence, of a concomitant development and expansion of nonsecure programs will be detrimental both to public protection and to the needs of most DYS youth.

DYS Administrative Reform

The *Preliminary Report* (July, 1976) focused on administrative reform as the most critical immediate need in addressing the issue of security. More than seventy changes were recommended. Since then, DYS has begun to implement many of the recommendations and must continue to give priority to these reforms. Some of the key ones are noted here and in *SECURE PROGRAMS* below.

• Organizational and managerial changes, and articulation of the framework and principles for the administration of security, to permit positive problem solving instead of crisis management.

• The development and application of minimum standards and uniform policies and procedures.

• A dramatic upgrading of the intake, assessment, placement and review processes to ensure effective and appropriate placements of youth.

• The implementation of a reliable system of data gathering, monitoring, evaluation and quality control in the interest of accountability and effective planning.

• Effective personnel recruitment, selection, training, supervision and performance review programs and policies.

Secure Programs

Secure programs in the community-based system have the dual purposes of public protection and quality care, both geared to the individualized needs of youth. The

Task Force identified the elements which are critical to the achievement of these objectives.

• The intake criteria must be clearly delineated. The eligibility of a youth for a secure placement should be determined by demonstrable, objective criteria which relate directly to public protection concerns. All youths who meet these criteria may not need secure placements; however, a secure placement is not appropriate unless these criteria are met.

• No one level or type of placement is appropriate or necessary for all youths in need of security. Security can generally be provided without a primary reliance on traditional high-level security designs. Therefore, there should be a gradated range of secure placements which includes a variety of levels and types of programs.

• Individualized plans and goals for services and care must exist for each youth placed in a secure program and effective aftercare planning and community reintegration services must be provided.

• The quality of the secure programs is the single most important factor. The essential ingredients for quality programs, consistent with public protection, reasonable costs, and decent, humane care, are the following:

- An adequate number of trained and qualified staff is required to address constructively the needs of the most difficult youth in noninstitutional settings. Staff/youth ratios should range from 1 1/2-to-1 to an optimum of 2-to-1.
- Youth populations in each program must be small in number. Large populations in secure settings inevitably result in the "warehousing" of youth, a primary reliance on traditional, dehumanizing custodial control, excessive costs, and do not necessarily enhance physical security. To avoid these negative effects and to achieve positive results, the population size should be limited to twelve to fifteen youths.
- Minimum standards for program content and quality control methods must be established and applied by DYS to every program.
- The program facilities must afford a decent, humane living environment. This requires adequate interior and exterior space and the maintenance of a low profile security design. Security is primarily a function of program size, staff and content, not the physical character of the facility.

The Number of Secure Placements

In the *Preliminary Report* the Task Force concluded that even though only a small percentage and a limited number of youth needed secure placements, there was a need for an increase. However, there was no rational or responsible basis for quantifying this need. Therefore, the Task Force undertook an independent study — the first objective examination of the controversial subject of the secure placement needs of DYS.

• The study, based on a 10 percent sample of DYS youths, was designed to establish the *presumptive eligibility* of a youth for a secure placement, using only public protection criteria, i.e. offenses involving violence toward others and/or a pattern of other serious offenses. The study also included a determination in each case of the level and type of security required.

• The Task Force concluded that the vast majority of DYS youth (88.7 percent) were *not* even presumptively eligible for secure placements. *Secure treatment* placements were needed for a maximum of 11.2 percent of DYS youths. Since DYS had secure placements for only 3 percent of its youths (49), increases were needed.

• In terms of numbers, depending upon the DYS population, a maximum of 129 to 168 secure treatment placements are needed for DYS youth, but 25 percent of them should be in Department of Mental Health secure programs. DYS itself needs to provide only 100 to 130. Of this number, approximately 40 percent (46 to 60) only need a "light" level of security for public protection purposes, and the majority of the new placements should be of this type. DYS is now meeting most of the need for youths requiring a "heavy" level of security.

• DYS now has 114 *secure detention* placements. That number is clearly adequate and should not be increased. Any need in this area can be met by reforms of the intake/placement process to ensure appropriate uses of these placements and to limit the duration of a detention placement. The majority of youths in secure detention are there only because of the lack of other secure or nonsecure alternatives.

• The Task Force "numbers" are not targets. They represent the maximum, or outer limit, of the secure placement needs of DYS. In a viable and effective system, the number of secure placements actually needed should be lower, since the study did not consider whether an appropriate nonsecure placement, based on comprehensive case-by-case assessments, could be made without detriment to public protection. Such considerations are highly relevant to actual placement decisions.

Budgetary Impact of Security

The reforms recommended by the Task Force will require budget increases because security is an expensive proposition in any system and DYS has been significantly underfunded in the past. The Task Force analyzed the DYS budget for Fiscal Year 1977 and the 1978 appropriation. It estimated the maximum amount of increased funding DYS needed to address security effectively, identified the specific areas where the increases were needed, and recommended guidelines, conditions and alternatives to ensure the most efficient use of these funds. Some of the salient features of the budget review included:

• Secure programs are far more expensive than any other DYS program level or type. Secure programs in the institutions and those which are predominantly "state run" have the highest average costs, even with larger populations. In general, purchase-of-service and nonsecure programs are significantly more economical.

• Even with limited resources, DYS has been according priority in funding to secure programs. In Fiscal Year 1977, DYS devoted 25-30 percent of its program resources to secure detention and treatment placements for 12.5 percent of the DYS youth population.

• The 1978 DYS appropriation dramatically increased the amount and percentage of funds for security. Of the $2.5 million increase from 1977 ($15.9 million to $18.4 million), 92 percent was for security. As a result of this increase, 35 percent of

·the program resources of DYS will be devoted to security. This should be the maximum percentage.

• Nonsecure program funds continued to decrease as a percentage of the budget; even though they are far more economical and provide appropriate services to the vast majority of DYS youth. To preserve a viable program balance in the community-based system, the 65 percent allocation to this area should be the minimum.

• Throughout the Report, the Task Force specifically conditions its recommendation for an increased emphasis on security on (a) administrative reform, (b) quality programs and (c) a proportionate emphasis on nonsecure programs. While the 1978 appropriation will permit DYS to increase its secure placements to the *number* recommended, it does not permit DYS to do that *and* comply with the conditions the Task Force deemed critical to an effective and economical approach to security. The unmet needs include adequate preplacement, "light" secure and aftercare programs; increases in the average cost of secure programs necessary to meet the recommended quality standards; and funding increases for nonsecure programs. Therefore, to address security effectively, DYS should have a budget of $22.5 million, an increase of $4.1 million.

• A corollary to the maximum flexibility DYS must have in resource allocations to administer the community-based system is the need for clear accountability. The present DYS budget is a maze which deters independent analysis; yet it is required by the appropriations process and is not subject to remedy by DYS alone. However, DYS should supplement its budget submissions with a clear, comprehensive budget overview.

The Responsibilities of Others

In reviewing the problems and issues of security in DYS, the Task Force repeatedly encountered problem areas which either cannot be remedied by DYS alone or for which it may not have the primary remedial responsibility.

• In addressing those problem areas, DYS is entitled to the support and assistance of a variety of state agencies and officials, including the governor, the legislature and the judiciary.

• The Report identifies the areas where action by others is both feasible and necessary and sets forth a recommended agenda for each one, consistent with their respective roles and responsibilities. Their response may well bear on the capacity of DYS to meet its obligations to youth and the public.

Implementation of the Report

The Report sets forth a comprehensive agenda for change which can be substantially implemented within one year. The responsibility must be affixed to individuals in specific positions, rather than to corporate entities, if that goal is to be met.

• The primary and final responsibility must rest with the *Commissioner of DYS*.

• *The Secretary of Human Services* must assume the critical, secondary responsibilities for general oversight of DYS and facilitating interagency coordination.

• The *Chairman of the DYS Advisory Committee* must ensure that that group performs the role of the Task Force on an on-going basis, that of a reasonably independent ally and advisor and a constructive critic.

NOTES

1. In July, 1976, the Task Force issued a thirty-five page *Preliminary Report* which was the product of an intensive three-month effort to arrive at conclusions and offer advice to the Commissioner at the earliest possible time. The primary focus was on the administration by DYS of its secure system. The Task Force recommended more than seventy reforms as preconditions for DYS to address the issue of security effectively. . . .

Epilogue

Juveniles continue to commit countless offenses, ranging from murder to petty theft and runaway. The public is tired of crime, both personal victimization and the fear of crime, and wants something done about it regardless of the age of the offender. While resolution of the crime problem awaits some unclear change in the structure and values of our society, and to some degree the anticipated demographic trend which shortly will provide a lowered rate of young persons in the most crime-prone ages, important changes are occurring in the juvenile justice world.

A punishment response has become more acceptable and juvenile court sanctions are increasingly related to the offense rather than the offender. It is not that a rehabilitation rationale is being discarded. Though research evaluations of rehabilitation programs have not been encouraging, rehabilitation efforts are continuing with lesser offenders, as an add-on to court ordered punishment stratagems, and in our institutions. Observers have suggested that punishment can be rehabilitative, and may be a deterrent against criminal activity for the punished offender and others who are aware of a court's use 'of more punitive sanctions. These observers and others, however, are concerned that a broad brush approach to punishment will capture in its net many youngsters who do not require severe sanctions, and that the open acknowledgement of a punishment purpose for the court will, in part, further dehumanize the programs and facilities erected to service and care for these youths.

The punishment direction is not universal. Many states and communities still emphasize the best interests of the child more than public protection, and continue to diagnose why youngsters "went wrong" and to prescribe individualized remedies aimed at enhancing improved future adjustment.

The new punishment approach is taking a variety of forms, among them: laws directing judges to sentence youths based on their age, present offense seriousness, and prior criminal history; direct criminal filings for certain offenses committed by juveniles above a specified age; easing the criteria for transferring youths from juvenile to criminal court jurisdiction; mandatory institutional sentences under specified conditions; mandatory minimum institutional stays; judges more readily institutionalizing delinquent youngsters; money restitution paid to victims; community service work orders; and a greater use of fines.

However, certain of the readings included here support the recognition that a punishment direction is not the only change visible on the landscape. Recent legislation and appellate case decisions have provided increased legal protections to juvenile offenders, alleged and proven. Status offenders decreasingly experience juvenile court sanctions. It has become much more difficult for judges to lock up incorrigible youths "for their own good." Detention screening, an array of detention alternatives, and the wide application of detention hearings have curbed unnecessary and unnecessarily prolonged secure pretrial confinement. Police and probation intake screening practices continue to expand, and together with prosecutor review at the intake stage exit huge numbers of lesser juvenile offenders and limited merit offenses from the formal system through warning conferences, dismissal, diversion, informal probation, and consent decree resolution. Community-based program alternatives are more numerous and varied, enriching the options available to judges who seek more than probation but less than an institution. Public defenders and appointed private counsel more commonly represent accused juveniles.

The juvenile court is in transition. Clearly, it provides more regularized legal procedures. There is a developing consensus that juveniles should be held accountable for their actions, and that more than counseling and guidance are needed to achieve law-abiding behavior. There is also more awareness that courts, probation, institutions, public child welfare services, and external agencies working with court youths should be accountable for what they do and do not do. At present, there is more interest in extending an equity or equal justice model to the handling of juveniles, a direction that comports more with a proportionality direction. But proportionality and just deserts can be rigid approaches that result in harsh treatment of certain individual offenders. There are ways to combine a more equal justice with individualized justice, and the future of juvenile justice is likely to seek such an accommodation.

The law is here to stay in the juvenile courts, and there is more justice in juvenile justice. Despite an occasional call for the abolition of juvenile courts, specialized handling of juveniles remains both wise and practical, and a specialized forum for the review of juvenile offenses will most likely continue indefinitely. Despite shortcomings and inconsistencies, the juvenile justice system remains a vital humanitarian enterprise which merits our understanding, support, and criticism.